A Course in Nepali

A Course in Nepali

David Matthews

LONDON AND NEW YORK

Published by
Routledge
2 Park Square, Milton Park, Abingdon, Oxon, OX14 4RN
270 Madison Ave, New York NY 10016

Transferred to Digital Printing 2008

This Edition 1998

British Library Catalogue in Publication Data
A catalogue record for this book is available from the British Library

Library of Congress Cataloguing in Publication Data
A catalogue record for this book has been requested

ISBN 0–7007–1070–1

Publisher's Note
The publisher has gone to great lengths to ensure the quality of this reprint but points out that some imperfections in the original may be apparent

CONTENTS

PREFACE

Nepali[1], the official language of the Kingdom of Nepal, is widely spoken throughout the Eastern Himalayas, where it functions as one of the major vehicles of communication. Nepali has also been adopted by peoples of the Himalayan region who belong to different linguistic groups, and is now understood throughout the whole of Nepal, the Darjeeling region of West Bengal, Sikkim, Bhutan and parts of Tibet, where it has functioned as a language of trade and commerce for well over two centuries.

Like most of the languages of the northern subcontinent, Nepali belongs to the Indo-Aryan family, being ultimately derived from Sanskrit, the classical language of India. The Indo-Aryan languages are historically related to many of the languages of Europe, including English, though at first sight the relationship may appear to be remote. Linguistically, Nepali is most closely related to Hindi, with which it shares a large proportion of its technical vocabulary, and a script, which differs from that of Hindi in only a few minor details. The two languages are in fact so close to each other (Italian and Spanish would be a fair European parallel) that early Western grammarians regarded Nepali merely as a dialect of Hindi. The two languages are, however, by no means mutually comprehensible and are now considered to be completely distinct from each other.

Although there is enough evidence to show that Nepali has been spoken in the Eastern Himalayas for several centuries, literature, in the real sense of the term, was not written in it until the beginning of the nineteenth century when classical Sanskrit was gradually abandoned in favour of the vernacular. One of the earliest and most revered Nepali works is the *Rāmāyaṇ* of the Brahmin poet, Bhānubhakta Āchāryā, who completed his long epic relating the exploits of Rāma in 1853. The collapse of the Rāṇā regime in 1949 led to a great upsurge in Nepali writing, and since that time many novels, short stories, plays and poetical works have been published from the two major centres of Kathmaṇdu and Darjeeling.

When learning Nepali, a number of peculiar difficulties are encountered which do not have to be faced when beginning the more frequently studied European languages.

[1]Nepali is often referred to as *Gorkhālī* 'the language of the people of Gorkha'. In the past the terms *Khas Kurā* and *Parbatīya* were also used.

As might be expected, Nepali, which is spoken over a large and fairly remote area, where the rate of illiteracy is still high, has a number of dialects. In some cases, the difference between the dialects is not very great and amounts only to slight variations in pronunciation or the preference of one word or grammatical form to another. On the other hand, an inhabitant of Kathmandu might find the dialect spoken in the hills of the far west of Nepal difficult to understand without a good deal of practice. However, over the last three decades, a rapid increase in education and an improvement in communications have greatly eased the dialect problem and a standard form of Nepali, based largely on the speech of the educated Brahmins and Chetris of central Nepal is gradually emerging, and this is now understood over the greater part of the language area.
area.

Another difficulty lies in the fairly big differences which exist between the spoken and the written language. The latter, which is employed in most printed works, newspapers and the broadcasts of Radio Nepal, is characterised by the large number of words taken over from Sanskrit, a more or less consistent use of grammatical gender and certain verbal forms which feature only sporadically in everyday speech. Although in the first half of this century, the literary language would have been regarded as artificial, and understood only by the educated elite, an increase in literacy and the growing use of the transistor and in some areas the television have radically altered the situation. The effect of the written style on speech has given rise to a certain inconsistency, and it is no longer uncommon to hear both literary and colloquial forms of the same word in the space of a few sentences. The debate among Nepali speakers about which form is 'correct' is endless!

Orthography, which tended to be erratic and inconsistent in earlier printed works, has now, largely by the efforts of the Royal Nepal Academy, been standardised, though variant spellings of the same word are still occasionally encountered. Most of the variants are obvious and the slight inconsistency which still prevails causes little difficulty once the nature of the script has been understood.

The aim of this course is to present a full description of both the spoken and written forms of modern standard Nepali, and to enable the student to understand, speak and read most types of Nepali he or she is likely to encounter. The earlier lessons concentrate mainly on the spoken style, and the conversation passages contain material which will prove useful for those who are about to travel in Nepal, as one usually does, on foot! The reading passages in the later lessons concern religious, political and literary topics, and will enable those who wish to read more widely in Nepali to do so without much difficulty.

The Nepali script has been employed throughout the course, and the spelling, based on that suggested by Bālchandra Sharmā in his excellent dictionary, *Nepālī Shabdakosh,* is consistent throughout. However the most commonly encountered orthographical and dialectal variants have been pointed out at various stages in the course.

The introductory chapter deals with the pronunciation of Nepali and the script used for writing the language. The script is logical and can be learnt without much difficulty. Correct pronunciation is obviously difficult to learn from a book, and if possible should be learnt with a native Nepali speaker.

Each lesson consists of a discussion of the grammar and the words required for tackling the reading passages and exercises which follow. The material of one lesson should be thoroughly mastered before the next lesson is started. Nepali vocabulary may at first seem difficult to learn, since few words (unlike those of French and German for example) bear any resemblance to those of English. The vocabulary, which is listed in each lesson in the correct alphabetical order, should always be memorized. The best test of whether you have learnt the words is to proceed from the English side of the list to the Nepali.

The course covers the whole grammar and all the constructions of modern Nepali, and introduces most of the spoken and written styles of the language.

For the preparation of the course I am indebted to the help given to me by many Nepali friends. Special thanks are due to Maṇī Rāṇā, Padma Prakāsh Shreṣṭha, Drubha Adhikārī and Miss Shāntā Shreṣṭha who have checked the material and offered many invaluable suggestions.

Nepal is a land which already provides great enjoyment to the increasing number of visitors from the West. A knowledge of the language leads to a deeper understanding of the culture of its people, and the object of this course is to provide the means of learning it without too much difficulty.

Publishers' note: We have taken the opportunity of this new edition to correct omissions and errors in the text which have become evident in the eight years since first publication, and to amend and update topical references in the content of the teaching examples.

Five C60 cassettes to accompany the book may be obtained from the Publications Office, School of Oriental and African Studies, Thornhaugh Street, Russell Square, London WC1H 0XG.

Abbreviations

adj.	adjective
adv.	adverb
affirm.	affirmative
cf.	compare
colloq.	colloquial
e.g.	for example
emph.	emphatic
esp.	especially
fem.	feminine
fut.	future
HGH	High Grade Honorific
hon.	honorific
i.e.	that is
inf.	infinitive
intrans.	intransitive
LGH	Low Grade Honorific
lit.	literally
masc.	masculine
MGH	Middle Grade Honorific
n.	noun
neg.	negative
obl.	oblique
part.	participle
perf.	perfect
plup.	pluperfect
pl.	plural
pron.	pronoun
ps.	person
sing.	singular
syn.	synonymous with
trans.	transitive
vb.	verb

PRONUNCIATION AND SCRIPT

In this introductory chapter, we shall be concerned with the pronunciation of Nepali, and the script which is used for writing the language.

In the sections below, the sounds of Nepali are first introduced by means of a transcription into Roman letters. The sounds are briefly described, where possible, with reference to the nearest equivalent sounds in English, or in one of the commonly studied European languages.

Each section is followed by a discussion of the various symbols necessary for writing the words which have been introduced in the pronunciation exercises. You should learn how to read and write the Nepali script as quickly as possible, and should not come to rely on the transcription, which is merely a convenient guide to the pronunciation.

Fortunately, the Nepali script (known as the **devanāgarī** script), though far from being 'phonetic', is a good deal more logical than those used to represent most European languages, and the spelling of Nepali presents far fewer problems than that of English or French. In most cases, therefore, once a number of fairly simple rules have been learnt, it is possible to deduce the correct pronunciation of a word from the way it is written.

As we have pointed out in the Preface, the spelling encountered in many Nepali books and newspapers (especially those printed during the first half of this century) tends to be somewhat erratic. Even though the situation is now greatly improved, spelling has not yet been completely standardized, and even in modern works one word may have two or more possible spellings.

In this course, consistency in spelling has been aimed at, but common alternatives have been given. You should, therefore, have no difficulty when you eventually come to reading original Nepali texts.

Section 1

Vowels **a ā**
Consonants **g n b m r l s**
Pronunciation

a This vowel varies from something like the Southern English pronunciation of *u* in *but* to something like the *o* in *not*.
After and before velars (**k, g, kh, gh, ŋ**) and labials (**p, b, ph, bh,**

m) the pronunciation of **a** approaches that of the *o* in *not*. In other contexts it is more like the *u* in *mug*. There is, however, considerable variation.

ā Similar to the *a* in *father*.

g Like the *g* in *go, mug*.

n Like the *n* in *not*.

b (i) In initial position like the *b* in *bull.*
(ii) Between vowels and in final position, **b** is pronounced laxly, with the lips hardly touching.
In some words final **-b** is pronounced like *p* (see Section 6 below) and is occasionally written so. For instance, the word **kitāb** (a book) is also written **kitāp.**

m Like the *m* in *may, time.*

r is tapped, like the *r* sometimes heard in *very* or in Italian *Maria*. It is never very strongly rolled.
r must be pronounced clearly in all positions. Special care must be taken when it is preceded by a vowel, which must not become a diphthong like the English vowels heard in *care, mere, poor,* etc.

l is always 'clear' like the *l* in *leaf*, and never like the *l* in *milk, feel.*

s in all positions like the *s* in *sing*.

Pronunciation Exercise 1

aba 'now' **ma** 'I' **ra** 'and' **la** 'there' **basa** 'sit' **gara** 'do' **laga** 'take' **nagara** 'do not do' **bā** 'father' **mā** 'in' **āmā** 'mother' **māra** 'kill' **ā** 'come' **bas** 'bus' **ban** 'forest' **sab** 'all' **rām** 'Ram' **sāl** 'year' **māl** 'goods' **sāgar** 'sea' **bās** 'lodging'

Script

Nepali is written in the **devanāgarī** script. The same script, with a few minor differences, is used for Sanskrit, Hindi and several other Indian languages.

The **devanāgarī** script is written from left to right. There are no special forms for capital letters.

Simple consonant characters represent not 'letters' but syllables containing the vowel **-a**. This vowel is known as the *inherent* vowel. Thus the character ग represents the syllable **ga** and not merely the consonant **g**.

The consonants introduced so far are :

ग **ga** न **na** ब **ba** म **ma** ल **la** र **ra** स **sa**

The word **basa** is then written बस , **nagara** नगर , **ra** र etc., each consonant being pronounced with its inherent vowel **-a.**

Vowels, with one exception, each have two symbols:

(i) vowel character – used in initial position and after other vowels, or when the vowel is isolated.

(ii) vowel signs – used after consonants.

The vowel character आ **ā** has the corresponding vowel sign ा .

The word **āmā** is then written आमा , the initial vowel being represented by the vowel character आ , and the second vowel by the vowel sign ा , because it occurs after the consonant character म . The addition of the vowel sign cancels the inherent vowel of the consonant.

The vowel character अ has no corresponding vowel sign, since the vowel **a** is already inherent in the consonant. Thus the word **aba** is written अब . The vowel character अ is used in initial position. The second vowel **-a** is already inherent in ब .

अ and आ have alternative forms ऄ,ऄा **a** and **ā**. In printed works both forms are encountered.

The inherent vowel **-a** is cancelled by placing the sign ् (known as **virām**) at the foot of the consonant character.[1] Thus बस् is pronounced **bas** as opposed to बस **basa**. The **virām** indicates that the inherent vowel in the consonant is not to be pronounced.

The use of the **virām** in Nepali books is unfortunately sporadic. As a rule it is used only when the editor feels that confusion is likely to arise: for instance, to distinguish forms like गर् **gar** (the 2nd person singular imperative of the verb 'to do') and गर **gara** (the 2nd person plural imperative). Of course, a Nepali speaker would usually know whether the inherent vowel is to be pronounced or not, and would not need the device to tell him. But since there is no way in which a foreign student of the language could know, the **virām** has been used consistently throughout this course.

The examples given in transcription in Pronunciation Exercise 1 are written in the **devanāgarī** script as follows:

अब म र ल बस गर लग नगर

बा मा आमा मार आ

बस् बन् सब् राम् साल् माल् सागर् बास्

Section 2

Vowels **i ī u ū**
Consonants **ch y h**
Pronunciation

i, ī Both vowels are pronounced the same, like the *ee* in *seem* but

[1]The sign is also referred to as **halanta.**

without the diphthongisation of the English sound. The *i* of French *dit* is much nearer to the Nepali sound.

u, ū Both pronounced the same, like the *oo* in *boot* or the *ou* in French *coup*.
Although there are good reasons for maintaining the difference between **u** and **ū, i** and **ī** in writing, they are pronounced the same in similar contexts. In unstressed positions they tend to be shorter and in stressed and final positions longer.

ch This is one of a number of strongly aspirated consonants. The aspiration is indicated in the transcription by the letter **-h** as the second element of the symbol. **ch**, however, represents only *one* character of the **devanāgarī** script. The same applies to other aspirated consonants such as **jh, dh, bh** etc. which are discussed later.
In order to pronounce **ch** press the blade of the tongue behind the upper teeth and try to say **ts**, at the same time exerting strong breath pressure.

y Like the *y* in *yes*. Before **i** and **ī**, the *y* is almost inaudible.

h Like the *h* in *horse, aha*.

Pronunciation Exercise 2

binā 'without' **sīmānā** 'frontier' **chu** 'am' **cha** 'is' **unī** 'he/she' **u** 'he/she' **banāī** 'she made' **banāū** 'make' **āū** 'come' **linu** 'to take' **lugā** 'clothes' **hāla** 'put' **lāī** 'she wore' **chānā** 'roof' **māchā** 'fish' **mahārānī** 'queen' **ālu** 'potato' **basūn** 'let them sit' **lāūn** 'let them wear' **yinī** 'he/she' **yī** 'these' **yī āimāīharū** 'these women'

Script

	i	**ī**	**u**	**ū**
Vowel characters	इ	ई	उ	ऊ
Vowel signs	ि	ी	ु	ू

The vowel sign ि is written before the consonant after which it is pronounced:

बि **bi-** गि **gi-** लि **li-**

The vowel sign ी follows the consonant:

सी **sī-** गी **gī-** री **rī-**

The vowel signs ु and ू are written at the foot of the consonant:

लु **lu-** लू **lū-** नु **nu-** नू **nū-**

When joined to र the vowels ु and ू are written thus: रु **ru** रू **rū**.

Consonants

छ **ch** य **y** ह **h**

(From now on, it is assumed that a consonant character, unless modified by the **virām** or a vowel sign, contains the inherent vowel **-a**. When individual consonants are referred to, the inherent vowel will not be included in the transcription. Thus ग will simply be transcribed **g,** य **y,** etc.)

Script version of Pronunciation Exercise 2

बिना सीमाना छु छ उनी उ बनाई बनाऊ आऊ

लिन् लुगा हाल लाई छाना माछा महारानी

आलु बसून् लाऊन् यिनी यी यी आइमाईहरू

Section 3

Vowels **ā ã̄ ū ū̃ o**

Consonant **ŋ**

Pronunciation

The sign ˜ placed above vowels indicates nasalisation.

ã̄ Rather like the French syllable in *élan*. First, the vowel **ā** is pronounced and the air stream is diverted through the nose. The same process is followed for **ã, ũ, ū̃.**

o A 'pure' vowel with rounded lips, like the *o* in French *tôt*.

ŋ Like the *ng* in *hanger*. This sound never occurs in initial position, and is almost always followed by the consonant *g*.
The Nepali word **sãga** (with), may also be written **saŋga,** but in either case it is always pronounced **saŋa** (almost rhyming with 'hanger'). In this course, we shall use the first spelling **sãga,** which is now preferred by most Nepali editors.

-y- When **-y-** occurs between two vowels, it is merely a glide sound, resembling, if anything, the *e* in *hen*.

Pronunciation Exercise 3

hã 'yes' **chāyā̃** 'shade' **hā̃go** 'branch' **nayā̃** 'new' **garū̃** 'may I do?'
gāū 'village' **āyo** 'came' **gayo** 'went' **āgo** 'fire' **āūcha** 'comes'
banāūcha 'makes' **sãga** 'with' **chorāsãga** 'with the boy' **gāūchu** 'I sing'
gāū 'sing' **gāū̃** 'may I sing' **yo** 'this' **hoina** 'is not' **ramāilo** 'nice'
os 'dew' **royo** 'wept' **āinā** 'I did not come' **garinā** 'I did not do'

Script

The mark of nasalisation has two signs in the **devanāgarī** script. The first we shall consider is ँ, known as **candrabindu** (literally 'moon-dot'). This is placed above vowel characters and vowel signs, no part of which extends above the top line. Thus:

अँ **ã** हँ **hã** आँ **ā̃** हाँ **hā̃** उँ **ũ** हुँ **hũ** ऊँ **ū̃** हूँ **hū̃**

Vowel character ओ } **o**

Vowel sign ो }

ओस् **os** होइन **hoina** आयो **āyo**

Consonant ङ **ŋ**

This consonant rarely appears by itself, but is mostly combined with ग which is written underneath it. Thus: ङ्ग **ŋg.**

ङ्ग **ŋg** may alternatively be written ँग **˜g.** Thus the word **hā̃go** has two possible spellings: हाङ्गो or हाँगो . The latter is rather more common.

The word **sā̃ga** is written either सँग or सङ्ग, the former being more common. (Note that the spelling सङ **saŋa,** adopted by some European grammarians is not found in Nepali works.)

Script version of Pronunciation Exercise 3

हँ छायाँ हाँगो (हाङ्गो) नयाँ गरूँ गाउँ आयो

गयो आगो आउँछ बनाउँछ सँग (सङ्ग) छोरासँग

गाउँछु गाऊ गाऊँ यो होइन रमाइलो ओस्

गेयो आइनँ गरिनँ

Section 4

Vowels **e ẽ ĩ ī̃**

Consonants **ḍ ṛ d**

Pronunciation

e A pure vowel like the *é* in French *été.*

ẽ The nasal counterpart of **e.**

ĩ, ī̃ The nasal counterparts of **i** and **ī,** both pronounced the same.

ḍ One of a series of retroflex consonants. **ḍ** sounds not unlike the *d* in *day*, but at the point of articulation the tip of the tongue is curled back.
Retroflex d's and t's are the most noticeable feature of the 'Indian' pronunciation of English. When an English loan word is taken into Nepali containing *d*, the English consonant is represented as **ḍ.** e.g. **soḍiam** 'sodium'.

ṛ This is in fact the medial (i.e. between vowels) and final form of **ḍ.** The articulation is similar to that of **ḍ**, but the tongue is very rapidly flapped forward and down.

d A dental consonant, like the *d* of French and Italian. The tongue is spread out, the tip touching the cutting edge of the upper front teeth.

We have noted that the English *d* suggests the sound of **ḍ** to a Nepali. On the other hand, the dental **d** is felt to be nearer to the *th* in English *the* which would be transcribed in Nepali as **dī**.

Pronunciation Exercise 4

ḍarāunu 'to fear' **ḍolī** 'sedan chair' **ḍūgā** 'boat' **laṛe** 'they fought'
hāṛ 'bone' **ḍā̃ṛo** 'ridge' **hĩṛera** 'having walked' **dāl** 'lentils'
dinu 'to give' **de** 'give' **dui** 'two' **bādal** 'cloud' **e** 'oh' **garẽ** 'I did'
ḍarāẽ 'I feared' **naḍarāū** 'do not fear' **nadagura** 'do not run'
dagurẽ 'I ran' **āena** 'did not come' **āẽ** 'I came' **diinā** 'I did not give'
diera 'having given'

Script

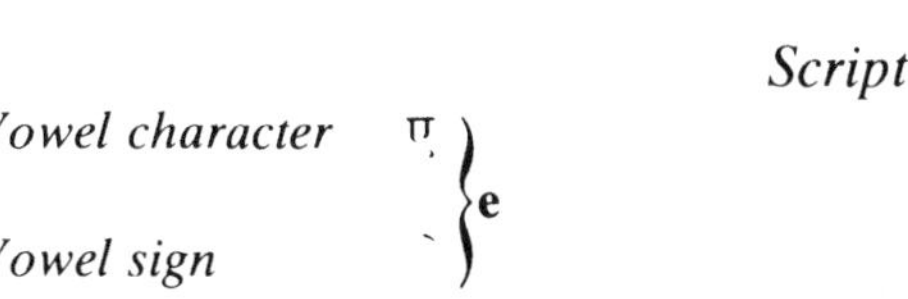

आए **āe** ले **le** गरे **gare**

The second mark of nasalisation (referred to in 3) is ं (known as **anusvār**). This is placed above vowel characters and vowel signs which extend above the top line.

एँ **ẽ** (nasalisation marked with **candrabindu**), but the corresponding vowel sign ें **ẽ** is marked with **ansuvār** because it is written above the top line. Similarly:

इँ **ĩ**, vowel sign िं
ईं **ĩ**, vowel sign ीं

एँ **ẽ**	हें **hẽ**
इँ **ĩ**	हिं **hĩ**
ईं **ĩ**	हीं **hĩ**

It should be noted that some editors prefer the **candrabindu** ँ as a mark of nasalisation in all cases, writing हेँ, हीँ etc., reserving the **anusvār** to represent one of the nasal consonants, as explained in Section 11 below. In this course the rule outlined above will be followed.

Consonants ड **ḍ** **ṛ**
द **d**

It will be noted that the same sign is used to represent both **ḍ** and **ṛ**. The pronunciation **ṛ** is sometimes indicated by a dot written under the character.

Thus ड **ḍ**, ड़ **ṛ**.

This is in fact a convention borrowed from Hindi and only very occasionally observed in Nepali. Throughout this course, however, the sound **ṛ** will be consistently written ड़ .

Script version of Pronunciation Exercise 4

डराउनु डोली डुँगा लड़े हाड़् डाँड़ो हिंड़ेर

दाल् दिनु दे दुइ बादल् ए गरें डराएँ

नडराऊ नदगुर दगुरें आएन आएँ दिइनँ दिएर

Section 5

Diphthong **əy**
Consonants **kh ṭh th ph**
Pronunciation

əy A diphthong. The first element (**ə**) is pronounced like the *a* in *arise*, the second element (**y**) like the *i* in *city*.

kh Strongly aspirated. Try saying *bulkhead* with the stress on the second syllable.

ṭh Try saying *hothouse*, dividing it thus: *ho-'thouse* with the stress on the second syllable. **ṭh** is articulated with the tongue curled back (see note on **ḍ** in Section 4).

th A dental aspirated consonant (see note on **d** in Section 4).

ph Try saying *haphazard*, dividing it thus: *ha-'phazard* with the stress on the second syllable. Some speakers pronounce the sound by bringing the lips closely together without interrupting the air stream. It will then sound something like *f*, but the upper teeth do not rest on the lower lip.

Pronunciation Exercise 5

(*a*) **khəy** 'what' **chəyna** 'is not' **həy** (interrogative particle) **əyn** 'law' **āūdəyna** 'does not come' **lāūdəyna** 'does not wear' **khela** 'play' **ā̃khā** 'eye' **rākha** 'put' **rukh** 'tree' **ṭhāū** 'place' **ṭhūlo** 'big' **āṭh** 'eight' **thiyo** 'was' **māthi** 'above' **phul** 'egg' **pheri** 'again' **āphəy** 'oneself' **māph** 'forgiveness'

(*b*) **mānche** 'man' **huncha** 'becomes' **lāgcha** 'seems' **khelcha** 'plays' **khelnu** 'to play' **kheldəyna** 'does not play' **garnu** 'to do' **garcha** 'does' **gardəyna** 'does not do' **basnu** 'to sit' **hā̃scha** 'laughs' **bascha** 'sits'

(*c*) **rāmsāga** 'with Ram' **sagarmāthā** 'Mt. Everest' **darbār** 'court' **banmā** 'in the forest' **choṛnu** 'to give up' **choṛcha** 'gives up'

Script

Vowel character	ऐ	**əy**
Vowel sign	ै	

Thus: ऐन् **əyn,** आउँदैन **āūdəyna**

Consonants ख **kh**
ठ **ṭh**
थ **th**
फ **ph**

Script version of Pronunciation Exercise 5a

खै छैन है ऐन् आउँदैन लाउँदैन खेल आँखा
राख रुख् ठाउँ ठूलो आठ् थियो माथि
फुल् फेरि आफै माफ्

Conjunct consonants

When two or more consonants occur together without an intervening vowel, e.g. **sch** in **bascha** (sits) or **nch** in **mānche** (man), the combination is written as a single unit, known as a *conjunct consonant.*

For example, स and छ are joined together thus: स्छ **sch** as in बस्छ **bascha,** न and छ are joined thus: न्छ **nch** as in मान्छे **mānche.** In these two conjunct consonants, the elements स्‍ and न्‍ preceding छ are easily recognizable as parts of the consonant characters स and न respectively.

Similarly, in the conjunct consonant ग्छ **gch,** the first element is recognizable as part of the full consonant ग, in ल्न **ln,** the first element is recognizable as part of the full consonant ल. Thus when joined to other consonants in this way स, न, ग, ल, become स्‍, न्‍, ग्‍, ल्‍.

The various elements of some conjunct consonants are not so easily recognizable. When र **r** precedes another consonant, it is written र्‍, and placed directly over the consonant character to which it is joined. If part of that character extends above the top line र्‍ is placed to the right of it. Thus:

र्छ **rch** as in गर्छ **garcha,** र्न **rn** as in गर्नु **garnu,** र्द **rd** as in गर्दैन **gardəyna** (note that the sign is written to the right of the vowel sign). The sign र्‍ is known as **reph** रेफ्.

In this section the following conjuncts are used:
ग्छ **gch** न्छ **nch** ल्छ **lch** ल्द **ld** ल्न **ln** र्छ **rch** र्द **rd** र्न **rn** स्छ **sch** स्न **sn**.

Script version of Exercise 5b

मान्छे हुन्छ लाग्छ खेल्छ खेल्नु खेल्दैन गर्नु गर्छ
गर्दैन बस्नु हाँस्छ बस्छ

Some consonants like ड **ḍ**, ड़ **ṛ** ठ **ṭh** have no special conjunct form. The junction is then effected by means of the **virām**. Thus **choṛnu** (to give up) is written छोड़्नु , the inherent vowel in ड़ being cancelled by the **virām**. In a compound word like **sagarmātha** (Mt. Everest), which is formed from two components **sagar** and **māthā**, the consonant junction is again effected by the **virām**. Thus: सगर्माथा

Similarly, when a word like **-mā** (in) or **-sãga** (with) is attached to a word ending in a consonant,[1] the **virām** is employed at the junction of the consonants. Thus: राम्सँग **rāmsãga** (with Ram), **banmā** बन्मा (in the forest).

In certain loanwords, the **virām** is employed at a consonant junction rather than a conjunct consonant. One example (a loanword from Urdu) is दर्बार् **darbār** (court, palace).

Script version of Exercise 5c

राम्सँग सगर्माथा दर्बार् बन्मा छोड़्नु
छोड़्छ

Section 6

Diphthong **əw**
Consonants **k ṭ t p**
Pronunciation

əw A diphthong, the first element of which is like the *a* in *arise* and the second like the *u* in *put*.

k An unaspirated consonant, released with the minimum of breath. Note that in English, *k, t,* and *p* are almost always aspirated. This breathiness must as far as possible be eliminated, otherwise the unaspirated consonants of Nepali will sound more like their aspirated counterparts.

ṭ A retroflex consonant articulated with the tip of the tongue curled back.

t A dental consonant, resembling the *t* in French *tu*.

p Unaspirated as in English *spin*.

Pronunciation Exercise 6

əwlo 'malaria' **chəw** 'you are' **məwsam** 'climate' **kalam** 'pen' **gareko** 'done' **khukurī** 'Nepalese knife' **ke** 'what' **ko** 'who?' **keṭākeṭī** 'childhood' **bāṭo** 'road' **basbāṭa** 'by bus' **pasal** 'shop' **nepāl** 'Nepal' **pānī** 'water' **aksar** 'often' **raksəwl** 'Raxaul'

[1]Such words, corresponding to English prepositions, always follow the noun they govern, and are thus termed 'postpositions'.

dekhnu 'to see' **dekhchəw** 'you see' **kāṭyo** 'cut' **sāṭnu** 'to change' **pugyo** 'arrived' **tyo** 'that' **pasyo** 'entered' **pākistān** 'Pakistan'

Script

Vowel character औ } **əw**
Vowel sign ौ }

Thus: औलो **əwlo** मौसम् **məwsam** गर्छौ **garchəw**

Consonants क **k**
ट **ṭ**
त **t**
प **p**

Conjunct consonants

क्स **ks** ख्छ **khch** ख्न **khn** ग्य **gy** ट्न **ṭn** ट्य **ṭy** त्य **ty** न्त **nt** न्द **nd** स्त **st** स्द **sd** स्य **sy**

Note that ट **ṭ** usually has no special conjunct form and the **virām** is used to effect the junction as in काट्न **kāṭnu.** When य **y** follows ट and certain other letters it has a special form य as in काट्यो **kāṭyo.**

The other conjunct letters are easily recognisable from their full form:

Script version of Exercise 6

औलो छौ मौसम् कलम् गरेको खुकुरी के को

केटाकेटी बाटो बस्बाट पसल् नेपाल् पानी

अक्सर् रक्सौल् देख्न् देख्छौ काट्यो साट्न् पग्यो

त्यो पस्यो पाकिस्तान्

Section 7

Diphthongs **əỹ** **əw̃**
Consonants **c** **j**
Pronunciation

əỹ The nasalised counterpart of the diphthong **əy.**

əw̃ The nasalised counterpart of the diphthong **əw.**

c An unaspirated consonant, like the initial *ty* sound in *tutor* but pronounced with the tip of the tongue pointing downwards and touching the lower teeth.

j Something like *dz* pronounced with the tip of the tongue pointing downwards and touching the lower teeth.

Double consonants must be given their full force, as they are in Italian for instance. The double **kk** in **pakkā** (decided) is like the long 'k' sound in *bookcase*, but of course, without any trace of aspiration.

In Nepali, most consonants can be doubled.

Pronunciation Exercise 7

pəỹtīs 'thirty-five' **sātəw̃** 'seventh' **əw̃lo** 'finger' **kāṭhmāṛəw̃** 'Kathmandu' **pāyəw̃** 'we found' **əỹc** 'subjection' **jānu** 'to go' **hajārəw̃** 'thousands' **bajār** 'market' **lāj** 'shyness' **ciso** 'cold' **pā̃c** 'five' **pā̃cəw̃** 'fifth' **kəỹcī** 'scissors' **akkal** 'intelligence' **pakkā** 'decided' **saṭṭā** 'instead' **hāttī** 'elephant' **baccā** 'child' **aḍḍā** 'office' **kinnu** 'to buy'

Script

Vowel character	ऐं } **əỹ**	औं } **əw̃**
Vowel sign	ैं	ौं
Thus:	ऐंच् **əỹc**	पैंतीस् **pəỹtīs**
	औंलो **əw̃lo**	सातौं **sātəw̃**
Consonants	च **c**	
	ज **j**	

Conjunct consonants

क्क **kk**	or क्क	च्च **cc**	or च्च
ट्ट **ṭṭ**	or ट्ट	ड्ड **ḍḍ**	or ड्ड
ड़्य **ṛy**	त्त **tt**	न्न **nn**	or न्न

Note that double consonants are often written one on top of the other.

Script version of Exercise 7

पैंतीस्   सातौं   औंलो   काठ्माड़ौं   पायौं   ऐंच्   जानु

हजारौं   बजार्   लाज्   चिसो   पाँच्   पाँचौं   कैंची

अक्कल्   पक्का   सट्टा   हात्ती   बच्चा   अड्डा   किन्नु

Section 8

Consonants

gh **ḍh** **ṛh** **dh** These are aspirated counterparts of **g, ḍ, ṛ,** and **d,** enunciated with strong breath pressure. Care must be taken not to pronounce **gha** as if it were **gaha.** (See the note on **cha** in Section 2 above.)

Pronunciation Exercise 8

ghoṛā 'horse' **aghi** 'before' **māgh** (10th Nepalese month) **ḍhokā** 'door' **ḍhīlo** 'late' **aṛhāī** 'two and a half' **sīṛhī** 'stairs' **paṛha** 'read' **dhulo** 'dust' **ādhā** 'half' **paṛhnu** 'to read' **paṛhyo** 'read' **paryo** 'fell' **caṛhcha** 'goes up' **sodhnu** 'to ask' **ā̃dhyāro** 'darkness' **pradhānmantrī** 'Prime-Minister' **dhūmrapān** 'smoking' **timro** 'your' **grām** 'village' **natra** 'else' **mahendra** 'Mahendra'

Script

Consonants घ **gh**
ढ **ḍh**
ढ़ **ṛh**
ध **dh**

Conjunct consonants ढ़्न **ṛhn** ढ़्छ **ṛhch** ढ़्य **ṛhy** ध्न **dhn** ध्य **dhy**

When र follows a consonant, it is usually written as a small stroke and joined to the right hand vertical line of the consonant character, or in the case of characters without vertical lines (like ड , ट , द etc.) it is placed directly underneath. Thus: ग्र **gr,** द्र **dr,** प्र **pr,** म्र **mr.** But note त्र **tr** and the combinations न्त्र **ntr,** न्द्र **ndr.**

reph (Section 5) is often joined to य thus: र्‍य **ry.** In certain words (mostly loans from Sanskrit), the combination **ry** is written र्य. In Nepali words र्‍य is preferred. Thus **paryo** is written पर्‍यो and seldom पर्यो

Script version of Exercise 8

घोड़ा अघि माघ् ढोका ढीलो अढ़ाई सिंढ़ी पढ़
धुलो आधा पढ़्नु पढ़्यो पर्‍यो चढ़्छ सोध्नु
अँध्यारो प्रधान्मन्त्री धूम्रपान् तिम्रो ग्राम् नत्र
महेन्द्र

Section 9

Consonants **jh** **bh** **ṇ** **ṣ** **ʃ**

Pronunciation

jh The aspirated counterpart of **j.**

bh The aspirated counterpart of **b.**

ṇ A retroflex nasal consonant, i.e. **n** pronounced with a slight curling back of the tongue. For this reason **ṇ** is written instead of **n** before a retroflex consonant, e.g. **ghaṇṭā** (hour). Most speakers pronounce it exactly like **n.**

ṣ A retroflex sibiliant, i.e. **s** pronounced with a slight curling back of the tongue, sounding something like the *sh* in *wished.* Most speakers, however, pronounce **ṣ** like **s.** It occurs only in words borrowed from Sanskrit.

ʃ Like the *sh* in *ship.* Many speakers, however, pronounce it like **s.**

The combination **kṣ** is pronounced like the *cti* in *auction.* In colloquial speech **kṣa-** is often pronounced **che-.** For example the colloquial pronunciation of **kṣamā** (forgiveness) is **chemā.** In medial position, there is a tendency to pronounce **-kṣa-** as **-kcha-**: e.g. **rakṣak** (defender) is often pronounced **rakchak.**

Pronunciation Exercise 9

jhan 'all the more' **jhul** 'net' **ajha** 'yet' **bhāt** 'rice' **lobhī** 'greedy' **bhandenəw̃** 'we do not say' **bhitra** 'inside' **āʃā** 'hope' **ʃākā** 'doubt' **paʃu** 'cattle' **ʃeṣ** 'remainder' **uṣā** 'dawn' **əwṣadhi** 'medicine' **jhyāl** 'window' **bujhnu** 'to understand' **kṣaṇ** 'moment' **akṣar** 'letter' **kṣamā** 'forgiveness' **ʃyām** 'Shyām' **ʃrī** 'Mr.' **ʃreṇī** 'rank' **ghaṇṭā** 'hour' **paṇḍit** 'scholar'

Script

Consonants झ **jh** भ **bh** ण **ṇ** ष **ṣ** श **ʃ**

Note that झ may be alternatively written झ and ण as ण.

There is now a tendency in Nepal to use the letter झ for **jh.** Over the past few years, this form of the letter has been frequently employed in official notices and publications.

Conjunct consonants

क्ष **kṣ** च्छ **cch** ण्ट **ṇṭ** (or ण्ट) ण्ड **ṇḍ** (or ण्ड) झ्म **jhm** (or झ्म) झ्य **jhy** (or झ्य) श्र **ʃr** श्च **ʃc** श्य **ʃy**

क्ष is also found written क्ष .

Script version of Exercise 9

झन् झुल् अझ भात् लोभी भन्दैनौं भित्र आशा

शँका पशु शेष् उषा औषधि झ्याल् बुझ्नु क्षण्

अक्षर् क्षमा श्याम् श्री श्रेणी घण्टा पण्डित्

Section 10

Vowel **ɹ**

Consonants **ɲ v**

Pronunciation

ɹ The so-called 'vocalic r' occurs only in words borrowed from Sanskrit. It is pronounced like the syllable *ri* in *river.*

ɲ A palatal nasal consonant pronounced like the *ni* in *opinion*. For this reason it most frequently occurs before the palatal consonants *c* and *j*.

v Usually like the *b* in *book.*
When *v* occurs after another consonant or immediately after *u*, it is pronounced like the *w* in *away.* In a few words *v* is pronounced like *w* in initial and intervocalic position. Such cases will be indicated as they occur.

ya When the syllable **ya** occurs before **t, n** and **s** it is pronounced like the *e* in *bed* (e.g. **yati** 'so much', **tyasto** 'such').

-h- When **h** occurs between vowels (e.g. **yahā̃** 'here') or after a vowel and before another consonant (e.g. **gāhro** 'hard'), it is almost inaudible, amounting only to a slight breathiness. Thus **yahā̃** sounds almost like **yā̃,** the vowel being rather longer than usual.

Pronunciation Exercise 10

ɹtu 'weather' **hɹdaya** 'heart' **kɹṣṇa** 'Krishna' **paɲcāyat** 'Panchayat' **aɲjuli** 'cupped hands' **tyasko** 'his' **tyati** 'so much' **yasarī** 'in this way' **ahile** 'now' **pahiro** 'landslide' **kohī** 'someone' **gāhro** 'hard' **sāhrəy** 'very' **yahā̃** 'here'

Words in which **v** *is pronounced* **b**
vidyārthī 'student' **viʃvavidyālaya** 'university' **avasthā** 'condition' **vyavasthā** 'arrangement' **vikram** (name of Nepalese era)

Words in which **v** *is pronounced* **w**
varipari 'around' **vāstā** 'care' **muvā** 'mother' **mvāī** 'kiss' **vahā̃** 'there' **svād** 'taste' **svatantra** 'independent' **dhvāŋg** 'bucket'

Script

Vowel character ऋ } **ɹ**
Vowel sign ृ }

Thus: ऋतु **ɹtu** कृषि **kɹṣi**

Note हृ **hɹ** as in हृदय **hɹdaya**

Consonants ञ[1] **ɲ,** व **v**

Conjunct consonants
क्र **kr** ञ्च **ɲc** ञ्ज **ɲj** ध्व **dhv** द्य **dy** म्व **mv** व्य **vy** र्थ **rth** ष्ण **ṣɳ** स्क **sk** स्त **st** स्थ **sth** स्व **sv** श्व **ʃv** (or श्व)[2] ह्र **hr**

Script version of Exercise 10

ऋतु हृदय कृष्ण पञ्चायत् अञ्जुलि त्यस्को त्यति यसरी अहिले पहिरो
कोही गाह्रो साह्रै यहाँ
विद्यार्थी विश्वविद्यालय अवस्था व्यवस्था विक्रम्
वरिपरि वास्ता मुवा म्वाई वहाँ स्वाद् स्वतन्त्र ध्वाङ्ग

[1]In Nepal, there is a growing tendency to spell the nasalised diphthong **-āī** as आञि . Thus the spelling तपाञि for तपाईं is sometimes encountered.
[2]Note the conjunct form श्‍ which is commonly used as an alternative to श ; and the conjunct consonant श्र **ʃr.**

Section 11

Special points

(*a*) The **anusvār** as a nasal consonant

In certain words, the **anusvār** (Section 3) may be used to represent one of the nasal consonants (**ŋ, ɲ, ɳ, n, m**) in combination with the letter that follows.

Before **k, kh, g, gh, ŋ,**	the **anusvār** may stand for	**ŋ.**
Before **c, ch, j, jh, ɲ**	the **anusvār** may stand for	**ɲ.**
before **ṭ, ṭh, ḍ, ḍh, ɳ,**	the **anusvār** may stand for	**ɳ.**
Before **t, th, d, dh, n,**	the **anusvār** may stand for	**n.**
Before **p, ph, b, bh, m**	the **anusvār** may stand for	**m.**
Before **s, ʃ, h,**	the **anusvār** may stand for	**m.**

In many cases either the **anusvār** or the relevant nasal consonant may be written, but there is a growing tendency to use the nasal consonant in preference to the **anusvār.** Thus:

संबन्ध	or	सम्बन्ध	**sambandha** connection
अंग्रेज्	or	अङ्ग्रेज्	**aŋgrej** Englishman
अंजुलि	or	अञ्जुलि	**aɲjuli** cupped hands

In certain words (all loans from Sanskrit), the **anusvār** is preferred:

सिंह **simha** (sometimes pronounced **siŋha**) lion
वंश **vamʃa** (usually pronounced **bamsa**) race, lineage

(*b*) **z** in loanwords

The word अंग्रेज् **aŋgrej** is in fact a loan from Urdu **aŋgrez.** The Urdu *z* is represented in Nepali by **j.** Similarly *z* in a number of loans from English is represented by **j** in Nepali. For example, the English words *zoo* and *visa* are written in Nepali as जू **jū,** भीजा **bhījā** (भ representing as often the English *v*).

(*c*) **Visarga**

The symbol **:** (known as विसर्ग **visarga**) occurs only in a few loanwords from Sanskrit. In most cases it is disregarded in pronunciation. Thus, प्राय: (usually, mostly) is transcribed and pronounced **prāya.** However, the word दु:ख is pronounced **dukkha** (pain). In this particular case, the **visarga** has the effect of doubling the consonant.

Pronunciation Exercise 11

sambandha 'connection' **vamʃa** 'lineage' **aŋgrej** 'Englishman' **simha** 'lion' **jū** 'zoo' **bhījā** 'visa' **prāya** 'usually' **dukkha** 'pain'

Script version of Exercise 11

संबन्ध वंश अंग्रेज् सिंह ज़ू भीजा प्राय: दु:ख

Section 12

Punctuation and numerals

The most commonly used punctuation signs are: । full stop, , comma, ? question mark, ' ' quotation marks.

The numerals are written as follows:

१	1	६	6
२	2	७	7
३	3	८	8
४	4	९	9
५	5	१०	10

The numerals are written from left to right:

१९७८ 1978
३२९८ 3298 etc.

Section 13

Stress in Nepali words

The rules which determine the position of the stress in Nepali words are complicated. The following guidelines, which should constantly be referred to, apply to the majority of cases.

1. The position of the stress depends upon both the length of the vowels and the nature of the syllables in a given word. The following vowels are regarded as *short*:

अ **a**	इ **i**	उ **u**	ऋ **ɹ**
अँ **ã**	इँ **ĩ**	उँ **ũ**	

The following vowels are regarded as *long*:

आ **ā**	ई **ī**	ऊ **ū**	ए **e**	ऐ **əy**	ओ **o**	औ **əw**
आँ **ā̃**	ईँ **ī̃**	ऊँ **ū̃**	एँ **ẽ**	ऐँ **əỹ**	ओँ **õ**	औँ **əw̃**

Syllables which end in a vowel are termed *open*. Syllables which end in a consonant are termed *closed*. Thus:

अब	**a-ba**	open-open
सामान्	**sā-mān**	open-closed
पश्चिमी	**paʃ-cim-ī**	closed-closed-open

In general, Nepali words may be stressed on the last syllable, the penultimate (last but one) syllable or the antepenultimate (preceding the last but one) syllable:

सामान्	**sā-mā́n**	last syllable

खैरो	**khəý-ro**	penultimate syllable
पश्चिमी	**páʃ-cim-ī**	antepenultimate syllable

In words of two syllables, the stress is on the *first* (penultimate) syllable when the final syllable is open: अब **á-ba,** उनी **ú-nī,** खैरो **khəý-ro,** सधैं **sá-dhəỹ,** घण्टा **gháṇ-tā.**

or if the final syllable is a closed syllable containing a short vowel: खबर **khá-bar** भारत् **bhá-rat,** पश्चिम् **páʃ-cim,** संस्कृत् **sám-skɹt.**

The stress is on the *final* syllable, if the final syllable is closed and contains a long vowel: सामान् **sā-mā́n,** प्राचीन् **prā-cī́n,** चुरोट् **cu-róṭ.**

The following exceptions to the above rules should be noted:

(a) certain adverbial and pronominal forms ending in the syllables **-hā̃, -hī** and **hī̃** are stressed on the final syllable: वहाँ **va-hā̃́,** कहाँ **ka-hā̃́,** त्यही **tya-hī́,** उहीं **u-hī̃́,** etc.

(b) the emphatic suffix **-əy** (see Lesson 5.9) is often stressed: घरै **gharəý,** जानै **jānəý,** etc.

In words of more than two syllables, if the penultimate syllable is long, it is stressed: सीमाना **sī-mā́-nā,** भारतीय **bhā-rat-ī́-ya,** अवलोकित् **avalókit.**

If the final syllable is closed and contains a long vowel or if the final syllable ends in two consonants, the final syllable is stressed: हिन्दुस्तान् **hin-du-stā́n,** इतिहास् **i-ti-hā́s,** अमरलोक् **a-mar-lók,** बन्दोबस्त् **ban-do-bást.**

If the penultimate syllable is short and the final syllable is open or a closed syllable containing a short vowel followed by only one consonant, the antepenultimate syllable is stressed: हलुको **há-lu-ko,** समानता **sa-mā́-na-ta,** परिषद् **páriṣad.**

4. The plural suffix हरू **-harū** is never stressed and the word to which it is added retains its original stress (see Lesson 2.2): राजा राजाहरू **rā́jā rā́jāharū,** तपाईं तपाईंहरू **tapāī̃ tapā́ī̃harū** etc.

5. The negative prefix न **na-** always attracts the stress: गर नगर **gára nágara,** गर्नुहोला नगर्नुहोला **gárnuholā nágarnuholā** etc.

6. All verbal infinitives are stressed on the first syllable (Lesson 5.3). This stress remains fixed in most forms of the verb. The major exceptions are:

(*a*) negative forms of the Simple Indefinite Tense formed with the suffix **-dəy-**, which is stressed (Lesson 6.2).

(*b*) negative forms with the stressed prefix **na-** (see 5 above).

Thus	गर्नु	गरेको	गर्दै छौ
	gárnu	**gáreko**	**gárdəy chəw** etc.

but गर्दैन गर्दैनन् नगरिएको
gardəýna **gardəýnan** **nágarieko** etc.

The devanāgarī syllabary

All the symbols of the *devanāgarī* syllabary have now been introduced. In the table below, the symbols are set out in the traditional order employed in Nepali dictionaries. The following points should be noted.

(*a*) The table is read from left to right. Thus in alphabetical listing, the vowel अ precedes the vowel आ, the consonant क precedes the consonant ख etc.

(*b*) In dictionaries, letters bearing the marks of nasalisation (**anusvār** and **candrabindu**) are listed first. Thus कँ and कं precede क.[1]

(*c*) It will be seen that consonants are grouped according to the mode and point of their articulation. In the first line, all the sounds are *velar*, the first (e.g. क) being voiceless and non-aspirated, the second (e.g. ख) being voiceless and aspirated, the third (e.g. ग) being voiced and non-aspirated, the fourth (e.g. घ) being voiced and aspirated, and the fifth (e.g. ङ) being nasal.

The sounds in the second line are all palatal, in the third line all retroflex, in the fourth line all dental, in the fifth line all labial.

The remaining letters follow in the order indicated.

(*d*) The letters ड़ and ढ़, though often distinguished from ड and ढ by means of a subscript dot are not listed separately in dictionaries. Thus पढ़्नु **paṛhnu** is listed as if it were written पढ्नु.

There are several different systems found in European works for the transliteration of the **devanāgarī** script into Roman letters. The most common alternatives are listed on page 20.

A handwritten version of the script is given on pages 21 and 22.

[1]Some dictionaries list letters bearing **candrabindu** before those bearing **anusvār,** whereas some make no distinction between the two.

Anusvār	ं										
Candrabindu	ँ										
Vowel characters	अ	आ	इ	ई	उ	ऊ	ऋ	ए	ऐ	ओ	औ
Vowel signs		ा	ि	ी	ु	ू	ृ	े	ै	ो	ौ
	a	ā	i	ī	u	ū	ɹ	e	əy	o	əw

Consonants							
Velar	क	ख	ग	घ	ङ		
	k	kh	g	gh	ŋ		
Palatal	च	छ	ज	झ	ञ		
	c	ch	j	jh	ɲ		
Retroflex	ट	ठ	ड	ढ	ण	ड़	ढ़
	ʈ	ʈh	ɖ	ɖh	ɳ	ɽ	ɽh
Dental	त	थ	द	ध	न		
	t	th	d	dh	n		
Labial	प	फ	ब	भ	म		
	p	ph	b	bh	m		

	य	र	ल	व	श	ष	स	ह
	y	r	l	v	ʃ	ʂ	s	h
Visarga	:							
Virām	्							

Alternative forms	अ	आ	ओ	औ	झ or झ	ण
	a	ā	o	əw	jh	ɳ

A note on other systems of transliteration

When transliterating Nepali names into English (in translations, learned articles etc.), the following signs are often used, and should be noted:

ऋ	**ṛi** or **ṛ**
ऐ	**ai**
औ	**au**
ङ	**ṅ**
च	**ch**
छ	**cch**
ञ	**ñ**

ट	**ṭ**
ठ	**ṭh**
ड	**ḍ**
ढ	**ḍh**
ण	**ṇ**
श	**sh** or **ś**
ष	**ṣ**

Nasalised vowels are often written: **aṅ, āṅ, iṅ** etc.

For other letters, the system of transcription described above is most commonly used.

The following examples illustrate the two types of transliteration. The first is that used in the text of this course, and the second is that most often found elsewhere:

	कृष्ण	भैरव	पौड्याल्	खुम्जुङ्ग	चामे	छेत्री
(1)	**kɹṣṇa**	**bhəyrava**	**pəwɽyāl**	**khumjuŋg**	**cāme**	**chetrī**
(2)	**kṛṣṇa**	**bhairava**	**pauḍyāl**	**khumjuṅg**	**chāme**	**chhetrī**

	अञ्जलि	ठकुर्	ढोका	शिव	भाद्गाउँ
(1)	**aɲjali**	**ṭhākur**	**ḍhokā**	**ʃiva**	**bhādgāū̃**
(2)	**añjali**	**ṭhākur**	**ḍhokā**	**śiva** **shiva**	**bhādgāuṅ**

Proper names transliterated according to the second system are usually written with a capital letter: e.g. **Kṛṣṇa, Śiva** etc.

Nepali handwriting

Here is a handwritten version of the *devanāgarī* syllabary given on page 20. An examination of the letters will show you that the differences between the written and printed characters are small. Just as in writing any other language you should adapt the letters to suit your own style.

Anusvār	ं
Candrabindu	ँ
Vowels	अ आ इ ई उ ऊ ऋ ए ऐ ओ औ
Velar	क ख ग घ ङ
Palatal	च छ ज झ ञ
Retroflex	ट ठ ड ढ ण ड़ ढ़

Dental	त	थ	द	ध	न			
Labial	प	फ	ब	भ	म			
	य	र	ल	व	श	ष	स	ह

Visarga ः

Virām ्

Alternatives अ आ ओ औ झ or रु ण

The following is a handwritten version of Exercise 1a (p. 26).

१. मेरो किताब् कहाँ छ ? टेबुल्मा छ ।

२. त्यो मान्छे को हो ? हाम्रो नोकर् हो ।

३. राम् कहाँ छ ? स्कूल्मा छ ।

४. त्यो मन्दिर् धेरै पुरानो हो ।

५. सगर्माथा नेपाल्मा छ ।

६. काठ्माडौं कहाँ छ ? नेपाल्मा छ ।

७. तिम्रो घर् कहाँ छ ? त्यहाँ छ ।

८. काठ्माडौं ठूलो शहर् हो तर पोखरा धेरै सानो हो ।

९. तिम्रो नाउँ के हो ? मेरो नाउँ राम् हो ।

१०. धोबी कहाँ छ ? मेरो घर्मा छ ।

११. ढोकामा को छ ? मेरो छोरा छ ।

१२. त्यो मान्छे को हो ? धोबी हो ।

LESSON 1

1. Nepali has no equivalent of the English definite or indefinite articles 'the', 'a'. Thus शहर् **ʃahar** means *a* town or *the* town, मान्छे **mānche** *a* man or *the* man. (Note that शहर् is sometimes written सहर् **sahar**.)

2. Adjectives always precede the noun they qualify:

पुरानो मन्दिर्	**purāno mandir**	the/an old temple
ठूलो शहर्	**ṭhūlo ʃahar**	the/a big city
राम्रो सिनेमा	**rāmro sinemā**	the/a good film

The English loan word सिनेमा means both *cinema* and *film*.

3. The demonstrative adjectives are: यो **yo** 'this' and त्यो **tyo** 'that'.

यो किताब्	**yo kitāb**	this book	त्यो देश्	**tyo deʃ**	that country
यो केटा	**yo keṭā**	this boy	त्यो आइमाई	**tyo āimāī**	that woman

(Note that किताब् is often pronounced *kitāp* – Introduction, Section 1.)

4. The third person singular forms छ **cha** and हो **ho** both mean 'is'. The difference between them is that, generally speaking, छ locates (i.e. indicates *where* someone or something is) and हो defines (i.e. indicates *how, who* or *what* someone or something is). The verb usually comes at the end of the sentence.

किताब् कहाँ छ?	**kitāb kahā̃ cha?** where is the book? (छ locates)
कलम् राम्रो हो	**kalam rāmro ho** the pen is good (हो defines)
नोकर् त्यहाँ छ	**nokar tyahā̃ cha** the servant is there
त्यो मान्छे को हो?	**tyo mānche ko ho?** who is that man?

5. छ is often used in contexts where according to the above rule हो would be expected. For instance, it would be quite correct to say कलम् राम्रो छ without any real difference being made to the sense. In certain idiomatic expressions like ठीक् छ **ṭhīk cha** 'it's all right', हो would in fact be incorrect. In statements, therefore, छ is often used in place of हो to define. In questions asking for a definition (usually with के **ke** 'what?' and को **ko** 'who?') हो is invariably used. Thus in the question तिम्रो नाउँ के हो? **timro nāũ ke ho?** 'what is your name?' छ would be incorrect.

6. The possessive adjectives मेरो **mero** 'my', तिम्रो **timro** 'your', हाम्रो **hāmro** 'our', like all other adjectives precede the noun they qualify.

मेरो घर् त्यहाँ छ **mero ghar tyahā̃ cha** my house is there
हाम्रो देश् नेपाल् हो **hāmro deʃ nepāl ho** our country is Nepal

7. यो and त्यो are also used as third person singular pronouns 'he', 'she', 'it'. यो refers to the person or thing nearer the speaker, and त्यो to the person or thing farther away. When no such distinction is implied, त्यो is usually employed.

त्यो को हो? **tyo ko ho?** who is he?
यो के हो? **yo ke ho?** what is this? or, what is it?
त्यो त्यहाँ छ **tyo tyahā̃ cha** he/she/it is there

Obviously the translation *he, she, it* will depend on the context.

Unless ambiguity is likely to arise, the pronominal subject of the verb may be omitted. Thus छ, हो could mean 'he/she/it is'. The translation will be decided by the context.

हाम्रो नोकर् कहाँ छ ? त्यहाँ छ
hāmro nokar kahā̃ cha? tyahā̃ cha
Where is our servant? He is there

मेरो किताब् कहाँ छ? यहाँ छ
mero kitāb kahā̃ cha? yahā̃ cha
Where is my book? It is here

त्यो मान्छे को हो ? धोबी हो
tyo mānche ko ho? dhobī ho
Who is that man? He is the washerman

8. Words like -मा **-mā** 'in, at, on', -सित **-sita** 'with', -सँग **sā̃ga** 'with', follow the word they govern and are known as *postpositions*. In writing they are joined to the word they follow. If that word ends in a consonant, the junction is effected by means of the **virām.**

नेपाल्मा	**nepālmā**	in Nepal
स्कूल्मा	**skūlmā**	at school
टेबुल्मा	**ṭebulmā**	on the table
ढोकामा	**ḍhokāmā**	at the door
मान्छेसित	**mānchesita**	with the man
मेरो छोरासँग	**mero chorāsā̃ga**	with my son

The translation of -मा 'in, at, on' is decided by the context. -सँग and -सित are largely synonymous. In certain idiomatic phrases, which will be discussed later, one may be preferred to the other.

सगर्माथा नेपाल्मा छ
sagarmāthā nepālmā cha
Mt. Everest is in Nepal

राम् स्कूल्मा छ
rām skūlmā cha
Ram is at school

किताब् टेबुल्मा छ
kitāb ṭebulmā cha
The book is on the table

नोकर्सँग को छ?
nokarsãga ko cha?
Who is with the servant?

Vocabulary 1

आइमाई	**āimāī**	woman
कलम्	**kalam**	pen
कहाँ	**kahā̃**	where?
काठ्माड़ौं	**kāṭhmāṛəw̃**	Kathmandu
किताब्	**kitāb**	book
के	**ke**	what?
को	**ko**	who?
घर्	**ghar**	house, home
छोरा	**chorā**	son
टेबुल्	**ṭebul**	table
ठीक्	**ṭhīk**	all right
ठूलो	**ṭhūlo**	big
ढोका	**ḍhokā**	door
तर	**tara**	but
तिम्रो	**timro**	your
त्यहाँ	**tyahā̃**	there
त्यो	**tyo**	that
देश्	**deʃ**	country, land
धेरै	**dherəy**	much, very
धोबी	**dhobī**	washerman
नाउँ	**nāũ**	name
नेपाल्	**nepāl**	Nepal
नोकर्	**nokar**	servant
पुरानो	**purāno**	old
पोखरा	**pokharā**	Pokhara
मन्दिर्	**mandir**	temple
-मा	**-mā**	in
मान्छे	**mānche**	man, person
मेरो	**mero**	my
यहाँ	**yahā̃**	here
यो	**yo**	this
राम्	**rām**	Ram (man's name)
राम्रो	**rāmro**	nice, good, beautiful
शहर् (सहर्)	**ʃahar (sahar)**	city
सगर्माथा	**sagarmāthā**	Mt. Everest
-सँग	**-sãga**	with

साइकल्	**sāikal**	cycle
सानो(सानु)	**sāno (sānu)**	small
-सित	**-sita**	with
स्कूल्	**skūl**	school
हाम्रो	**hāmro**	our

Exercise 1a

Translate into English

१ . मेरो किताब् कहाँ छ? टेबुल्मा छ।

२ . त्यो मान्छे को हो? हाम्रो नोकर् हो ।

३ . राम् कहाँ छ? स्कूल्मा छ।

४ . त्यो मन्दिर् धेरै पुरानो हो।

५ . सगर्माथा नेपाल्मा छ।

६ . काठ्माडौं कहाँ छ? नेपाल्मा छ।

७ . तिम्रो घर् कहाँ छ? त्यहाँ छ।

८ . काठ्माडौं ठूलो शहर् हो तर पोखरा धेरै सानो हो।

९ . तिम्रो नाउँ के हो? मेरो नाउँ राम् हो।

१०. धोबी कहाँ छ? मेरो घर्मा छ।

११. ढोकामा को छ? मेरो छोरा छ।

१२. त्यो मान्छे को हो? धोबी हो।

Exercise 1b

Translate into Nepali

1. Our house is in Pokhara.
2. Where is my cycle?
3. The servant is at the door.
4. This book is very good.
5. Kathmandu is in Nepal. It is a very big city.
6. What is your name?
7. Who is in your house?
8. My town is Kathmandu.
9. This temple is very old.
10. My son is with the servant.

Exercise 1c

Use छ *or* हो *as appropriate*

1. मेरो किताब् कहाँ ---- ?
2. त्यो के ----?
3. हाम्रो घर् नेपाल्मा ----।
4. राम् यहाँ ----।
5. त्यो शहर् धेरै ठूलो ----।

6. तिम्रो नाउँ के ---- ?
7. ढोकामा को ---- ?
8. मेरो छोरा स्कूलमा ---- ।

Exercise 1d

Translate into Nepali

In the house; on the table; with Ram; this country is Nepal; he is a washerman; who is that? he is in Nepal; it's all right; where is Kathmandu? she is in the temple; with the little boy.

LESSON 2

1. *New conjunct consonants*

ज्य	**jy**	as in	दाज्यू	**dājyū**	elder brother
थ्व	**thv**	as in	पृथ्वी	**pṛthvī**	earth
प्त	**pt**	as in	हप्ता	**haptā**	week
र्ख	**rkh**	as in	गोर्खा	**gorkhā**	Gorkha[1]
ल्त	**lt**	as in	खल्ती	**khaltī**	pocket
ल्ल	**ll**	as in	दिल्ली	**dillī**	Delhi
स्व	**sv**	as in	स्वास्नी	**svāsnī**	wife

2. The plural of nouns is formed by adding the plural suffix -हरू **harū** directly to the noun. When the noun to which the suffix is added ends in a consonant, the junction is effected by means of the **virām.**

राजा	**rājā**	king	राजाहरू	**rājāharū**	kings
मान्छे	**mānche**	man	मान्छेहरू	**mānceharū**	men
शहर्	**ʃahar**	city	शहर्हरू	**ʃaharharū**	cities
बाहुन्	**bāhun**	Brahmin	बाहुन्हरू	**bāhunharū**	Brahmins
खेत्	**khet**	field	खेत्हरू	**khet-harū**	fields
किताब्	**kitāb**	book	किताब्हरू	**kitāb-harū**	books

3. Before plural nouns, the demonstratives यो and त्यो (1.3) become यी **yī** and ती **tī** respectively.

यो मन्त्री	**yo mantrī**	this minister
यी मन्त्रीहरू	**yī mantrīharū**	these ministers
त्यो घोड़ा	**tyo ghoṛā**	that horse
ती घोड़ाहरू	**tī ghoṛāharū**	those horses

4. In spoken Nepali, other adjectives usually have the *same* form before both singular and plural nouns.

पुरानो मन्दिर्हरू	**purāno mandirharū**	old temples
मेरो छोराहरू	**mero chorāharū**	my sons
ठूलो शहर्हरू	**ṭhūlo ʃaharharū**	big cities

[1]This word is often written गोरखा

In written and occasionally in the spoken language, adjectives ending in **-o** change their endings to **-ā** before a plural noun.

ठूला राजाहरू	**ṭhūlā rājāharū**	great kings
पुराना शहरहरू	**purānā ʃaharharū**	old cities
मेरा किताब्हरू	**merā kitāb-harū**	my books

Some adjectives in **-o** have an alternative form in **-u,** e.g. सानो **sāno** or सानु **sānu** 'small'. These also have a plural form in **-ā.** Thus साना **sānā.**

5. When a plural suffix is added to 'non-countable' nouns denoting inanimate objects (e.g. words like *rice, tea, clothes* etc.), it implies 'and other things'.

भात्	**bhāt**	'cooked rice'	भात्हरू	**bhāt-harū**	rice and other things to eat
लुगा	**lugā**	'clothes'	लुगाहरू	**lugāharū**	clothes and other things to wear

Note that लुगा 'clothes' is singular in Nepali:
मेरो लुगा त्यहाँ छ my clothes are there

6. When हरू is added to a proper name, it implies 'the person and his family or people'.

राम्हरू	**rāmharū**	Ram and his family
सीताहरू	**sītāharū**	Sita and her friends

7. The plural forms corresponding to छ and हो are छन् **chan** and हुन् **hun,** both meaning 'are'.

ती मान्छेहरू कहाँ छन् ?	Where are those men?
ती आइमाईहरू को हुन्?	Who are those women?

In sentences like 'my sons are students', where in English both nouns are plural, in Nepali the plural suffix -हरू is added only to the first noun. The noun in the predicative position does not usually require the plural suffix.

मेरो (मेरा) छोराहरू विद्यार्थी हुन्
mero (*or* merā) chorāharū vidyārthī hun
My sons are students

8. In spoken Nepali, the singular form of the demonstrative यो , त्यो and the singular form of the verb छ , हो are often used even when the subject of the sentence is plural. Thus the following would be acceptable in the spoken language.

त्यो मान्छेहरू कहाँ छ?
त्यो आइमाईहरू को हो ?
मेरो छोराहरू विद्यार्थी हो

The replacement of plural endings by the singular is a common feature of the spoken language.

9. The numerals are set out in Appendix 1 (p. 251). At this stage numerals 1 to 10 should be learnt.

When preceded by a numeral, the noun usually remains singular. Thus: दुइ दिन् **dui din** 'two days', पाँच् साल् **pā̃c sāl** 'five years', दस् महीना **das mahīnā** 'ten months', छ हजार् मील् **cha hajār mīl** 'six thousand miles', सात् कोस् **sāt kos** 'seven *kos*'. (**kos** is a measure of distance approximately two miles. In villages **kos** is used more frequently than मील् or किलोमीटर् **kilomīṭar**.)

10. When a noun is qualified by धेरै **dherəy** 'much, many', the addition of the plural suffix is optional and in spoken Nepali is often omitted. Thus: धेरै किताब् or धेरै किताब्हरू .

In spoken Nepali verbal concord may be singular or plural. In the written language it is usually plural.

पुस्तकालयमा धेरै किताब्हरू छन्
pustakālayamā dherəy kitāb-harū chan
In the library there are many books

In spoken Nepali, the same sentence may be expressed:

पुस्तकालयमा धेरै किताब् छ।

11. All Nepali verbs have special negative forms. The negative forms corresponding to छ and हो are छैन **chəynan** and होइन **hoina** respectively. The plural negative forms are छैनन् **chəynan** and होइनन् **hoinan.**

मेरो किताब् यहाँ छैन
My book is not here
त्यो मान्छे बाहुन् होइन
That man is not a Brahmin
मेरो छोराहरू स्कूल्मा छैनन्
My sons are not at school
यी आइमाईहरू नेपाली होइनन्
These women are not Nepalis

12. Questions may be asked by using an interrogative word like कहाँ **kahā̃?** 'where?' के **ke?** 'what?', को **ko?** 'who?', कुन् **kun** 'which?'. Note that कुन् is an adjective. कुन् देश्मा **kun deʃmā?** 'in which country?' कुन् किताब् **kun kitāb?** 'which book?' कुन् किसिम् **kun kisim?** 'which sort?'

In questions which require the answer 'yes' or 'no', the order of words remains the same as in the statement, but the pitch of the voice rises at the end of the sentence.

यो किताब् हो?	Is this a book?
त्यो मान्छे नेपाली हो ?	Is that man a Nepali?
ती विद्यार्थीहरू विश्वविद्यालयमा छन्?	Are those students at university?

Such questions are answered by repeating the main verb in the affirmative for 'yes' and in the negative for 'no'.

मेरो किताब् टेबुल्मा छ? छ	Is my book on the table? Yes (it is)
त्यो मान्छे बाहुन् हो? होइन	Is that man a Brahmin? No (he is not)

The word हजुर् **hajūr** (literally 'sir') is often added to the answer for the sake of politeness.

चिया छ? छ, हजुर्
ciyā cha? cha hajūr
Is there (any) tea? Yes, sir

Questions are commonly asked by using the expressions छ कि छैन? **cha ki chəyna?** हो कि होइन? **ho ki hoina?** 'is there or isn't there?'

पसल्मा फल्फुल् छ कि छैन?
pasalmā phalphul cha ki chəyna?
In the shop is there any fruit (or not)?

त्यो मान्छे छेत्री हो कि होइन?
tyo mānche chetrī ho ki hoina?
Is that man a Chetri[1] (or not)?

तर्कारी मीठो छ कि छैन?
tarkārī mīṭho cha ki chəyna?
Are the vegetables good (or not)?

Note that तर्कारी 'vegetables' is singular in Nepali.

13. In Nepali there are a number of words for 'good':

(*a*) राम्रो **rāmro,** though strictly speaking means 'pleasing to the eye', 'beautiful', is now used in most senses of the English 'good'.

(*b*) मीठो means 'good to the taste' and is only used for food and drink.

(*c*) असल् means 'of good quality' or 'morally good'.

त्यो राम्रो मान्छे हो	He's a good-looking man
त्यो असल् मान्छे हो	He's a good man (ref. to character)
पानी मीठो छ	The water tastes good
पानी असल् छ	The water is good (for drinking)

(*d*) बेस् **bes** and its emphatic form[2] बेसै **besəy** again refers to quality:

त्यो होटेल् बेस् छ	That hotel is good
सिनेमा बेसै छ	The film is fairly good

14. The informal greeting कस्तो छ? **kasto cha?** 'how goes it?', 'how are you?'

[1]A Nepalese caste.

[2]Emphatic forms (Lesson 5.9) all end in the suffix **-əy.** All words may have emphatic forms, which are not always very different in meaning from the simple form. **ṭhīk cha** and **ṭhīkəy cha** are more or less synonymous. Note that the emphatic forms **besəy** and **ramrəy** are used in the sense of 'fairly good', 'not too bad'.

may be answered:

बेस् छ *or* बेसै छ **bes/besəy cha,**
ठीक् छ *or* ठीकै छ **ṭhīk/ṭhīkəy cha**
राम्रो छ *or* राम्रै छ **rāmro/rāmrəy cha,**
सन्चो छ *or* सन्चै छ **sanco/sancəy cha**

All these expressions may be translated 'all right'.

The most common form of greeting in Nepal is नमस्ते **namaste** or नमस्कार् **namaskār**, used at any time of the day. When taking leave of someone नमस्ते is used where we should say 'goodbye'. In this case it may be preceded by some remark like म जाऊँ है त? **ma jāū̃ həy ta?** (literally 'may I go now?').

15. The interrogative pronouns को 'who?' and के 'what?' have no separate plural forms. Plurality is indicated by repeating the pronoun.

तिम्रो घर्मा को को छ ? (छन्)
Who (i.e. what people) are in your house?

पसल्मा के के छ?
What things are in the shop?

Similarly, repetition of an adjective indicates plurality:

त्यो पसल्मा असल् असल् माल् छ
tyo pasalmā asal asal māl cha
There are all kinds of good things in the shop

Note especially the reduplicated forms सान्साना **sānsānā** 'small', and ठुल्ठुला **ṭhūlṭhūlā** 'big' which always have the plural ending **-ā.**

खोलामा सान्साना माछा धेरै छन्
kholāmā sānsānā māchā dherəy chan
In the river there are lots of little fish

भारत्मा ठुल्ठुला शहर्हरू छन्
bhāratmā ṭhūlṭhūlā ʃaharharū chan
In India there are many big cities

16. The postposition -को **-ko** 'of' deserves special attention. 'The book of the boy' or 'the boy's book' is expressed छोराको किताब् **chorāko kitāb** 'boy-of book'. Compare the following sentences:

नोकर्को नाउँ के हो?
nokarko nāū̃ ke ho?
What is the servant's name?

राम्को पसल् कहाँ छ?
rāmko pasal kahā̃ cha?
Where is Ram's shop?

नेपाल्को राज्धानी काठ्माडौं हो
nepālko rājdhānī kāṭhmāṛəw̃ ho
The capital of Nepal is Kathmandu

रामको पसलमा कुन किसिमको माल छ?
rāmko pasalmā kun kisimko māl cha?
What sort of goods are there in Ram's shop?

In written and sometimes in spoken Nepali, -को changes to -का **kā** before plural nouns. In this respect it behaves like an adjective:

नेपालका मान्छेहरू	**nepālkā mānchehārū**	men of Nepal
छोराका किताबहरू	**chorākā kitāb-harū**	the boy's books
रामका बहिनीहरू	**rāmkā bahinīharū**	Ram's sisters

17. Nepali possesses a large number of relationship terms, which will be encountered throughout the course.[1] बहिनी **bahinī** is a term applied to a sister younger than oneself. दिदी **didī** is an elder sister. Similarly, भाइ **bhāi** is a younger brother, and दाइ **dāi** or दाज्यू **dājyū** is an elder brother.

These terms are commonly used even when addressing strangers. If we stopped a man of about our own age, or a little older, in the street to enquire the way to the teashop, we might say:

ए दाज्यू, चियापसल कहाँ छ?
e dājyū, ciyāpasal kahã cha
Excuse me ('o elder brother!'), where is the teashop?

In the same way, a woman might be politely addressed as दिदी. If she is much older than oneself, she would be addressed as आमा **āmā** 'mother', or if very much older as बज्यै **bajyəy** 'grandmother'. Younger men may be addressed as भाइ and younger women as बहिनी. Children are frequently addressed as नानी **nānī.**

The honorific suffix -ज्यू **-jyū** when added to male proper names is the equivalent of 'Mr.'

गणेशज्यू	**gaṇeʃjyū**	Mr. Ganesh
बिष्टज्यू	**biṣṭajyū**	Mr. Bista

Occasionally, the Hindi form of the suffix -जी **-jī** is also used.

18. The postpositions -बाट **-bāṭa** and -देखि **-dekhi** both mean 'from'.

काठमाडौंदेखि पोखरा कति टाढा छ?
kāṭhmāṛəw̃dekhi pokharā kati ṭāṛhā cha?
How far is Pokhara from Kathmandu?

लन्दनबाट नेपाल छ हजार मील टाढा छ
landanbāṭa nepāl cha hajār mīl ṭāṛhā cha
Nepal is six thousand miles away from London

(Note the use of the adjective **ṭāṛhā** 'far' in the second sentence.)

In sentences like the following only -देखि may be used:

[1] A list of relationship terms is given on p.256.

त्यो मान्छे पाँच् महीनादेखि यहाँ छ
tyo mānche pā̃c mahīnādekhi yahā̃ cha
That man has been here *for* five months ('is here from five months')
मेरो छोरा तीन् हप्तादेखि बिरामी छ
mero chorā tīn haptādekhi birāmī cha
My son has been ill for three weeks

19. Postpositions may be added to adverbs like यहाँ, त्यहाँ, कहाँ
त्यो मान्छे यहाँको होइन
That man is not from ('of') here
यो मान्छे कहाँको हो?
Where does he come from? (lit. 'He is a man of where?')
यहाँबाट शहर् कति टाढा छ?
How far is the city from here?

Vocabulary 2

अरू	**arū**	other, else
अरू के	**arū ke**	what else?
अलि	**ali**	rather, a little
असल्	**asal**	good, sound
ऊ त्यहीं	**ū tyahī̃**	over there
उकालो	**ukālo**	steep
कति	**kati**	how much?
कति टाढा?	**kati ṭāṛhā**	how far?
कस्तो	**kasto**	how
किसिम्	**kisim**	kind, sort
कुन्	**kun**	which
खल्ती	**khaltī**	pocket
खेत्	**khet**	field
खोला	**kholā**	river
गाउँ	**gāū̃**	village
घोड़ा	**ghoṛā**	horse
चिया	**ciyā**	tea
चियापसल्	**ciyāpasal**	teashop
छेत्री	**chetrī**	Chetri
-ज्यू	**-jyū**	honorific suffix, Mr.
टाढा	**ṭāṛhā**	far
ठूल्ठूला	**ṭhūlṭhūlā**	big (pl. adj.)
तर	**tara**	but
तर्कारी	**tarkārī**	vegetables
दर्बार्	**darbār**	court, palace
दाइ (दाज्यू)	**dāī (dājyū)**	elder brother

दिन्	**din**	day
दिल्ली	**dillī**	Delhi
दिदी	**didī**	elder sister
दूध्	**dūdh**	milk
-देखि	**-dekhi**	from, since
धेरै	**dherəy**	much, many
नमस्ते (नमस्कार्)	**namaste (namaskār)**	hello, goodbye
नानी	**nānī**	child
नेपाली	**nepālī**	Nepali
पण्डित्	**paṇḍit**	scholar (of Sanskrit)
पनि	**pani**	also, even
पसल्	**pasal**	shop
पुस्तकालय	**pustakālaya**	library
पृथ्वीनारायण्	**pɹthvīnārāyaṇ**	Prithvinarayan
पैसा	**pəysā**	money
फल्फुल्	**phalphul**	fruit
बजार्	**bajār**	bazaar, market
बहिनी	**bahinī**	younger sister
बज्यै	**bajyəy**	grandmother
-बाट	**-bāṭa**	from
बाटो	**bāṭo**	road
बाहुन्	**bāhun**	Brahmin
बिरामी	**birāmī**	ill
बूढो	**būṛho**	old man
बेस्	**bes**	good, fine
भाइ	**bhāi**	younger brother
भात्	**bhāt**	cooked rice
भारत्	**bhārat**	India
मन्त्री	**mantrī**	minister
महीना	**mahīnā**	month
माछा	**māchā**	fish
माथि	**māthi**	on, above, up
माल्	**māl**	goods, wares
मास्टर्	**māsṭar**	schoolmaster
मीठो	**mīṭho**	pleasant tasting
मील्	**mīl**	mile
राम्रो	**rāmro**	good, beautiful
राज्धानी	**rājdhānī**	capital
रुपियाँ	**rupiyā̃**	rupee[1]
लन्दन्	**landan**	London
लुगा	**lugā**	clothes
विद्यार्थी	**vidyārthī**	student

[1]The major unit of currency in Nepal.

विश्वविद्यालय	**viʃvavidyālaya**	university
सन्चो	**sanco** (*emph.* **sancəy**)	in good health, well
सान्साना	**sānsānā**	little (pl. adj.)
साल्	**sāl**	year
सिपाही	**sipāhī**	soldier, seepoy
स्वास्नी	**svāsnī**	wife
हजार्	**hajār**	thousand
हजूर्	**hajūr**	sir
हप्ता	**haptā**	week
होटेल्	**hoṭel**	hotel, restaurant

Reading Passage

अ. दाज्यू नमस्ते।
आ. नमस्ते
अ. यहाँबाट गोर्खा कति टाढ़ा छ ?
आ. धेरै टाढ़ा छैन हजूर् , ऊ त्यहीं छ , माथि।
अ. बाटो कस्तो छ? उकालो छ ?
आ. अलि उकालो छ हजूर् ।
अ. शहर् कस्तो छ? ठूलो छ कि छैन?
आ. धेरै ठूलो छैन, तर बजार्मा पसल्हरू धेरै छन्।
अ. शहर्मा अरू के के छ? मन्दिर्हरू छन्?
आ. छन् हजूर्। पृथ्वीनारायणको पुरानो दर्बार् पनि छ।
मेरो गाउँ यहाँ छ। म जाउँ है त हजूर्।नमस्ते।
अ. नमस्ते ।

Exercise 2a

Translate into English

१. त्यो पसल्मा धेरै किसिम्को माल् छ।
२. तिम्रो छोराको नाउँ के हो? गणेश् हो हजूर् ।
३. ती मान्छेहरू को हुन्? ती मान्छेहरू सिपाही हुन्।
४. तिम्रो पसल्मा चिया छ कि छैन? छ हजूर् तर दूध् छैन ।
५. भारत्को राज्धानी के हो? दिल्ली हो ।
६. ए दाज्यू नमस्ते । कस्तो छ? राम्रै छ ।
७. काठ्माड़ौं कुन् देश्मा छ? नेपाल्मा छ ।
८. त्यो तर्कारी मीठो हो कि होइन? धेरै मीठो हो ।
९. गोर्खा काठ्माड़ौंबाट अलि टाढ़ा छ ।
१०. काठ्माड़ौंमा धेरै पुराना मन्दिर्हरू छन् ।
११. शहर्देखि विश्वविद्यालय कति टाढ़ा छ? धेरै टाढ़ा छैन ।
१२. मेरो छोराहरू विद्यार्थी हुन्। विश्वविद्यालयमा छन्।
१३. त्यो ठूलो होटेल् कस्तो छ ? बेसै छ ।

१४. त्यो मान्छे दुइ महीनादेखि नेपाल्मा छ ।
१५. तिम्रो गाउँ कहाँ छ? ऊ त्यहीं छ हजुर् ।
१६. राम्को पसल्मा असल् असल् माल् छ ।
१७. त्यो बूढो यहाँको मान्छे होइन । गोर्खाको हो।
१८. तिम्रो खल्तीमा के के छ?
१९. मेरो भाइ पोखरामा छ ।
२०. नेपाल्का शहर्हरू ठूला छैनन् ।

Exercise 2b

Translate into Nepali

1. How far is the hotel from here?
2. Where is Ram's shop? It is in the city.
3. Is there (any) milk in the shop?
4. What is the capital of Nepal? It is Kathmandu.
5. That man has been in Kathmandu for two years.
6. My sisters are at the university.
7. Is this temple old? Yes, it is very old.
8. Excuse me. How far is the library from here?
9. How is the rice? It is very tasty.
10. My son's name is Ganesh.
11. Hello, how are you? I am very well.
12. There are many big cities in India.

Exercise 2c

Translate into Nepali using the plural form of the adjective where necessary

my books; eight rupees; many great cities; our servants; five days; great kings; your clothes; those villages; three *kos*.

Exercise 2d

Put the following into the plural

शहर्, स्वास्नी, छेत्री, विद्यार्थी, यो किताब्, त्यो घोड़ा,
ठूलो मान्छे, पुरानो मन्दिर्, तिम्रो छोरा मेरो भाइ,
सानु खेत् ,

Exercise 2e

Translate into Nepali

the servant's house; the capital of India; Gaṇesh's wife; the university of Kathmandu; this old man is not from here; he comes from Gorkhā; the villages of India; the big cities of Pākistān.

Exercise 2f

Translate into English

१ . नेपाल्मा गाउँहरू धेरै छन् ।
२ . राम्को बहिनीको नाउँ सीता हो ।
३ . गणेश्ज्यू, नमस्कार्, कस्तो छ? बेसै छ ।
४ . ए नानी, तिम्रो घर् यहाँबाट कति टाढ़ा छ ।
धेरै टाढ़ा छैन, हजूर् । ऊ त्यहीं छ ।
५ . पोखरा कहाँ छ? नेपाल्मा छ ।
६ . दिल्ली कहाँ छ? दिल्ली भारत्मा छ। दिल्ली भारत्को राज्धानी हो।
७ . काठ्माड़ौंमा पुराना मन्दिरहरू धेरै छन्।
८ . हिमालयमा ठूल्ठूला नदीहरू छन् ।
९ . यो तर्कारी मिठो छैन। तिम्रो पसल्मा अरू के के छ?
१०. मेरो भाइ तीन् महीनादेखि भारत्मा छ ।

LESSON 3

1. *New conjunct consonants*

ग्ल	gl	as in	अग्लो	**aglo**	high
र्ज, ङ्ग	rj, ŋg	as in	दार्जीलिङ्ग	**dārjīliŋg**	Darjeeling
द्ध	ddh	as in	बुद्धिमान्	**buddhimān**	clever
ध्य	dhy	as in	अध्यापक्	**adhyāpak**	lecturer
फ्र	phr	as in	फ्रान्स्	**phrāns**	France
ल्क	lk	as in	कल्कत्ता	**kalkattā**	Calcutta
ष्ट्र	ṣṭr	as in	राष्ट्रपति	**rāṣṭrapati**	president
ज्ञ	jñ	as in	ज्ञानी	**jñānī**	well behaved

The combination of ज and ञ (written ज्ञ) is pronounced *gy* exactly the same as ग्य . In the word ज्ञानी the **ā** is pronounced like the *a* in Southern English *hat.*

2. We shall now discuss the rather complex system of personal pronouns and the full conjugation of the verbs छ and हो which you have met in the first two lessons.

Second person pronouns ('you') and third person pronouns ('he', 'she', 'it', 'they') may be grouped into three major honorific grades:

(*a*) Low Grade Honorific (LGH) pronouns – used mainly for children in one's own family, family retainers and animals.

(*b*) Middle Grade Honorific (MGH) pronouns – used mainly for other children, social inferiors, younger relations and intimate friends.

(*c*) High Grade Honorific (HGH) pronouns – used mainly for older relations, acquaintances of equal status, and people to whom one owes a measure of respect.

For example, a family servant, one's son or daughter might be addressed as तँ **tã** 'you' (LGH). The pronoun can equally be used to insult or to express endearment. A child belonging to someone else, a waiter in a hotel or a taxi driver might be addressed as तिमी **timī** 'you' (MGH). An elder relation, one's father, teacher or any older acquaintance would be addressed as तपाईं **tapāī̃** 'you' (HGH). Although one might compare French *tu* and *vous*, it should be noted that the form of address, once established, is never changed.

The honorific scale also extends to third person pronouns. Thus उ **u** 'he/she' is LGH, उनी **unī** is MGH, and वहाँ **vahā̃** and यहाँ **yahā̃** are HGH. Whereas in third person pronouns there is no distinction of gender (उ ,उनी mean both 'he' and 'she'), a distinction of nearness and farness is maintained. See for example Lesson 1.7. where we found that यो denotes the person nearer to and त्यो the person farther from the speaker.

In most cases, plural pronouns are formed by adding the plural suffix-हरू to the singular form. Thus तपाईं **tapāī̃** 2. sing. HGH, तपाईंहरू **tapāī̃harū** 2. plur. HGH.

The following is a complete list of the personal pronouns:

Singular

1	म	**ma**					I
2 LGH	तँ	**tã**					you
2 MGH	तिमी	**timī**					you
2 HGH	तपाईं	**tapāī̃**					you
3 LGH	उ	**u**					he/she
3 LGH	यो	**yo**	त्यो	**tyo**			he/she/it
3 MGH	यिनी	**yinī**	तिनी	**tinī**	उनी	**unī**	he/she
3 HGH	यहाँ	**yahā̃**	वहाँ	**vahā̃**			he/she

Plural

1	हामी	**hāmī**			we
	हामीहरू	**hāmīharū**			
2 LGH/MGH	तिमी	**timī**			you
	तिमीहरू	**timīharū**			
2 HGH	तपाईंहरू	**tapāī̃harū**			you
3 LGH/MGH	यिनीहरू	**yinīharū**	तिनीहरू	**tinīharū**	they
	उनीहरू	**unīharū**			
3 HGH	यहाँहरू	**yahā̃harū**	वहाँहरू	**vahā̃harū**	they

The 2nd person LGH pronoun तँ has no plural form. Instead, the MGH form is used. The 3rd person LGH pronoun उ and the 3rd person plural pronouns refer only to persons, not to things. The usage of the personal pronouns is discussed in section 4 below.

3. The affirmative and negative paradigms of the verbs छ and हो are as follows:

(*a*)

Personal pronoun	*Affirmative*		*Negative*	
म	छु	**chu**	छैन	**chəyna**
तँ	छस्	**chas**	छैनस्	**chəynas**
यो त्यो उ	छ	**cha**	छैन	**chəyna**
उनी, यिनी, तिनी	छन्	**chan**	छैनन्	**chəynan**
तपाईं, तपाईंहरू	हुनुहुन्छ	**hunuhuncha**	हुनुहुन्न	**hunuhunna**

हामी, हामीहरू	छौं	**chəw̃**	छैनौं	**chəynəw̃**
तिमी, तिमीहरू	छौ	**chəw**	छैनौ	**chəynəw**
उनीहरू, यिनीहरू, तिनीहरू	छन्	**chan**	छैनन्	**chəynan**
यहाँ, वहाँ	हुनुहुन्छ	**hunuhuncha**	हुनुहुन्न	**hunuhunna**
यहाँहरू, वहाँहरू	हुनुहुन्छ	**hunuhuncha**	हुनुहुन्न	**hunuhunna**

(*b*)

Personal pronoun		*Affirmative*		*Negative*	
म		हुँ	**hũ**	होइन	**hoina**
तँ		होस्	**hos**	होइनस्	**hoinas**
उ	etc.	हो	**ho**	होइन	**hoina**
उनी	etc.	हुन्	**hun**	होइनन्	**hoinan**
तपाईं	etc.	हुनुहुन्छ	**hunuhuncha**	हुनुहुन्न	**hunuhunna**
हामी	etc.	हौं	**həw̃**	होइनौं	**hoinəw̃**
तिमी	etc.	हौ	**həw**	होइनौ	**hoinəw**
उनीहरू	etc.	हुन्	**hun**	होइनन्	**hoinan**
वहाँ	etc.	हुनुहुन्छ	**hunuhuncha**	हुनुहुन्न	**hunuhunna**
वहाँहरू	etc.	हुनुहुन्छ	**hunuhuncha**	हुनुहुन्न	**hunuhunna**

From the above tables it will be clear that the 3rd person MGH pronouns (उनी , तिनी , यिनी) require the 3rd person plural verb forms छन् and हुन् and that all the HGH pronouns (तपाईं, वहाँ etc.) take the same forms. It will also be noted that the HGH forms of छ and हो are identical.

The two verbs also share a common infinitive हुनु **hunu** 'to be'. In English both verbs are translated as 'I am', 'you are', 'he/she is' etc., but as we have already seen, the function of छ is to *locate* and that of हो is to *define*.

4. The following sentences illustrate the use of the personal pronouns. 1 sing. म **ma** 'I' requires little comment:

म विश्वविद्यालयमा छु
I am in the university

म अड्डामा छैन
I am not in the office

म अँग्रेज् हुँ । हिन्दुस्तानी होइन
I am English, not Indian

Note that the personal pronoun may be omitted in cases where confusion is not likely to arise.

2 sing. LGH तँ **tã** 'you' is reserved for social inferiors usually in the family. Children and servants of the speaker's family are often addressed as तँ . It is also used when speaking to animals and often used in poetry, something like English 'thou'.

ए नानी तँ कहाँ छस्?
Child, where are you?
तँ ज्ञानी होइनस्?
Aren't you good (little boy)?

2 sing. MGH तिमी **timī**'you' is reserved for social inferiors and for children not of the speaker's family. It may be used to address younger members of the family (sisters, brothers etc.). A man may address his wife as तिमी but she would not generally use it for her husband. A foreigner would do well not to use तिमी when addressing adult strangers.

2 sing. HGH तपाईं **tapāī̃** 'you' is used for anyone to whom respect is due. It is becoming customary to use तपाईं for any adult stranger regardless of his or her social status. A woman usually addresses her husband as तपाईं

तपाईं हिजोआज कहाँ हुनुहुन्छ, बिष्टज्यू?
Where are you nowadays, Mr. Bista?
ए दाइ, तपाईं बाहुन् हुनुहुन्छ?
Excuse me, are you a Brahmin?

2 pl. MGH and HGH तिमीहरू **timīharū,** तपाईंहरू **tapāī̃harū** 'you' are used to address several people who would individually be addressed as तिमी and तपाईं. Occasionally in books and speeches, when a number of people are addressed as a group, the singular forms are used.

तपाईंहरू विद्यार्थी हुनुहुन्छ?
Are you students?
तपाईंहरू छेत्री हुनुहुन्छ?
Are you Chetris?

Note that the noun in predicative position remains singular.

1 pl. हामी **hāmī** 'we' and the form हामीहरू **hāmīharū** are in most respects synonymous and interchangeable. If there is any difference, हामी means 'we as a group'; हामीहरू 'we as individuals'. Occasionally हामी may be used by the speaker to refer to himself, in which case it would be translated 'I'.

हामीहरू मज्दुर हौं
We are labourers
हामी नेपाली हौं
We are Nepalis

3 sing. LGH उ **u** 'he/she', यो, त्यो **yo, tyo** 'he/she/it'. We have already seen that the demonstratives may be used as 3rd person singular pronouns (see Lesson 1.7.). When proximity or distance is not implied त्यो is used rather than यो. These pronouns refer to persons, to whom no particular respect is due, and to things. उ is used only for persons.

उ घर्मा छ
He/she is at home

त्यो दार्जीलिङ्गमा छ
He/she is in Darjeeling

त्यो धेरै राम्रो हो
That's very good

यो नेपाल्मा छ तर त्यो भारत्मा छ
He is in Nepal, but he (the other one) is in India

3 sing. MGH यिनी **yinī,** तिनी **tinī** उनी **unī** 'he/she' are used for persons to whom a certain measure of respect is due. They are frequently used to refer to persons in novels and historical narrative, but not usually to refer to the royalty of Nepal or their ancestors. यिनी refers to the person nearer the speaker and तिनी to the person farther away. उनी is more or less synonymous with तिनी and perhaps used more frequently in speech.

यिनी को हुन्?
Who is he/she?

उनी लन्दन्मा छन्
He is in London

तिनी कहाँ छन्?
Where is he?

Nouns denoting persons who would be referred to with a MGH pronoun take a 3rd person *plural* verb:

राम् कहाँ छन्? उनी घर्मा छन्
Where is Ram? He is at home

The plural verb in the question and the use of उनी in the answer makes the sentences more polite than if the singular छ and त्यो had been used.

3 sing. HGH यहाँ **yahā̃** वहाँ **vahā̃** (sometimes written उहाँ **uhā̃**) 'he, she' are used to refer to people who would be addressed as तपाईं in the 2nd person. The difference between यहाँ and वहाँ is again one of proximity.[1]

वहाँ अड्डामा हुनुहुन्छ
He is at the office

यहाँ बाहुन् हुनुहुन्छ
He (the person here) is a Brahmin

Nouns denoting persons referred to with a HGH pronoun require the honorific form of the verb.

मेरो बुवा कल्कत्तामा हुनुहुन्छ । वहाँ मन्त्री हुनुहुन्छ
My father is in Calcutta. He is a minister

मेरो दिदी घरै हुनुहुन्छ। बिरामी हुनुहुन्छ
My elder sister is at home. She is ill

[1]**yahā̃** and **vahā̃** are occasionally used in place of **tapāī̃** to address a second person, in which case, of course, they would be translated 'you' in English. This usage is felt to be extra polite.

When such a noun is preceded by the postposition -को in written and occasionally in spoken Nepali, -को becomes -का **-kā** (the plural concord denotes respect).

जापान्का प्रधान्मन्त्री टोक्योमा हुनुहुन्न
The Prime Minister of Japan is not in Tokyo

फ्रान्स्का राष्ट्रपति बेलायत्मा हुनुहुन्छ
The President of France is in England.

3 pl. LGH/MGH यिनीहरू **yinīharū** तिनीहरू **tinīharū** उनीहरू **unīharū** 'they' are used only for persons:

यिनीहरू बाहुन् हुन्
They are Brahmins

उनीहरू हिजोआज विश्वविद्यालयमा छैनन्
They are not at the university nowadays

तिनीहरू कहाँ छन्?
Where are they?

Note that 'they' referring to things is left unexpressed:

मेरो (मेरा) किताब्हरू कहाँ छन् ? यहाँ छन्
Where are my books? They are here

In colloquial speech the singular forms of the adjectives and verbs may be used:

तिनीहरू कहाँ छ ?
मेरो किताब्हरू कहाँ छ ?

3 pl. HGH यहाँहरू **yahā̃harū,** वहाँहरू **vahā̃harū** correspond to their singular counterparts.

वहाँहरू दर्बार्मा हुनुहुन्छ
They are at court

5. *Feminine forms*

We have seen that there is usually no distinction of gender in the 2nd and 3rd person forms of pronouns and verbs. A number of separate feminine verb forms, however, do exist, and these are found in both written and spoken Nepali, though usage is by no means consistent. The following feminine forms of छ are the most common:

2 sing. LGH	तँ छेस्	**tã ches**	you (f.) are
3 sing. LGH	उ, त्यो, यो छे	**u, tyo, yo che**	she is
3 sing. MGH	उनी, तिनी, यिनी छिन्	**unī, tinī, yinī chin**	she is

Adjectives ending in ओ **-o** and the postposition -को have a feminine singular form in -ई **-ī** (e.g. बूढ़ी, मेरी, -की), which is occasionally used with nouns denoting females. Thus:

मेरी स्वास्नी	**merī svāsnī**	my wife
बूढ़ी आइमाई	**būṛhī āimāī**	an old woman
राम्की केटी	**rāmkī keṭī**	Ram's daughter

The use of a feminine verb with a feminine noun is obligatory:

राम्की स्वास्नी कहाँ छे?
Where is Ram's wife?

मेरी बहिनी मन्दिर्मा छे
My little sister is in the temple

तपाईंकी स्वास्नी कहाँ छिन् ? उनी घर्मा छिन्
Where is your wife? She is at home

Note तपाईंकी **tapāĩkī** 'of you', 'your'

Feminine forms, though occasionally employed in spoken Nepali, are largely a feature of the written language. In normal colloquial speech, राम्को स्वास्नी... छ, मेरो बहिनी.....छ, तपाईंको स्वास्नी....छन् etc. are more frequently heard than the forms given in the examples above.

6. At first sight, the Nepali pronominal system, with its three honorific grades and special forms denoting nearness and farness, appears extremely complicated. Added to this is the fact that in speech the system is not always consistently employed and many speakers change grade within the space of a short conversation. The foreign student of the language might do well to follow the rough guidelines set out below:

(*a*) When addressing a second person, always use तपाईं except for children who should be addressed as तिमी .

(*b*) A third person, who is not present, may usually be referred to by one of the LGH pronouns उ, यो, त्यो, unless special respect is due, in which case the HGH pronouns यहाँ , वहाँ should be used. For example, an absent friend or acquaintance might be referred to as उ , the parent, relation, teacher of the interlocutor would usually be referred to as वहाँ .

(*c*) The MGH pronouns (उनी , यिनी , तिनी) which are now largely a feature of the written language, can for most purposes be ignored in speech.

(*d*) Feminine forms can also be ignored in speech. It will be enough to recognize them when they occur.

(*e*) Nepalese royalty should be referred to by the HGH pronouns, or by the special form हजूर् which will be discussed later in the course (Lesson 20).

(*f*) Older people frequently address younger people as तिमी or तँ. The younger person, however, would not respond with the same pronoun, but would show respect by using तपाईं .

7. Comparison of adjectives is effected by means of the postposition -भन्दा **-bhandā** than'.

(*a*) *Comparative*

कल्कत्ता दिल्लीभन्दा ठूलो छ
kalkattā dillībhandā ṭhūlo cha
Calcutta is bigger than Delhi (lit. 'than-Delhi is big')

यो तरकारी त्यो तरकारीभन्दा मीठो छैन
These vegetables are not as nice as those vegetables

तपाईंको घर मेरो घरभन्दा राम्रो छ
Your house is more beautiful than my house

(*b*) *Superlative*

This is effected by means of the phrase सब्भन्दा **sab-bhandā** 'than all':

स्कूल्को सब्भन्दा बुद्धिमान् विद्यार्थी राम् हो ।
skūlko sab-bhandā buddhimān vidyārthī rām ho
Ram is the cleverest boy in the school (lit. 'than all clever student')

काठ्माडौं नेपाल्को सब्भन्दा ठूलो शहर् हो
Kathmandu is the biggest city in ('of') Nepal

The adjective सब् **sab** 'all', 'every' usually takes a singular noun:

शहर्को सब् पसल् बन्द छ
ʃaharko sab pasal banda cha
Every shop in the city is closed

8. Nepali possesses a number of particles, which are mostly monosyllabic words like पो **po,** नि **ni,** है **həy,** त **ta** etc. The meaning given to these particles depends very much on the context in which they are used, and may often be rendered in English merely by a change of tone. Here we shall deal with a few of the most common particles. Others will be introduced in later lessons.

(*a*) पो **po,** usually precedes the main verb of the sentence and implies a contradiction of something that has already been said. For example, if someone says त्यो होटेल् राम्रो छ । **tyo hoṭel rāmro cha** 'that hotel is good', when *you* have found that it is not, you may contradict the statement by replying नराम्रो पो छ । **narāmro po cha** 'it's not, I tell you'. The pitch on which पो is uttered is higher than that of the other words in the sentence. The sentence तपाईं ब्राह्मण् पो हुनुहुन्छ **tapāī̃ brāhmaṇ po hunuhuncha** might be translated as, 'oh, I see you are a Brahmin' (whereas I thought you were something else). (Note that ब्राह्मण् **brāhmaṇ** is a literary form of बाहुन् 'a Brahmin'.)

(*b*) The particle नि **ni** usually comes at the end of the sentence. In statements it implies that the information given is common knowledge and may be translated 'you know'.

त्यो सगरमाथा हो नि
That's Mt. Everest, you know

In short interrogative phrases, it may be translated 'what about . . .'.

यो होटेल् धेरै राम्रो छैन । त्यो होटेल् नि
This hotel is not very good. What about that hotel?

(*c*) The particle त **ta,** which never stands as the first word in the sentence, has a number of functions. One is to emphasise the word or phrase it follows.

म त ब्राह्मण् हुँ
I am a Brahmin

मेरो भाइ त कलेज्मा छ
My brother is at college

When linking two sentences, त may be translated 'but'.

तपाईं धनी हुनुहुन्छ , म त गरीब् छु ।
You are rich but I am poor

होइन त? **hoina ta?** (or simply होइन?), standing at the end of a sentence turns the statement into a question (something like French *n'est-ce pas*?):

त्यो सगर्माथा होइन त ?
That's Mt. Everest, isn't it?

रक्सौल् भारत्मा छ , होइन?
Raxaul's in India, isn't it?

The affirmative answer to such a question is हो **ho** 'yes'.

त and पो may occur in the same sentence, giving emphasis to an assertion:

त्यो होटेल् त राम्रो पो छ त
tyo hoṭel ta rāmro po cha ta
But that hotel *is* nice, I tell you

(*d*) The particle है **həy** is interrogative, often used in polite requests. We have already seen the expression:

म जाऊँ है त
All right if I go now?

The other uses of particles are discussed in later lessons.

9. कोही **kohī** 'someone' and केही **kehī** 'something' are 3rd person singular indefinite pronouns. (Note that they are often pronounced *koī* and *keī* respectively.) In English they may also be translated 'anyone', 'anything', and in negative sentences 'no one', 'nothing'.

ढोकामा कोही छ?
Is there anyone at the door?

घर्मा कोही छैन
There isn't anyone at home

हिजोआज पसल्हरूमा केही छैन
There's nothing in the shops these days

ढोकामा कोही छैन
There's no one at the door

In negative sentences, the indefinite pronouns are often emphasised with the adverb पनि **pani** 'at all', 'also':

मेरो खल्तीमा केही पनि छैन
There's nothing at all in my pocket.

त्यो गाउँमा कोही पनि छैन
There isn't anyone at all in that village.

Vocabulary 3

अंग्रेज् (अङ्ग्रेज्)	**angrej**	Englishman
अंग्रेजी (अङ्ग्रेजी)	**angrejī**	English language
अग्लो	**aglo**	high
अड्डा	**aḍḍā**	office
अध्यापक्	**adhyāpak**	lecturer
अमेरिका	**amerikā**	America
आज	**āja**	today
आज्कल् (आज्काल्)	**ājkal (ājkāl)**	nowadays
आयो	**āyo**	came, has come
एक् दम् (एक् दमै)	**ek dam** (emph. **ek daməy**)	extremely, very
कपड़ा	**kapṛā**	cloth
कलेज्	**kalej**	college
कल्कत्ता	**kalkattā**	Calcutta
काम्	**kām**	work
केही	**kehī**	something
कोठा	**koṭhā**	room
कोही	**kohī**	somebody
गरीब्	**garīb**	poor
घरै	**gharəy**	at home
चीन्	**cīn**	China
जात्	**jāt**	caste
जापान्	**jāpān**	Japan
ज्ञानी	**jñānī**	well-behaved
त	**ta**	but, however
दार्जीलिङ्ग	**dārjīling**	Darjeeling
दुनियाँ	**duniyā̃**	world
धनी	**dhanī**	rich
नराम्रो	**narāmro**	bad
नि	**ni**	'you know', 'what about'
नेपाल्	**nepāl**	Nepal
पल्टन्	**palṭan**	army, regiment
पो	**po**	'on the contrary'
प्रधान्मन्त्री	**pradhānmantrī**	Prime Minister
फ्रान्स्	**phrāns**	France
बन्द	**banda**	closed, shut
बस्	**bas**	bus
बिजुली	**bijulī**	electricity
बिदा	**bidā**	holiday
बुद्धिमान्	**buddhimān**	clever
बुवा	**buvā**	father
बेलायत्	**belāyat**	England
मज्दूर्	**majdūr**	labourer

महँगो	**mahãgo**	expensive
र	**ra**	and
राष्ट्रपति	**rāṣṭrapati**	President
ल	**la**	look, there
विभाग्	**vibhāg**	department
सब्	**sab**	all
सस्तो	**sasto**	cheap
सीमाना	**sīmānā**	frontier
हिजोआज	**hijoāja**	nowadays
हिन्दुस्तानी	**hindustānī**	Indian
हिमाल्	**himāl**	mountain
है	**həy**	interrogative particle

Reading Passage

अ. नमस्ते। कस्तो छ?
आ. सन्चो छ ।
अ. तिमी हिजोआज कहाँ छौ?
आ. म विश्वविद्यालयमा छु । तिमी नि?
अ. म त अड्डामा छु। मेरो भाइ विश्वविद्यालयमा छ । अंग्रेजी विभाग्मा ।
आ. उनी आज कहाँ छन्?
अ. घरै छ । आज विश्वविद्यालय बन्द छ , होइन ?
आ. हो , आज बिदा छ ।
अ. तिम्रो दाइ आज्काल् कहाँ हुनुहुन्छ?
आ. भारत्मा हुनुहुन्छ , पल्टन्मा ।
अ. ल, मेरो बस् आयो । म जाऊँ है त? आज घर्मां अलि काम् छ । नमस्ते ।
आ. नमस्ते ।

Exercise 3a

Translate into English

१. त्यो ठूलो होटेल् नि ? सस्तो छ? सस्तो छैन , महँगो पो छ ।
२. आज हाम्रो घर्मा कोही पनि छैन ।
३. ती मान्छेहरू को हुन् ? तिनीहरू बाहुन् हुन् ।
४. मेरो बुवा अध्यापक् हुनुहुन्छ ।
५. नेपाल्मा ठूला शहर्हरू धेरै छैनन् । काठ्माडौं नेपाल्को सब्भन्दा ठूलो शहर् हो ।
६. यो बाटो त्यो बाटोभन्दा राम्रो छ ।
७. तिम्रो जात् के हो? म छेत्री हुँ, हजुर्।
८. सगर्माथा दुनियाँको सब्भन्दा अग्लो हिमाल् होइन त ? हो ।
९. हामी त नेपाली हौं , हजूर् । हिन्दुस्तानी होइनौं।
१०. मेरो दाज्यू दार्जीलिङ्गमा हुनुहुन्छ।
११. त्यो ठूलो पसल्मा कुन् किसिम्को माल् छ? कप्ड़ा र लुगाहरू ।
१२. हामी गरीब् छौं , हजूर् । हाम्रो घर्मा बिजुली छैन ।
१३. त्यो कोठामा केहि पनि छैन ।

१४. अमेरिकाका राष्ट्रपति हिजोआज चीन्‌मा हुनुहुन्छ ।
१५. रामका छोराहरू एक् दम् ज्ञानी छन् ।
१६. मेरी बहिनी घर्‌मा छे । आज स्कूल्‌मा छैन ।
१७. आज त बिदा छ । सब् पसल् बन्द छ ।
१८. नेपाल्‌को सीमाना दार्जीलिङ्‌बाट टाढ़ा छैन ।
१९. त्यो किताब् तिम्रो होइन । मेरो पो हो त ।
२०. त्यो बाटो एक्‌दम् उकालो छ , हजूर् । सब्‌भन्दा राम्रो यो बाटो हो ।

Exercise 3b

Translate into Nepali

1. There is nothing at all in my pocket.
2. Calcutta is the biggest city in India.
3. My elder sister is (HGH) in Darjeeling.
4. What is your (HGH) caste? I am a Brahmin, sir.
5. In which country is Delhi? It is the capital of India.
6. What about that hotel? Is it good?
7. It is a holiday today. The college is closed, isn't it?
8. My elder brother is (HGH) a lecturer in the university. He is in the Nepali department.
9. The Prime Minister is (HGH) in India nowadays.
10. Tokyo is the biggest city in the world, you know.
11. How far is your (MGH) village from here? It's not very far.
12. Mr. Pradhān's shop is in Kathmandu. He (LGH) is very rich, you know.

Exercise 3c

Translate into Nepali

All the shops; the biggest temple; he (MGH) is a Nepali; that's my book, isn't it? is there anyone there? I must be going now; where is your (MGH) little sister? my mother is (HGH) at the market; she is (MGH) not from here, she is from England.

Exercise 3d

Complete the following sentences with the correct negative forms of the verbs छ *and* हो *:*

१. हाम्रो घर्‌मा कोही पनि ------ । २. म त अंग्रेज् ------ । ३. आज राम्‌को पसल् बन्द ------ । ४. त्यो होटेल् सस्तो ------ । ५. हामीहरू त मज्दूर् ---- । ६. काठ्‌माड़ौं भारत्‌मा -- । ७. वहाँ धनी ------ ।

LESSON 4

1. *New conjunct consonants*

ग्ग	**gg**	as in	जग्गा	**jaggā**	land, estate
ग्द	**gd**	as in	चाख्लाग्दो	**cākhlāgdo**	interesting
ब्द	**bd**	as in	शब्द	**ʃabda**	word
र्ष	**rṣ**	as in	वर्ष	**varṣa**	year[1]
श्च	**ʃc**	as in	निश्चय	**niʃcaya**	certainty
ह्र	**hr**	as in	बाह्र	**bāhra**	twelve

2. Postpositions may be added directly to the personal pronouns, with a few exceptions discussed below: **मसित masita** 'with me', **तँलाई tãlāī** 'to/for you' (-लाई 'to', 'for'), **तिमीसँग timīsãga** 'with you', **तपाईंको** 'of you, your', हामीकहाँ **hāmīkahā̃** 'at our house' (-कहाँ 'at the house of', like French *chez*), **केमा kemā** 'in what?', **उनीहरूको unīharūko** 'of them, their'.

3. -को may *not* be added to the pronouns म, तँ, हामी, or तिमी. Instead, the possessive adjectives **मेरो mero** 'of me, my'; **तेरो tero** 'of you, your' (LGH); हाम्रो 'of us, our'; तिम्रो 'of you your' (MGH) are used.

4. Before the majority of postpositions, यो and त्यो change to **यस् yas** and **त्यस् tyas** respectively (see note on pronunciation, Section 12). Similarly, before postpositions, उ changes to **उस् us,** तिनी to **तिन् tin,** यिनी to **यिन् yin,** and उनी to **उन् un.** Thus:

यस्को	**yasko**	of him/her, his/her
त्यस्सँग	**tyassãga**	with him/her
उस्को	**usko**	of him/her, his/her
उन्लाई	**unlāī**	to him/her (MGH)
त्यस्पछि	**tyaspachi**	after that, afterwards (-पछि 'after')

Note that **उस्लाई uslāī** is often pronounced **ullāī** and sometimes written उल्लाई 'to him/her' (LGH). Similarly यस्लाई and त्यस्लाई are often pronounced **yallāī** and **tyallāī** and occasionally written यल्लाई, त्यल्लाई.

The forms **यस्को yasko, त्यस्को tyasko, उस्को usko, यिन्को yinko, तिन्को tinko, यहाँको yahā̃ko, वहाँको vahā̃ko, तिनीहरूको tinīharūko,**

[1] Also commonly written **बर्ष barṣa.**

उनीहरूको **unīharūko** are used as 3rd person possessives: 'his', 'her', 'their'. They are illustrated in the following sentences:

यस्को नाउँ के हो?
What is his/her name? (LGH)

यिन्को अड्डा कहाँ छ ?
Where is his office? (MGH)

उस्को कपाल् कालो छ
His/her hair is black (LGH)

वहाँको किताब् चाख्लाग्दो हो ?
Is his/her book interesting? (HGH)

तपाईंहरूको देश् कहाँ छ?
Where is your country (HGH plur.)

उनीहरूको गाउँ ऊ माथि छ
Their village is up there (LGH/MGH)

The adverb ऊ **ū** is always uttered on a high pitch. It occurs in expressions like ऊ माथि **ū māthi** 'up there', ऊ त्यहीं **ū tyahī̃** 'over there'.

तिमीहरूको गाउँ कहाँ छ ?
Where is your village? (MGH, plur.)

तपाईंको बुवा भारत्मा हुनुहुन्छ ?
Is your father in India? (HGH)

5. The forms यस् , त्यस् , उस् , यिन् , तिन् ,etc. are often referred to as the *oblique* forms of the pronouns. These forms usually occur only before postpositions, but in certain expressions they are used idiomatically with nouns not governed by a postposition. For example:

यस् बेला	**yas belā**	at this time
त्यस् ताक	**tyas tāk**	at that moment
त्यस् कारण्	**tyas kāraṇ**	for that reason

6. In written, but only occasionally in spoken, Nepali, the oblique forms of the demonstratives (यस् , त्यस्) are used to qualify a noun governed by a postposition.

यस् शब्दको माने के हो?
yas ʃabdako māne ke ho?
What is the meaning of this word?

त्यस् देश्को राज्धानी राम्रो हो
tyas deʃko rājdhānī rāmro ho
The capital of that country is beautiful

In spoken Nepali, यो शब्दको . . ., त्यो देश्को . . . would be rather more common.

7. The postposition -लाई **-lāī** 'to/for' is used idiomatically in expressions like:

मलाई थाहा छ
malāī thāhā cha

I know ('to me there is knowledge')
उस्लाई थाहा छैन
He/she does not know ('to him/her there is not knowledge')
त्यस्लाई रुचि छैन
tyaslāī ruci chəyna
He has no appetite
उस्लाई निश्चय छ
He/she is certain

निश्चय niʃcaya 'certainty' is often pronounced **niscəy** or **nissəy.** Note also the expressions:

तपाईंलाई कस्तो छ?
tapāīlāī kasto cha?
How are you ('to you how is it')?
राम्लाई कस्तो छ?
How is Ram?

8. The numerals 11-20 should now be learnt (Appendix 1 p. 251).
Numerals in their simple form are used:
(*a*) when counting or enumerating.
(*b*) with **बजे** . . . **baje** 'at . . . o'clock' and **बज्यो** . . . **bajyo** 'it is . . . o'clock'

कति बजे?	At what time? ('at how much o'clock?')
एक् बजे	At one o'clock.
पाँच् बजे	At five o'clock.
बाह्र बजे	At twelve o'clock.
कति बज्यो ?	What time is it?
नौ बज्यो	It is nine o'clock.
एघार बज्यो	It is eleven o'clock.

मेरो घड़ीमा तीन् बज्यो
mero ghaṛīmā tīn bajyo
According to my watch it is three o'clock.

Note the use of **-मा** in this expression.

(*c*) with nouns denoting periods of time, measures, weights and receptacles:

दुइ हप्ता	two weeks
पन्द्र दिन्	fifteen days
बीस् मील्	twenty miles
सोह्र वर्ष	sixteen years
चौद्ध किलो	fourteen kilos
तीन् कप् चिया	three cups of tea

After numerals nouns always retain their singular form.

(*d*) in expressions of age:

तिम्रो उमेर् कति हो?
timro umer kati ho?
How old are you? ('how much is your age?')

म बीस् बर्षको हुँ
ma bīs barṣako hũ
I am twenty ('I am of twenty years')

9. When a numeral precedes a noun denoting a human being, the classifier **-जना -janā** is added to the numeral:

दुइजना मान्छे	**duijanā mānche**	two men
चार्जना छोरा	**cārjanā chorā**	four sons
छजना आइमाई	**chajanā āimāī**	six women

As usual, the noun remains singular.

10. When a numeral qualifies a noun denoting an animal or an inanimate object, the classifier **-वटा -vaṭā** (pronounced **-əwṭā** and occasionally written **-औटा**) is added to the numeral. The first two numerals have slightly irregular forms: **एउटा euṭā** (often pronounced **yəwṭā**), **दुइटा duiṭā** (occasionally written **दुइवटा** and pronounced **duiəwṭā**). Thereafter **तीन्वटा tīnvaṭā,** चार्वटा **cārvaṭā,** दस्वटा **dasvaṭā,** बीस्वटा **bīsvaṭā,** etc.

एउटा किताब्	**euṭā kitāb**	one book
चार्वटा भैंसी	**cārvaṭā bhəỹsī**	four buffaloes
बीस्वटा धर्	**bīsvaṭā ghar**	twenty houses

11. The classifiers are also added to the interrogative adjective कति 'how much?, how many'.

कतिजना मान्छे ?	**katijanā mānche**	how many men
कतिवटा चुरोट्	**kativaṭā curoṭ**	how many cigarettes?

Note that कतिवटा is pronounced **katiəwṭā.**

12. एक्जना , एउटा may sometimes be translated by the English indefinite article 'a, an'.

नेपाल् हिमालयको एउटा सानो राज्य हो
Nepal is a small kingdom in the Himalayas

ढोकामा एक्जना मान्छे छ
There is a man at the door

13. 'To have' may be expressed in Nepali by means of the verb छ used with the postposition -को or a possessive adjective (मेरो , हाम्रो , तिम्रो etc.)

यस्को तीन्वटा घर् छ
He has three houses ('of him there are three houses')

तपाईंको कतिजना छोरा छ(न्)?
How many sons do you have?

उसको पाँचजना छोराछोरी छन्
He has five children

If the thing possessed is portable and is with the possessor, the postpositions -सँग and -मित are used:

तपाईंसँग कलम् छ कि छैन ?
Do you have a pen (with you) or not?

मसँग पैसा छैन
I have no money (with me)

मसँग पाँच रुपियाँ मात्रै छ
I only have five rupees (on me)

14. The third person singular verb रहेछ **rahecha** is used in place of छ and हो implying that a fact has just been discovered or that it was contrary to what had been expected. It may often be translated 'Oh, I see that . . . is'. रहेछ is frequently used with the particle पो .

मेरो किताब् तिम्रो कोठामा रहेछ
Oh, I see that my book is in your room

त्यो होटेल् महँगो पो रहेछ
No, in fact that hotel is expensive.

The negative form is रहेनछ **rahenacha:**

मेरो खल्तीमा केही पनि रहेनछ ।
I find that I have nothing in my pocket

त्यो गाउँमा चियापसल् रहेनछ।
It seems that there is no teashop in that village.

The last sentence may also be idiomatically expressed:

त्यो गाउँमा चियापसल् छैन रहेछ

Vocabulary 4

अहिले	**ahile**	now
ऊ माथि	**ū māthi**	up there
उमेर्	**umer**	age
कपाल्	**kapāl**	hair
-कहाँ	**-kahā̃**	at the house of
कारण्	**kāraṇ**	reason
कालो	**kālo**	black
किलो	**kilo**	kilogramme
कप्	**kap**	cup
खाना	**khānā**	food, meal
चाखलाग्दो	**cākhlāgdo**	interesting
चुरोट्	**curoṭ**	cigarette

छोराछोरी	**chorāchorī**	children
टुक्रा	**ṭukrā**	piece
ठाउं	**ṭhāũ**	place
ठाउं ठाउंमा	**ṭhāũ ṭhāũmā**	in places, here and there
जग्गा	**jaggā**	land, estate
ताक	**tāk**	moment
त्यस् ताक	**tyas tāk**	at that moment
थाहा	**thāhā**	knowledge
धने	**dhane**	Dhane (man's name)
निक्कै	**nikkəy**	very, extremely
निश्चय	**niʃcaya**	certainty
-पछि	**-pachi**	after
पाटन्	**pāṭan**	Patan (town in Kathmandu Valley)
वर्ष (बर्ष)	**varṣa (barṣa)**	year
बेला	**belā**	time, occasion
भाषण	**bhāṣan**	speech
मात्रै	**mātrəy**	only
माने	**māne**	meaning
राज्य	**rājya**	kingdom
रुचि	**ruci**	appetite
–लाई	**-lāī**	to, for
विदेशी	**videʃī**	foreigner
शब्द	**ʃabda**	word
हिमालय	**himālaya**	Himalayas
हिलो	**hilo**	mud
हुलाक्	**hulāk**	post
हुलाक्घर्	**hulākghar**	post-office[1]

Reading Passage

अ. ए दाइ नमस्ते । कस्तो छ तपाईंलाई ?

आ. सन्चै छ हजूर्, तपाईं नि ।

अ. राम्रो छ । तपाईंको गाउँ यहाँबाट कति टाढा छ ?

आ. धेरै टाढा छैन । ऊ माथि छ ।

अ. गाउँमा चियापसल् छ कि छैन ?

आ. छ हजूर् । राम्रो चियापसल् छ । त्यहाँ चिया पनि छ भात् पनि ।[2]

अ. तपाईंको नाउँ के हो दाइ ?

आ. मेरो नाउँ रण् बहादुर् हो ।

अ. र तपाईंको जात् ?

आ. म त छेत्री हुँ, हजूर् ।

अ. तपाईंको कतिजना छोराछोरी छन्?

[1] हुलाक् refers to the Nepalese postal service only. The postal service of other countries is called डाँक् **dāk.**

[2] **bhāt** 'boiled rice', the staple diet of many Nepalis.

आ. दुइजना छोरा र एक्जना छोरी छन् । तपाईं कहाँको हुनुहुन्छ ?
अ. म अंग्रेज् हुँ । मेरो देश् बेलायत् हो नि । तर हिजोआज म नेपाल्मा छु ।
आ. तपाईंसँग चुरोट् छ , हजुर् ?
अ. छ , धेरै छ । दुइटा चुरोट् लिनुहोस् (take)। ल त म जाऊँ है त ? नमस्ते।
आ. नमस्ते

Exercise 4a

Translate into English

१. तपाईंको घड़ीमा कति बज्यो ? अहिले चार् बज्यो ।
२. त्यो मान्छे एक दम् धनी हो । शहर्मा त्यस्को दुइटा पसल् छन्।
३. यहाँबाट पाटन् कति टाढ़ा छ ? निक्कै टाढ़ा छ हजुर्।
४. तपाईंसँग पैसा छ कि छैन ? धेरै छैन । मेरो खल्तीमा दुइ रुपियाँ मात्रै छ ।
५. धनेको कतिजना छोराछोरी छन् ? उनको दुइजना छोरा र एक्जना छोरी छन् ।
६. यो बाटो राम्रो रहेनछ । ठाउँ ठाउँमा धेरै हिलो छ।
७. ए भाइ, कति बज्यो ? थाहा छैन , मसँग घड़ी छैन ।
८. ती मान्छेहरू एक् दम् गरीब छन् । तिनीहरूको गाउँमा केही पनि छैन ।
९. काठ्माडौंको विश्वविद्यालयमा कतिजना विद्यार्थी छन्?
१०. त्यो होटेल्को खाना नि ? सस्तो छ? सस्तो छैन । महँगो पो छ ।
११. उस्को घर्भन्दा तिम्रो घर् ठूलो छ।
१२. रामको पसल् कहाँ छ? तपाईंलाई थाहा छ? थाहा छ हजुर् । त्यो हुलाक्घर् छ नि , हो , त्यहीं छ ।
१३. ए नानी , तिम्रो उमेर् कति हो? म बाह्र बर्षको हुँ , हजुर् ।
१४. यस् बेला काठ्माडौंमा धेरै विदेशीहरू छन् ।
१५. तिम्रो अध्यापक् कहाँको हुनुहुन्छ? वहाँ भारत्को हुनुहुन्छ ।
१६. मेरी स्वास्नी आज्काल् दार्जीलिङ्गमा छे। उस्को घर् त्यहाँ छ नि।
१७. प्रधानमन्त्रीको भाषण् निक्कै चाखलाग्दो रहेछ, होइन त ?
१८. टोक्यो लन्दन्भन्दा ठूलो हो? हो , दुनियाँको सब्भन्दा ठूलो शहर् हो ।

Exercise 4b

Translate into Nepali

1. Dhane has three sons and two daughters.
2. How old is your daughter? She is five years old.
3. What is the meaning of this word? I don't know.
4. What is the time now? It is seven o'clock.
5. Is the water in (of) that river good to drink?
6. Oh, I see you have electricity in your house.
7. My little sister has been ill for two weeks. She has no appetite.
8. Where is Mr. Pradhān's house? It is over there.
9. Is the university far from the city? Yes, sir. It is six miles away ('far') from the city.
10. How many children do you have? I have no children, sir.

Exercise 4c

Translate into Nepali

With you (HGH); to him (LGH); he knows (HGH); our books; my sons; his fields (LGH); do you know (HGH); with his son (HGH); at Ram's house; what is his age (MGH); I am not certain; five men; how many books; at six o'clock; what time is it by your (HGH) watch; two cups of tea; four kings; do you (HGH) have a cigarette? I see that you (HGH) have no money.

Exercise 4d

Complete the following sentences, using affirmative forms of the verbs

१. मेरो दाज्यु लन्दन्मा ––––– ।
२. तपाईंलाई कस्तो –––– ।
३. रण् बहादुरको गाउँ यहाँबाट टाढ़ा ---- ।
४. तिमी हिजोआज कहाँ ---- ?
५. मेरी स्वास्नी काठ्माड़ौंमा ---- । उन्को घर् त्यहाँ ---- नि ।
६. फ्रान्स्का प्रधान्मन्त्री बेलायतमा ---- ।
७. तपाईंसँग चुरोट् ---- , हजूर् ?
८. उहाँ कहाँको ---- ?

Exercise 4e

Translate into Nepali

I have two sons; he (LGH) has nothing in his pocket; do you have (MGH) a cigarette? she (MGH) has four rupees; I have a house in Kathmandu; they (HGH) have a nice library; they (LGH) have three fields.

Exercise 4f

Answer the following questions in Nepali

१. तपाईंको नाउँ के हो ?
२. तपाईंको घर् लन्दन्बाट टाढ़ा छ कि छैन ?
३. तपाईंका कतिजना दाइहरू छन् ?
४. तपाईंको घर् कुन् शहर्मा छ?
५. तपाईंको देस् कुन् हो ?

LESSON 5

1. *New conjunct consonants*

ड्य	**ḍy**	as in	ड्यूटी	**ḍyūṭī**	duty, shift
त्छ	**tch**	as in	सुत्छ	**sutcha**	sleeps
त्न	**tn**	as in	सुत्नु	**sutnu**	to sleep
म्म	**mm**	as in	-सम्म	**-samma**	up to, until
र्स	**rs**	as in	बिर्सनु	**birsanu**	to forget
ल्प	**lp**	as in	पाल्पा	**pālpā**	Palpa

2. The Nepali verb has several infinitives. The infinitive by which the verb is referred to in dictionaries ends in the suffix -नु **-nu.** Thus: गर्नु **garnu** 'to do', आउनु **āunu** 'to come', जानु **jānu** 'to go'. We have already seen that the verbs छ and हो share a common infinitive हुनु **hunu** 'to be'.

3. The *Primary Base* of the verb, to which suffixes are added to form certain tenses and participles, is obtained from the infinitive by dropping the suffix -नु .

Group	*Infinitive*		*Primary Base*		
(i)	गर्नु	**garnu**	गर्-	**gar-**	to do
	बस्नु	**basnu**	बस्-	**bas-**	to sit, to stay
(ii)	खानु	**khānu**	खा-	**khā-**	to eat
	जानु	**jānu**	जा-	**jā-**	to go
	दिनु	**dinu**	दि-	**di-**	to give
	उभिनु	**ubhinu**	उभि-	**ubhi-**	to stand
(iii)	धुनु	**dhunu**	धु-	**dhu-**	to wash
	रुनु	**runu**	रु-	**ru-**	to weep
(iv)	बिर्सनु	**birsanu**	बिर्स-	**birsa-**	to forget
	दुहुनु	**duhunu**	दुहु-	**duhu-**	to milk
(v)	आउनु	**āunu**	आउ-	**āu-**	to come
	पठाउनु	**paṭhāunu**	पठाउ-	**paṭhāu-**	to send
	पिउनु	**piunu**	पिउ-	**piu-**	to drink

Verbs are then divided into five groups according to the nature of their Primary Base.

(i) Base ending in a consonant: गर्, बस् **gar-, bas-**
(ii) Base ending in the vowels **-ā** and **-i:** खा-**khā-,** जा-**jā-,** दि-**di-**
(iii) Base of one syllable ending in the vowel **-u:** धु-**dhu-,** रु-**ru-**
(iv) Base of more than one syllable ending in the vowels **-a** and **-u:** बिर्स-**birsa-,** दुहु- **duhu-**
(v) Base ending in the vowels **-āu,** and **-iu:** पठाउ-**paṭhāu-,** आउ-**āu** पिउ- **piu-**

Verbs belonging to groups (iii), (iv) and (v) also have a secondary base which is discussed in Lesson 9.

4. The affirmative suffixes of the *Simple Indefinite Tense* are as follows:

1 sing. (म) -छु	1 plur. (हामी etc.) -छौं
2 sing. (तँ) -छस्	2 MGH (तिमी etc.) -छौ
3 sing. LGH (उ etc.) -छ	3 MGH, plur. (उनी, उनीहरू) -छन्

There are also four special feminine suffixes:
2 LGH -छेस् 3LGH -छे 2 MGH -छ्यौ 3 MGH छिन्
It will be noted that the suffixes of the Simple Indefinite are identical to the forms of छ given in Lesson 3.

5. The suffixes are added directly to the *Primary Base* of the verbs belonging to Group (i).

म गर्छु	**ma garchu**	I do
तँ बस्छस्	**tā baschas**	you sit
तिनीहरू सुत्छन्	**tinīharū sutchan**	they sleep

Verbs belonging to Groups (ii), (iii), (iv) have **-n-** infixed between the vowel of the Primary Base and the suffix:

म खान्छु	**ma khānchu**	I eat
उ दिन्छे	**u dinche**	she gives
त्यो जान्छ	**tyo jāncha**	he goes
हामी बिर्सन्छौं	**hāmī birsanchəw**	we forget

Verbs belonging to Group (v) have the second vowel of the Primary Base nasalised before the suffix:

म पठाउँछु	**ma paṭhāũchu**	I send
हामी आउँछौं	**hāmī āũchəw̃**	we come
तिनीहरू पिउँछन्	**tinīharū piũchan**	they drink

6. HGH (तपाईं, वहाँ etc.) forms of *all* groups have the suffix -हुन्छ **-huncha** added to the infinitive:

तपाईं गर्नुहुन्छ	**tapāĩ garnuhuncha**	you do
वहाँहरू आउनुहुन्छ	**vahā̃harū āunuhuncha**	they come
मेरो बुवा पठाउनुहुन्छ	**mero buvā paṭhāunuhuncha**	my father sends

7. The full conjugation of the Simple Indefinite Tense of गर्नु is as follows:

1 sing.	म	गर्छु		**garchu**
2 sing. LGH	तँ	गर्छस्	(गर्छेस्)	**garchas** (f. **garches**)
3 sing. LGH	उ, त्यो, यो	गर्छ	(गर्छे)	**garcha** (f. **garche**)
1 plur.	हामी (-हरू)	गर्छौं		**garchəw̃**
2 sing. pl. MGH	तिमी (-हरू)	गर्छौ	(गर्छ्यौ)	**garchəw** (f. **garchyəw**)
3 sing. MGH	उनी, तिनी, यिनी	गर्छन्	(गर्छिन्)	**garchan** (f. **garchin**)
3 plur. LGH, MGH	उनीहरू	गर्छन्		
2 sing. pl. HGH	तपाईं (-हरू)	गर्नुहुन्छ		**garnuhuncha**
3 sing. pl. HGH	वहाँ (-हरू)	गर्नुहुन्छ		**garnuhuncha**

Similarly:	म	खान्छु	**khānchu**
	तँ	खान्छस्	**khānchas**, etc.
	म	धुन्छु	**dhunchu**
	तँ	धुन्छस्	**dhunchas**, etc.
	म	बिर्सन्छु	**birsanchu**
	तँ	बिर्सन्छस्	**birsanchas**, etc.
	म	आउँछु	**āũchu**
	तँ	आउँछस्	**āũchas**, etc.

8. The Simple Indefinite Tense refers to action performed at regular intervals or as a matter of habit. It can often be translated by the English simple present tense: 'I do', 'I eat', 'I go' etc.

म दिनहुँ काम् गर्छु
I work ('do work') every day

मेरो छोरा महाविद्यालयमा पढ्छ
My son studies ('reads') at the college

हिजोआज वहाँ नेपाल्मा बस्नुहुन्छ
Nowadays he lives in Nepal

Note that बस्नु means both 'to sit down' and 'to reside':

म बेलायत्मा बस्छु
I live in England

म मेच्मा बस्छु
I sit down in a chair

तपाईं चुरोट् खानुहुन्छ?
Do you smoke cigarettes?

Note the expression चुरोट् खानु 'to consume cigarettes', i.e. 'to smoke'. खानु means both *to eat* and *to drink*:

त्यो मान्छे मासु खान्छ
That man eats meat

त्यो जोगी पानी मात्रै खान्छ
The holy man (**jogī**) drinks only water

The verb पिउनु 'to drink', though it may be used for any liquid, is frequently used in the context of alcohol.

हामी त कहिले कहीं मात्रै रक्सी पिउँछौं
We sometimes drink spirits

रक्सी **raksī** Nepalese spirit may be used loosely for any alcoholic drink.

नेपालीहरू अक्सर भात् नै खान्छन्
The Nepalese often eat only (cooked) rice

The particle नै **nəy** emphasises the word it follows. It may often be translated 'only' when it follows a noun.

9. Most Nepali words have emphatic forms (already briefly mentioned in 2.14). They are formed thus:

(*a*) When a word ends in a vowel, the final vowel is changed to **əy.** Thus:

बिहान	**bihāna**	morning	emph.	बिहानै	**bihānəy**
गर्नु	**garnu**	to do	emph.	गर्नै	**garnəy**
म	**ma**	I	emph.	मै	**məy**

(*b*) When a word ends in a consonant, the syllable **-əy** is added to the word:

घर्	**ghar**	house	emph.	घरै	**gharəy**
त्यस्	**tyas**	obl. of **tyo**	emph.	त्यसै	**tyasəy**
सब्	**sab**	all	emph.	सबै	**sabəy**

Note that सबै is often pronounced **sappəy.**

Many emphatic forms have special or modified meanings, which cannot be explained simply in terms of emphasis. For example: घरै 'at home', बिस्तारै 'slowly', एकाबिहानै 'early in the morning', बिहानै बेलुकै 'morning and evening'.

The emphatic form मात्रै **mātrəy** (often pronounced **mattəy**) is used in preference to the ordinary form मात्र **mātra** 'only'.

गाउँलेहरू बिहानै बेलुकै दिन्को दुई पटक् नै दाल् र भात् खान्छन्
gāũleharū bihānəy belukəy dinko dui paṭak nəy dāl ra bhāt khānchan
Villagers eat rice and lentils twice a day morning and evening

Note the expression दिन्को दुइ पटक् 'two times a day'. Similarly, महीनाको चार् पटक् 'four times a month'.

The particle नै, itself an emphatic form, adds further emphasis.

त्यो त धेरै नै लामो बाटो छ
But that's an extremely long way round (lit. 'long road')

(*c*) In some cases the final consonant of a word may be doubled before the emphatic suffix **-əy.** For example निको **niko** 'good', 'well', निक्कै **nikkəy** 'extremely well', 'very much'.

10. The Simple Indefinite Tense is also used with reference to future time and in some contexts may be translated, 'I shall do', 'I am doing', etc.

आउने साल् म नेपाल् जान्छु
Next year I am going to Nepal[1]
आउने बिहिबार् त्यो मकहाँ आउँछ
Next Thursday he is coming to my place
म बेलुका आठ् बजे तपाईंकहाँ आउँछु है
I'll come to your house at eight in the evening, all right?

Note the use of the interrogative particle है in the above sentence.

ए दाइ, यो बाटो कता जान्छ ? दार्जीलिङ्गसम्म जान्छ
Excuse me, where does this road go to? It goes to Darjeeling

कता **katā** 'to where', 'to which place'. Whereas कहाँ may be used both in the sense of 'in which place' and 'to which place', कता may only be used in the latter sense.

The postposition -सम्म **-samma** means 'up to', 'as far as', 'until':

तपाईं नेपाल्मा कति बस्नुहुन्छ ?
जून्सम्म बस्छु
How long (lit. 'how much') will you stay in Nepal?
I'll stay until June

11. A Present Continuous Tense (corresponding to the English 'I am doing') is formed with the Imperfect Participle in -दै **-dəy** followed by the auxiliary verb छ.

The Imperfect Participle is formed by adding the suffix -दै directly to the base of verbs belonging to group (i). The final vowel of the Primary Base of verbs belonging to other groups is nasalised before the addition of the suffix.

गर्दै **gardəy,** बस्दै **basdəy,** खाँदै **khā̃dəy,** जाँदै **jā̃dəy,** दिंदै **dĩdəy,** धुँदै **dhū̃dəy,** आउँदै **āũdəy,** पिउँदै **piũdəy,** etc.

The Present Continuous Tense is then formed thus:

म गर्दै छु	**ma gardəy chu**	I am doing
उ खाँदै छ	**u khā̃dəy cha**	he/she is eating
हामी जाँदै छौं	**hāmī jā̃dəy chəw̃**	we are going
तपाईं आउँदै हुनुहुन्छ	**tapāī̃ āũdəy hunuhuncha**	you (HGH) are coming
उनीहरू धुँदै छन्	**unīharū dhū̃dəy chan**	they are washing etc.

This tense, examples of which will be found in later reading passages, is frequently used in colloquial speech. Like the Simple Indefinite Tense, it may also be used with reference to future time.

तपाईं के गर्दै हुनुहुन्छ? म काम् गर्दै छु
What are you doing? I am working

[1]आउने **āune** 'next', 'coming' is the infinitival participle of the verb आउनु. This participle which functions as a verbal adjective is fully discussed in Lesson 15.

राम् शहर् जाँदै छ
Ram is going to town
आउने बिहिबार् त्यो मकहाँ आउँदै छ
Next Thursday he is coming to my house

Vocabulary 5

अक्सर्	**aksar**	usually, often
अलि अलि	**ali ali**	very little
अलिकति	**alikati**	a little, few
आउनु	**āunu**	to come
आउने	**āune**	next
उपहार्	**upahār**	gift
उभिनु	**ubhinu**	to stand
कता	**katā**	whither, to where
कसरी	**kasarī**	how?, by what means?
कहिले कहीं	**kahile kahī̃**	sometimes
काम्	**kām**	work (noun)
काम् गर्नु	**kām garnu**	to work
खानु	**khānu**	to eat
गर्नु	**garnu**	to do
गाउँले	**gāũle**	villager
चामल	**cāmal**	rice (in grain)
चुरोट्	**curoṭ**	cigarette
चुरोट् खानु	**curoṭ khānu**	to smoke
जानु	**jānu**	to go
ठाउँ	**ṭhāũ**	place
डराउनु	**ḍarāunu**	to fear, be frightened
ड्यूटी	**ḍyūṭī**	shift, duty
दाल्	**dāl**	lentils
दिनहुँ	**dinahũ**	daily, every day
दिनु	**dinu**	to give
दुहुनु	**duhunu**	to milk
देख्नु	**dekhnu**	to see
धुनु	**dhunu**	to wash
निक्कै	**nikkəy**	very, much
पटक्	**paṭak**	time, occasion
एक् पटक्, दुइ पटक्	**ek paṭak, dui paṭak**	once, twice, etc.
पठाउनु	**paṭhāunu**	to send
पढ्नु	**paṛhnu**	to read, study
पाल्पा	**pālpā**	Palpa (town in Nepal)
पिउनु	**piunu**	to drink
बस्नु	**basnu**	to sit, reside
बानेश्वर्	**bāneʃvar**	Baneshvar (suburb of Kathmandu)

बिर्सन्	**birsanu**	to forget
बिस्तारै	**bistārəy**	slowly
बिहान	**bihāna**	morning
बिहिबार्	**bihibār**	Thursday
बेरा	**berā**	waiter (Eng. 'bearer')
बेलुका	**belukā**	evening
भोलि	**bholi**	tomorrow
मासु	**māsu**	meat
महाविद्यालय	**mahāvidyālaya**	college
मेच्	**mec**	chair
रक्सी	**raksī**	wine, spirits
लामो	**lāmo**	long
शुरू हुन्छ	**ʃurū huncha**	will begin
-सम्म	**-samma**	up to, until
साथी	**sāthī**	friend
हवाईजहाज्	**havāījahāj**	aeroplane
हवाईजहाज्मा	**havāījahājmā**	by air
हेर्नु	**hernu**	to look at

Reading Passage

अ. नमस्ते।
आ. नमस्ते हजूर्।
अ. तपाईं कहाँको हुनुहुन्छ ?
आ. म पाल्पाको हुँ हजूर्। तर हिजोआज म काठ्माड़ौंमा बस्छु ।
अ. यहाँ के काम् गर्नुहुन्छ ?
आ. म होटेल्मा बेरा काम् गर्छु ।[1]
अ. तपाईं कहिले कहीं घर् जानुहुन्छ ?
आ. कहिले कहीं मात्रै जान्छु हजूर । पाल्पा यहाँबाट एक् दम् टाढ़ा छ । तपाईं कहाँको हुनुहुन्छ नि ?
अ. म त अंग्रेज् हुँ । म लन्दन्मा बस्छु । तपाईंलाई लन्दन् कहाँ छ थाहा छ ?[2]
आ. थाहा छ हजूर् । बेलायत्मा छ , होइन ? तपाईं यहाँ कुन् ठाउँमा बस्नुहुन्छ ?
अ. म एक्जना साथीकहाँ बानेश्वर्मा बस्छु ।
आ. नेपाल्मा कति बस्नुहुन्छ ?
अ. यहाँ छ महीना बस्छु । त्यस्पछि म भारत् जान्छु । कल्कत्तामा अलिकति काम् छ ।
आ. बेलायत्मा के काम् गर्नुहुन्छ ?
अ. म विद्यार्थी हुँ । लन्दन्को विश्वविद्यालयमा पढ़्छु।
आ. तपाईंको घड़ीमा कति बज्यो हजूर् ?
अ. मेरो घड़ीमा चार् बज्यो ।
आ. ए , मेरो ड्यूटी पाँच् बजे शुरू हुन्छ[3]। म जाउँ है त ?
अ. नमस्ते

[1]**berā kām** 'the work of a waiter'.
[2]Literally, 'to you where is London is it known?' Do you know where London is?
[3]The English word **ḍyūṭī** 'a shift', 'a turn of duty'.

Exercise 5a

Translate into English

१. तिमी चुरोट् खान्छौ? कहिले कहीं मात्रै खान्छु, हजूर्। तपाईं नि ? म त निक्कै खान्छु ।
२. तपाईं कुन् होटेल्‌मा बस्नुहुन्छ ? त्यो ठूलो होटेल् छ नि, हो, म त्यहाँ बस्छु ।
३. ए दिदी, त्यो बाटो कता जान्छ ? थाहा छ ? दार्जीलिङ्गसम्म जान्छ ।
४. मेरो बुवा दिनहुँ शहर् जानुहुन्छ । वहाँको अड्डा त्यहाँ छ ।
५. नेपाल्‌का धेरै मान्छेहरू दाल् र भात् मात्रै खान्छन्।
६. तपाईं भोलि कति बजे मकहाँ आउनुहुन्छ? बेलुका सात् बजे आउँछु ।
७. ए नानी, स्कूल्‌मा पढ्छस् ? पढ्छु हजूर् ।
८. मेरो दाइ महीनाको दुइ पटक् कलकत्ता जानुहुन्छ ।
९. ती मान्छेहरू के काम् गर्छन् ? बेरा काम् गर्छन् ।
१०. म छ महीनापछि लन्दन् जान्छु । केमा जानुहुन्छ ? हवाईजहाज्‌मा ।
११. त्यो मान्छे हिन्दुस्तानी पो रहेछ । नेपाली त होइन रहेछ ।
१२. उनी आउने बिहिबार् हवाईजहाज्‌मा दिल्ली जान्छन् ।
१३. म काठ्माडौंमा पन्ध्र दिन् बस्छु, त्यस्‌पछि म पोखरा जान्छु ।
१४. त्यो पसल्‌मा चामल् धेरै नै महँगो रहेछ ।
१५. मेरो साथी आउने हप्ता दार्जीलिङ्ग जाँदै छ।
१६. तपाईं के गर्दै हुनुहुन्छ, दाइ ? म किताब् पढ्दै छु।

Exercise 5b

Translate into Nepali

1. Excuse me, where does this road lead to? It leads to Patan.
2. How many children do you have? I have one son and two daughters.
3. Next week, I am going to Pokhara. How are you going? I am going by air.
4. How long will you be staying in Darjeeling? I'll stay only two weeks.
5. What time are you coming to our house? I'll come at five o'clock.
6. Oh, I see there is no one in the house.
7. How many cigarettes do you smoke? I smoke ten.
8. Mr Bista lives in India nowadays. He only sometimes comes to Nepal.
9. What time is it by your (HGH) watch? It is now twelve o'clock.
10. Does his (HGH) son study in Patan College? I don't know.
11. These days many foreigners are in Nepal.
12. My office is closed today. There's a holiday, you know.

Exercise 5c

Complete the following sentences by giving the correct affirmative form of the verb in brackets:

१. तपाईं कुन् होटेल्‌मा (बस्नु)
२. उनीहरू बेरा काम् (गर्नु)
३. मेरो बुवा शहर्‌मा काम् (गर्नु)
४. वहाँहरू हामीकहाँ कति बजे (आउनु)

५. मेरी बहिनी महाविद्यालयमा (पढ्नु)
६. तपाईं आज्काल् कहाँ (हुनु)
७. हामी पाल्पामा (बस्नु)
८. म अलिकति भात् (खानु) त्यस्पछि म घर् (जानु)

Exercise 5d

Read the following passage, then answer the questions in Nepali

रण् बहादुर् छेत्री हुनुहुन्छ । वहाँ पाल्पाको मान्छे हुनुहुन्छ तर हिजोआज काठ्माडौंमा बस्नुहुन्छ। वहाँ शहर्को एउटा ठूलो अड्डामा काम् गर्नुहुन्छ । रण् बहादुर्का दुइजना छोरा र एक्जना छोरी छन् । एक्जना छोरा राष्ट्र बैंकमा काम् गर्छ, उस्को भाई त्रिचन्द्र महाविद्यालयमा पढ्छ , र छोरी स्कूल्मा पढ्छे । रण् बहादुरको घर् अड्डाबाट धेरै टाढ़ा छैन । त्यस् कारण् वहाँ दिनहुँ अड्डामा हिंड़ेरै जानुहुन्छ । वहाँको जहान् धेरैजसो घर्मा बस्नुहुन्छ ।

१. रण् बहादुर्को जात् के हो ?
२. वहाँका कतिजना छोराछोरी छन् ?
३. वहाँ अड्डामा कसरी जानुहुन्छ ?
४. वहाँ हिजोआज कहाँ बस्नुहुन्छ ?
५. वहाँको जहान् के गर्नुहुन्छ ?

त्रिचन्द्र महाविद्यालय	Trichandra College (a famous college in Kathmandu, founded by the Prime Minister, Chandra Shamsher)
राष्ट्र बैंक्	The State Bank
जहान्	wife (a politer term than स्वास्नी)
हिंड़ेरै	on foot
धेरैजसो	usually
कसरी	how?, in what manner?

LESSON 6

1. *New conjunct consonants*

क्ल	**kl**	as in	क्लास्	**klās**	class
ख्द	**khd**	as in	देख्दैन	**dekhdəyna**	does not see
ज्न	**jn**	as in	बज्नु	**bajnu**	to strike
ट्छ	**ṭch**	as in	भेट्छ	**bheṭcha**	meets
ट्ठ	**ṭṭh**	as in	अट्ठाईस्	**aṭṭhāīs**	twenty-eight
ट्न	**ṭn**	as in	भेट्नु	**bheṭnu**	to meet
ढ्द	**ṛhd**	as in	पढ्दैन	**paṛhdəyna**	does not read
ब्ब	**bb**	as in	छब्बीस्	**chabbīs**	twenty-six
म्च	**mc**	as in	नाम्चे	**nāmce**	Namche
म्ब	**mb**	as in	खुम्बु	**khumbu**	Khumbu
र्म	**rm**	as in	गर्मी	**garmī**	heat, summer
र्य	**ry**	as in	पर्यटक्	**paryaṭak**	tourist

2. We have already seen that all Nepali verbs have special negative forms (2.11). The negative suffixes of the Simple Indefinite Tense are as follows:

-दिन	**-dina**
-दैनस्	**-dəynas**
-दैन	**-dəyna**
-दैनौं	**-dəynəw̃**
-दैनौ	**-dəynəw**
-दैनन्	**-dəynan**

The final vowel of the 1st person singular suffix is sometimes nasalised -दिनँ **-dinã.**

3. The negative suffixes are added directly to the base of verbs belonging to group (i):

गर्दिन	**gardina**	I do not do, etc.
गर्दैनस्	**gardəynas**	
गर्दैन	**gardəyna**	
गर्दैनौं	**gardəynəw̃**	

गर्दैनौ	**gardəynəw**
गर्दैनन्	**gardəynan**

When the base ends in an unvoiced consonant, i.e. क, ख, च, छ, ट, ठ, त, थ, प, फ, स, the द of the suffix may be 'devoiced' to त, i.e. -दिन **-dina** becomes -तिन **-tina.** Thus म बस्तिन **ma bastina** 'I do not sit', उ सुत्तैन **u suttəyna** 'he does not sleep'. There is, however, a growing tendency to use the suffix in -द-, whatever the nature of the base, and बस्दैन **basdəyna** etc. is now commonly written and spoken.

4. Verbs belonging to all other groups (i.e. with primary bases ending in a vowel) have the final vowel nasalised before the suffix is added:

म जाँदिन	**ma jā̃dina**	I do not go
तँ खाँदैनस्	**tā̃ khā̃dəynas**	you do not eat
उ धुँदैन	**u dhū̃dəyna**	he does not wash
हामी बिर्साँदैनौँ	**hāmī birsā̃dəynəw̃**	we do not forget
उनीहरू आउँदैनन्	**unīharū āū̃dəynan**	they do not come

5. HGH forms have the suffix -हुन्न **-hunna** added to the infinitive in -नु.

तपाईं जानुहुन्न	**tapāī̃ jānuhunna**	you do not go
वहाँ देख्नुहुन्न	**vahā̃ dekhnuhunna**	he does not see
मेरो बुवा निस्कनुहुन्न	**mero buvā niskanuhunna**	my father does not go out

The negative of the Simple Indefinite Tense has the following feminine forms:
3 sing. LGH उ गर्दिन **gardina,** 3 sing. MGH उनी गर्दिनन् **gardinan.**

6. Verbs belonging to groups (ii), (iii), (iv) and (v) have alternative negative forms of which the suffixes are:

म	-न्न	**-nna**
तँ	-न्नस्	**-nnas**
उ	-न्न	**-nna**
हामी	-न्नौँ	**-nnəw̃**
तिमि	-न्नौ	**-nnəw**
उनी (हरू)	-न्नन्	**-nnan**

These suffixes are added directly to the Primary Base.

म जान्न	**ma jānna**	तँ आउन्नस्	**tā̃ āunnas**
उ खान्न	**u khānna**	उनी पिउन्नन्	**unī piunnan**
हामी धुन्नौँ	**hāmī dhunnəw̃**	तिमी बिर्सन्नौ	**timī birsannəw**
उनीहरू जान्नन्	**unīharū jānnan,** etc.		

7. Verbs which may take a direct object are known as *transitive verbs.* For example गर्नु 'to do', भेट्नु 'to meet', पिट्नु 'to hit', हेर्नु 'to look at', दुहुनु 'to milk' are all transitive verbs.

Verbs which cannot take a direct object, such as जानु 'to go', आउनु 'to come', बस्नु 'to sit/remain', are known as *intransitive verbs.*

When the object of a transitive verb is (*a*) a proper noun (राम् ,गणेश् etc.) or (*b*) a noun or pronoun referring to a person (मान्छे, बहिनी , म , उ , त्यो , etc.), the postposition -लाई **-lāī** must be added to the object of the verb.

The *oblique case* of 3rd person pronouns (Lesson 4.4) is, of course, used before -लाई

केटालाई किन पिट्छौ ?
Why do you beat the boy?

म राम्लाई हेर्दै छु ।
I am looking at Ram

म तपाईंलाइ एक् बजेतिर भेट्छु है ?
I'll meet you at about one o'clock, shall I?

Note the postposition -तिर **-tira** 'towards', 'about', 'approximately'.

त्यस् मान्छेलाई चिन्नुहुन्छ ?
Do you recognise that man?

म त्यस्लाई चिन्दिन
I do not know him

The verb चिन्नु **cinnu** 'to recognise/know (a person)' is like French *connaître*.

When the object of a verb is a noun denoting a thing or an animal, the postposition -लाई is not usually required:

राम् गाई दुहुन्छ
Ram milks the cow

त्यो सिनेमा हेर्दैन
He does not watch films

हामी दिनहुँ काम् गर्छौं
We work ('do work') every day

8. The postposition-ले **-le** deserves special attention. It may be translated 'by', 'with', 'from', 'of', 'in' etc. according to the context in which it occurs. It is encountered in many idiomatic expressions which must be learnt as they are found. Note the following:

मेरो बिचार्ले	**mero bicārle**	*in* my opinion
औलोले मर्नु	**əwlole marnu**	to die *of* malaria
पानीले भिजेको	**pānīle bhijeko**	soaked with water
ठूलो स्वर्ले बोल्नु	**ṭhūlo svarle bolnu**	to talk *in* a loud voice
मान्छेहरूले भरिभराउ	**mānceharūle bharibharāu**	packed with people

बिचार् is also written विचार् **vicār** 'opinion' स्वर् is usually pronounced *sor* (but rarely spelt सोर्).

मेरो बिचार्ले आज पानी पर्दैन
In my opinion, it will not rain today

Note पर्नु **parnu** 'to fall' and पानी पर्छ 'water falls', i.e. 'it rains'

गर्मीमा धेरै मान्छे हैजाले मर्छन्
In the hot season many people die of cholera

काठ्माडौंको होटेल्हरू पर्यटक्हरूले भरिभराउ छन्
The hotels of Kathmandu are packed with tourists

त्यो सधैं ठूलो स्वर्ले बोल्छ
He always speaks in a loud voice/shouts

तिम्रो लुगा पानीले भिजेको छ
Your clothes are soaked with water

9. The postposition -ले is often added to the third person *subject* of a transitive verb in the Simple Indefinite:

प्रधान्मन्त्रीले आज भाषण् गर्नुहुन्छ
The Prime Minister will make a speech today

ट्याक्सीले कति लिन्छ?
How much will the taxi take (i.e. 'how much will it cost by taxi?')

लिनु **linu** 'to take'

त्यो बाटोले कहाँ कहाँ लान्छ हँ ?
Where does that road lead to?

लानु **lānu** 'to take away'. The repetition of कहाँ implies 'to which different places?' हँ **hã** is an interrogative particle, something like English 'huh', 'eh'.

When the 3rd person singular pronouns are used, -ले requires the oblique case: उस्ले , यस्ले , त्यस्ले , उन्ले , तिन्ले , यिन्ले . The LGH forms are often pronounced *yalle, tyalle, ulle* (c.f. 4.4.).

उस्ले मलाई चिन्दैन
He does not know me

उस्ले मलाई भन्छ
He says to me/tells me

When -ले is added to the pronouns म and तँ , their forms are मैले **məyle** and तैँले **tə̃yle** respectively.

The addition of the postposition -ले to the 3rd person subject of a verb in the Simple Indefinite Tense makes no difference to the meaning. It will be noted that with certain verbs the addition of the postposition is optional while with others it is obligatory. We shall see later that with certain past tenses the addition of -ले to the subject of a transitive verb is obligatory in all cases. Correct usage can only be learnt by observation and experience.

10. The indirect object of a transitive verb is indicated by the postposition -लाई **-lāī** 'to', 'for'.

म तिमीलाई पैसा दिन्छु
I'll give you some money

त्यस्ले मलाई केही पनि भन्दैन
He does not tell me anything at all ('say to me')

The verb भन्नु **bhannu** 'to say' with an indirect object may be translated 'to tell':

म यस्लाई भन्छु
I'll tell him

उस्ले मलाई भन्छ
He will tell me

11. The interrogative adverb कहिले **kahile?** means 'when?'[1]

तपाईं मकहाँ कहिले आउनुहुन्छ ?
When are you coming to my house?

राम् दिल्ली कहिले जान्छ ?
When is Ram going to Delhi?

The phrase कहिले कहीं **kahile kahī̃** means 'sometimes':

त्यो कहिले कहीं मात्रै मासु खान्छ
He eats meat only sometimes

म कहिले कहीं नेपाल् जान्छु
I sometimes go to Nepal

कहिले पनि **kahile pani** followed by a negative verb means 'never', 'not ever';

म त कहिले पनि रक्सी पिउँदिन
I never drink spirits

हामी उस्लाई कहिले पनि भेट्दैनौं
We never meet him

Similarly, the adverb कतै **katəy** 'somewhere' followed by a negative verb may be translated 'nowhere', 'not anywhere'.

त्यो त कतै जान्न
He does not go anywhere/he goes nowhere

The interrogative adverb कसरी **kasarī** 'how?', 'by what means?' must be distinguished from the adjective कस्तो **kasto** 'how?', 'of what quality?' 'in what state'. Compare the following:

कसरी जानुहुन्छ ? म हवाईजहाज्मा जान्छु
How are you going? I'm going by aeroplane

सिनेमा कस्तो छ ? बेसै छ
What is the film like? It is not too bad

Note that adverbs and adverbial phrases often directly precede the verb they qualify:

तपाईं कहाँ जाँदै हुनुहुन्छ ? म त कतै जान्न
Where are you going? I'm not going anywhere

12. We have already seen that the verbs छ and हो share a common infinitive हुनु 'to be'.

[1] कहिले has the emphatic form कहिल्यै.

A Simple Indefinite Tense is also regularly formed from the Primary Base हु- **hu-**:

	Affirmative		*Negative*	
म	हुन्छु	**hunchu**	हुँदिन	**hũdina**
तँ	हुन्छस्	**hunchas**	हुँदैनस्	**hũdəynas**
उ	हुन्छ	**huncha**	हुँदैन	**hũdəyna**
हामी	हुन्छौं	**hunchəw̃**	हुँदैनौं	**hũdəynəw̃**
तिमी	हुन्छौ	**hunchəw**	हुँदैनौ	**hũdəynəw**
उनी (हरू)	हुन्छन्	**hunchan**	हुँदैनन्	**hũdəynan**
तपाईं / वहाँ	हुनुहुन्छ	**hunuhuncha**	हुनुहुन्न	**hunuhunna**

The alternative negative forms are:

हुन्न	**hunna**	हुन्नौं	**hunnəw̃**
हुन्नस्	**hunnas**	हुन्नौ	**hunnəw**
हुन्न	**hunna**	हुन्नन्	**hunnan**

13. हुन्छ, though usually translated 'is', differs from छ and हो in that it is used to denote a *general* fact or occurrence. For this reason हुन्छ is frequently used with adverbs like अक्सर् **aksar** 'often', सधैं **sadhəỹ** 'always' (often pronounced **sãdəy**), and धेरैजसो **dherəyjaso** 'mostly, usually'. For example, the sentence 'mangoes are sweet' states a general fact. They are sweet by nature. This is rendered in Nepali as आँप् गुलियो हुन्छ **ãp guliyo huncha.** In the sentence 'This mango is sweet', a particular instance is referred to: यो आँप् गुलियो छ **yo ãp guliyo cha** (or **ho**). Compare the following:

यहाँको बस्हरू सधैं भरिभराउ हुन्छन्
The buses are always crowded (general)

यो बस् भरिभराउ छ
This bus is crowded (particular)

नेपाली केटीहरू एक् दमै राम्रो हुन्छन्
Nepalese girls are extremely pretty (general)

सुन्दरी राम्री केटी हो
Sundari is a pretty girl (particular)

काठमाडौंमा धेरैजसो त्यतिको गर्मी हुँदैन
It is not usually so hot in Kathmandu[1] (general)

यो कोठामा धेरै गर्मी छ
It is very warm in this room (particular)

14. The Simple Indefinite Tense हुन्छ is also used with reference to future time. Thus म हुन्छु also means 'I shall be' etc.

[1]Literally 'there is not usually so much (**tyatiko**) heat'. **garmī** means both 'the hot season', and 'heat' (of the weather, a fire etc.)

आउने हप्ता शहर्को सबै अड्डा बन्द हुन्छन् तर पसल् बन्द हुँदैनन्
Next week all the offices in the city will be closed, but the shops will not be

म आज दुइ बजेदेखि पाँच् बजेसम्म घरै हुन्छु
I'll be at home today from two o'clock till five o'clock

मेरो डचूटी ठीक् पाँच् बजे शुरू हुन्छ
My shift will start at five o'clock precisely

शुरू **ʃurū** is a noun meaning 'beginning', 'start'. Note the expression शुरूमा **ʃurūmā** 'in the beginning'. The verbal phrase शुरू हुनु **ʃurū hunu** means 'to begin'. ठीक् in expressions of time means 'precisely'.

आज सिनेमा कति बजे शुरू हुन्छ ? ठीक सात् बजे शुरू हुन्छ
At what time will the film start today? It will start at seven sharp

15. So far we have met four verbs which can be translated by the English verb 'to be':

(i) हो used only to define and obligatory in questions of the type: के हो?, को हो? 'what is?', 'who is?'
(ii) छ used mainly to locate, but also frequently in statements in place of हो to define.
(iii) हुन्छ used to denote a generality or a regular occurrence, and also with reference to future time.
(iv) रहेछ used in place of छ and हो indicating surprise.

The above points are illustrated in the following sentences:

यो के हो ? आँप् हो । गुलियो हो ? हो
What is this? It is a mango. Is it sweet? Yes

आँप् टेबुल्मा छ । धेरै मीठो छ
The mango is on the table. It is nice-tasting

आँप् सधैं गुलियो हुन्छ। स्याउ अक्सर् गुलियो हुँदैन
A mango is always sweet. Apples are frequently not sweet

यो आँप् गुलियो पो रहेछ
Why, this mango is sweet after all

Vocabulary 6

अनि	**ani**	and, and then
आँप्	**ā̃p**	mango
आइत्बार्	**āitbār**	Sunday
औलो	**əwlo**	malaria
किन	**kina**	why?
क्लास्	**klās**	class
खुम्बु	**khumbu**	Khumbu (N.E. Nepal)
गर्मी	**garmī**	heat, hot season
गाई	**gāī**	cow

गाईको मासु	**gāiko māsu**	beef
गुलियो	**guliyo**	sweet
चिन्नु	**cinnu**	to know (someone)
जाडो	**jāṛo**	cold, cold season
ट्याक्सी	**ṭyāksī**	taxi
डिल्ली बजार्	**ḍillī bajār**	Dilli Bazar (area of Kathmandu)
–तिर	**-tira**	about
त्रिभुवन	**tribhuvan**	Tribhuvan (King of Nepal, d. 1955)
त्रिभुवन् विश्वविद्यालय	**tribhuvan viʃvavidyālaya**	Tribhuvan University (Kathmandu)
त्यतिको	**tyatiko**	so much
दिउँसो	**diũso**	in the afternoon
धेरैजसो	**dherəyjaso**	generally, often
नाम्चे बजार्	**nāmce bajār**	Namche Bazar (Sherpa town)
निस्कनु	**niskanu**	to go out
पच्चीस	**paccīs**	twenty-five
पकाउनु	**pakāunu**	to cook
पट्ना	**paṭnā**	Patna (town in India)
पर्यटक्	**paryaṭak**	tourist
पानी	**pānī**	water
पानी पर्छ	**pānī parcha**	it rains/will rain
पिट्नु	**piṭnu**	to hit, beat
पुग्नु	**pugnu**	to arrive
बाहिर	**bāhira**	out, outside
बोल्नु	**bolnu**	to speak
भने	**bhane**	however (syn. **ta**)
भन्नु	**bhannu**	to say, tell (with **-lāī**)
भरिभराउ	**bharibharāu**	full, crowded
भरे	**bhare**	this evening
भाषण्	**bhāṣaṇ**	speech
भेट्नु	**bheṭnu**	to meet
मर्नु	**marnu**	to die
मासु	**māsu**	meat
राति	**rāti**	at night
रेल्	**rel**	rail, train
रेल्मा	**relmā**	by rail
लानु	**lānu**	to take away, lead to
लिनु	**linu**	to take
विचार् (बिचार्)	**vicār (bicār)**	opinion
मेरो विचार्ले	**mero vicārle**	in my opinion, I think that
सधैं	**sadhəỹ**	always

सञ्चरबार्	**sancarbār**	Saturday
सिपाही	**sipāhī**	soldier
स्याउ	**syāu**	apple
सुन्नु	**sunnu**	to hear
हजारौं	**hajārəw̃**	thousands of
हरेक् (हरएक्)	**harek**	every, each
हिंडेर (हिंडेरै)	**hĩṛera** (*emph.* **hĩṛerəy**)	on foot, walking
हिंडेरै जानु	**hĩṛerəy jānu**	to go on foot
हैजा	**həyjā**	cholera

Reading Passage

अ. नमस्ते
आ. नमस्ते
अ. तपाईंको घर् कहाँ छ ?
आ. मेरो घर् डिल्ली बजार्मा छ ।[1]
अ. तपाईं के गर्नुहुन्छ ?
आ. म विद्यार्थी हुँ । त्रिभुवन् विश्वविद्यालयमा पढ्छु । [2]
अ. कुन् विभाग्मा हुनुहुन्छ ?
आ. म अंग्रेजी विभाग्मा छु ।
अ. तपाईंको क्लास्मा कतिजना विद्यार्थी पढ्छन् ?
आ. पच्चीस्जना पढ्छन् ।
अ. विश्वविद्यालय तपाईंको घर्देखि कति टाढ़ा छ ?
आ. धेरै टाढ़ा छैन । हाम्रो घर्देखि दुई मील् टाढ़ा छ ।
अ. तपाईं कसरी जानुहुन्छ ? बस्मा ?
आ. धेरैजसो म बस्मा जान्छु । कहिले कहीं हिंडेरै पनि जान्छु ।
अ. तपाईं दिनहुँ विश्वविद्यालय जानुहुन्छ ?
आ. दिनहुँ भने जान्न ।[3] हप्ताको पाँच् पटक् मात्रै जान्छु । सञ्चर्बार् बिदा हुन्छ नि ।
अ. तपाईंको बुवा के काम् गर्नुहुन्छ ?
आ. मेरो बुवा शहर्को एउटा अड्डामा काम् गर्नुहुन्छ ।
अ. तपाईंको आमा नि ?
आ. आमा त घरै बस्नुहुन्छ । कहिले पनि बाहिर जानुहुन्न ।

Exercise 6a

Translate into English

१. भोलि बिहान ठीक् नौ बजे हामी तपाईंकहाँ आउँदै छौं।
२. मेरो बिचार्ले आज पानी पर्छ । म त बाहिर जान्न ।
३. मेरो बुवा आज अड्डा जानुहुन्न। बिदा छ नि।
४. हामी कहिले पनि गाईको मासु खाँदैनौं ।

[1]Dilli Bazaar – an area of Kathmandu, about a mile from the centre.
[2]Tribhuvan University – named after the present King's grandfather.
[3]**bhane** is used like the particle **ta.** Trans. 'I don't go *every* day'. In Nepal Saturday is a holiday, Sunday is a normal working day.
gāiko māsu 'the meat of a cow' = 'beef', never eaten by Hindus or Buddhists.

५. प्रधान्मन्त्रीज्यूले आज पाटन्मा तीन् बजेतिर भाषण् गर्नुहुन्छ, होइन त ?
६. बाहुन्हरू मासु खान्दैनन् । दाल्, भात् र तर्कारी मात्रै खान्छन् ।
७. जाड़ोमा त पानी पर्दैन । गर्मीमा त धेरै नै पर्छ ।
८. तिमी नाम्चे बजार् कसरी जान्छौ ? हिंड़ेरै जान्छु ।
९. यो बाटोले कहाँ लान्छ, दाइ ? तपाईंलाई थाहा छ ? थाहा छ, हजूर् । गोर्खासम्म जान्छ ।
१०. मदेस्मा धेरै गर्मी हुन्छ, तर काठ्माड़ौंमा त्यतिको गर्मी हुँदैन।[1]
११. जाड़ोमा हजारौं अमेरिकी पर्यटक्हरू नेपाल् जान्छन् ।
१२. नेपाल्मा सञ्चरबार् बिदा हुन्छ । आइत्बार् बिदा हुँदैन।
१३. आउने हप्ता बुवाले मलाई एउटा राम्रो उपहार् दिनुहुन्छ ।
१४. तिमी आज शहर् जान्छौ ? आज त म जान्न । घर्मा धेरै काम् छ ।
१५. म आउने हप्ता दिल्ली जाँदै छु ।
केमा जानुहुन्छ?
म हवाईजहाज्मा पट्नासम्म जान्छु, अनि त्यस्पछि रेल्मा जान्छु ।
१६. तपाईं मकहाँ कति बजे आउनुहुन्छ ? म भरे आठ् बजेतिर आउँछु ।
१७. ए दाइ, तपाईंको घड़ीमा कति बज्यो ? मेरो घड़ीमा एघार बज्यो ।
१८. यो किताब् त मेरो पो हो । म तिमीलाई दिंदिन ।
१९. आज त म खान्न । रुचि छैन ।
२०. आउने महीना मेरो दाज्यू भारत् जाँदै हुनुहुन्छ । म त यहाँ बस्छु ।

Exercise 6b

Translate into Nepali

1. My elder sister is going to England next month. How is she going? She is going by aeroplane.
2. Will it rain today or not? I don't know.
3. What time are you going to the university? I'm not going today. It's a holiday, you know.
4. Where does that road lead to? It leads to our village. But it's a terribly long way round.
5. In the hot season tourists do not usually go to the Terai. It's very hot there at that time.
6. Brahmins never eat beef. They usually only eat vegetables.
7. Oh, I don't seem to have any money in my pocket. I'll go on foot.
8. The buses in ('of') London are always crowded at five o'clock.
9. This week he will not give me anything. Next week he'll give me ten rupees.
10. Why are you hitting your son? He is very well behaved.
11. Where are you studying these days? I'm not studying. I'm in an office, you know. But **(ta)**, my young brother is in the English department of the university.
12. I won't have anything to eat now. I have no appetite.

[1] **mades,** derived from the Sanskrit term **madhya-deś** 'midlands', is applied to the plains of India and to the Terai region of Nepal.

Exercise 6c

Translate into Nepali

I do not go; she (MGH) does not eat; we do not send; you (HGH) do not drink; they (LGH) do not take; he (LGH) milks the cow; do you know that man; I do not know him; they MGH never speak in a loud voice; we sometimes go to Kathmandu; it is always hot in Calcutta; Nepali girls are very pretty; the film begins at two o'clock sharp.

Read the following passage, then answer the questions in Nepali

नेपाल्मा सञ्चर्बार् बिदा हुन्छ । अड्डा र धेरैजसो पसल्हरू बन्द हुन्छन् । म दिनहुँ अड्डामा काम् गर्छु, तर सञ्चर्बार् म अड्डामा जान्न । राम्रो छ । म दस् बजेसम्म सुत्छु, त्यस्पछि बजार्तिर जान्छु । त्यहाँ कुनै[1] चियापसल्मा साथीहरूलाई भेट्छु। चिया खान्छु, अनि त्यस्पछि घर्तिर जान्छु । हामी बाह्र बजेतिर भात् खान्छौं । दिउँसो म बाहिर निस्कन्न । घर्मै आराम् गर्छु ।

१. नेपाल्मा बिदा कहिले हुन्छ ?

२. सञ्चर्बार् अड्डाहरू बन्द हुन्छन् कि हुँदैनन्?

३. तपाईं धेरैजसो कति बजे सुत्नुहुन्छ ?

४. तपाईं कति बजे भात् खानुहुन्छ ?

५. बेलायत्मा सञ्चर्बार् बिदा हुन्छ कि हुँदैन?

[1] कुनै 'any', 'some'.

LESSON 7

1. *New conjunct consonants*

क्न	**kn**	as in	हाँक्नु	**hā̃knu**	to drive
क्ष्य	**kṣy**	as in	उपलक्ष्य	**upalakṣya**	occasion
त्त्व	**ttv**	as in	महत्त्व	**mahattva**	importance
न्ध	**ndh**	as in	गान्धी	**gāndhī**	Gandhi
न्म, त्स	**nm, ts**	as in	शुभजन्मोत्सव	**ʃubhajanmotsava**	birthday
भ्र	**bhr**	as in	भ्रमण	**bhramaṇ**	tour
र्च	**rc**	as in	खर्च	**kharca**	expense

2. The numerals 21 to 30 (page 251) should now be learnt. Remember that *all* numerals take the classifiers –जना and –वटा (Lesson 4.9).

पच्चीस्‌जना सिपाही 'twenty-five soldiers', उनन्तीस्‌वटा किताब्‌ 'twenty-nine books', एक्काइस्‌वटा घर 'twenty-one houses'. But तीस्‌ दिन्‌ 'thirty days', तैंतीस्‌ मिनेट्‌ 'thirty-three minutes'.

3. The most important fractions are:

पाउ	**pāu**	a quarter	तिहाई	**tihāī**	a third
आधा	**ādhā**	half	डेढ्‌	**deṛh**	one and a half
अढ़ाई	**aṛhāī**	two and a half			

These function in the same way as other numerals: आधा मील्‌ 'half a mile', डेढ्‌ महीना 'one and a half months', अढ़ाई रुपियाँ 'two and a half rupees'.

The word रुपियाँ **rupiyā̃** may also be written and pronounced रुपैयाँ **rupəyā̃.**

4. The words सवा **savā** 'plus one quarter', साढ़े **sāṛhe** 'plus one half', पौने **pəwne** 'less one quarter' are always followed by another numeral.

सवा चार्‌	'four plus one quarter'	four and a quarter
साढ़े चार्‌	'four plus one half'	four and a half
पौने पाँच्‌	'five less one quarter'	four and three quarters

Occasionally साढ़े एक्‌ and साढ़े दुइ are used in place of डेढ्‌ ($1\frac{1}{2}$) and अढ़ाई ($2\frac{1}{2}$).

5. In telling time, divisions of the hour are expressed as follows:

चार्‌ बजे	at four o'clock
सवा चार्‌ बजे	at a quarter past four

साढ़े चार् बजे   at half past four
पौने पाँच् बजे   at a quarter to five

In other words, one says 'at four and a quarter o'clock' etc. Note in particular:

डेढ़ बजे or साढ़े एक् बजे   at half past one
अढ़ाई बजे or साढ़े दुइ बजे   at half past two

6. Minutes to and past the hour are expressed as follows:

चार् बज्नलाई पाँच् मिनेट् बाँकी छ
cār bajnalāī pāc mineṭ bā̃ki cha
It is five to four (lit. 'for four striking five minutes are left')[1]

बाह्र बज्नलाई पच्चीस् मिनेट् बाँकीमा
bārha bajnalāī paccīs mineṭ bā̃kīmā
At twenty-five to twelve.

Note that बाँकी **bā̃kī** is an adjective meaning 'left over, remaining':

पैसा बाँकी छैन   there is no money left
केही पनि बाँकी रहेनछ   why, there is nothing left at all

दस् बजेर बीस् मिनेट् गयो
das bajera bīs mineṭ gayo
It is twenty past ten (lit. 'ten having struck twenty minutes have gone')

एघार बजेर दस् मिनेटमा
eghāra bajera das mineṭmā
at ten past eleven

7. The postposition–तिर **-tira** 'towards, about' is used in expressions of time for a rough approximation:

तीन् बजेतिर   at about three o'clock
साढ़े पाँच् बजेतिर   at about half past five

–तिर is also used with reference to place:

म खुम्बुतिर जाँदै छु
I'm going towards Khumbu/I'm heading for Khumbu

उ पहाड़तिर जाँदै छ
He is going towards the hills

पहाड़् **pahāṛ** 'hills, mountains' is a term generally used in Nepal for the Himalayan foothills. पहाड़ी **pahāṛī** or पहाड़िया **pahāṛiyā** is a 'hillman' who lives in the hill villages, as distinct from मदेसी **madesī** – someone who lives in the southern Nepalese plains (मदेस् **mades** or तराई **tarāī**).

[1]**bajnalāī** 'for striking' is the second infinitive of the verb **bajnu** 'to strike' (Lesson 12) followed by the postposition **-lāī.**

8. *Other points*

(*a*) ठीक् with expressions of time means 'exactly, precisely'

ठीक् छ बजे	at exactly six o'clock
	at 9.15 precisely

(*b*) The adverbs **bihāna** 'in the morning', दिउँसो **diūso** 'in the afternoon', भरे **bhare** 'this evening', बेल्का **belukā** 'in the (early) evening', राति **rāti** 'at night' precede the expression of time:

हवाईजहाज् बिहान नौ बजे काठ्माडौं पुग्छ
The aeroplane reaches Kathmandu at nine in the morning

म भरे सात् बजेतिर तपाईंकहाँ आउँछु
I'll come and see you this evening at about seven

(*c*) The postposition -मा is used in the following expressions:

बस् दुइ दुइ घण्टामा आउँछ
The bus comes every two hours

The repetition of the numeral implies that the bus comes at regular intervals:

रेल् कति कति बेलामा आउँछ ?
How often do the trains run?

बजेमा / साढेमा / सवामा / आउँछ
They come on the hour/on the half hour/on the quarter

रेल् हरेक् घण्टामा आउँछ
The train comes every hour

Note हरेक् **harek** (sometimes written हरएक्) 'every': हरेक् मान्छे 'every man', हरेक् किसिम् 'every kind', हरेक् दिन् 'every day'.

9. The suffix चाहिं **-cāhī** may be added to adjectives, nouns and pronouns.

(*a*) When added to adjectives, चाहिं has the effect of turning them into nouns, and may usually be rendered into English as 'the . . . one'.

ठूलोचाहिं	**ṭhūlocāhī**	'the big one'
मेरोचाहिं	**merocāhī**	'my one', 'mine'

In the same way चाहिं may be added to demonstrative and pronominal adjectives, and to a possessive formed with the postposition -को:

त्योचाहिं	**tyocāhī**	that one
योचाहिं	**yocāhī**	this one
कुन्चाहिं	**kuncāhī**	which one?
रामकोचाहिं	**rāmkocāhī**	Ram's one
त्यस्कोचाहिं	**tyaskocāhī**	his/her one
उनीहरूकोचाहिं	**unīharūkocāhī**	their one, theirs etc.

(*b*) When added to nouns and pronouns, चाहिं has the effect of emphasising them and may be translated in English as 'as for', or simply by a change of tone.

मचाहिं	**macāhī**	as for me

उचाहिं	**ucāhī**	as for him/her
रामचाहिं	**rāmcāhī**	as for Ram
गर्मीमाचाहिं	**garmīmācāhī**	in the *hot* season (as opposed to others)

Note the use of चाहिं in the following sentences:

त्यो गाउँमा कुन्चाहिं चियापसल् सब्भन्दा राम्रो छ ?
Which (one) is the best tea shop in that village?

मेरो घर् रामकोचाहिंभन्दा ठूलो रहेछ
I see that my house is bigger than Ram's (one)

यो घड़ी राम्रो हो तर त्योचाहिं त्यति राम्रो होइन
This watch is nice but that one is not so nice

Note that त्यति **tyati** is an adverb which modifies an adjective: त्यति ठूलो 'so big', त्यति अग्लो 'so high', त्यति राम्रो 'so nice'.

The adjective त्यतिको **tyatiko** (plural form त्यतिका **tyatikā**) qualifies a noun: त्यतिको गर्मी 'so much heat', त्यतिका किताब्हरू 'so many books'.

मचाहिं जे पनि खान्छु । उचाहिं खाली भात् र दाल् मात्रै खान्छ
As for me, I eat anything. *He* eats only rice and lentils

जे पनि	**je pani**	'anything at all'
खाली मात्रै	**khālī mātrəy**	very emphatic 'only', 'nothing but'

10. The oblique forms of को **ko?** 'who?', कोको **koko?** 'who?' (plural), and कोही **kohī** 'someone' are कस् **kas,** कसकस् **kaskas,** and कसै **kasəy** respectively. The oblique forms are used before postpositions:

कस्को किताब्	**kasko kitāb?**	whose book?
कस्कस्कहाँ	**kaskaskahā̃**	at whose place? ('of which people')
म कसैलाई दिंदिन	**ma kasəylāī dīdina**	I shan't give it to anyone

Note that कस्लाई **kaslāī** 'to whom?' and कस्ले **kasle** are often pronounced **kallāī** and **kalle** respectively (cf. 4.4).

त्यो उपहार् कस्लाई दिन्छौ ?
To whom are you giving that present?

कस्ले भन्छ ?
Who says so?

11. के **ke?** 'what?' and केही **kehī** 'anything' have no oblique forms.

केमा जानुहुन्छ ? हवाईजहाज्मा जान्छु
How (in what) are you going? I'm going by air

केको हतपत् ?
What's the hurry (lit. 'of what . . .')?

12. Certain postpositions or postpositional phrases consist of two or more words, the first of which is –को. Such expressions are:

–को लागि	**-ko lāgi**	for, for the sake of
–को बारेमा	**-ko bāremā**	about, concerning

–को निम्ति	**-ko nimti**	for, for the sake of
–को निमित्त	**-ko nimitta**	for (a literary synonym of **-ko nimti**)
–को बाद्	**-ko bād**	after (syn. with -पछि)

म पन्ध्र दिन्को लागि भारत् जाँदै छु
I'm going to India for a fortnight

Note that भारत् **bhārat** is synonymous with हिन्दुस्तान् **hindustān.** Both terms are used for 'India', the former being more frequently used in official contexts.

नेपाल्को बारेमा के थाहा छ ?
What do you know about Nepal?

When a postpositional phrase with -को as the first element follows one of the pronouns म, तँ, हामी, तिमी, the possessive adjective is used.

उस्ले मेरो निम्ति केही पनि गर्दैन
He does nothing for me ('for my sake')

विवाहको निमित्त नेपालीहरू धेरै पैसा खर्च गर्छन्
Nepalis spend a lot of money on weddings ('for the sake of a wedding')

खर्च गर्नु **kharca garnu** 'to spend (money)'
विवाह **vivāha** – the literary form of the colloquial बिहा **bihā** 'wedding'. In spoken Nepali the latter is more common.

मेरो बिहा आउने महीना हुन्छ
My marriage will take place next month

त्यस्को बाद् म घर् जान्छु
After that I shall go home

त्यस्पछि **tyaspachi** could also have been used.

13. Certain postpositional expressions consist of –को and a noun followed by –मा.

–को विषयमा	**-ko viṣayamā**	on the subject of, about
को उपलक्ष्यमा	**-ko upalakṣyamā**	on the occasion of

वहाँले नेपाली साहित्यको विषयमा भाषण् गर्नुहुन्छ
He is making a speech on the subject of Nepali literature

महाराजाधिराज्को शुभजन्मोत्सवको उपलक्ष्यमा
On the occasion of the birthday of His Majesty

महाराजाधिराज् **mahārājādhirāj** is the title of the King of Nepal.

14. A member of the Nepalese royal family is given the honorific title श्री ५ **ʃrī pā̃c** (lit. 'five times Lord'), and is often referred to in this way. The full title of the present King is:

श्री ५ महाराजाधिराज् बिरेन्द्र वीर् विक्रम् शाह देव्
ʃrī pā̃c mahārājādhirāj birendra vīr vikram ʃāh dev

वीर् and विक्रम literally mean 'hero', 'brave'; शाह is the family name; देव् 'a god' indicates the King's considered divinity.

The term श्री **ʃrī** and the feminine counterpart श्रीमती **ʃrīmatī** are used on formal occasions before proper names corresponding to the English titles Mr. and Mrs. Verbal concord is of course HGH.

श्री प्रधान् आज पीकिङ्गबाट इस्लामाबाद् फर्कनुहुन्छ
Mr. Pradhan will return from Peking to Islamabad today
श्रीमती श्रेष्ठले आउने महीना बिहार्को भ्रमण् गर्नुहुन्छ
Mrs. Shrestha will make a tour of Bihar next month.

श्रीमती also means 'wife' and is used in preference to स्वास्नी when talking about someone else's wife:

तपाईंकी श्रीमती पनि पाल्नुहुन्छ ?
Will your wife also be coming?

पाल्नु **pālnu** 'to come/go' is used only in HGH contexts.

Note that the word शुभजन्मोत्सव 'birthday' in the example above is a combination of three Sanskrit words: शुभ **ʃubha** 'auspicious', जन्म **janma** 'birth', उत्सव **utsava** 'festival'. शुभनाम् **ʃubhanām** (lit. 'auspicious name') is a polite word for नाउँ. The polite way to ask someone's name is: तपाईंको शुभनाम् के हो ?

15. In written Nepali, the first element –को in compound postpositional phrases, like those considered above, is often changed to –का **-kā,** which is the oblique form of the postposition:

–का लागि **-kā lāgi**
–का निमित्त **-kā nimitta**

Similarly, adjectives ending in **-o** have the ending changed to **-ā** if they qualify a noun which is governed by a postposition (i.e. they become oblique):

त्यस् साना देश्का राज्धानीमा
tyas sānā deʃkā rājdhānīmā
in the capital of that small country

This, however, is entirely restricted to the written language and consistency is not always observed. The last sentence would be spoken:

त्यो सानो देश्को राज्धानीमा

16. The postposition –बाट **-bāṭa** is used idiomatically in certain expressions like:

बस्बाट	**basbāṭa**	by bus
हवाईजहाज्बाट	**havāījahājbāṭa**	by air
यो बाटोबाट	**yo bāṭobāṭa**	by this road
कुन् बाटोबाट ?	**kun bāṭobāṭa**	by which road?

–बाट is also used with adverbs like बाहिर **bāhira** 'outside', नजीक् **najīk** 'nearby':

पर्यटक्हरू धेरैजसो काठ्माड़ौंबाट बाहिर जाँदैनन्
Tourists do not usually go outside Kathmandu

यहाँबाट सब्भन्दा नजीक्को गाँउ कन्चाहिं हो ?
Which is the nearest village to here?

नजीक् may also be used as a postposition:

त्यो मेरो घर्नजीक् बस्छ
He lives near my house

पाटन् काठ्माड़ौंनजीक् छ
Patan is near Kathmandu

17. जस्तो **jasto** 'like', 'such as' may be used as an adjective and an adverb. When used as an adjective it follows the noun it qualifies:

मेरो कोट् उस्को (कोट्) जस्तो रहेछ
My coat is like his (coat)

कल्कत्ता र शाङ्हाई जस्ता एशियाका ठूला शहर्हरू
The great cities of Asia like Calcutta and Shanghai

When used adverbially जस्तो immediately precedes the verb:

उस्को कुरा साँचो जस्तो छैन
What he says does not sound true (lit. 'his word is not like true')

आज पानी पर्छ जस्तो छैन
It does not look as if it will rain today (lit. 'today it will rain as if it is not')

आज आउँदैन जस्तो छ
It looks as if he is not coming today

Note that कुरा **kurā** may mean 'a thing' in the general sense, but often refers to something said. Thus तपाईंको कुरा may be translated 'what you said'. The expression कुरा गर्नु means 'to talk', 'to have a word':

म भोलि तपाईंसँग कुरा गर्छु
I'll have a word with you tomorrow

18. अर्को **arko** 'other' (usually 'the other of two') is used mainly with singular nouns. अरू **arū** 'other', 'else', 'more' is used mainly with plural nouns and non-countable nouns like चिया, भात् , etc.

तपाईंलाई अर्को किताब् दिन्छु
I'll give you the other book

यस्को सट्टा अर्को मान्छे आउँछ
The other man is coming in place of this one

–को सट्टा
-ko saṭṭā 'in place of'

म अर्को महीना आउँदै छु
I'll come next month

अरू चिया खानुहोस्
Drink some more tea (see below 19)

यो घर्मा अरू कोही बस्दैन
No-one else lives in this house

अरू कोही साथ्मा छ ?
Is anyone else with you?

मेरो खल्तीमा अरू केही पनि छैन
I have nothing else at all in my pocket

अरू के लिनुहुन्छ ?
What else will you take?

अरू कुन् किताब् पढ्नुहुन्छ ?
Which other book will you read?

19. The HGH imperative is formed by adding –होस -hos to the infinitive of the verb:

गर्नुहोस्	**garnuhos**	do
बस्नुहोस्	**basnuhos**	sit
आउनुहोस्	**āunuhos**	come
भित्र पाल्नुहोस्	**bhitra pālnuhos**	please come in

Note that भित्र is used both as an adverb and a postposition 'in', 'inside':

म भित्र जान्छु	I'll go inside
हाम्रो घरभित्र	inside our house
काठ्माडौंभित्र	inside Kathmandu

The negative of the HGH imperative is formed by adding the prefix न– **na-** to the positive form.

नआउनुहोस्	**naāunuhos**	do not come
नरिसाउनुहोस्	**narisāunuhos**	do not be angry

The ending -नुहोस् **-nuhos** is often pronounced and sometimes written as –नोस् **-nos:**

पाल्नुहोस्	or	पाल्नोस्	**pālnos**	come, go
नआउनुहोस	or	नआउनोस्	**naāunos**	do not come
गर्नुहोस्	or	गर्नोस्	**garnos**	do

The suffix –होला **-holā** instead of –होस् **-hos** may be used to convey extra politeness.

मोटर् बिस्तारै हाँक्नुहोला
Please drive the car slowly

नरिसाउनुहोला
Please do not be angry

The particles न **na** and त **ta,** following the imperative, have the effect of making the command less brusque. They may be rendered in English as 'won't you?', 'please' etc.

मलाई भन्नुहोस् त
Please tell me

चिया खानुहोस् न
Have some tea, won't you?

20. The particle रे **re** (always coming at the end of a sentence) indicates that the words which precede it are reported or that the information is at second hand. It may be translated: 'they say that . . .', 'he says that . . .', 'I hear that . . .' etc.

भरे पानी पर्छ रे
They say that it's going to rain this evening

आउने हप्ता बिदा छ रे
I hear there's a holiday next week

उसको खल्तीमा केही पनि छैन रे
He says that he's got nothing at all in his pocket

के रे ?
What does he say?

Vocabulary 7

अचेल्	**acel**	now, nowadays
अढ़ाई	**aṛhāī**	two and a half
अत्यन्त	**atyanta**	extremely
अन्तर्राष्ट्रीय	**antarrāṣṭrīya**	international
अर्थ–व्यवस्था	**artha-vyavasthā**	economy
आधा	**ādhā**	half
–को उपलक्ष्यमा	**-ko upalakṣyamā**	on the occasion of
एशिया	**eʃiyā**	Asia
ओहोर् दोहोर् गर्नु	**ohor dohor garnu**	to come and go, to make a round trip
औद्योगिक्	**əwdyogik**	industrial
काख्	**kākh**	lap, heart
कुरा	**kurā**	thing, matter
कैयन्	**kəyyan**	several
खाली...मात्रै	**khālī . . . mātrəy**	only, nothing but
खर्च गर्नु	**kharca garnu**	to spend
खुला	**khulā**	open
घण्टा	**ghaṇṭā**	hour
चालु	**cālu**	operating, in motion
छिन्	**chin**	moment
एक् छिन्	**ek chin**	just a moment
जस्तो	**jasto**	like, as if
जे पनि	**je pani**	whatever, anything at all
जोड़्नु	**joṛnu**	to join, link
जोड़्ने	**joṛne**	linking

टुँड़िखेल्	**ṭũṛikhel**	Tundikhel (a parade ground in Kathmandu)
डेढ़	**ḍeṛh**	one and a half
ढाका	**ḍhākā**	Dacca (Bangladesh)
तराई	**tarāī**	the Terai
त्यति	**tyati**	so, that much
नजीक्	**najīk**	near, nearby
नाउँ गरेको	**nāũ gareko**	by name, called
–को निमित्त	**-ko nimitta**	for the sake of
–को निम्ति	**-ko nimti**	for the sake of
पाल्नु	**pālnu**	to come, go (HGH)
पीकिङ्ग	**pīkiŋg**	Peking
पूजा	**pūjā**	worship
पूजा गर्नु	**pūjā garnu**	to worship
पौने	**pəwne**	less a quarter
फर्कनु	**pharkanu**	to come back, return
बँग्लादेश्	**bãglādeʃ**	Bangladesh
बाहिर	**bāhira**	out, outside
–को बाद्	**-ko bād**	after
–को बारेमा	**-ko bāremā**	about, concerning
–बाहेक्	**-bāhek**	except
बिराट्नगर् (विराट्नगर)	**birāṭnagar (virāṭnagar)**	Biratnagar (town in Terai)
बिस्तारै	**bistārəy**	slowly
बिहा	**bihā**	wedding
बिहार्	**bihār**	Bihar
बीच्	**-bīc**	between
बीर्गंज्	**bīrganj**	Birganj (town in Terai)
ब्याँकक्	**byā̃kak**	Bangkok
भन्ने	**bhanne**	by name, called
भित्र	**bhitra**	inside, in tour
भ्रमण्	**bhramaṇ**	tour
भ्रमण गर्नु	**bhramaṇ garnu**	to make a tour
महत्त्व	**mahattva**	importance
महाराजाधिराज्	**mahārājādhirāj**	title of King of Nepal
मिनेट्	**mineṭ**	minute
मोटर्	**moṭar**	motor car
मौसम्	**məwsam**	season, weather
जाड़ो मौसम्	**jāṛo məwsam**	cold season, winter
रक्सौल्	**raksəwl**	Raxaul (border town in India)
रङ्गून्	**raŋgūn**	Rangoon
राज्पथ्	**rājpath**	Rajpath (the name of the road running between Kathmandu and Raxaul)

रिसाउनु	**risāunu**	to be angry
–को लागि	**-ko lāgi**	for, for the sake of
वाशिङ्टन	**vāʃiŋgtan**	Washington
विमान्	**vimān**	aeroplane
विमान्सेवा	**vimānsevā**	airservice
विमान्स्थल्	**vimānsthal**	airport
विवाह	**vivāha**	wedding
विषय	**viṣaya**	subject
–को विषयमा	**-ko viṣayamā**	on the subject of
व्यवस्था	**vyavasthā**	arrangement[1]
शाङ्हाई	**ʃāŋghāī**	Shanghai
शुभनाम्	**ʃubhanām**	name (polite word)
शुभजन्मोत्सव	**ʃubhajanmotsava**	birthday
–को सट्टा	**-ko saṭṭā**	instead of
सड़क्	**saɽak**	road (syn. **bāṭo**)
सवा	**savā**	plus one quarter
साँचो	**sā̃co**	true
साढ़े	**sāɽhe**	plus one half
साथ्मा	**sāthmā**	along with
साहित्य	**sāhitya**	literature
सीमाना	**sīmānā**	border, frontier
सुन्दर्	**sundar**	beautiful
हत्पत्	**hatpat**	hurry
हावापानी	**hāvāpānī**	climate[2]
हाँक्नु	**hā̃knu**	to drive (a car etc.)

Reading Passage

The following Reading Passage is a reasonably straightforward piece of connected prose, but is rather more complicated than anything encountered so far. The style of the passage tends to be more literary than colloquial and is fairly typical of (though simpler than) the Nepali found in modern newspapers. It will be noted that plural verbal and adjectival concord is observed throughout.

The passage also contains a number of terms (largely borrowings from Sanskrit) which, though common in the literary language, would not be used so frequently in everyday speech. For example, the word विमान् **vimān** 'aeroplane' is almost entirely restricted to the written language – an official term for the colloquial हवाईजहाज् . Similarly, the term विमान्स्थल् **vimānsthal** 'airport' is used much less frequently than its colloquial synonyms गौचरन् **gəwcaran** (originally meaning 'cow-pasture') and हवाईघाट् **havāīghāṭ.** The expression भारत्का कैयन् शहरहरू **bhāratkā kəyyan ʃaharharū** would usually be rendered in

[1]Usually pronounced **bebasthā**

[2]A compound of **hāvā** 'wind' and **pānī** 'water'.

the spoken language as भारत्को केही शहर **bhāratko kehī ʃahar,** and the expression अत्यन्त सुन्दर् **atyanta sundar** as एक् दम् राम्रो **ek dam rāmro.**

Words such as औद्योगिक् **əwdyogik** 'industrial', अर्थ–व्यवस्था **artha-vyavasthā** 'economy', महत्त्व **mahattva** 'importance' etc., which have no colloquial synonyms, though nowadays quite familiar to any Nepali who reads the newspaper or listens to the radio, tend to be used only in comparatively sophisticated circles.

Finally, the passage contains one or two verbal forms and constructions which are fully dealt with in later lessons. The expressions in which they occur have been explained in the footnotes and for the moment may be learnt as items of vocabulary.

हिमालयको काख्मा नेपाल् नाउँ गरेको[1] एउटा सानो राज्य छ। नेपाल्को राज्धानी काठ्माडौं हो । काठ्माडौंमा एउटा अन्तर्राष्ट्रीय विमान्स्थल् छ। भारत्का कैयन् शहर्हरूबाट यहाँ विमान्हरू ओहोर् दोहोर् गर्छन् र एशियाका अरू शहर्हरू जस्ता ढाका, ब्याँकक् र रङ्गुन्बाट पनि यहाँ विमान्हरू आउँछन्। काठ्माडौंबाहेक् नेपाल्मा एक् दुइवटा[2] अरू पनि ठूला शहर्हरू छन् । तराईका बीर्गंज् र बिराट्नगर् जस्ता ठूला शहर्हरू औद्योगिक् शहर्हरू हुन् । यस् कारण् नेपाल्को अर्थ-व्यवस्थामा यी शहर्हरूको ठूलो महत्त्व छ।

काठ्माडौंलाई भारत्सँग जोड्ने[3] दुइटा सड्क्हरू छन् । सब्भन्दा पुरानोचाहिं राज्पथ् हो । यो बाटो भारत्को रक्सौल् भन्ने[4] एउटा सानो शहर्सम्म जान्छ । काठ्माडौंलाई चीन्को सीमानासँग जोड्ने बाटो पनि अहिले खुला छ ।

नेपाल्मा पोखरा नाउँ गरेको एउटा सानो तर अत्यन्त सुन्दर् शहर् पनि छ । काठ्माडौं र पोखराबीच् विमान्सेवा चालू छ[5] र दिन्दिनै विमान्हरू ओहोर् दोहोर् गर्छन् । नेपाल्मा अचेल् निक्कै पर्यटक्हरू आउँछन् । जाडोको मौसम्मा काठ्माडौंका सबै होटेल्हरू पर्यटक्हरूले भरिभराउ हुन्छन् ।

Notes

1. **nepāl nāũ gareko** 'Nepal by name', 'called Nepal'. **gareko** is the 1st perfect participle of the verb **garnu** lit. 'having done'. This participle is dealt with in Lesson 12.
2. **ek duivaṭa arū** 'one (or) two others'. For the form of the numeral, see Lesson 4, 10.
3. **kāṭhmāɽəw̃lāī bhāratsãga joɽne . . . :** 'linking Kathmandu with India'.

joṛne is the infinitival participle of the verb **joṛnu** 'to link, join'. The infinitival participle is often used as a verbal adjective. Cf. **āune** 'coming, next'.

4. **raksəwl bhanne:** 'called Raxaul'. **bhanne,** here translated 'called', is the infinitival participle of the verb **bhannu.** The Rajpath runs almost due north from the Indian border (Bihar) to Kathmandu. It is one of the oldest roads linking Nepal with India.
5. **vimānsevā:** 'air-service'. **sevā** literally means 'service' (of any kind). Cf. the expression **kasəyko sevā garnu** 'to serve someone'. The Royal Nepal Airlines Corporation (R.N.A.C.) is known in Nepali as शाही नेपाल् वायुसेवा निगम् **ʃāhī nepāl vāyusevā nigam** – a literal rendering of the English words. **vāyu** is a Sanskrit word meaning 'air, wind'. Thus **vāyusevā** 'air-service'. वायुयान् **vāyuyān** is yet another term for aeroplane, commonly used in the written language. **yān** is literally 'a carriage'.

Exercise 7a

Translate into English

१. आउने हप्ता म दुइ महीनाको लागि नेपाल् जाँदैछु।
२. केको हतपत् दाइ? एक छिन् बस्नुहोस् न ।
३. श्री ५ का भाषणहरू धेरै मान्छे पढ्छन् ।
४. यो बाटोमा धेरै हिलो छ । मोटर् बिस्तारै हाँक्नुहोस् ।
५. काठ्माड़ौंको सब्भन्दा महँगो होटेल् त्योचाहिं होइन त ?
६. हाम्रो घर्नजीक् एउटा सानो मन्दिर् छ । मेरा बहिनीहरू त्यहाँ दिनहुँ पूजा गर्छन् ।
७. त्यो बाटोबाट नजानुहोस् है । एक् दम् उकालो छ ।
८. जाड़ोमा नेपाल्को हावापानी धेरैजसो राम्रो हुन्छ । गर्मीमाचाहिं त्यति राम्रो हुँदैन ।
९. महाराजाधिराज्को शुभजन्मोत्सवको उपलक्ष्यमा प्रधान्मन्त्रीले दुइ बजे दिउँसो टुँड़िखेल्मा भाषण् गर्नुहुन्छ ।
१०. भित्र पाल्नुहोस् हजूर् । एक् छिन् बस्नुहोस् त ।
११. राम्को बिहा आउने हप्ता हुन्छ रे ।
१२. मेरो छोरा आज स्कूल् जाँदैन । बिदा छ रे ।
१३. मेरो आमा सधैं घरै बस्नुहुन्छ । कहिले पनि बाहिर निस्कनुहुन्न ।
१४. बेलुकाको हवाईजहाज् कति बजे पुग्छ ? पाँच बजे पुग्छ रे ।
१५. तपाईं नेपाल्मा कस्कहाँ बस्नुहुन्छ ? धेरैजसो म एक्जना साथीको घर्मा बस्छु ।
१६. मेरी बहिनी आज त खाँदिन । रुचि छैन रे ।
१७. छेत्रीहरू अक्सर् जे पनि खान्छन् । बाहुन्हरूचाहिं खाली तर्कारी मात्रै खान्छन् ।
१८. त्यो गाउँमा सब्भन्दा राम्रो चियापसल् कुन्चाहिं हो ? राम्कोचाहिं ।
१९. तपाईंको नोकर्को कुरा साँचो जस्तो छैन ।
२०. आज पानी पर्छ जस्तो छैन । म त बाहिर जान्छु । बेलुका पाँच् बजे फर्कन्छु ।

Exercise 7b

Translate into Nepali

1. Which is the best cinema in Kathmandu? In my opinion that one is the best. The one in Patan is also very good.

2. What time are you coming home this evening? I'll be home about half past seven.
3. They say the President of Pakistan will meet Mrs. Gandhi next month.
4. Nowadays there is an air-service between Kathmandu and Jumla. The aeroplanes go twice a month.
5. They say the road is very bad. Drive slowly won't you?
6. Excuse me, how far is the airport away from the hotel? It is not very far. A bus leaves every hour.
7. When are you getting married? I'm getting married next year.
8. What is the climate of England like (How is . . .)? The climate of England is very good usually.
9. Why, your pen is just like mine! Give it to me a moment, will you?
10. They say that all the shops in ('of') the city will be closed tomorrow. Is it true? Yes, there's a holiday you know.
11. What's the hurry? Sit down. Have some tea won't you? No, we are going to the cinema, and the film starts in ten minutes.
12. On the occasion of His Majesty's birthday, many tourists come to Kathmandu. At that time the hotels are crowded with people.

Exercise 7c

Translate into Nepali

How many men? twenty-five days; three and a half hours; half a kilo; twice a day; after three months; five and a half miles; one cup of tea; two sons and one daughter; four times a fortnight; nine men.

Exercise 7d

Translate into English

१. हामी दुइ बजेतिर तपाईंकहाँ आउँदै छौं।
२. रेल् पट्नाबाट हरेक् घण्टामा रक्सौल् जान्छ रे ।
३. सिनेमा ठीक् छ बजे शुरू हुन्छ ।
४. बस् यहाँ कति कति बेलामा आउँछ ? साढ़ेमा आउँछ, हजूर् ।
५. तिम्रो घड़ीमा कति बज्यो ? मेरो घड़ीमा ८ बज्नलाई १० मिनेट् बाँकी छ ।
६. कति बज्यो अहिले त ? अहिले ठीक् सवा नौ बज्यो ।

Exercise 7e

Complete the following sentences by giving the correct affirmative form of the verb in brackets

१. हामी धेरैजसो त्यो होटल्मा (बस्नु)
२. तपाईं के काम् (गर्नु)
३. हाम्रो नोकर् बिहान बेलुकै दिन्को दुइ पटक् गाई (दुहुनु)
४. तपाईं कति बजे (सुत्नु)
५. मेरो बुवा पोखरामा (बस्नु) । म त काठ्माड़ौंमा काम् (गर्नु)

LESSON 8

1. *New conjunct consonants*

थ्य	**thy**	as in	थ्याङ्बोचे	**thyāŋboce**	Thyangboche
न्थ्य	**nthy**	as in	हुनुहुन्थ्यो	**hunuhunthyo**	was, were (HGH)
म्न	**mn**	as in	घुम्नु	**ghumnu**	to travel
ल्ढ	**lḍh**	as in	ओखल्ढुङ्गा	**okhalḍhuŋgā**	Okhaldhunga
श्न	**ʃn**	as in	प्रश्न	**praʃna**	question

2. In Lesson 5, we saw that Nepali verbs are divided into five groups, according to the Nature of their *Primary Base*.

Verbs belonging to groups (i) and (ii) i.e. bases ending in a consonant like गर्नु and बस्नु or in the vowels **-ā** or **-i** like खानु and दिनु in fact only have one base.

Verbs belonging to group (iii) – monosyllabic base ending in **-u** like धुनु, group (iv) – base of more than one syllable ending in **-a** or **-u** like बिर्सनु and दुहुनु, and group (v) – base ending in **-āu** or **-iu** like आउनु and पिउनु also have a *Secondary Base*, which is used in the formation of certain tenses and participles.

The Secondary Base of verbs belonging to group (iii) is formed by changing the Primary Base vowel **-u** to **-o.** That of verbs belonging to groups (iv) and (v) is formed by dropping the final vowel of the Primary Base. Thus:

	Infinitive		*Primary Base*		*Secondary Base*	
(iii)	धुनु	**dhunu**	धु	**dhu-**	धो	**dho-**
(iv)	बिर्सनु	**birsanu**	बिर्स	**birsa-**	बिर्स्	**birs-**
	दुहुनु	**duhunu**	दुहु	**duhu**	दुह	**duh-**
(v)	आउनु	**āunu**	आउ	**āu-**	आ	**ā-**
	पिउनु	**piunu**	पिउ	**piu-**	पि	**pi-**

The group (ii) verb जानु **jānu** (Primary Base जा **jā**) has an irregular Secondary Base ग **ga-.**

3. The personal suffixes of the Simple Past Tense, which are added to the Primary Base of Verbs belonging to groups (i) and (ii) and to the Secondary Base of Verbs belonging to groups (iii), (iv) and (v) are as follows:

Pronoun	*Affirmative*		*Negative*	
म	एँ	**-ẽ**	इनँ	**-inã**

तँ	–इस्	**-is**	–इनस्	**-inas**
उ,त्यो,यो	–यो	**-yo**	–एन	**-ena**
हामी (–हरू)	–यौं	**-yəw̃**	–एनौं	**-enəw̃**
तिमी (–हरू)	–यौ	**-yəw**	–एनौ	**-enəw**
उनी (–हरू)	–ए	**-e**	–एनन्	**-enan**

The HGH forms of the Simple Past Tense have the suffixes -भयो **-bhayo** (affirm.) and–भएन **bhaena** (neg.) added to the infinitive. The subject of a *transitive* verb in the Simple Past Tense *always* takes the postposition –ले.

4. The Simple Past Tenses of गर्नु (transitive) and आउनु (intransitive) are thus:

(*a*) गर्नु	*Affirmative*		*Negative*	
मैले	गरें	**garẽ**	गरिनँ	**garinã**
तैंले	गरिस्	**garis**	गरिनस्	**garinas**
उसले	गर्‍यो	**garyo**	गरेन	**garena**
हामीले	गर्‍यौं	**garyəw̃**	गरेनौं	**garenəw̃**
तिमीले	गर्‍यौ	**garyəw**	गरेनौ	**garenəw**
उनले,उनीहरूले	गरे	**gare**	गरेनन्	**garenan**
तपाईंले, वहाँले	गर्नुभयो	**garnubhayo**	गर्नुभएन	**garnubhaena**

(*b*) आउनु	*Affirmative*		*Negative*	
म	आएँ	**āẽ**	आइनँ	**āinā**
तँ	आइस्	**āis**	आइनस्	**āinas**
उ	आयो	**āyo**	आएन	**āena**
हामी	आयौं	**āyəw̃**	आएनौं	**āenəw̃**
तिमी	आयौ	**āyəw**	आएनौ	**āenəw**
उनी (-हरू)	आए	**āe**	आएनन्	**āenan**
तपाई वहाँ	आउनुभयो	**āunubhayo**	आउनुभएन	**āunubhaena**

Similarly:

म बसें	I sat/stayed	मैले खाएँ	I ate	मैले दिएँ	I gave
मैले बिर्सें	I forgot	मैले दुहें	I milked	मैले धोएँ	I washed
मैले पठाएँ	I sent	म गएँ	I went		

Take each of these verbs and conjugate them with the pronouns in the Simple Past Tense as was done above with गर्नु and आउनु . When the verb is transitive, be careful to add the postposition -ले to the pronoun. Note that म and तँ with -ले become मैले **məyle** and तैंले **təỹle**.

5. Third person forms have the following optional feminine suffixes

Pronoun	*Affirmative*		*Negative*	
उ	-ई	**-ī**	-इन	**-ina**
उनी	-इन्	**-in**	-इनन्	**-inan**

त्यो गई **tyo gaī** she went

मेरी बहिनीले गरिन	**merī bahinīle garina**	my sister did not do
तिनी आइन्	**tinī āin**	she (MGH) came
यिन्ले धोइनन्	**yinle dhoinan**	she (MGH) did not wash

The feminine forms of the Past Simple Tense, though optional alternatives to the masculine forms in spoken Nepali, tend to be used more frequently in speech than the feminine forms of the Simple Indefinite Tense.

6. The Simple Past Tense denotes action completed at some time in the past, and as we have seen in the above examples may usually be translated by the English past tense: 'I went', 'he did not go', 'you saw' etc.

पोहोर् साल् म नेपाल् गएँ
Last year I went to Nepal

Note पोहोर् साल् **pohor sāl** or simply पोहोर् **pohor** 'last year'

तपाईंको छोरा कहिले आयो ? अस्ति आयो
When did your son come? He came the other day

अस्ति **asti** strictly means 'the day before yesterday', but is frequently used loosely in the sense of 'the other day'. अस्तिको **astiko** preceding the days of the week means 'last'.

अस्तिको बिहिबार् म घरै बसें
Last Thursday, I stayed at home

गएको **gaeko** (often pronounced **gāko**) means 'last' in all contexts.

गएको महीना पानी परेन
Last month it did not rain

गएको सञ्चर्बार् उ मकहाँ आयो
He came to my house last Saturday

In written Nepali गत **gata** is used for 'last'. Thus गत बिहिबार् 'last Thursday', गत वर्ष 'last year' (वर्ष **varṣa** is an alternative literary spelling of बर्ष **barṣa** 'year').

तीन् बर्ष अघि मैले नेपाल्मा पाँच् महीना बिताएँ
Three years ago, I spent five months in Nepal

तपाईंले के भन्नुभयो ? मैले त केही पनि भनिनँ
What did you say? *I* did not say anything

7. The past tense of the verbs छ and हो (corresponding to English 'was' and 'were' is formed from the base थि **thi-**, to which the suffixes are added regularly.

Pronoun	*Affirmative*		*Negative*	
म	थिएँ	**thiẽ**	थिइनँ	**thiinā̃**
तँ	थिइस्	**thiis**	थिइनस्	**thiinas**
उ	थियो	**thiyo**	थिएन	**thiena**

हामी	थियौं	**thiyəw̃**	थिएनौं	**thienəw̃**
तिमी	थियौ	**thiyəw**	थिएनौ	**thienəw**
उनी (-हरू)	थिए	**thie**	थिएनन्	**thienan**
F. उ	थिई	**thiī**	थिइन	**thiina**
उनी (-हरू)	थिइन्	**thiin**	थिइनन्	**thiinan**
HGH तपाईं वहाँ	हुनुहुन्थ्यो	**hunuhunthyo**	हुनहुन्नथ्यो	**hunuhunnathyo**

Note that the HGH suffixes हुन्थ्यो **-hunthyo** (affirmative) and हुन्नथ्यो **-hunnathyo** (neg.) are added to the infinitive.

थियो is used both to locate and define.

अस्तिको शुक्रबार् म राम्कहाँ थिएँ
Last Friday I was at Ram's place
तपाईं कहाँ हुनुहुन्थ्यो ? घर्मा हुनुहुन्नथ्यो
Where were you? You were not at home
मेरी बहिनी सिकिस्त बिरामी थिई
My little sister was seriously ill
हिजो उनी अड्डामा थिएनन्
Yesterday he (MGH) was not at the office

8. The base भ- **bha-** is used only with past tense and past participle suffixes. Strictly speaking भ- functions as the Secondary Base of the verb हुनु though usage of the tenses and participles formed from this base should be carefully noted. The Simple Past Tense is formed from the base भ- regularly:

Pronoun	*Affirmative*		*Negative*	
म	भएँ	**bhaẽ**	भइनँ	**bhainã**
तँ	भइस्	**bhais**	भइनस्	**bhainas**
उ	भयो	**bhayo**	भएन	**bhaena**
हामी	भयौं	**bhayəw̃**	भएनौं	**bhaenəw̃**
तिमी	भयौ	**bhayəw**	भएनौ	**bhaenəw**
उनी (-हरू)	भए	**bhae**	भएनन्	**bhaenan**
F. उ	भई	**bhaī**	भइन	**bhaina**
उनी (- हरू)	भइन्	**bhain**	भइनन्	**bhainan**
HGH तपाईं, वहाँ	हुनुभयो	**hunubhayo**	हुनुभएन	**hunubhaena**

The 3rd person singular form भयो **bhayo** is often pronounced and sometimes written भो **bho.**

भयो may literally be rendered in English as 'has become', 'became'. The alternative translations in the following examples should, however, be carefully noted:

म बिरामी भएँ
I became ill/I fell ill

but म बिरामी थिएँ
I was ill

पसल् बन्द भयो
The shop has (become) closed/the shop is closed

but पसल् बन्द थियो
The shop was closed

वहाँ मन्त्री हुनुभयो
He became/was appointed minister

but वहाँ मन्त्री हुनुहुन्थ्यो
He was a minister

त्यो साइकल् एक् दम् पुरानो भयो
That cycle has become/is terribly old

मेरो घड़ी ढीलो भयो
My watch is ('has become') slow

गाउँको सबै घर् नाश् भयो
Every house in the village was ('became') destroyed

नाश् हुनु **nāʃ hunu** 'to be destroyed'

Note the following idiomatic expressions:

के भयो ? (के भो ?)	What's the matter?
गर्मी भयो	It has got warm
अबेर् भयो	It is late already (has become late)
धेरै नोक्सान् भयो	Much damage has been done

भयो is used as an interjection, meaning 'enough', 'stop'. In this case it is usually pronounced **bho.**

भो, भो, अब त खान्न
That's enough. I can't eat any more

भो, भो, त्यो त धेरै नै भयो
Stop. That's plenty

9. *The days of the week*

आइत्बार्	**āitbār**	Sunday
सोम्बार्	**sombār**	Monday
मङ्गल्बार्	**maŋgalbār**	Tuesday
बुध्बार्	**budhbār**	Wednesday
बिहिबार्	**bihibār**	Thursday
शुक्रबार्	**ʃukrabār**	Friday
सञ्चर्बार्	**saɲcarbār**	Saturday

The suffix -बार् **-bār** is often written वार् **-vār.** Note the expression: आज के बार् ? **āja ke bār?** 'What day of the week is it today?'

Three days have alternative literary forms, which are often used in newspapers and other official contexts:

रविवार्	**ravivār**	Sunday
वृहस्पतिवार्	**vɹhaspativār**	Thursday
शनिवार्	**ʃanivār**	Saturday

Vocabulary 8

अघि	**aghi**	ago
अतिनै	**atinəy**	very much, all that
अब	**aba**	now, from now on
अबेर्	**aber**	late
अस्ति	**asti**	day before yesterday, the other day
आखिरी	**ākhirī**	end, last day (of month, etc.)
एक्लै	**ekləy**	alone
ओखल्ढुङ्गा	**okhalḍhuŋgā**	Okhaldhunga (town in East Nepal)
कहीं कहीं	**kahī̃ kahī̃**	here and there
किन ?	**kina?**	why
केटाकेटी	**keṭākeṭī**	children, childhood
खूब् (खूप्)	**khūb (khūp)**	very, extremely
खुम्जुङ्	**khumjuŋg**	Khumjung (Sherpa village in Khumbu)
गत	**gata**	last (with days of week)
गएको	**gaeko**	last (with days of week)
घण्टाघर्	**ghaṇṭāghar**	clock-tower
घुम्नु	**ghumnu**	to travel, stroll
चल्नु	**calnu**	to go, run (of buses, planes)
छाड्नु (छोड्नु)	**chāɽnu (choɽnu)**	to leave, give up
छापा	**chāpā**	newspaper
जून्	**jūn**	June
ढीलो	**ḍhīlo**	slow (of watch, etc.)
तरीका	**tarīkā**	method, way
त्यसैले	**tyasəyle**	therefore, for that reason
त्यही	**tyahī**	emph. of **tyo** 'that very'
थ्याङबोचे	**thyāŋgboce**	Thyangboce (Sherpa village)
दोहोऱ्याउनु	**dohoryāunu**	to repeat
नाश्	**nāʃ**	destroyed
नाश् हुनु	**nāʃ hunu**	to be destroyed
नोक्सान्	**noksān**	loss, destruction
पहिले	**pahile**	first of all
पहिलो	**pahilo**	first (adj.)
पहिलो पटक्	**pahilo paṭak**	the first time
पाहुना	**pāhunā**	guest

पोहोर्	**pohor**	last year
प्रश्न	**praʃna**	question
फेरा	**pherā**	time, turn
फेरि	**pheri**	again
बिताउनु	**bitāunu**	to spend (time)
भर्खर्	**bharkhar**	recently, just now
भीजा	**bhījā**	visa
बुझ्नु	**bujhnu**	to understand
माइती (माइत)	**māitī (māita)**	wife's father's home
माफ् गर्नु	**māph garnu**	to excuse
माफ् गर्नुहोस्	**māph garnuhos**	excuse me, forgive me
मैलो	**məylo**	soiled, dirty
रेडियो	**reḍiyo**	radio
शेर्पा	**ʃerpā**	Sherpa
साह्रै	**sāhrəy**	very, absolutely
सिकिस्त	**sikista**	gravely (ill)
हिजो	**hijo**	yesterday
हिजोआज	**hijoāja**	nowadays
हिजो राति	**hijo rāti**	last night

The ordinal numerals are as follows: पहिलो **pahilo** 'first', दोस्रो **dosro** 'second', तेस्रो **tesro** 'third', चौथो **cəwtho** 'fourth', पाँचौं **pā̃cəw̃** 'fifth', छटौं **chaṭəw̃** 'sixth', सातौं **sātəw̃** 'seventh'. Thereafter the suffix औं **-əw̃** is added to the cardinal numeral: दसौं **dasəw̃** 'tenth', बीसौं **bīsəw̃** 'twentieth', etc.

Reading Passage

अ. नमस्ते ज्यू । कस्तो छ तपाईंलाई ? सन्चै छ ?

आ. राम्रो छ । तपाईं नि ?

अ. ठीकै छ। तपाईंले सुन्नुभयो? म आउने साल् छ महीनाको लागि नेपाल् जाँदै छु । तपाईं पनि नेपाल् जानुभयो, होइन त ?

आ. हो । म पोहोर् साल् नेपाल्मा थिएँ । कस्तो राम्रो थियो । भन्नुहोस्, तपाईं कहिले जानुहुन्छ ?

अ. मलाई निश्चय छैन। मेरो विचार्ले म जून्को आखिरीमा जान्छु ।

आ. तपाईं त्यहाँ कहाँ कहाँ जानुहुन्छ ?

अ. पहिले म भीजा लिन काठ्माडौं जान्छु।[1] त्यस्पछि, ओखल्ढुङ्गातिर जान्छु। भन्नुहोस् मलाई, काठ्माडौंदेखि हवाईजहाज् पनि जान्छ त्यहाँ ? [2]

आ. हवाईजहाज् छन त छ,[3] तर जून् महीनामा धेरै पानी पर्छ नि ।[4] कहिले कहीं हवाईजहाज् चल्दैन ।

अ. तपाईं नेपाल्मा कहाँ जानुभयो ? काठ्माडौंबाट बाहिर पनि जानुभयो ?

आ. गएँ । धेरै ठाउँहरू घुमें । पहिलो दुइ महीना मैले काठ्माडौंमा बिताएँ । त्यस्पछि, खुम्बुतिर गएँ ।

अ. ए । केमा जानुभयो ?

आ. धेरैजसो पैदल् नै घुमें । [5] नेपाल्मा घुम्ने तरीका त्यही मात्रै हो नि ।[6]
अ. तपाईं एक्लै जानुभयो कि साथ्मा अरू पनि थिए ?
आ. होइन । एक्जना साथी पनि मसँग थियो ।
अ. खुम्बुको बाटो कस्तो थियो ?
आ. कहीं कहीं त बाटो एक् दम् नराम्रो थियो । ठाउँ ठाउँमा उकालै उकालो ।[7] तर मौसम् त खूब् राम्रो थियो ।
अ. खुम्बुमा कस्कहाँ बस्नुभयो ?
आ. म एक्जना शेर्पाको घर्मा बसें । खुम्जुङ्ग नाउँ गरेको गाउँमा । त्यहाँबाट हामी दुइ फेरा थ्याङ्बोचे गयौं । त्यो त धेरै सुन्दर् ठाउँ हो नि ।
अ. थ्याङ्बोचे खुम्जुङ्गनजीक् छ होइन त ? त्यहाँबाट कति टाढ़ा छ ?
आ. धेरै टाढ़ा छैन, तर बाटो अलि उकालो रहेछ ।

Notes

1. **bhījā lina kāṭhmāṛə̃w jānchu:** 'I'm going to get (lit. 'take') a visa'. **lina** is the Second Infinitive of the verb **linu.** In this case it is used to express purpose: 'in order to take'. The Second Infinitive is discussed in Lesson 11.
2. 'Aeroplanes go there as well, don't they?' In speech the adverb is often placed at the end of the sentence.
3. **havāījahāj chana ta cha:** 'Well, there are aeroplanes but . . .' **chana ta cha** is a colloquial expression.
4. **jūn mahīnāmā:** 'in the month of June' cf. **jāṛo mahīnāmā** 'in the winter months'.
5. 'I usually travelled on foot': **pəydal jānu** is the same as **hīṛerəy jānu.**
6. **ghumne tarīkā tyahī mātrəy ho:** 'that is the only way of travelling'. **ghumne** is the infinitival participle 'the travelling way'. Cf. **joṛne bāṭo** 'a linking road'.
7. **ukāləy ukālo:** 'terribly steep' – the adjective is repeated for emphasis.

Exercise 8a

Translate into English

१. म आज बजार् गएँ तर सबै पसल् बन्द थियो ।
२. तिमी शहर्बाट कहिले आयौ ? म भर्खर् आएँ ।
३. हिजो राति त म सुतिनँ । अतिनै गर्मी थियो ।
४. तपाईंले हिजो राति रेडियो सुन्नुभयो ? अहँ, सुनिनँ । हाम्रो घर्मा पाहुनाहरू थिए ।
५. मेरो साथी सिकिस्त बिरामी थियो । अहिले त सन्चै छ ।
६. माफ् गर्नुहोला तर मैले तपाईंको नाउँ बिर्सें ।
७. मैले तपाईंको प्रश्न बुझिनँ । एक् फेरा फेरि दोहोऱ्याउनुहोला कि? [1]
८. अस्ति मैले उस्लाई पहिलो पटक भेटें ।
९. राम् कता गयो ? मैले त्यस्लाई पसल् पठाएँ । घर्मा तर्कारी थिएन ।
१०. मेरी स्वास्नी दुइ हप्ता अघि दार्जीलिङ्ग गइन् । उन्को माइत त्यहाँ छ नि ।
११. तिमी हिजो किन आएनौ ? माफ् गर्नुहोला । घर्मा धेरै काम् थियो ।

[1] Here **ki** is used as an interrogative particle. Translate 'Would you mind repeating?'.

१२. अहिले कति बज्यो दाइ ? मेरो घड़ीमा नौ बजेर पच्चीस् मिनेट् गयो, तर घण्टाघर्मा साढ़े नौ बज्यो । मेरो घड़ी ढीलो रहेछ ।

१३. मेरो लुगा साह्रै मैलो भयो । भोलि म धोबीलाई दिन्छु ।

१४. अलिकति भात् खानुहोस् न । भो भो । अब त म खान्न ।

१५. नेपाल्मा कहाँ कहाँ घुम्नुभयो ? धेरै ठाउँहरू घुमें ।

१६. पोहोर् साल् पानी परेन । त्यसैले खेत्मा धेरै नोक्सान् भयो ।

१७. बिष्टज्यू मन्त्री हुनुभयो रे । तपाईंलाई थाहा छ ? मलाई थाहा छ । आज छापामा पढ़े ।

१८. पोहोर् साल् उन्ले दुइ महीना खुम्जुङ्मा बिताए रे ।

Exercise 8b

Translate into Nepali

1. What did he (HGH) say? I did not understand his question.
2. Where did you (HGH) study? I studied in London.
3. At the end of June, my father went to Calcutta. How did he go? He went by aeroplane to Delhi first of all, and from there he went to Calcutta by rail.
4. Where were you yesterday? Why didn't you come to my place? Yesterday I was at home. There was a lot of work (to do).
5. Three years ago, the President of America went to Peking.
6. I am sorry, but I did not understand your question. Would you mind repeating it please.
7. The shops have closed. I'll go to the market tomorrow morning.
8. His pen was just like mine.
9. Did you wash my clothes? (MGH) No I didn't. I'll wash (them) tomorrow.
10. They say that it did not rain ('much water did not fall') in the Tarai last year.
11. What time did you (go to) sleep last night? I went to sleep at about ten o'clock.
12. Did you (MGH) not see that new film? It was very good indeed.
13. My wife went (MGH fem.) to India two years ago. She spent three months in Delhi. Her father's house (**māitī**) is there, you know.
14. It was extremely hot in Biratnagar. I was there last week.
15. When did he (MGH) come to Kathmandu? He arrived last month, and says he will spend one year here. After that he will return to England.

Exercise 8c

Translate into Nepali

We ate; he (LGH) did not work; my lecturer said; the servant did not come; who says so?; do you (HGH) smoke?; he (MGH) drank some tea; they (LGH) forgot; my friend became (LGH) ill; it did not rain last month; drive carefully;

we spent two days in a village; my little sister is gravely ill; she (LGH) fell ill; please do not be angry.

LESSON 9

1. *New conjunct consonants*

न्च	**nc**	as in	उनन्चालीस्	**unancālīs**	thirty-nine
न्य	**ny**	as in	धन्यवाद्	**dhanyavād**	thank you
र्त	**rt**	as in	फिर्ता	**phirtā**	back, again

2. Many Nepali verbs have passive or impersonal counterparts which are formed by adding the suffix **-i** to the base of verbs belonging to groups (i) and (ii) and to the secondary base of verbs belonging to groups (iii), (iv) and (v). Thus the active verb गर्नु **garnu** 'to do' is made passive by extending the base with the suffix **-i:** गरिनु **garinu** 'to be done'. Such verbs are often referred to as 'I-stem' verbs. In general only the infinitive, 3rd person forms and certain participles of such verbs are used.

I-Stem verbs are conjugated like other verbs belonging to group (ii) with a base ending in **-i,** e.g. दिनु **dinu,** and have the full range of tenses and participles. Firstly we shall consider the I-Stem forms of गर्नु.

I-Stem base	गरि-	**gari-**	
Infinitive	गरिनु	**garinu**	to be done
Simp. Indef. 3 s. aff.	गरिन्छ	**garincha**	it is done
Simp. Indef. 3 s neg.	गरिंदैन	**garīdəyna**	it is not done
	गरिन्न	**garinna**	
Simp. Indef. 3 pl. aff.	गरिन्छन्	**garinchan**	they are done
Simp. Indef. 3 pl. neg.	गरिंदैनन्	**garīdəynan**	they are not done
	गरिन्नन्	**garinnan**	
Simp. Past 3 s. aff.	गरियो	**gariyo**	it was done
Simp. Past 3 s. neg.	गरिएन	**gariena**	it was not done, etc.

Similarly with other verbs:

भन्नु **bhannu** 'to say', I-Stem Base भनि- **bhani-,** भनिनु **bhaninu** 'to be said', भनिन्छ **bhanincha** 'it is said', भनिंदैन **bhanīdəyna** 'it is not said', भनियो **bhaniyo** 'it was said', भनिएन **bhaniena** 'it was not said', etc.

सुन्नु **sunnu** 'to hear', सुनिनु **suninu** 'to be heard', सुनिन्छ **sunincha** 'it is heard', etc.

देख्नु **dekhnu** 'to see', देखिनु **dekhinu** 'to be seen', देखिन्छ **dekhincha** 'it is seen', etc.

चाहनु **cāhanu** 'to want/require', चाहिनु **cāhinu** 'to be wanted/required', चाहिन्छ **cāhincha** 'it is wanted/required', etc.

पाउनु **pāunu** 'to find/get/acquire', पाइनु **pāinu** 'to be found/got/acquired', पाइन्छ **pāincha** 'it is found', etc.

Note that all I-Stem verbs may have the alternative Simple Indefinite negative forms: गरिन्न **garinna,** देखिन्न **dekhinna,** चाहिन्न **cāhinna,** पाइन्न **pāinna.**

3. In the following examples which illustrate the use of the I-Stem verbs the English translation should be carefully noted. Whereas English usually prefers a personal construction – 'you want', 'they say', 'you can see' etc. – Nepali tends to prefer the passive or impersonal construction – 'it is wanted', 'it is said', 'it is seen' etc.

काठ्माडौंबाट पनि सगर्माथा देखिन्छ
You can see Mt. Everest even from Kathmandu (lit. E. 'is seen')

हवाईजहाज् आकाश्मा देखियो
The aeroplane was seen in the sky

त्यहाँबाट केही पनि देखिंदैन
You can't see anything at all from there (lit. 'nothing is seen')

त्यस्को स्वर् यहाँबाट सुनिन्छ
You can hear his voice from here (lit. 'his voice is heard')

Note that स्वर् **svar** 'voice' is usually pronounced **sor.**

केही पनि सुनिएन
You could not hear a sound (lit. 'nothing at all was heard')

अलि महँगो होटल्हरूमा हरेक् कुरा पाइन्छ
In the rather more expensive hotels you can get anything (lit. 'everything is acquired')

म बजार् गएँ तर पसल्हरूमा केही पनि पाइएन
I went to the market but couldn't get anything in the shops (lit. 'nothing at all was found')

The transitive verb पाउनु **pāunu** means 'to find', 'to receive', 'to get', 'to earn money', etc. Thus:

मैले गएको मङ्गल्बार् तपाईंको चिठी पाएँ
I received your letter last Tuesday

म चालीस् रुपियाँ पाउँछु
I earn forty rupees

तिमीले के पायौ ? केही पनि पाइनँ
What did you get? I got nothing at all

The Simple Past forms of the transitive verb पायो,पाएन **(usle) pāyo** 'he got', **(usle) pāena** 'he did not get' must be carefully distinguished from the impersonal forms पाइयो **pāiyo** 'it was found' and पाइएन **pāiena** 'it was not found'.

यो शब्द नेपालीमा भनिंदैन
You can't use this word in Nepali (lit. 'this word is not said')

नेपालीमा 'chair' को लागि के भनिन्छ ?
What do they say for 'chair' in Nepali (lit. 'what is said')?
नेपालमा 'मेच्' भनिन्छ तर दार्जीलिङ्गमा 'कुर्सी' भनिन्छ। 'कुर्सी' त हिन्दी शब्द हो नि
In Nepal they say **mec** but in Darjeeling they say **kursī. kursī** is a Hindi word, you know

In such sentences, the 3rd person singular of the transitive verb **bhannu** may also be used:

यस्लाई नेपालीमा के भन्छ ? यस्लाई किताब् भन्छ
What do they call this (**yaslāī**) in Nepali? They call it **kitāb**
समाचार्पत्रमा निक्कै संस्कृत् शब्दहरू प्रयोग् गरिन्छन्
In the newspapers many Sanskrit words are used

समाचार्पत्र **samācārpatra** is a rather official word for 'newspaper'. More common terms are छापा **chāpā** (derived from छाप्नु **chāpnu** 'to print') and अख्बार् **akhbār** (a loan from Urdu).

प्रयोग् गर्नु **prayog garnu** 'to use', प्रयोग् गरिनु **prayog garinu** 'to be used'.

4. The I-Stem verb चाहिनु **cāhinu** 'to be required', 'to be needed' is formed from the comparatively rarely used transitive verb चाहनु **cāhanu** 'to want'.

The Simple Indefinite form चाहिन्छ **cāhincha** is mainly used to express 'it is generally required' or 'it will be required', whereas the Simple Past चाहियो **cāhiyo** expresses 'it is required now' or 'it was required'. Thus:

मान्छेहरूलाई रोटी सधैं चाहिन्छ
Men always need bread (lit. 'to men bread is required')
तपाईंलाई अब के चाहियो ? मलाई चिया चाहियो
What do you want (now)? I want some tea
बाटोको लागि हामीहरूलाई के के चाहिन्छ ?
What things shall we need for the journey?

Note the use of लाई in this construction.

In practice the Simple Indefinite चाहिन्छ is sometimes used where according to the above rule चाहियो would be expected. Thus चिया चाहिन्छ ..... is also correct, but less common.

यो रोटी बासी रहेछ । मलाई त चाहिन्न बा
This bread is stale. I don't want it

बा **bā** is an exclamation of disgust.

5. In general, only transitive verbs possess I-Stem counterparts. There are, however, a few intransitive verbs which also possess them. One common example is पुगिनु **puginu** 'to be reached', formed from the intransitive verb पुग्नु **pugnu** 'to arrive':

हाम्रो घर् सजिलैसँग यहाँबाट पुगिन्छ
You can reach our house easily from here (lit. 'our house is arrived at')

सजिलैसँग **sajiləysāga** 'with ease', 'easily'

बेलामा पुगिएन
We did not arrive on time (lit. 'it was not arrived')

In these examples the verb is used impersonally. However if a subject word is expressed, the transitive verb पुग्नु must be used:

तपाईं कति बजे पुग्नुहुन्छ ? छ बजे पुग्छु
What time will you arrive? I'll arrive at six o'clock

6. The verb पुग्नु may also mean 'to suffice', 'to be enough'. In this case the postposition -ले is always added to the subject word:

त्यति पैसाले पुग्दैन रे
He says that that much money is not enough
त्यति भात्ले मलाई पुग्छ
That's enough rice for me (*lit.* 'that much rice will suffice to me')

7. In spoken Nepali, पुग्छ and पुग्दैन are often used impersonally instead of their *I-stem* counterparts:

बेलुकासम्म पुग्छ कि पुग्दैन ?
Can we get there by evening or not?

Strictly speaking पुगिन्छ and पुगिंदैन would be correct.

In the same way, पाउँछ is often used in place of पाइन्छ . This usage, though 'grammatically' incorrect, is so common in speech, that it should be noted.

यहाँ चिया पाउँछ कि पाउँदैन ? पाउँछ, साहेब्
Can I get some tea here? Yes, sir.

साहेब् **sāheb** (often pronounced *sāhab* or *sāb*) is a loan from Urdu and is frequently used by Nepalis to address foreigners.

8. The transitive verb खोल्नु **kholnu** 'to open' has an intransitive counterpart खुल्नु **khulnu** 'to be opened', 'to come open' (roughly the difference between French *ouvrir* and *s'ouvrir*).

कोठामा गर्मी छ । म झ्याल् खोल्छु
It is hot in the room. I'll open the window
पँखा खोल्नुहोस् त
Switch (lit. 'open') the fan please

Note that 'to switch on a light' is बत्ती बाल्नु **battī bālnu**:

अँध्यारो भयो, बत्ती बाल्नुहोस् है
It's dark (lit. 'darkness has become'). Switch on the light, will you?
पसल् कति बजे खुल्छ ? आज त खुल्दैन । बिदा छ नि
What time will the shop open? It won't open today. It's a holiday

The adjective खुला **khulā** means 'open'

बाटो अहिले खुला छ रे
They say the road is now open

9. Open Conditional Sentences (i.e. in which nothing is implied as to the

fulfilment of the condition) of the type, 'If he comes, I shall go' are expressed as follows.

The subordinate 'if' clause consists of a verb in the Simple Past Tense followed by the word भने **bhane.** The verb in the main clause is in the Simple Indefinite Tense:

त्यो आयो भने म जान्छु
If he comes, I shall go
तिमीले काम् गरेनौ भने पैसा पाउँदैनौ रे
He says that if you don't do any work, you won't get any money
भोलि पानी परेन भने म बाहिर जान्छु
If it does not rain tomorrow, I shall go out
रोटी भएन भने म भात् नै खान्छु
If there is no bread, I'll just have boiled rice
नोकरले आज पनि ढीलो गऱ्यो भने खुब् झाँट्नुहोस्
If the servant is late again today, give him a good scolding

The expressions ढीलो गर्नु and ढीलो आउनु both mean 'to be late (in arriving)'.

माफ् गर्नुहोला, म ढीलो आएँ
Excuse me, I am late
ढीलो नगर्नुहोस् है
Don't be late, will you

Note also the expression अबेर् भयो 'it is already late' (ref. to time).

10. The numerals 31 to 50 (p.251) should now be learnt. Remember that the classifiers -जना and -वटा are added in the usual manner: चौंतीस्‌वटा घर् '34 houses', छयालीस्‌जना मान्छे '46 men', अठ्तीस् रुपियाँ '38 rupees'.

11. *Expressions of price, weight and measure etc.*

(*a*) The Nepalese and Indian rupee (रुपियाँ) consists of 100 paisa (पैसा). रुपियाँ **rupiyā̃** is often written and pronounced रुपैयाँ **rupəyā̃.** In writing, रुपियाँ is usually abbreviated to रु. Thus रु १०० is read एक् सय् रुपियाँ **ek say rupiyā̃.** पैसा **pəysā** is used as a general term for money:

कति पैसा चाहिन्छ ?
How much money will be needed?
मेरो खल्तीमा पैसा रहेनछ
I have no money in my pocket

(*b*) In Nepal (but not in India) the term मोहर् **mohar** (often pronounced *mor*) is used to denote half a rupee (i.e. 50 paisa) and the term सुका **sukā** to denote a quarter of a rupee (i.e. 25 paisa). All over Nepal, small sums of money are usually reckoned in terms of *mohars* and *sukās*. Thus:

एक् मोहर् 50 paisa
एक् मोहर् सुका 75 paisa

तीन् मोहर् 1 rupee 50 paisa
पाँच् मोहर् सुका 2 rupees 75 paisa

However, only uneven numbers can be used before these terms, i.e. 2 rupees cannot be expressed as चार् मोहर् . In Nepal, Indian rupees are often referred to as कम्पनी **kampanī** i.e. East India Company rupees.

(*c*) Price is indicated in various ways. The following expressions are among the most common:

यो कलम्को मोल् कति हो ?
What (lit. 'how much') is the price of this pen?
यो (यस्) कलम्लाई कति पर्छ ?
How much does this pen cost? (lit. 'how much falls to . . .')
फुल्को कति पैसा ? *or* फुल्को कति ?
How much do eggs cost?
एउटाको एक् सुका
25 paisa (one **sukā**) each/for one
यो कप्ड़ा गज्को कति ?
How much a yard is this cloth?

गज् **gaj** is roughly a yard (equal to four spans बित्तो **bitto**)

मसिनो चामल्को भाउ के हो ?
What is the market price of fine quality rice?

मसिनो **masino** 'soft', 'fine', चामल् **cāmal** 'rice' in grain as opposed to भात् **bhāt** 'boiled rice'.

तीन् मोहर् माना
It is one and a half rupees a **mānā** (approx. 1 lb.)
सुन्तला कसरी छ ? सैकड़ा कतिमा दिन्छ रे ?
How much do the oranges cost? How much is he asking for a hundred? (lit. 'in how much will he give per hundred')

Note कतिमा **katimā** '*for* how much':

त्यो मोटर् कतिमा लिनुभयो ?
How much did you buy ('take') that car for?
बीस् हजार् रुपियाँमा किनें
I bought it for twenty thousand rupees
मैले यो कोट् सस्तोमा किनें
I bought this coat cheaply
यो कोट्को कति त ? तपाईंलाई एक् सय् बीस्मा दिन्छु
How much for this coat then? I'll let you have it for 120

After कोट्को a word like मोल् 'price' must be understood.

नेपाल्मा चीनिया माल् सस्तोमा पाइन्छ
In Nepal you can get Chinese goods cheaply

त्यो त अलि महँगो भयो नि, साहूजी
That's a bit expensive, you know

Any shopkeeper (पसले **pasale**) may be addressed as साहूजी **sāhūjī.** साहू means 'a rich man', 'a trader'.

12. *The imperative*

So far, we have met only the HGH imperative forms. These are the forms you will need to use most often. The LGH (तँ) imperative is formed as follows:

(*a*) Verbs belonging to groups (i) and (ii) – the LGH imperative is identical with the base of the verb:

गर् **gar** do   बस् **bas** sit down
खा **khā** eat   उभि **ubhi** stand

(*b*) Verbs belonging to groups (iii) and (v) – the LGH imperative is identical with the Secondary Base of the Verb:

धो **dho** wash   पठा **paṭhā** send
पि **pı** drink   आ **ā** come

(*c*) Verbs belonging to group (iv) in most cases have the suffix ई **-ī** or इँ **-ĩ** added to the secondary base of the verb:

दुही **duhī** milk   बिर्सिइँ **birsĩ** forget
सम्झी **samjhī** remember

(*d*) दिनु and लिनु have irregular LGH imperatives: दे **de** 'give', ले **le** 'take'. The LGH imperative of आउनु is sometimes आइज **āija** as well as आ **ā.**

The MGH (तिमी) imperative is formed as follows.

(*a*) Verbs belonging to group (i) have the suffix **-a** added to the base:

गर **gara** do   बस **basa** sit down

(*b*) Verbs belonging to group (ii) have the suffix **-ū** and sometimes the suffix **-o** added to the base:

खाऊ **khāū** eat   जाऊ **jāū** go   उभिऊ **ubhiū** or उभिओ **ubhio** stand up

(*c*) Verbs belonging to groups (iii) and (v) have the suffix **-ū** added to the secondary base:

धोऊ **dhoū** wash   आऊ **āū** come   ल्याऊ **lyāū** 'bring'

(*d*) Verbs belonging to group (iv) have the suffix **-a** added to the secondary base:

दुह **duha** milk   बिर्स **birsa** forget   सम्झ **samjha** remember

(*e*) दिनु and लिनु have irregular imperative forms for the MGH:

देऊ **deū** give   लेऊ **leū** take

The verb हो has the imperative forms:

LGH हो **ho**   MGH होऊ **hoū** be

The negative of the imperative is formed by adding the prefix न **na-:**

नगर **nagara**   नखाऊ **nakhāū**   नदेऊ **nadeū**
नआ **naā**   नहोऊ **nahoū**   नबिर्सिइँ **nabirsĩ,** etc.

Examples of the imperative

LGH

भात् खा त, नानी
Eat your dinner, won't you, child
यता आइज । त्यहाँ नबस्
Come here. Don't sit there

यता **yatā** 'to here', 'hither'
ए रामे, मलाई त्यति भात् नदे, हैं
Rame, don't give me so much rice

MGH

यो कोठामा गर्मी छ । पँखा खोल त
It's hot in this room. Switch on the fan, please
ए भाइ, चिया ल्याऊ, पानी पनि ल्याऊ
Waiter, bring some tea. Bring some water as well

Note that waiters may be addressed as ए भाइ and the MGH imperative may be used.

यहाँ चुरोट् नखाऊ । मनाई छ । सुन्यौ तिमीले ?
Don't smoke here. It's forbidden. Didn't you hear?

The official term for 'no smoking', written in buses, cinemas etc., is: धूम्रपान् मनाई छ **dhūmrapān manāī cha.** मनाई **manāī** 'forbidden' is sometimes spelt मनाही

HGH

नमस्कार् विष्टज्यू । भित्र पाल्नुहोस् । बस्नुहोस् त
Good morning, Mr. Bista. Come in and sit down
मोटर् बिस्तारै हाँक्नुहोला । बाटोमा हिलो छ
Drive the car slowly. There's mud on the road

Vocabulary 9

अँध्यारो	**ādhyāro**	darkness
आकाश्	**ākāʃ**	sky, heaven
उभिनु	**ubhinu**	to stand up
ऊनी	**ūnī**	woollen
कपड़ा	**kapṛā**	cloth
कम्	**kam**	less
कहीं पनि	**kahī̃ pani**	anywhere at all
किन्नु	**kinnu**	to buy
कुर्सी	**kursī**	chair
खल्बल्	**khalbal**	noise, commotion
खुल्नु	**khulnu**	to be opened, come open
खोल्नु	**kholnu**	to open
गज्	**gaj**	yard

चढ्नु	**caṛhnu**	to go up, mount
चाँडै	**cā̃ṛəy**	soon, quickly
चाहनु	**cāhanu**	to wish, want
चाहिनु	**cāhinu**	to be required, wanted
चिठी (चिट्ठी)	**ciṭhī (ciṭṭhī)**	letter
चीनिया	**cīniyā**	Chinese
चोमोलोङ्मो	**comoloŋgmo**	the Tibetan name for Mt. Everest
छिटो छिटो	**chiṭo chiṭo**	quickly
जुत्ता	**juttā**	shoes
जोर्	**jor**	pair
झाँट्नु	**jhā̃ṭnu**	to scold
झ्याल्	**jhyāl**	window
ढीलो	**ḍhīlo**	slow, late
ढीलो गर्नु	**ḍhīlo garnu**	to be late
थोरै	**thorəy**	a little, few
दाम्	**dām**	price
देखिनु	**dekhinu**	to be seen, to appear, to seem
धन्यवाद्	**dhanyavād**	thank you
धूम्रपान्	**dhūmrapān**	smoking
-नेर	**-nera**	next to, nearby
पँखा	**pā̃khā**	fan
पसले	**pasale**	shopkeeper
पाउनु	**pāunu**	to find, get, acquire
पाइनु	**pāinu**	to be found, etc.
पिरो	**piro**	spicy, hot (of food)
पुगिनु	**puginu**	to be reached
पुग्नु	**pugnu**	to reach, to arrive
प्रयोग् गर्नु	**prayog garnu**	to use, employ
फिर्ता	**phirtā**	back, returned
बत्ती	**battī**	lamp, light
बर्सादी	**barsādī**	raincoat
बा	**bā**	exclamation of disgust
बाक्लो	**bāklo**	thick, heavy (of cloth)
बाल्नु	**bālnu**	to burn, switch on (lights)
बास्	**bās**	lodging for the night[1]
बासी	**bāsī**	stale (of food)
बेलामा	**belāmā**	on time, in time
भाउ	**bhāu**	market rate, price
भैगो (भइगयो)	**bhəygo (bhaigayo)**	very well, all right
भोट्	**bhoṭ**	Tibet
भोटे	**bhoṭe**	a Tibetan, Tibetan speaking person

[1]Note especially: बास् पाइन्छ ? **bās pāincha**? 'can I get a lodging for the night?' When travelling in Nepal lodgings in villagers' houses can usually be arranged.

मनाई	**manāī (manāhī)**	forbidden
मसिनो	**masino**	soft, good quality (rice)
मेच्	**mec**	chair
मोल्	**mol**	price
यता	**yatā**	to here, hither
रँग्	**rãg**	colour
रहनु	**rahanu**	to stay, remain
रातो	**rāto**	red
रोटी	**roṭī**	bread
लाइहेर्नु	**lāihernu**	to try on (clothes)
ल्याउनु	**lyāunu**	to bring
संस्कृत्	**samskɹt (sāskɹt)**	Sanskrit
सजिलो	**sajilo**	easy
साहेब्	**sāheb**	Sir, Mr.
साहूजी	**sāhūjī**	term of address for shopkeepers
सुनिनु	**suninu**	to be heard
सुन्तला	**suntalā**	orange
सेतो	**seto**	white
सैकड़ा	**səykaṛā**	per hundred
हिंड़्नु	**hĩṛnu**	to walk

Reading Passage

पसल्मा

अ. भन्नुहोस् हजूर् । के चाहिन्छ ?

आ. कोट्हरू हेरूँ न,[1] साहूजी । तपाईंकहाँ कस्तो कस्तो कोट् छ ? मलाई अलि बाक्लो ऊनी कोट् चाहियो । म आउने हप्ता पहाड़्तिर पैदल् जाँदै छु ।

अ. मकहाँ किसिम् किसिम्का कोट्हरू छन् हजूर् । तपाईंलाई जस्तो चाहिन्छ म दिन्छु ।

आ. यो कोट् ऊनी हो कि होइन ?

अ. हो । असल् कपड़ा हो,हजूर् ।

आ. यो कोट्को कति त ?

अ. तपाईंलाई एक् सय् बीस्मा दिन्छु ।

आ. ओहो, साहूजी । त्यो त अलि भएन,[2] धेरै नै महँगो भयो ।

अ. के महँगो भन्नुहुन्छ ? योभन्दा कम् दाम्मा त कहीं पनि पाउनुहुन्न[3]।

आ. यो सेतो रहेछ । अरू के रँग छ तपाईंकहाँ ?

अ. ई[4]। एउटा रातो छ । यस्कोचाहिं सय् रुपियाँ, हजूर् ।

आ. हो । रातोचाहिं त अलि राम्रो रहेछ, तर सय् रुपियाँ त अलि महँगो भयो । सत्तरी (७०) रुपियाँमा दिनुहोस् न त ।

अ. ल, तपाईंको नब्बे (९०) रुपियाँ भयो । योभन्दा सस्तो त हुँदैन । लाइहेर्नुहोस् न एक् फेरा ।

आ. अँ, ठीक् छ । ल, पचासी (८५) रुपियाँमा लिएँ ।

अ. ल भैगो[5]। त्यतिमै लिनुहोस् ।

आ. मलाई एक् जोर् जुत्ता पनि चाहियो साहूजी । तपाईंसँग छ कि छैन ?

अ. जुत्ता त मकहाँ छैन । ऊ त्यहाँनेर[6] जुत्तापसल् छ नि, हेर्नुहोस् न । ल, तपाईंको पैसा फिर्ता लिनुहोस्[7] ।

आ धन्यवाद्, साहूजी, नमस्ते ।

अ. नमस्ते ।

Notes

1. **herũ na?** 'may I see?' **herũ** is the 1st person singular of the injunctive of **hernu** (cf. **ma jāũ həy ta?** 'may I go now?').
2. **tyo ta ali bhaena:** 'that will not do at all'.
3. Lit. 'you will not find (them) anywhere at all for (**-mā**) less price than this'. **dām** 'price' is synonymous with **mol.**
4. **ī:** an exclamation of surprise or hesitation 'er', 'ah'. Note, the numerals in the following sentences: **sattarī** 'seventy', **nabbe** 'ninety', **pacāsī** 'eighty five'.
5. **bhəygo:** a contraction of **bhai-gayo** lit. 'having become it went' – used as an exclamation 'all right', 'let it pass', etc.
   tyatiməy: 'for that much'. **-məy** the emphatic form of the postposition **-mā.**
6. **ū tyahā̃nera:** 'just near there', 'just over there'.
7. **pəysā phirtā linuhos:** 'take back your money', i.e. 'here's your change'. The word **cāncun** is used for 'small change' (coins).

Exercise 9a

Translate into English

१. भोलि पानी परेन भने म तपाईंलाई दस् बजेतिर भेट्छु । पानी पर्‍यो भने म घरै बस्छु ।

२. छिटो छिटो हिंड्यौं भने बेलुकासम्म पुगिन्छ रे ।

३ नेपालीमा निक्कै हिन्दी शब्द प्रयोग् गरिन्छन् ।

४. आजकाल् नेपाल्मा चीनिया माल्ताल एक् दम् सस्तोमा पाइन्छ । हिजो मात्रै मैले दस् रुपियाँमा एउटा राम्रो बर्सादी किनें ।

५. काठमाडौंमा पसल्हरू धेरैजसो बिहान साढ़े आठ् बजे नै खुल्छन् ।

६. यो बाटोबाट जानुभयो भने चाँडै नै पुग्नुहुन्छ ।

७. ए नानी, ज्ञानी होऊ । खल्बल् नगर त ।

८. माफ् गर, म ढीलो आएँ । सिनेमा कति बजे शुरू हुन्छ ?

९. तपाईंले योचाहिं लिनुभयो भने पैंतालीस् रुपैयाँ पर्छ ।

१०. यो पहाड् चढ्यौं भने सगर्माथा राम्ररी देखिन्छ रे ।

११. अ. ए भाइ, महीनामा कति पैसा पाउँछौ ?
आ. एक् सय् बीस् रुपियाँ पाउँछु, हजूर ।
अ. त्यो त अलि थोरै जस्तो छ । त्यतिले पुग्छ ?
आ. पुग्दैन, हजूर ।

१२. त्यो कुरा ठीक् जस्तो सुनिंदैन । फेरि भन त ।

१३. माउन्ट् एभरेस्ट्लाई नेपालीमा सगर्माथा भनिन्छ । भोटेहरूचाहिं यस्लाई चोमोलोङ्मो भन्छन् ।

१४. ए दाइ, तपाईंको घर्मा बास् पाइन्छ कि पाइँदैन ? पाइन्छ, हजूर । भित्र पाल्नुहोस् न ।

१५. बत्ती बाल त । यहाँ केही पनि देखिन्न ।

१६. मलाई एक् जोर् जुत्ता चाहियो, साहूजी तपाईंकहाँ कस्तो कस्तो जुत्ता छ ?

Exercise 9b

Translate into Nepali

1. How much do the oranges cost? They cost twenty-five pice each, sir.
2. It looks as if it will rain today. Do you have a raincoat with you?
3. If you go by air, you will arrive there in about an hour.
4. That watch is very nice. You can't get such good ones in Nepal.
5. This woollen cloth is very good, but it costs sixteen rupees a yard.
6. Nowadays on (**-mā**) Radio Nepal they use many Sanskrit words.
7. How far is Gorkha from here? Can we get there by evening?
8. In the shops in Kathmandu you can get anything you want. In the hill villages it is rather difficult.
9. My elder brother is in Darjeeling these days. I got a letter ('I received his letter') the day before yesterday.
10. Excuse me, can I get a night's lodging in your village?
11. How much does this raincoat cost? Only twenty-five rupees, sir. But that's far too much. Take twenty rupees. Oh, very well, I'll let you have it for twenty-two.
12. The university library usually remains open till half past six, but on Saturday it closes at one o'clock.
13. It's dark in here. I can't see anything at all. Switch the light on, will you (MGH)?
14. If you go by this road, you will arrive in Darjeeling. If you go by that one, you will come to Kalimpong.
15. How much did you pay for that watch? I bought it cheaply. It cost me only 145 rupees.

Exercise 9c

Give the HGH and MGH imperatives of the following verbs:

आउनु लिनु पठाउनु धुनु दोहोऱ्याउनु भन्नु जानु
पढ्नु खोल्नु सुन्नु उभिनु

Exercise 9d

Translate into Nepali

this word is used only in the Nepali of Darjeeling; the Sherpa says that eight rupees is not enough; switch on (MGH) the fan; that's enough, I can't eat any more; Nepali cigarettes cost four or five rupees; how much is he asking for that red hat?; I'm sorry to be late; we shall need three hundred rupees for the road; it is hot in this room. I'll open the window; my watch appears to be (**rahecha**) slow; we spent five days in Pokhara; he (LGH) arrived at six o'clock sharp; what's the hurry?; have some tea (HGH); last year it did not rain; another servant is coming in place of this one.

LESSON 10

1. *New conjunct consonants*

क्ख	**kkh**	as in	सुक्खा	**sukkhā**	dry
ग्न	**gn**	as in	लाग्नु	**lāgnu**	to seem
ल्ट	**lṭ**	as in	भोलिपल्ट	**bholipalṭā**	the next day

2. The Conjunctive Participles are formed by adding one of the three suffixes: (*a*) -एर **-era,** (*b*) -ई **-ī,** (*c*) -ईकन **-īkana** to the Base of verbs belonging to groups (i) and (ii) and to the Secondary Base of verbs belonging to groups (iii), (iv), (v). Thus:

Group (*a*)			(*b*)		(*c*)	
(i)	गरेर	**garera**	गरी	**garī**	गरीकन	**garīkana**
	बसेर	**basera**	बसी	**basī**	बसीकन	**basīkana**
(ii)	खाएर	**khāera**	खाई	**khāī**	खाईकन	**khāīkana**
	दिएर	**diera**	दिई	**diī**	दिईकन	**diīkana**
(iii)	धोएर	**dhoera**	धोई	**dhoī**	धोईकन	**dhoīkana**
(iv)	बिर्सेर	**birsera**	बिर्सी	**birsī**	बिर्सीकन	**birsīkana**
	दुहेर	**duhera**	दुही	**duhī**	दुहीकन	**duhīkana**
(v)	आएर	**āera**	आई	**āī**	आईकन	**āīkana**
	पिएर	**piera**	पिई	**piī**	पिईकन	**piīkana**
जानु	गएर	**gaera**	गई	**gaī**	गईकन	**gaīkana**
हुनु	भएर	**bhaera**	भई	**bhaī**	भईकन	**bhaīkana**

Of the three forms , the participle in **-era** is by far the most common. The other two forms are by and large stylistic alternatives. The form of the participle is invariable.

The negative of the conjunctive participle is formed by prefixing the negative particle न- **na-** to the positive form:

नगरेर	**nagarera**	नगरी	**nagarī**	नगरीकन	**nagarīkana**
नआएर	**naāera**	नआई	**naāī**	नआईकन	**naāīkana**

3. In sentences where the subject of the conjunctive participle is the same as the subject of the main verb, the participle may literally be translated 'having done', 'having come' etc.

भात् खाएर म घर् जान्छु
Having eaten dinner, I shall go home

English, however, often prefers a sentence containing two main clauses linked by the conjunction 'and', or a subordinate clause introduced by an adverb like 'when', 'after', 'as soon as' etc. Thus the sentence above could be translated: 'I'll go home after I've had something to eat'. Note the way in which the following sentences are translated:

काम् गरेर त्यो घर् जान्छ रे
He says he'll finish his work and go home ('having done . . . he'll go')
एक् छिन्पछि गृहकृत्य गरेर उसकी स्वास्नी कोठामा पसी
After a while his wife finished the housework and entered the room ('having done . . . entered')
यहाँ बसेर आराम् गर्नुहोस् है
Sit down and rest for a moment ('having sat . . . rest')

4. The Conjunctive Participle in ई may be used in exactly the same way.
म हवाईजहाज्मा चढी बेलायत् गएँ
I boarded the plane and went to Britain

When a long narrative contains several conjunctive participles, the participle in -ई is often used to avoid the monotonous repetition of the syllable एर **-era.** Note the forms in the following passage:

घर्बाट दाज्यु र म बिहानै हिंडेर कालिम्पोङ्ग पुग्यौं र एक् रात् त्यहाँ सुत्यौं । भोलिपल्ट गेल् स्टेशन्मा झर्‍यौं र टिकट् काटी, रेल्मा चढी, राति सात् बजेतिर हामी सिलिगुडी पुग्यौं । त्यहाँदेखि बिहानै उठी, हामी सिलिगुडी स्टेशन् पुग्यौं

My elder brother and I left home ('having walked. . .') early in the morning and arrived at Kalimpong, and stayed one night there. The next morning we went down to Gel station, took our tickets, got into the train and arrived at Siliguri about seven o'clock ('having taken . . . having mounted . . . arrived'). We got up early in the morning and from there arrived at Siliguri station ('from there having got up . . . arrived')

रात् सुत्नु **rāt sutnu** 'to stay the night'.
बास् बस्नु **bās basnu** 'to stay the night in lodgings'
टिकट् काट्नु **ṭikaṭ kāṭnu** lit. 'to cut a ticket' i.e. 'to buy a ticket'

5. The participle in -ईकन is more emphatic than the other two forms and is used rather less frequently:
भात् खाइकन घर्बाट हिंड्यौं
We left just as soon as we had eaten
घरमा पसीकन त्यस्लाई खूब् झाँटें
I went straight into the house and scolded him

6. When the subject of the conjunctive participle is *different* from the subject of the main verb of the sentence, it may often be rendered by a causal clause in English. The postposition -ले is added to the subject of the conjunctive participle of a transitive verb:

उसले भनेर मैले त्यो काम् गरें
I did it because he told me to ('he having said . . . I did')

पोहोर् साल् पानी नपरेर जमीन् साह्रै सुक्खा भयो
Because it did not rain last year the ground has become very dry. ('rain not having fallen . . . the ground became . . .')

7. In the following sentences, the conjunctive participle is used idiomatically. The expressions in which it occurs should be carefully noted:

चिया लिएर आउनुहोस् न
Bring us some tea please ('having taken . . . come')

लिएर आउनु **liera āunu** (often pronounced and written लेराउनु **lerāunu**) is synonymous with the verb ल्याउनु **lyāunu** 'to bring'. Distinguish these verbs from लिनु **linu** 'to take' and लानु **lānu** 'to take away' 'to lead to'.

बस् त छुट्यो । अब गाली गरेर के काम ?
We've missed the bus (lit. 'the bus has been missed'). It's no use cursing now ('having cursed, what work?')

आज सब् पसल् बन्द छ नि । बजार् गएर के फाइदा ?
All the shops are closed today, you know. What's the point of going to the market? ('having gone . . . what use?')

दूध् त पोखियो । अब रोएर के काम् ?
The milk has got spilled. What's the use of crying about it?

हवाईजहाज् कल्कत्ता भएर आयो
The aeroplane came via Calcutta ('having been to C.')

यो पोको धेरै गह्रुँगो छ। होश् गरेर बोक है ।
This package is very heavy. Be careful how you carry it, now.

होश् गर्नु **hoʃ garnu** 'to take care'

8. We have already seen that speech may be reported by using the particle रे . This is largely a feature of spoken Nepali.

An alternative method of reporting speech is to quote the words exactly as they were spoken. The spoken words are followed by the conjunctive participle भनेर **bhanera** or भनी **bhanī** 'having said', and then by some part of the verbs भन्नु **bhannu** 'to say', सोध्नु **sodhnu** 'to ask', अह्राउनु **ahrāunu** 'to command' etc. Thus the statement म भोलि आउँछु may be reported:

उसले म भोलि आउँछु भनेर भन्यो
He said he would come tomorrow ('he, "I am coming tomorrow", having said, said')

Similarly, the statement पोहोर् साल् म नेपाल्मा थिएँ may be reported:

वहाँले पोहोर् साल् म नेपाल्मा थिएँ भनेर भन्नुभयो
He (HGH) told me he was in Nepal last year

When reporting questions, the verb सोध्नु must be used:

मेरो बुवाले तिमी कति बजे जान्छौ भनेर सोध्नुभयो
My father asked me what time I was going ('having said asked . . .')
रामे कहाँ छ भनेर उस्लाई सोधें
I asked him where Rame was ('where is Rame having said I asked')

When the original question does not contain an interrogative word like कति, कहाँ, कहिले, को, etc., the interrogative particle कि **ki** is usually placed at the end of the reported question.

वहाँले तिमी आज शहर् गयौ कि भनेर सोध्नुभयो
He asked (me) if I had been to town today

The question is spoken with a rising intonation, the highest pitch falling on the interrogative particle कि which is followed by a short pause.

यहाँ चिया पाइन्छ कि भनी पसलेलाई सोध्यौं
We asked the shopkeeper if we could get some tea there

When reporting commands, the verb भन्नु is used:

बिष्टज्यूले भोलि तीन् बजेतिर मकहाँ आउनुहोस् भनेर हामीलाई भन्नुभयो
Mr. Bista told us to come to his house at about three o'clock tomorrow

The verb अह्राउनु 'to command' is used when the command is addressed to an inferior:

बाले यसो गर भनेर मलाई अह्राउनुभयो
My father ordered me to do it this way

यसो **yaso** 'in this manner', 'thus'

सुबेदार्ले राइफल् सीधा समाऊ भनेर सिपाहीलाई अह्राए
The Subedar ordered the soldier to hold his rifle straight

Unless another word intervenes between भनेर and the main verb, e.g., as in मलाई भन्यो 'he said *to me*', the conjunctive participle may be omitted:

उस्ले म भोलि आउँछु भन्यो
He said he would come tomorrow

Occasionally, speech may be reported by using the conjunction कि **ki** 'that':

त्यस्ले भन्यो कि म भोलि आउँदै छु
He said that he was coming tomorrow

Note that the statement is reported by using the words just as they were spoken.

The construction with कि (modelled on the Hindi construction) is often regarded as being inelegant or even incorrect. It is, however, common in speech and in long prose narratives where the construction with **bhanera** might lead to confusion.

9. The verb लाग्नु **lāgnu** (basically meaning 'to be applied', 'to become attached' then 'to be felt', 'to seem') deserves special attention. Some common expressions in which this verb is used are given in the following examples:

मेरो लुगामा हिलो लाग्यो
My clothes are muddy ('mud has been attached to my clothes')
मलाई भोक् लाग्यो
I feel hungry ('hunger has been applied to me')
मलाई तिर्खा लाग्यो
I feel thirsty (**tirkhā** 'thirst')
मलाई रुघा लाग्यो
I have a head cold (**rughā** 'a cold')
मलाई थकाई लाग्यो
I feel tired (**thakāī** 'tiredness')
मलाई उँग् लाग्यो
I feel drowsy (**ūg** 'drowsiness')

In the above examples, the Simple Past Tense लाग्यो has been translated by an English present tense. If one bears in mind the basic meaning of लाग्यो 'has become attached', the reason for this will be obvious. All these examples refer to particular instances. Thus मलाई भोक् लाग्यो means 'I feel hungry (at this particular moment)'. On the other hand, the Simple Indefinite लाग्छ denotes a general or regular occurrence:

बेलुका पाँच् बजेतिर मलाई सधैं भोक् लाग्छ
I always feel hungry about five in the evening ('hunger attaches itself')
but आज मलाई भोक लागेन
I do not feel hungry today
तपाईंलाई हिन्दुस्तानी खाना कस्तो लाग्छ ?
How do you like Indian food (in general)?
but तपाईंलाई नेपाल् कस्तो लाग्यो ?
How do you like Nepal/what do you think of Nepal (a particular instance)?
आज घाम् लाग्यो
It is sunny today ('sunshine has applied itself')
but जाड़ोमा खूब् घाम् लाग्छ ।
In the cold season, it is (generally) nice and sunny

घाम् **ghām** 'sunshine', as opposed to सूर्य **sūrya** (often pronounced **sūrje**) 'the sun'; e.g. सूर्य कति बजे अस्ताउँछ ? 'What time does the sun set?'

शुक्रबार् शुक्रबार् यहाँ बजार् लाग्छ
A market is held here every Friday.

The repetition of शुक्रबार् implies regularity.

आज राति मलाई दुइ बजेसम्म निद्रा लागेन
Last night I did not get to sleep ('sleep did not attach itself') till two o'clock

10. We have already met the verb पर्नु **parnu** (basically meaning 'to fall') in expressions like पानी पर्छ 'it rains', यस्लाई कति पर्छ ? 'how much does it cost'. The usage of this verb is often very idiomatic. Some of the common expressions in which it occurs are given in the following examples:

आज पानी पर्छ कि पर्दैन मलाई थाहा छैन
I don't know whether it will rain today or not
काठ्माड़ौंमा हिउँ कहिले पनि पर्दैन, पहाड़तिर त निक्कै पर्छ
It never snows in Kathmandu, but in the hills it snows a lot

हिउँ **hiũ** 'snow', 'ice'

मेरो साथी मदेस् गईकन सिकिस्त बिरामी पऱ्यो
As soon as my friend got to the Terai, he fell seriously ill
त्यो नयाँ सिनेमा कस्तो थियो ? तिमीलाई मन् पऱ्यो कि परेन ?
How was that new film? Did you like it or not?

मन् **man** literally means 'heart', 'mind'. The idiomatic expression कसैलाई मन् पर्नु **kasəylāī man parnu** (lit. 'to fall to the heart of someone') means 'to like (something)'.

मलाई मन् पर्छ **malāī man parcha** is more or less synonymous with मलाई राम्रो लाग्छ **malāī rāmro lāgcha.** In both these expressions, the Simple Past Tense refers to a particular instance and the Simple Indefinite to a general instance:

त्यो घड़ी कस्तो लाग्यो ? तिमीलाई मन् पऱ्यो कि परेन ?
How do you find that watch? Do you like it or not?
मलाई हिन्दुस्तानी खाना उस्तो मन् पर्दैन । कहिले कहीं त धेरै नै पिरो हुन्छ
I don't like Indian food all that much. Sometimes it's far too hot

उस्तो **usto** 'so much'

Note that पिरो **piro** means 'hot' in the sense of 'peppery'. तातो **tāto** means 'hot to the touch' e.g. तातो पानी 'hot water', तातो दूध् 'hot milk'. Referring to climate or weather, 'hot' and 'cold' are expressed by गर्मी **garmī** 'heat' and जाड़ो **jāṛo** 'coldness':

आज त अलि गर्मी छ
It's quite warm today
मदेस्मा धेरै गर्मी हुन्छ रे
They say that it gets very warm in the Terai
मलाई गर्मी भयो
I feel warm ('to me warmth has become')
जून्देखि गर्मी लाग्छ
It gets warm from June onwards
यो कोठामा जाड़ो छ
It's cold in this room
हिमाल्मा जाड़ो हुन्छ
It's usually cold in the mountains

चिसो **ciso** means 'cold' or 'damp' (to the touch)

चिसोमा बस्यौ भने रुघा लाग्छ । सुन्यौ तिमीले ?

If you sit in the cold/damp you'll get a cold. Did you hear me?

11. Age may be expressed in the following ways:

तिम्रो उमेर् कति हो/भयो ?

How old are you? (either **ho** or **bhayo**)

म तीस् बर्षको हूँ

or

म तीस् बर्ष लागें

or

म तीस् बर्ष पुगें

All the above expressions mean 'I am thirty'

त्यस्को उमेर् कति भयो ? पैंतालीस् बर्ष लाग्यो क्यारे

How old is he? He's about forty-five

क्यारे **kyāre** a particle used to express doubt, frequently used in the context of age.

Vocabulary 10

अथवा	**athavā**	or, or else
अनुसन्धान्	**anusandhān**	research
अन्डर्ग्राउन्ड्	**anḍargrāunḍ**	Underground
अलग्ग	**alagga**	separate
अलग्ग गर्नु	**alagga garnu**	to separate
अस्ताउनु	**astāunu**	to set (of the sun)
अह्राउनु	**ahrāunu**	to command
आदि	**ādi**	and so on
आराम्	**ārām**	rest
आराम् गर्नु	**ārām garnu**	to rest
आशा	**āʃā**	hope
आशा गर्नु	**āʃā garnu**	to hope
उठ्नु	**uṭhnu**	to get up, rise
उत्तर्	**uttar**	North
उस्तो	**usto**	so much, that much
उँग्	**ũg**	drowsiness
उँग् लाग्नु	**ũg lāgnu**	to feel drowsy
कमाउनु	**kamāunu**	to earn (money)
काट्नु	**kāṭnu**	to cut
कालिम्पोङ्ग	**kālimpoŋg**	Kalimpong (town in Bengal)
कुनै	**kunəy**	some, any, a certain
क्यारे	**kyāre**	about, roughly, I suppose
खड़ा हुनु	**khaṛā hunu**	to stand, be standing

खास् गरेर	**khās garera**	especially
गह्रुँगो	**gahrũgo**	heavy
गाली गर्नु	**gālī garnu**	to swear, curse
गेल्	**gel**	Gel (town near Darjeeling)
गृहकृत्य	**gɹhakɹtya**	housework
घाम्	**ghām**	sunshine
घाम् लाग्नु	**ghām lāgnu**	to be sunny
जीवन्	**jīvan**	life
जीविका	**jīvikā**	livelihood
चढ्नु	**caɽhnu**	to mount, go up, get in (a bus)
चमेनाघर्	**camenāghar**	restaurant, canteen
चिसो	**ciso**	cold, damp
चीनिया	**cīniyā**	Chinese
छुट्नु	**chuʈnu**	to be missed (of a bus, etc.)
चलाउनु	**calāunu**	to make move, to direct, drive
जमीन्,जिमीन्	**jamīn, jimīn**	land, earth
जल्पान्	**jalpān**	snack, breakfast
झर्नु	**jharnu**	to come down, descend
टिकट्	**ʈikaʈ**	ticket
तातो	**tāto**	hot, warm
तिर्खा	**tirkhā**	thirst
तिर्खा लाग्नु	**tirkhā lāgnu**	to feel thirsty
थकाई	**thakāī**	tiredness
थकाई लाग्नु	**thakāī lāgnu**	to feel tired
दक्षिण्	**dakṣiɳ**	South
दृष्टिकोण्	**dɹṣʈikoɳ**	point of view
नयाँ	**nayā̃**	new
निद्रा	**nidrā**	sleep
नुहाउनु	**nuhāunu**	to bathe, take a bath
नोभेम्बर्	**nobhembar**	November
पद्म	**padma**	Padma (man's name)
पर्खनु	**parkhanu**	to wait
पश्चिम् (पच्छिम्)	**paʃcim, pacchim**	West
पस्नु	**pasnu**	to enter
पिरो	**piro**	hot, spicy
पूर्व	**pūrva**	East
पोको	**poko**	package
पोखिनु	**pokhinu**	to be spilt
पोख्नु	**pokhnu**	to spill
फाइदा	**phāidā**	use, advantage
बगैंचा	**bagəȳcā**	garden, park
बस्-बिसौनी	**bas-bisəwnī**	bus stop
बाँड्नु	**bā̃ɽnu**	to distribute, divide

बा	**bā**	father (syn. **buvā**)
बास् बस्नु	**bās basnu**	to take lodgings for the night
बोक्नु	**boknu**	to carry
भोक्	**bhok**	hunger
भोक् लाग्नु	**bhok lāgnu**	to feel hungry
भोलिपल्ट	**bholipalṭa**	the next day
मद्रास्	**madrās**	Madras
मन् पर्नु	**man parnu**	to like
मिठाई	**miṭhāī**	sweets
मुख्	**mukh**	face, mouth
मौका	**məwkā**	opportunity
यसो	**yaso**	in this way, thus
रमाइलो	**ramāilo**	pleasant
रमाइलो गर्नु	**ramāilo garnu**	to have fun, enjoy oneself
राइफल्	**rāiphal**	rifle
रात्	**rāt**	night
रुनु	**runu**	to weep
रुघा	**rughā**	a cold
रुघा लाग्नु	**rughā lāgnu**	to have/catch a cold
लगाउनु	**lagāunu**	to put on (clothes)
लम्किनु	**lamkinu**	to hurry
लिएर आउनु (लेराउनु)	**liera āunu, lerāuna**	to bring (syn. **lyāunu**)
लेक्चर्	**lekcar**	lecture
विभिन्न	**vibhinna**	various
समाउनु	**samāunu**	to hold up, catch
समात्नु	**samātnu**	to catch (a bus, etc.)
सवेरै	**saverəy**	early in the morning
साहित्य	**sāhitya**	literature
सीधा	**sīdhā**	straight
सुक्खा	**sukkhā**	dried, dry
सुबेदार्	**subedār**	Subedar (military rank)
सूर्य	**sūrya**	sun
सोझै	**sojhəy**	direct(ly)
सोध्नु	**sodhnu**	to ask
हात्	**hāt**	hand
हालत्	**hālat**	state, condition
हिउँ	**hiũ**	snow
हिउँ पर्नु	**hiũ parnu**	snow to fall
होश् गर्नु	**hoʃ garnu**	to be careful

Reading Passage

अ. पद्मज्यू । नमस्कार् । तपाईं लन्दन्को विश्वविद्यालयमा विद्यार्थी हुनुहुन्छ, होइन त ? तपाईं कहाँको हुनुहुन्छ ?

आ. म काठ्माडौंको हुँ, तर हिजोआज म लन्दन्मा बस्छु । दुइ बर्षदेखि यहाँको

विश्वविद्यालयमा नेपाली साहित्यको विषयमा अनुसन्धान् गर्दै छु।

अ. तपाईंलाई लन्दन् कस्तो लाग्यो ? राम्रो लाग्यो कि लागेन ?

आ. धेरै नै राम्रो लाग्यो । काठ्माड़ौंभन्दा लन्दन् शहर् निक्कै ठूलो छ नि । एउटा दृष्टिकोण्बाट लन्दन्को जीवन् सजिलो देखिन्छ तर कहिले कहीं हामी नेपालीहरूको लागि गाह्रो पनि हुन्छ । साथीहरू त धेरै छन् । त्यस् कारण् मलाई रमाइलो लाग्यो ।

अ. तपाईं धेरैजसो हप्तामा के गर्नुहुन्छ ?

आ. धेरैजसो म बिहान सात् बजेतिर उठेर, मुख् हात् धोई,[1] अथवा कहिले कहीं नुहाएर आठ् बजे बस् बिसौनीतिर लम्किन्छु । त्यहाँबाट स्टेशन्सम्म दस् मिनेट्को बाटो मात्रै हो । फेरि अन्डरग्राउन्ड् समातेर मेरो अड्डासम्म जान्छु ।

अ. तपाईं बिहान अड्डामा काम् गर्नुहुन्छ कि ?

आ. गर्छु । हिजोआज विद्यार्थीको हालत् उस्तो राम्रो छैन । के गर्ने? त्यस् कारण् जीविका चलाउनलाई[2] अड्डामा काम् गरेर अलिकति पैसा कमाउँदै छु ।

अ. त्यहाँ तपाईं के गर्नुहुन्छ ?

आ. अड्डाको काम धेरै गाह्रो त छैन। बिहानको डाँक् अलग्ग गरेर विभिन्न विभाग्हरूमा बाँड़छु ।

अ. तपाईं कति बजेसम्म त्यहाँ काम् गर्नुहुन्छ ?

आ. म बाह्र बजेसम्म मात्रै काम् गर्छु । त्यस्पछि अड्डाको चमेनाघर्मा भात्[3] खाएर विश्वविद्यालयतिर जान्छु । त्यहाँ पुगेर दुइ बजेदेखि पुस्तकालयमा पढ्छु । हप्ताको दुइ पटक् अध्यापक्सँग भेट्छु । कहिले कहीं कुनै चाखलाग्दो विषयको बारेमा लेक्चर् भयो भने म सुन्न जान्छु ।[4]

अ. सन्चरबार् र आइत्बार् बिदा हुन्छ, होइन त ? बिदाको दिन् के के गर्नुहुन्छ ?

आ. बिदाको दिन् साथीहरूसँग भेटेर, रमाईलो गर्छु । घाम् लाग्यो भने लन्दन्को कुनै बगैंचामा हामी आराम् गर्छौं । पानी पर्‍यो भने सिनेमा हेर्न जान्छौं,[5] अथवा घर्मा बसेर रेडियो सुन्छौं। गर्मीमा कहिले कहीं लन्दन्बाट बाहिर निस्केर हामी समुद्रतिर घुम्न जान्छौं[6]। त्यो त धेरै नै राम्रो लाग्छ नि ।

अ. नेपाल् फर्केर के गर्ने बिचार् छ ?[7]

आ. अहिलेसम्म त थाहा छैन । तर मौका पाइयो भने काठ्माड़ौंको विश्वविद्यालयमा नेपाली साहित्य पढ़ाउने आशा गर्छु ।[8]

Notes

1. **mukh hāt dhunu**: 'to wash one's hands and face'. **hāt** is strictly speaking 'the forearm'.
2. **jīvikā calāunalāī**: 'in order to make (lit. 'to run') a living'. Note the use of **-lāī** with the second infinitive in **-na** to express purpose.
3. **bhāt**: 'cooked rice' is often used in the general sense of 'food'.
4. **ma sunna jānchu**: 'I go to hear it'. Here the second infinitive expresses purpose. Cf. note 2.
5. **sinemā herna jānchəw̃**: 'we go to watch a film'.
6. **ghumna jānchəw̃**: 'we go to stroll'.
7. **ke garne bicār cha**: 'what do you have in mind to do'. **garne** is the infinitival participle of **garnu.** Cf. **ke garne?** 'what to do?'
8. **paṛhāune āʃā garchu**: 'I hope to teach' (lit. 'I do a teaching hope'.)

Exercise 10a

Translate into English

१. भोलि घाम् लाग्यो भने म बिहान सवेरै उठेर तपाईंको घर् आउँछु ।
२. मेरो दाज्यू पट्ना भएर काठ्माड़ौं आउनुभयो ।
३. होश् गरेर मोटर् हाँक्नुहोस् त । हिजोआज बाटो एक्दम् नराम्रो छ ।
४. हामी ढीलो रक्सौल् पुग्यौं तर होटेल् सजिलैसँग पायौं । भोलिपल्ट बिहान सवेरै उठेर जल्पान् गरी स्टेशन्तिर हिंड्यौं ।
५. कस्ले भनेर तिमी मेरो कोठामा पस्यौ ?
६. त्यहाँ खड़ा होऊ सुबेदार्ले सिपाहीलाई अह्रायो।
७. यो बाटोले कहाँ कहाँ लान्छ भनेर उस्ले सोध्यो ।
८. हाम्रो देश् तपाईंलाई कस्तो लाग्यो ? मलाई त एक्दम् राम्रो लाग्यो ।
९. एक् छिन् पर्खनुहोस्, म छिटो नुहाएर आउँछु ।
१०. नेपाली मिठाई तपाईंलाई मन् पर्छ कि पर्दैन ? उस्तो मन् पर्दैन। मलाई अतिनै गुलियो लाग्छ ।
११. तिम्रो भाइको उमेर् कति भयो ? दस् बर्ष लाग्यो क्यारे ।
१२. यो उपन्यास् कस्तो लाग्यो ? मन् पर्‍यो कि परेन ? मलाई त उस्तो मन् परेन ।
१३. दक्षिण् भारत्मा, खास् गरी मद्रास् आदि शहर्हरूमा, जाड़ो कहिले पनि हुँदैन । तर उत्तर् भारत्मा जाड़ो महीनामा अतिनै जाड़ो हुन्छ ।
१४. यो चिया एक्दमै चिसो भयो । अलि तातो पानी लिएर आऊ न ।
१५. उस्ले त्यो गह्रुंगो पोको एक्लैले बोकेर ल्यायो ।
१६. तपाईंले मलाई यो होटेल् राम्रो हो भन्नुभयो तर नराम्रो पो रहेछ ।
१७. बिहानको हवाईजहाज् सोझै पोखरा जान्छ तर बेलुकाकोचाहिं गोर्खा भएर जान्छ ।
१८. पोहोर् साल् मदेस् गईकन म सिकिस्त बिरामी परें ।

Exercise 10b

Translate into Nepali

1. How old is that boy? He says he's fifteen.
2. I feel thirsty. Give (HGH) me a little water, please.
3. He said that he did not like Indian food. What about you? Do you like it? Yes, I do, but sometimes it is rather hot.
4. Tomorrow morning, I'll get up early and go to town. Do you know what time the shops open?
5. In countries like India and Nepal, most people eat only rice and vegetables. Meat is always very expensive.
6. Does the aeroplane go direct to Madras from here? No. It goes via Delhi.
7. I'll quickly have a bath and come. Wait a little while, will you?
8. The Subedar asked the soldier how old he was. The soldier said that he was about thirty.
9. Yesterday was a holiday. My elder sister got up early, had a bath, and went straight to the temple. But I ('as for me') slept until twelve o'clock.
10. I see this package is very heavy. Be careful how you (MGH) carry it.
11. How do you like Kathmandu? I find it very interesting.
12. These days the condition of students in ('of') many countries is not very good. But what's the use of moaning about it?

Exercise 10c

Translate into Nepali

Who says so?; which one; so many villages; I shall not tell anyone; how are you going?; he is getting married next week; my cycle is like his; the vegetables do not taste good; drive carefully; we feel thirsty; last year it did not rain very much; he is twenty-five years old; where does he (LGH) come from?; it is quite warm today; bring some tea (MGH).

Exercise 10d

Give correct forms of the verbs in brackets:

म दस् बजे (उठ्नु) तपाईंकहाँ (आउनु)
वहाँले तिम्रो उमेर् कति (हुनु) भनेर (सोध्नु)
मेरो भाइ भात् (खानु) घर्बाट (निस्कनु)
पानी पर्‍यो भने, म त (जानु)
ए नानी खल्बल् (गर्नु) भनेर बाले (भन्नु)
एक् छिन् (पर्खनु) । म छिटो (नुहाउनु) तपाईंकहाँ (आउनु)

LESSON 11

1. *New conjunct consonants*

त्न	**tn**	as in	प्रयत्न	**prayatna**	effort
च्न	**cn**	as in	बेच्नु	**becnu**	to sell
द्व	**dv**	as in	द्वीप्	**dvīp**	island

2. Obligation – 'must', 'have to', 'it is necessary to' is expressed by the infinitive in **-nu** followed by a 3rd person singular form of the verb पर्नु . The infinitive and the relevant part of पर्नु are written together as one word:

गर्नुपर्छ	**garnuparcha**	it is necessary to do/must do
खानुपर्दैन	**khānupardəyna**	it is not necessary to eat/must not eat
धुनुपर्‍यो	**dhunuparyo**	it was necessary to wash/had to wash
आउनुपरेन	**āunuparena**	it was not necessary to come etc.

The construction is impersonal. Therefore the subject is often omitted when it is clear on whom the obligation falls:

कहिले कहीं त आराम् गर्नुपर्छ
You have to/one has to rest sometimes

बिहानको हवाईजहाज् आउँदैन रे । बेलुकासम्म पर्खनुपर्छ
They say the morning plane is not coming. We'll have to wait till the evening

Emphasis may be conveyed by using the emphatic form of the infinitive:

काम् त गर्नैपर्छ
One just has to work

खल्तीमा त पैसा हुनैपर्छ
One really has to have some money in one's pocket ('it is necessary for there to be . . .')

3. When a subject word (i.e. a noun or pronoun denoting the person on whom the obligation falls) needs to be expressed, it takes either -लाई or -ले . -लाई is preferred for the 1st person sing. pronoun in all cases. Other words tend to take -लाई when the infinitival verb is intransitive and -ले when it is transitive. No hard and fast rule, however, can be given.

मलाई काम् गर्नुपर्छ
I have to/it is necessary for me to work

उस्ले खानुपऱ्यो
He had to eat
हामीले पर्खनुपरेन
We did not have to wait
उस्लाई घर् जानुपऱ्यो
He had to go home
आज त ट्याक्सी पाइएन । शहर्बाट हिंड़ेरै आउनुपऱ्यो
I could not get a taxi today. I had to walk back from town

When the infinitival verb is intransitive, the postposition is sometimes omitted from the subject word:

म जानुपर्छ
I'll have to go

Often, the Simple Past पऱ्यो tends to be used to denote a particular instance, while the Simple Indefinite पर्छ denotes a general or regular occurrence:

मलाई दिनहुँ काम्मा जानुपर्छ
I have to go to work every day (general)
अबेर भयो । अब त जानुपऱ्यो
It's late already. I must go now (particular)

4. The reflexive pronominal adjective आफ्नो **āphno** refers back to the subject of the sentence, and may be used in place of the other possessives when they denote the same person as the subject word. For example, in the sentence: '*he* is going to *his* room', where 'he' and 'his' refer to the same person, 'his' may be rendered आफ्नो .

त्यो आफ्नो कोठामा जाँदै छ
He is going to his (own) room
म आफ्नो कोठामा जाँदै छु
I am going to my (own) room
उद्योग्मन्त्रीले आफ्नो भाषण्मा नेपाल्को औद्योगिक् विकास्को लागि भर्सक् प्रयत्न गर्नुपर्छ भन्नुभयो
In his speech the minister of industry said that it was necessary to make every effort for the development of Nepal

भर्सक् प्रयत्न **bharsak prayatna** 'every possible effort' – a rather literary phrase.

In written Nepali, the reflexive possessive आफ्नो is invariably used in such sentences. In the spoken language, the other possessives may be employed: म मेरो कोठामा जाँदै छु , etc. would be acceptable in speech.

5. The Second Infinitive, examples of which have been encountered in earlier reading passages, is formed by changing the termination नु **-nu** of the First Infinitive to न **-na.** Thus: गर्न **garna,** बस्न **basna,** खान **khāna,** आउन **āuna,** etc.

6. The Second Infinitive may function as a verbal noun, and can be translated 'doing', 'to do' etc.

घाम्मा बस्न रमाइलो हुन्छ
It is pleasant to sit in the sunshine
गाईको मासु खान पाप् हो नि
It is a sin to eat beef, you know
जाड़ोमा हिमाल्मा हिंड़्न गाह्रो हुन्छ
It is difficult to walk in the mountains in winter
बस्मा जान बेस् हुन्छ
It is better to go by bus
माग्न राम्रो होइन
It is not good to beg

माग्नु **māgnu** 'to ask for', 'to beg'

The Infinitive in **-nu** may also be used in the same way, but is less frequent: Thus घाम्मा बस्नु रमाइलो हुन्छ is equally acceptable. The Infinitive in **-nu** is used before the adverb अगाड़ि **agāṛi** or the phrase भन्दा अगाड़ि **bhandā agāṛī** meaning 'before':

तपाईंकहाँ आउनुभन्दा अगाड़ि मलाई अलि काम् सिद्ध्याउनुपर्छ
Before coming to see you, I have to finish some work

सिद्ध्याउनु **siddhyāunu** 'to finish, complete'
सिद्धिनु **siddhinu** 'to be finished'

सुर्य अस्ताउनु अगाड़ि काम् सिद्धिनुपर्छ
The work must be finished before the sun sets
त्यो काम् त सिद्धियो
Well?, that job's finished

7. The Second Infinitive is used with हुन्छ and हुँदैन, which in this context may be translated 'it is all right to', 'one may' etc. The construction is impersonal and the subject word is often omitted:

त्यहाँ जान हुन्छ ?
Is it all right to go there?
ए नानी, गाली गर्न हुन्न
You should not swear, you naughty boy

If a subject word is expressed, -ले is added to the subject when the infinitival verb is transitive:

केटाकेटीहरूले रक्सी खान हुँदैन
Children should not drink *raksi*
मैले बत्ती बाल्न हुन्छ ?
Will it be all right if I switch on the light?
म भित्र जान हुन्छ ?
May I go inside?

8. हुन्छ and हुन्न may be used to answer a question or command:

भोलि म तपाईंकहाँ आउँछु । त्यो त हुन्न । म बाहिर जान्छु

I'll come and see you tomorrow. No, that won't do. I'm going out

चिया ल्याऊ। हुन्छ, साहेब्

Bring some tea. Very well, sir

हवस् **havas** (usually pronounced **hos**) means 'very well' in reply to questions and commands:

अ. म जाऊँ है त । भोलि भेटौंला

आ. हवस् म २ बजे आउँछु

A. I'll be off now. See you tomorrow

B. Very well. I'll come at two o'clock

भेटौंला **bheṭəw̃lā** 'we shall probably meet'. This form is discussed in Lesson 17. The expression should, however, be remembered.

9. The Second Infinitive is used to express purpose 'in order to', etc.

पहिले म भीजा लिन काठ्माडौं जान्छु

First of all I'm going to Kathmandu to get a visa

हामी भात् खान जान्छौं

We are going to have dinner

रामे आज ताश् खेल्न आउँदैन रे

Rame says he's not coming to play cards today

त्यो त ताश् खेल्न जहिले पनि तयार् छ

He's always ready to have a game of cards

जहिले पनि **jahile pani** 'whenever', 'at any time', 'always'

10. In the following sentences, the Second Infinitive is used in expressions involving लाग्छ and लाग्यो . The examples should be carefully noted:

बेलुका शहर्मा डुल्न मजा लाग्छ

It's fun strolling through the city in the evening

(गर्न) मजा लाग्छ **(garna) majā lāgcha** 'it's fun (to do)'

तपाईं अगाडि नेपाली बोल्नु मलाई लाज् लाग्छ

I am ashamed to speak Nepali in front of you

(गर्न) लाज् लाग्छ **(garna) lāj lāgcha** 'one feels ashamed (to do)'

सिनेमा हेर्न जान मन् लाग्छ कि लाग्दैन ?

Do you like going to the pictures or not?

(गर्न) मन् लाग्छ **(garna) man lāgcha** 'one likes (to do)'

Note that मन् लाग्नु is used with a verb:

मलाई जान मन् लाग्छ	I like to go
हामीलाई हेर्न मन् लाग्छ	we like to watch
तिमीलाई गर्न मन् लाग्छ	you like to do etc.

मन् पर्छ (Lesson 10) is used only with nouns:

त्यो सिनेमा मन् पर्‍यो कि परेन ?
Did you like that film or not?

The Simple Past मन् लाग्यो refers to a particular instance, and may often be translated: 'I want to', 'I feel like' etc.

सिनेमा हेर्न जान मन् लाग्यो
I want to go to see a film (now)
चिया खान मन् लाग्यो कि लागेन ?
Do you want to drink tea or not (at this moment)?
but मलाई बिहान चिया खान मन् लाग्दैन
I do not (usually) like to drink tea in the mornings

11. The verb चाहनु **cāhanu** 'to wish', 'to want', is used with the Second Infinitive:

तपाईं कहिले जान चाहनुहुन्छ ?
When do you wish to go?
म प्रधानमन्त्रीलाई भेट्न चाहन्छु
I want to meet the Prime Minister

चाहनु is, however, rather formal and literary. In speech it is more usual to find the construction with मन् लाग्नु

जुन् बेला मन् लाग्छ, त्यति बेला आऊ
Come at any time you wish ('whatever time you wish, come at such a time')

जुन् **jun** 'whichever'.

12. The Second Infinitive is used with लाग्नु in expressions like:

कति बेर् लाग्छ ? 'how much time does it take to . . .'
कति खर्च लाग्छ ? 'how much does it cost to . . .'

यहाँबाट गोर्खा पुग्न कति दिन् लाग्छ ?
How many days does it take to reach Gorkha from here?
मेरो बिचारले आउन जान दस् दिन् जति लाग्छ
In my opinion, it will take about ten days to go and come back

जति **jati** 'approximately' follows the word it qualifies.

काठ्माड़ौंबाट नाम्चे बजार् पुग्न तीन् हप्ता जति लाग्यो
It took about three weeks to get to Namche Bazar from Kathmandu

अ. यहाँबाट पाटन् कति टाढ़ा छ ?
आ. हिंड़ेर जान त टाढ़ा छ, बसमा जानुभयो भने दस् मिनेट् जति लाग्छ
A. How far is it to Patan from here?

B. It's quite a long way on foot, but if you go by bus it will take about ten minutes

In such sentences (especially if they are short) -लाई may be added to the infinitive:

त्यहाँ पुग्नलाई कति बेर लाग्छ ?
How long does it take to get there?
हवाईजहाज्मा बेलायत् जानलाई कति खर्च लाग्छ ?
How much does it cost to go to England by air?
यो काम् सिद्ध्याउनलाई धेरै बेर् लाग्छ
It takes a long time to finish this work

13. The verb दिनु is used with the Second Infinitive in the sense of 'to allow to', 'to let'.

धेरै हल्ला नगर । उस्लाई पढ्न देऊ न
Don't make such a noise. Let him read
दुइ बज्नु अगाडि सिंह दर्बार्मा कसैलाई पस्न दिंदैनन्
Before two o'clock, they don't let anyone go inside the Singha-Darbar

सिंह दर्बार् the H.Q. of the Nepalese Civil Service in Kathmandu

मेरो चश्मा लिएर उस्ले मलाई पढ्नै दिएन
He took my glasses away and just would not let me read

पढ्नै conveys emphasis, Cf. 2 above.

Vocabulary 11

अगाडि	**agāṛi**	before
आगो	**āgo**	fire
आगो ताप्नु	**āgo tāpnu**	to warm oneself by a fire
आफ्नो	**āphno**	one's own
उद्योग्	**udyog**	industry
उद्योग्मन्त्री	**udyogmantrī**	minister of industry
उपमहाद्वीप्	**upamahādvīp**	subcontinent
कम्सेकम्	**kamsekam**	at least
किन्नु	**kinnu**	to buy
किसान्	**kisān**	peasant, farmer
कोशिश्	**koʃiʃ**	effort
खाने कुरा	**khāne kurā**	food, 'things for eating'
खेल्नु	**khelnu**	to play (games)
चश्मा	**caʃmā**	glasses
चाहनु	**cāhanu**	to want, wish, desire
छाता	**chātā**	umbrella
जता ततै	**jatā tatəy**	everywhere, all over

जम्मा	**jammā**	altogether, in total
जुन्	**jun**	whichever
ज्यापु	**jyāpu**	peasant, farmer
झिक्नु	**jhiknu**	to pull out, take out
टचाक्सी	**ṭyāksī**	taxi
डाक्टर्	**ḍākṭar**	doctor
डुल्नु	**ḍulnu**	to stroll
तयार्	**tayār**	ready
तल	**tala**	down, below
ताप्नु	**tāpnu**	to warm oneself
ताश्	**tāʃ**	playing-cards
ताश् खेल्नु	**tāʃ khelnu**	to play cards
थोरै	**thorəy**	a few, very few
दराज्	**darāj**	drawer
दाँजो	**dā̃jo**	comparison
को दाँजोमा	**-ko dā̃jomā**	in comparison with
दाउरा	**dāurā**	firewood
धारा	**dhārā**	water-spout (for washing in villages)
पठाइदिनु	**paṭhāidinu**	to send for
पल्लो	**pallo**	next, neighbouring
पाप्	**pāp**	sin
पुरिया	**puriyā**	box, carton
प्रयत्न	**prayatna**	effort
बट्टा	**baṭṭā**	packet
बाबु	**bābu**	term of address for children
बिस्कुट्	**biskuṭ**	biscuit
बेच्नु	**becnu**	to sell
बेर्	**ber**	time, delay, lateness
बोलाउनु	**bolāunu**	to call, summon
भरसक्	**bharsak**	every possible, fullest
भुइँ	**bhuī̃**	ground[1]
मजा	**majā**	fun, pleasure
मन् लाग्नु	**man lāgnu**	to want to
माग्नु	**māgnu**	to ask for, beg
मुख्	**mukh**	face, mouth
रमाइलो	**ramāilo**	pleasant
लाज्	**lāj**	shame
लैजानु	**ləyjānu**	to take away[2]
विकास्	**vikās**	development, progress

[1]Usually pronounced **bhuē̃** or **bhəỹ**.
[2]Synonymous with **lānu.** It is only used in tenses derived from its Primary Base. The past tenses are supplied from **lānu.**

साँझ्	**sā̃jh**	evening
साँझ् पर्नु	**sā̃jh parnu**	of evening to fall
सिद्धिनु	**siddhinu**	to be completed
सिद्ध्याउनु	**siddyāunu**	to complete
हल्ला	**hallā**	noise
हल्ला गर्नु	**hallā garnu**	to make a noise
हवस् (होस्)	**havas (hos)**	very well
हात्	**hāt**	hand, forearm
होला	**holā**	maybe, perhaps

Reading Passage

बाटोमा

अ. ए दाज्यू । पल्लो गाउँ यहाँबाट कति टाढ़ा छ ? त्यहाँ पुग्नलाई कति बेर् लाग्छ होला ?[1]

आ. टाढ़ा छ, हजूर् । यहाँबाट कम्सेकम् दुइ घण्टा लाग्छ।

अ. साँझ् पर्नु अगाडि पुगिन्छ कि पुगिंदैन ?

आ. पुगिंदैन, हजूर् । बाटो अलि उकालो छ नि । हाम्रो गाउँ यहाँनजीक् छ । आज त्यहीं बस्नुहोस् । भोलि बिहान सवेरै उठेर जानुहोस् न ।

अ. हवस् । तपाईंको गाउँमा बास् पाइन्छ ?

आ. पाइन्छ, हजूर् । तपाईं मेरो घर्मा बस्न आउनुहोस् न । कतिजना हुनुहुन्छ ?

अ. हामी दुइजना मात्रै छौं ।

अलि बेर्पछि गाउँमा पुगेर

आ. ल मेरो घर् यही हो । भित्र पाल्नुहोस् । म एक् छिन्पछि आउँछु।

अ. खाने कुरा पनि पाइन्छ, दाइ ? हामीलाई धेरै भोक् लाग्यो ।

आ. पाइन्छ, हजूर् । दाल्,भात् र तर्कारी दिउँला नि ।[2]

अ. बास्को लागि कति पैसा लिनुहुन्छ त ?

आ. खाने कुराको तीन् मोहर्, दाउराको एक् रुपियाँ । जम्मा पाँच् मोहर् लिन्छु क्यारे।

अ. ल हुन्छ । ठीकै छ ।

किसान् गाई दुहुन र दाउरा लिन जान्छ । हामीचाहिं घर्मा पसेर जुत्ता खोली भूईंमा बस्छौं ।[3] १५ मिनेट्पछि किसान् घर्भित्र आउँछ ।

आ. चिया खानुहुन्छ त अहिले ?

अ. हुन्छ । तपाईंकहाँ बिस्कुट् पनि छ ?

आ. मकहाँ त छैन तर पसल्मा पाइन्छ होला । छोरालाई लिन पठाइदिन्छु । कति चाहिन्छ तपाईंलाई ?

अ. एक् पुरिया मात्रै । ल, एक् रुपियाँ लिनुहोस् । आज त अलि जाड़ो छ, होइन, दाज्यू ?

आ. हो । पहाड्मा साँझ् परेपछि अलि चिसो हुन्छ[4]। त्यहाँ बसेर आगो ताप्नुहोस् न ।

किसान्ले छोरालाई बोलाउँछ ।

आ. ए बाबू, जा त[5]। त्यहाँबाट एक् पुरिया बिस्कुट् किनेर लेर[6]। अरू केही ल्याउनुपर्छ पसल्बाट, हजूर् ?

अ. चुरोट् पनि बेच्छ भने दुइ बट्टा आसा लिन पठाउनुहोस्[7]। हामी धारामा हात् मुख् धोएर एक् छिनपछि आउँछौं ।[8]

आ. हवस् । धारा ऊ तल छ ।

Notes

1. **holā** 'maybe', 'perhaps', follows a verb, e.g. **ma āũchu holā** 'perhaps I'll come', **khāne kurā pāincha holā** 'you may be able to get something to eat'. **holā** is in fact the future tense of **ho,** discussed in lesson 17.
2. **diũlā**: the future tense of **dinu.** Translate 'I shall be able to give you'.
3. **juttā kholnu**: 'to untie ('open') one's shoes'.
4. **sā̃jh parepachi:** 'after sunset', lit. 'after the falling of the sun'. **pare** is the Second Perfect Participle of **parnu,** which will be discussed in full later.
5. **bābu**: a term of address, mostly for children and younger relations.
6. **lerā**: a colloquial form of **liera ā** 'bring'.
7. **āsā**: the name of a popular cheap brand of cigarettes, usually the only type available in Nepalese villages.
   beccha bhane 'if they sell'. The use of the Simple Indefinite rather than the Simple Past indicates that a specific time or instance is being referred to. For example: **timro khaltīmā pəysā cha bhane, malāī ek rūpiyā deu** 'If you have any money in your pocket (now), lend me a rupee'. Had **becyo bhane** been used, the meaning would be rather 'if ever they do sell . . .'
8. **dhārā**: 'a water spout', usually a small stream or pond outside a village serving as a communal washing place. In Kathmandu the **dhārās** are huge structures, where people still go to bathe.

Exercise 11a

Translate into English

१. काठ्माडौंबाट नाम्चे बजार् पुग्न कति दिन् लाग्छ ? छिटो हिंड्नुभयो भने दस् दिन् जति लाग्छ ।
२. घर् जान ढीलो भयो भनेर म बस्मा चढ्न गएँ ।
३. अबेर् भयो । अब मलाई जानुपर्‍यो । भोलि भेटौंला है । हवस् । मकहाँ दस् बजेतिर आउनुभयो भने म भेट्छु ।
४. कस्ले भनेर तिमीले मेरो किताब् दराज्बाट झिक्यौ ?
५. जाडोमाचाहिं मदेस् गएर बस्न एक्दम् मजा हुन्छ । घाम् मधैं लाग्छ र काठ्माडौंमा जस्तो जाडो कहिले पनि हुँदैन।
६. ए नानी, तिमीलाई माग्न लाज् लाग्दैन ?
७. मेरो लुगामा हिलो लाग्यो । भोलि त धोबीलाई दिनुपर्छ ।
८. नेपालीहरू गाईको मासु खान पाप् हो भन्छन् ।
९. साँझ् पर्नु अगाडि पुगेनौं भने गाउँमा बास् पाइँदैन रे ।
१०. हवाईजहाज्मा कल्कत्ता आउन जान कति खर्च लाग्छ ? तीन् सय पचास् रुपियाँ लाग्छ ।
११. बाटोमा सजिलैसँग बास् पाइँछ तर गाउँतिर खाने कुरा पाउन अलि गाह्रो हुन्छ । खाने कुराचाहिं काठ्माडौंमा नै किनेर लैजानुहोस् ।
१२. सगर्माथा राम्ररी हेर्नलाई खुम्बुतिर जानुपर्छ ।

१३. काठ्माड़ौं यूरोपका शहर्हरूको दाँजोमा त सानो भन्नुपर्छ तर त्यहाँ ठूल्ठूला होटेल्हरू पनि छन् र बजार्मा जे पनि पाइन्छ।

१४. खाली हिन्दुहरूलाई मात्रै पशुपतिनाथ्को मन्दिर्मा जान दिन्छन् ।

१५. यो काम् सिद्ध्याउनलाई कति बेर् लाग्छ ? कम्सेकम् दुइ घण्टा लाग्छ ।

१६. हल्ला नगर त । नानीलाई सुत्न देऊ । सुन्यौ तिमीले ?

१७. आज पानी पर्छ कि पर्दैन मलाई थाहा छैन, तर छाता लिईकन जान बेस् हुन्छ ।

१८. भरे पाँच बजे म आउन हुन्छ त ? हुन्छ ।

Exercise 11b

Translate into Nepali

1. The soldier said that we should not go into the temple. I think they only let Hindus go inside.
2. I'll be going now. We'll meet again tomorrow. All right. Come to my place about ten thirty. If it is sunny we'll go for a walk outside the town.
3. Do you like playing cards? Yes, I do occasionally.
4. What time shall I come? Come whenever you like.
5. How long does it take to go from London to Kathmandu by air? If you go by air, it takes about twenty-four hours.
6. How much did you pay for those shoes? They cost me twenty-eight rupees.
7. In the villages of Nepal, it is usually quite easy to get a lodging for the night.
8. In order to see the mountains well, you have to go to Khumbu. You can see Mt. Everest very well from there, you know.
9. After getting up in the morning, I wash my hands and face and then have breakfast at about half past seven.
10. It is very cold today. Sit here and warm yourself by the fire.
11. How do you like Nepal? I like it very much. Kathmandu is a very beautiful city. You can even see the Himalayas from here. Before coming, I didn't know that.
12. Before going into a temple, you have to take off ('open') your shoes.
13. In order to earn some money, I have to work in an office in the morning. But I only work until twelve o'clock, and the work is not very hard.
14. On weekdays, I get up early and go out of the house after I have breakfast. I usually arrive home after ten in the evening. On Saturdays and Sundays, I just have to have a rest.
15. Compared with the big cities of India, the towns of Nepal are quite small. But towns like Pokhara and Gorkha are very beautiful.

LESSON 12

1. *New conjunct consonants:*

ज्य	**jy**	as in	ज्योति	**jyoti**	light, flame
न्य	**ny**	as in	न्यानो	**nyāno**	warm, cosy
ह्म	**hm**	as in	ब्रह्मपुत्र	**brahmaputra**	Brahmaputra
र्ण	**rṇ**	as in	अन्नपूर्णा	**annapūrṇā**	Annapurna
ल्ड	**lḍ**	as in	खाल्डो	**khālḍo**	valley

2. The First Perfect Participle is formed by adding the suffix -एको **-eko** to the Base of verbs belonging to groups (i) and (ii) and to the Secondary Base of verbs belonging to groups (iii), (iv) and (v). Thus:

गरेको	**gareko**	done, having done
बसेको	**baseko**	sat, having sat
खाएको	**khāeko**	eaten, having eaten
दिएको	**dieko**	given, having given
धोएको	**dhoeko**	washed, having washed
बिर्सेको	**birseko**	forgotten, having forgotten
आएको	**āeko**	come, having come
गएको	**gaeko**	gone, having gone
भएको	**bhaeko**	been, having been

The negative is formed by prefixing the negative particle **na-** to the affirmative: नगरेको **nagareko,** नआएको **naāeko,** नभएको **nabhaeko,** etc. The HGH has the suffix -भएको **-bhaeko** added to the infinitive in **-nu:** गर्नुभएको **garnubhaeko** नआउनुभएको **naāunubhaeko,** etc.

3. In speech the suffix -एको **-eko** is often pronounced **-yā** (sounding a little like English *yeah*), when it occurs after a base ending in a consonant. Thus गरेको may be pronounced **garyā,** देखेको **dekhyā,** बसेको **basyā,** etc.

When the suffix -एको follows a base ending in **-ā** or **-a,** -आएको **-āeko** and -अएको **-aeko** are often pronounced **-āko,** or **-āyā** and **-ayā** respectively. Thus गएको may be pronounced **gāko** or **gayā,** खाएको **khāko** or **khāyā,** भएको **bhāko** or **bhayā,** etc. Both forms of pronunciation are heard in normal speech. In more formal situations (broadcasts, public speeches, etc.) only the forms in **eko** are used. In the initial stages, the student would be advised to use the 'formal' pronunciation, but be prepared to hear and recognise the variants.

4. The First Perfect Participle is a verbal adjective, and to some extent is used like the English past participle 'done', 'having done'. In earlier lessons we have met a few examples of the 1st Perf. Part., which have been translated in English by an adjective or an adjectival phrase:

गएको महीना **gaeko mahīnā** last month ('the having-gone month')
नेपाल् नाउँ गरेको **nepāl nāū gareko** called Nepal ('having-done-the-name . . .')

Compare the following:

मेरो साइकल् बिग्रेको छ
My cycle is broken (**bigranu** 'to be broken, to break')

मलाई उमालेको पानी चाहियो
I want some boiled water (**umālnu** 'to boil liquids')

त्यो उम्लेको पानीमा हात् नहाल है । हात् पोल्छ
Don't put your hand in that boiling water. Your hand will be scalded

उम्लनु **umlanu** – the intransitive counterpart of उमाल्नु – means 'to come to the boil' (of liquids). Thus उम्लेको पानी 'the having-come-to-the-boil-water' i.e. 'boiling water' as opposed to उमालेको पानी **umāleko pānī** 'boiled water'.

अहिलेसम्म पानी उम्लेको छैन
The water is not boiling yet

उमालेको पानी पिउनुपर्छ
You should drink boiled water

Note that उसिन्नु **usinnu** means 'to boil food'. Thus उसिनेको फुल् **usineko phul** 'a boiled egg'.

मेरो पेट् दुखेको छ
My stomach is aching ('is in a position of having ached')

दुख्छ **dukhcha** (Simp. Indef.) means 'aches' (usually) or 'will ache':

अग्लो हिमाल्मा सधैं टाउको दुख्छ
In the high Himalayas your head always aches

मेरो टाउको दुखेको छ
My head is aching (now)

राम त्यहाँ बसेको छ
Ram is sitting ('is having-sat') there

The Simp. Indef. बस्छ would mean 'usually sits':

उ सधैं त्यो मेच्मा बस्छ
He always sits in that chair

The difference between बस्छ and बसेको छ is comparable to the difference between French *il s'assied* and *il est assis.*

पानी परेको छ
It is raining ('water is having-fallen')

पानी पर्छ would mean 'it rains' or 'it will rain'.

5. In written and often in spoken Nepali, gender and number are distinguished in the 1st Perf. Part. as with other adjectives:

M. Sing.	*F. Sing.*	*M. F. Plur.*
गरेको **gareko**	गरेकी **garekī**	गरेका **garekā**
आएको **āeko**	आएकी **āekī**	आएका **āekā** etc.

उसकी स्वास्नी पल्लो कोठामा सुतेकी थिई
His wife was sleeping (was having-slept) in the next room
तिनीहरू मन्दिरमा बसेका थिए
They were sitting in the temple
उनी पढ़े-लेखेका मान्छे हुन्
He is a well read man (MGH)

In the last example, पढ़े-लेखेका is plural agreeing with the MGH pronoun उनी . Note पढ़े–लिखेका **paṛhe-lekhekā** 'having read and written'. Here पढ़े- may be regarded as a reduced form of the participle. This form is used when two closely related verbs occur in idiomatic phrases. cf. भत्के-बिग्रेको **bhatke-bigreko** 'smashed', 'destroyed'. भत्कनु **bhatkanu** 'to be smashed' is a near synonym of बिग्रनु .

6. The 1st Perf. Part. may also take a subject. When this is the case, it may usually be translated by a relative ('who', 'which') clause in English. The subject of the participle of a transitive verb *always* takes -ले .

म आएको बेला
The time at which I came ('the I-having-come-time')
हिजो आएकी नोकर्नी
The servant-girl who came yesterday
हाम्रो घरमा बस्न आएका पाहुनाहरू
The guests who have come to stay in our house
मैले लेखेको किताब्
The book which I wrote ('the I-having-written book')
त्यसले गरेको काम्
The work which he did
तपाईंले भन्नुभएको कुरा
The thing which you said/What you said
तपाईंको घरमा आएका पाहुनाहरू कहिलेसम्म बस्छन् ?
How long ('till when') are the guests who have come to your house going to stay?
तपाईंले लेख्नुभएको चिठी मसँग छ
I have the letter which you wrote

सूर्य अस्ताएको बेलामा हवाईजहाज् आकाश्मा देखियो
The aeroplane appeared in the sky just as ('at the time when') the sun was setting
मैले तिम्रो चिठी गएको हप्ता पाएँ । जवाफ् ढीलो भएकोमा माफ् गर, तर आज्काल् मलाई एक् छिन् फुर्सत् छैन
I got your letter the other week. I am sorry to have been late in replying ('in the answer-having-been-late forgive me'), but I just don't have a minute's leisure these days

जवाफ् **javāph** 'answer' (the *v* is pronounced like English *w*)

7. In the following sentences, all involving expressions of time, the 1st Perf. Part. is translated by a temporal clause or phrase in English:

म नेपाल्मा आएको दुइ बर्ष भयो
I have been in Nepal for two years ('I-having-come-in Nepal, two years have happened')
तपाईं यहाँ आउनुभएको कति दिन् भयो ?
How long ('how many days') have you been here?
मैले उस्लाई भेटेको अस्ति जस्तो लाग्छ
It seems just like the other day that I met him.

8. The 1st Perf. Participle, followed by -ले or हुनाले **hunāle** is translated by a causal ('since', 'because') clause in English:

नेपाल्मा थोरै दिन् मात्रै बसेकोले, म काठ्माडौं खाल्डोबाट बाहिर गइनँ
Because I stayed only for a few days in Nepal, I did not go outside the Kathmandu valley
मसँग पैसा नभएको हुनाले, हिंड़ेरै जानुपर्‍यो
Since I had no money, I had to go on foot
पानी नपरेको हुनाले, बाली-नाली सब् नोक्सान् भयो
Because it did not rain, all the crops were destroyed
जमीन् सुक्खा भएकोले, पहिरो गयो
Because the ground was dry, there was a landslide

पहिरो **pahiro** (sometimes also written and pronounced पैरो **pəyro**) 'a landslide'. Note the expression पहिरो गयो 'a landslide went').
-ले and हुनाले may sometimes be omitted:

पानीमा गएको, मेरो लुगा सबै भिज्यो
Because I went out in the rain, all my clothes got wet

भिज्नु **bhijnu** 'to become wet'. Note that भिजेको **bhijeko** means 'wet', 'soaked'.

मेरो लुगा भिजेको रहेछ
Why, my clothes are wet through

9. In the following sentences, the 1st Perf. Part. is translated by a participle or adjectival phrase in apposition to a noun or pronoun:

> उस्ले गीत् गाएको मैले सुनें
> I heard him singing a song

गाउनु **gāunu** 'to sing'. Do not confuse गाएको **gāeko** with गएको **gaeko.**

> एउटा खाली टचाकसी आएको देखेर त्यस्लाई रोकें र त्यसैमा घर् आएँ
> Seeing an empty taxi coming, I stopped it and came home in that

त्यसैमा **tyasəymā** the emphatic form of त्यस्मा .

> उस्ले के भनेको मलाई थाहा छैन
> I don't know what he's saying
> वहाँले नेपालीमा भाषण् गर्नुभएको सुन्यौं
> We heard him giving a speech in Nepali

10. The Second Infinitive is used in conjunction with a number of verbs such as सक्नु **saknu** 'to be able', पाउनु **pāunu** 'to manage to', थाल्नु **thālnu** 'to begin to', छोड्नु **choṛnu** 'to give up/stop' and लाग्नु **lāgnu** 'to begin to/to be in the process of'.

(*a*) सक्नु and पाउनु

In most contexts both verbs may be translated 'to be able', 'can' etc. सक्नु , however, is used mostly in the sense of *being physically able* to do something, while पाउनु implies that *permission has been given* or that *conditions are favourable*. Thus म जान सक्छु means 'I can go' (i.e. am capable of going). म जान पाउँछु means 'I can go' (i.e. am allowed to go, nothing is stopping me from going, etc.).

When the infinitival verb is transitive and the tense of सक्नु or पाउनु is past (i.e. Simple Past or one of the other past tenses which will be introduced later), the postposition -ले is added to the subject of the verb.

> म जान सकें
> I was able to go
> मैले त्यो काम् गर्न सकिनँ
> I could not do that job
> म पस्न पाएँ
> I managed to enter
> मैले तिम्रो चिठी पढ्न पाइनँ
> I did not manage to read your letter
> माफ गर्नुहोस्, हाम्रो घर्मा पाहुनाहरू आएकोले म हिजो तपाईंकहाँ आउन पाइनँ
> I'm sorry, but since we had guests, I could not get along to see you yesterday
> तिमी पौडी खेल्न सक्छौ ? पौडी त खेल्न सक्तिन, तर घोड़ा चढ्न सक्छु
> Can you swim ('play swimming')? I cannot swim, but I can ride a horse

तिमीले लेखेको चिठी हराएको हुनाले, मैले पढ्न पाइनँ
Because I lost your letter, I couldn't read it
तपाईं नेपाली बोल्न सक्नुहुन्छ? सक्छु, राम्ररी बोल्न सक्छु
Can you speak Nepali? Yes, I can speak it fluently

The last sentence could also have been expressed: तपाईंलाई नेपाली आउँछ ? lit. 'does Nepali come to you?'

तपाईंलाई नेवारी आउँछ ? अलि अलि मात्रै आउँछ
Do you speak Newari? I only know a little

The impersonal I-Stem forms सकिन्छ **sakincha** and पाइन्छ **pāincha** are frequently used:

त्यो बाटोबाट जान सकिन्छ ? सकिन्छ, हजूर्
Is it possible to go by that road? Yes, sir
साँझ् पर्नु अगाडि पुग्न सकिंदैन
It will be impossible to arrive before nightfall
अलिकति चिया खान पाइन्छ ?
Is it possible to get a little tea to drink?
मोटर् खराब् भएकोले, बेलामा पुग्न सकिएन
Since the car went wrong, it was impossible to arrive on time

(*b*) थाल्नु and छोड्नु

The subject takes -ले when the infinitival verb is transitive and the main verb past. Occasionally -ले may be added to the subject even when the infinitival verb is intransitive:

म आजदेखि काम् गर्न थाल्छु
I'll start working from today
उस्ले अंग्रेजी सिक्न थाल्यो
He began to learn English
पानी पर्न थाल्यो
It started to rain
उ आफ्नो साथीको घर्मा जान छोड्यो
He stopped going to his friend's house
मैले चुरोट् खान छोड्नैपर्छ
I really must give up smoking

(*c*) लाग्नु

Only past tenses of लाग्नु are used with the Second Infinitive, in the sense of 'has begun to', 'is in the process of':

पानी पर्न लाग्यो
It came on to rain
उनी बोल्न लागे
He began to speak

ए भाइ, कता जान लाग्यौ ? म घर् जान लागें
Where are you off to (where have you begun to go)? I'm going home
म शहर् जान लागेको बेलामा मेरो साथी आइपुग्यो
As I was going to town, my friend arrived

आइपुग्नु **āipugnu** 'to arrive' – a compound of आउनु and पुग्नु

11. सकेसम्म **sakesamma** before adjectives and adverbs means 'as ... as possible'.

त्यो सकेसम्म छिटो दगुरेर आयो
He came running as quickly as possible
सकेसम्म छिटो चिया ल्याऊ
Bring the tea as quickly as you can
सकेसम्म बिस्तारै मोटर हाँक्नुहोस्
Drive the car as slowly as possible

Vocabulary 12

अझै	**ajhəy**	yet, so far
अनि	**ani**	and then
अर्थ	**artha**	meaning
अन्नपूर्णा	**annapūrṇā**	Annapurna
अलिकति	**alikati**	a little
अहिलेसम्म	**ahilesamma**	till now, still
आइपुग्नु	**āipugnu**	to arrive
उँचाई	**ūcāī**	height, altitude
उत्पति	**utpati**	source, origin
उत्पन्न हुनु	**utpanna hunu**	to originate, to rise
उपमहाद्वीप	**upamahādvīp**	subcontinent
उमाल्नु	**umālnu**	to boil (trans.)
उम्लनु	**umlanu**	to boil (intrans.)
उसिन्नु	**usinnu**	to boil (of food)
औषधि	**əwṣadhi**	medicine
करीब्	**karīb**	about, approximately
खराब्	**kharāb**	spoilt, bad
खाल्डो	**khālḍo**	valley
खोज्नु	**khojnu**	to seek, look for
गंगा	**gaŋgā**	Ganges
गाउनु	**gāunu**	to sing
गीत्	**gīt**	song
घोड़ा	**ghoṛā**	horse
घोड़ा चढ़नु	**ghoṛā caṛhnu**	to ride ('mount') a horse
छुट्ट्याउनु	**chuṭṭyāunu**	to separate
जमुना (यमुना)	**jamunā (yamunā)**	Jamuna (river)

जवाफ्	**javāph**	answer
ज्योति	**jyoti**	flame, light
झैं	**jhəỹ**	like, as if, just as
टाकुरो	**ṭākuro**	peak (of mountain)
डाँड़ो	**ḍā̃ṛo**	ridge, crest
ढाकिनु	**ḍhākinu**	to be covered
तट्	**taṭ**	bottom, bank, level
त्यसो भए	**tyaso bhae**	in that case
दगुर्नु	**dagurnu**	to run
दुख्नु	**dukhnu**	to ache
दृश्य	**dɹʃya**	view
देखाउनु	**dekhāunu**	to show
धौलागिरि	**dhəwlāgiri**	Dhaulagiri
नगर्कोट्	**nagarkoṭ**	Nagarkot (a ridge in Kathmandu valley)
नदी	**nadī**	river
नेवारी	**nevārī**	Newari (language spoken in Nepal)
नोकर्नी	**nokarnī**	servant girl
न्यानो	**nyāno**	warm, cosy
पग्लनु	**paglanu**	to melt
पढ़े-लेखेको	**paṛhe-lekheko**	well-read, educated
पनि...पनि	**pani . . . pani**	both . . . and
पहिरो (पैरो)	**pahiro (pəyro)**	landslide
पहेंलो	**pahẽlo**	yellow
पेट्	**peṭ**	stomach
पोल्नु	**polnu**	to be burnt, scalded
पौड़ी खेल्नु	**pəwṛī khelnu**	to swim
फरक्	**pharak**	difference
फुट्	**phuṭ**	foot (measure)
फुर्सत् (फुर्सद्)	**phursat (phursad)**	leisure
बढ़ी	**baṛhī**	more (than), greater
बन्नु	**bannu**	to be made
बाली-नाली	**bālī-nālī**	crops
बिग्रनु	**bigranu**	to be broken
ब्रह्मपुत्र	**brahmaputra**	Brahmaputra
बोलाई	**bolāī**	the spoken language
भत्कनु	**bhatkanu**	to smash
भाषा	**bhāṣā**	language
भिज्नु	**bhijnu**	to be soaked
मकालु	**makālu**	Makalu (mountain in Himalayas)
मत्लब्	**matlab**	meaning
मध्ये	**madhye**	midst, middle

मनोहर्	**manohar**	charming
यसो	**yaso**	like this, in this way
यस्तो	**yasto**	such (as this)
रोक्नु	**roknu**	to stop (trans.)
रोकिनु	**rokinu**	to be stopped
विदेशी	**videʃi**	foreigner
शिखर्	**ʃikhar**	peak (of mountain)
शेर्पा	**ʃerpa**	Sherpa
सकेसम्म	**sakesamma**	as . . . as possible
सक्नु	**saknu**	to be able
सफर्	**saphar**	journey
समुद्र	**samudra**	sea
साँझ-सवेरै	**sā̃jh savere**	evening and morning
साधारण्	**sādhāraṇ**	ordinary
सिक्नु	**siknu**	to learn
सिंधु	**sindhu**	Indus (river)
सीमाना	**sīmānā**	frontier
सुन्	**sun**	gold
सुन्ले बनेको	**sunle baneko**	made of gold, golden
सेतो	**seto**	white
हराउनु	**harāunu**	to lose
हिमाल्	**himāl**	mountain (esp. in Himalayas)

Reading Passage

नेपाल् र हिमालय

संस्कृत् भाषामा 'हिम्' को अर्थ हिउँ र 'आलय' को अर्थ घर् हो । त्यसै कारण् भारतीय उपमहाद्वीप्को उत्तर्मा रहेका पहाड्हरूलाई हिमालय भनिएको हो[1]। हिमालयका सब्भन्दा अग्ला शिखरहरू सगर्माथा, मकालु, अन्नपूर्णा, र धौलागिरि हुन् । यी हिमाल्हरूले नेपाल् र भोट्को सीमाना छुट्टयाउँछन्। यी मध्येको[2] सब्भन्दा अग्लो हिमाल् सगर्माथा हो । यस्को उँचाई समुद्रको तट्बाट[3] उनन्तीस् हजार् फुट्भन्दा बढ़ी छ। समुद्रको तट्बाट धेरै नै माथि भएकोले यी हिमाल्का टाकुराहरू सधैं नै हिउँले ढाकिएका हुन्छन्।[4] गर्मीमा त्यहाँको हिउँ पग्लेर, नदीहरूको उत्पति हुन्छ । गंगा, जमुना, ब्रह्मपुत्र सिंधु र अरू ठूला ठूला नदीहरू यहींबाट उत्पन्न हुन्छन्। काठमाड़ौं खाल्डोमा नगर्कोट् नाउँ गरेको डाँड़ोबाट हिमाल्का टाकुराहरू राम्ररी हेर्न सकिन्छ । त्यहाँबाट साँझ्-सवेरै अत्यन्त मनोहर् दृश्य देखिन्छ। पहेंलो घाम्को ज्योति सेतो हिउँमा परेको बेलामा ती हिमाल्हरू सुन्ले बनेका झैं देखिन्छन् ।[5] यस्तो दृश्य हेर्नलाई टाढ़ा टाढ़ाबाट विदेशी पर्यटक्हरू त्यहाँ जान्छन् । तर सगर्माथा राम्ररी हेर्नलाईचाहिं नाम्चे बजार्तिर जानुपर्छ । नाम्चे

बजार् नेपाल्का शेर्पाहरूको सब्भन्दा ठूलो गाउँ हो । यो गाउँ काठ्माडौंबाट करीब्[7]एक् सय् मील् टाढ़ा छ । नाम्चे बजार् नजीकैको लुक्ला भन्ने[8] ठाउँसम्म काठ्माडौंबाट सान्साना हवाईजहाज्हरू जान्छन् । तर यसरी हवाईजहाज्मा जान धेरै नै महँगो पर्छ । साधारण् मानिस्हरूलेचाहिं पैदलै सफर् गर्नुपर्छ[9] ।

पश्चिम् नेपाल्मा पोखरा नाउँ गरेको अर्को एउटा सानो तर अत्यन्त सुन्दर् शहर् छ । यो शहर् अन्नपूर्णा र धौलागिरिको काख्मा छ । यस्को उँचाई समुद्रको तट्बाट २००० फुट् मात्रै भएको हुनाले जाड़ोमा पनि यहाँ न्यानो[10] हुन्छ, र दिन्दिनै हिउँले ढाकिएका हिमाल्हरूका टाकुराहरू हेर्न पर्यटक्हरू आउँछन् ।

Notes

1. **rahekā . . . bhanieko ho**: 'the mountains having-remained in the north of the subcontinent are called'.
2. **yī madhyeko**: 'among them . . .'
3. **samudrako taṭ**; 'sea level'.
4. **hiũle ḍhākiekā**: 'covered with snow'. Note the use of **-le.**
5. **pahēlo . . . belāmā**: 'at the time of the light of the yellow sunshine having fallen on the white snow'.
6. **sunle . . . dekhinchan**: 'are seen as if having-been-made-of-gold', i.e. 'seem to be made of gold'.
7. **karīb**: 'about', 'almost'. **ek say mīl jati** would mean the same thing.
8. Lukla is a small landing strip situated at about 10,000 feet near Namche Bazar, the principal Sherpa village of the area.
   bhanne: 'by name' (cf. Reading Passage 7).
9. **mānis**: 'a man', in the sense of a human being.
10. **nyāno** (also **nyānho**): 'warm and comfortable'.

Exercise 12a

Translate into English

१. तपाईं नेपाल् आउनुभएको कति दिन् भयो ? म यहाँ आएको तीन् हप्ता मात्रै भयो ।
२. पानी परेको बेलामा, बर्सादी नलिईकन बाहिर गयौ भने रुघा लाग्छ ।
३ तराईमा बिराट्नगर् नाउँ गरेको एउटा सानो औद्योगिक् शहर् छ ।
४. चियाको पानी अझै उम्लेको छैन । पाँच् मिनेट् पर्खनुहोस् अनि म लिएर आउँछु ।
५. पेट् दुखेको बेलामा औषधि खानैपर्छ ।
६. हिजो पानी परेको हुनाले म तपाईंकहाँ आउन पाइनँ । आज म आउन सक्छु ?
७. म भोलि तिमीलाई भेट्न आउन सक्तिन । घर्मा अलि काम् छ नि ।
८. ए भाइ, कता जान लाग्यौ ? म खेत्मा काम् गर्न जान लागें, हजूर् ।
९. म लन्दन् आएको अस्ति जस्तो लाग्छ। यहाँ मलाई धेरै राम्रो लाग्यो ।
१०. हामीहरू सकेसम्म छिटो हिंड्यौं तर साँझ पर्नु अगाड़ी घर् पुग्न सकिएन।

११. वहाँ नेपाल् आउनुभएको धेरै भयो । वहाँलाई नेपाली पनि आउँछ, नेवारी पनि ।
१२. पोहोर् साल् पानी नपरेकोले बाली–नाली सबै नाश् भयो ।
१३. मेरो चश्मा हराएको जस्तो लाग्छ । पल्लो कोठामा छ कि खोज त ।
१४. नेपाली समाचार्पत्र पढ्न अलि गाह्रो हुन्छ । बोलाई र लेखाईको भाषामा धेरै नै फरक् छ, होइन त ?
१५. ए दिदी, मलाई तिर्खा लाग्यो । अलिकति पानी खान पाइन्छ कि ?
१६. उस्ले नेपाली सिक्न थालेको छ महीना भयो रे ।
१७. उस्ले भनेको मैले त बुझिनँ । तपाईं बुझ्न सक्नुहुन्छ कि ?
१८. नाम्चे बजार्को उँचाई समुद्रको तट्बाट एघार हजार् फुट् भएको हुनाले जाड़ो महीनामा त्यहाँ धेरै हिउँ पर्छ ।

Exercise 12b

Translate into Nepali

1. How long have you been in London? I have been here for two years.
2. Because it did not rain last year, the people in ('of') the villages cannot get anything to eat.
3. Kathmandu is four thousand five hundred feet above sea-level.
4. Because the ridge of Nagarkot is so high, you can see many Himalayan peaks from there. Both morning and evening, you get the most exquisite views.
5. The shopkeeper charged ('took') a hundred and twenty rupees for this woollen coat. That was far too much, you know.
6. It took me six months to learn Nepali, but I still find it difficult to understand the newspaper. There are so many Sanskrit words used.
7. These days, small aeroplanes go to Lukla. From there you have to go on foot to Namche Bazar. But ordinary people have to walk from Kathmandu.
8. The big rivers of the Indian subcontinent all rise from the Himalayas.
9. Where are you going? I'm going to cut some firewood.
10. If you walk quickly, you will reach the village before three o'clock.
11. I have lived in Nepal for many years, but I cannot speak Newari. It is a very difficult language, you know.
12. Because we had guests in our house, I could not come to see you. Will it be all right if I come tonight?
13. Waiter, bring some tea. There is no tea, sir. The water has not boiled yet.
14. I feel hungry. Can I get anything to eat here?
15. He can speak Nepali very well. But because there are so many Sanskrit words used in the written language, he says he cannot understand the newspaper.

Exercise 12c

Translate into English

आउनुभन्दा अगाड़ी ; त्यो काम् त सिद्धियो ; भित्र आउन हुन्छ ?
भोलि भेटौंला; सिनेमा हेर्न मन् लाग्छ; यो किताब् मलाई मन् परेन;

उ जहिले पनि ताश् खेल्छ; उ पाँच् वर्ष पुग्यो क्यारे? यता आऊ; यहाँ बास् पाइन्छ ?
पँखा खोल है; ल, भैगो, त्यतिमै दिन्छु; यो कपड़ा गज्को कति ? पहिरो गयो.

Exercise 12d

Translate into Nepali

a boiled egg; about two hundred miles; can you ride a horse? as quickly as possible; it is raining; the village was destroyed; he arrived the other day; he was sitting in the room; my head aches; the village called Lukla; cities like Rangoon and Calcutta; waiter, bring (MGH) some tea; I'll wash my hands and face before going out; compared to Delhi, the capital of Nepal is small.

LESSON 13

1. *New conjunct consonants*

क्ट	**kṭ**	as in	डाक्टर्	**ḍākṭar**	doctor
ड़्ब	**ṛb**	as in	गड़्बड़्	**gaṛbaṛ**	disorder
ण्ड	**ṇḍ**	as in	झण्डै	**jhaṇḍəy**	almost

2. The First Perfect Tense consists of the First Perfect Participle followed by some part of the verb छ which acts as an auxiliary. The subject of a transitive verb always takes -ले .

म आएको छु	**ma āeko chu**	I have come
उस्ले गरेको छ	**usle gareko cha**	he/she has done

In written and frequently in spoken Nepali, gender and number are indicated by the participle (Lesson 12.5). However, the feminine forms of the auxiliary (छे,छिन्) are not commonly used.

MGH 3rd person pronouns require plural concord.

मेरी बहिनी आएकी छ
My little sister has come

हाम्रो घर्मा पाहुनाहरू आएका छन्
Guests have come to our house

उन्ले देखेका छैनन्
He/she has not seen

The HGH forms consist of the HGH First Perfect Participle followed by the auxiliary छ (affirm.), छैन् (neg.). Gender and number are not indicated in the participle:

तपाईं जानुभएको छ	**tapāı̃ jānubhaeko cha**
मेरी दिदीले भन्नुभएको छ	**merī didīle bhannubhaeko cha**
वहाँहरूले हेर्नुभएको छैन	**vahā̃harūle hernubhaeko chəyna**

3. In the following table, the First Perfect Tense of गर्नु is set out in full:

	Pronoun	Affirmative	Negative
M. sing.	मैले	गरेको छु	गरेको छैन
	तैंले	गरेको छस्	गरेको छैनस्
	उस्ले	गरेको छ	गरेको छैन

M. F. Pl.	हामी (हरू) ले	गरेका छौं	गरेका छैनौं
	तिमी (हरू) ले	गरेका छौ	गरेका छैनौ
	उनीहरूले	गरेका छन्	गरेका छैनन्
F. Sing.	मैले	गरेकी छु	गरेकी छैन
	तैंले	गरेकी छस्	गरेकी छैनस्
	उसले	गरेकी छ	गरेकी छैन
MGH	उन् / यिन / तिन } ले	गरेका छन्	गरेका छैनन्
HGH	तपाईं (हरू) / वहाँ (हरू) } ले	गर्नुभएको छ	गर्नुभएको छैन

Note that ले is not added to the subject of an intransitive verb. Thus:
म आएको छु त्यो गएको छैन   हामी भएका छौं   तिनीहरू बसेका छैनन्

4. *Spoken forms*

In spoken Nepali, feminine and plural forms of the First Perfect Tense are used, but with no great consistency. Many speakers ignore the distinctions and use only the masculine singular form of the participle, regardless of the gender and number of the subject. Thus the following examples might be heard in the speech of many people:

मेरो बहिनी आएको छ	**mero bahinī āeko cha**
पाहुनाहरू आएको छ (न्)	**pāhunāharū āeko cha(n)**
उनीहरूले गरेको छ (न्)	**unīharūle gareko cha(n)**

The participle may also be pronounced as described in Lesson 12.3.

म आएको छु	**ma āyā** or **āko chu**
उसले गरेको छैन	**usle garyā chəyna**
तिमी गएको छौ	**timī gāko chəw**

In radio broadcasts, speeches and other formal contexts, the participle is pronounced as it is written (i.e. **ma āeko chu** rather than **ma āyā chu**) and this is often the case in less formal speech also. In the first stages, you would do well to use the standard (written) pronunciation which will be acceptable at all times.

5. The First Perfect Tense in many cases corresponds to the English perfect tense 'I have come', 'you have done' etc. and denotes a present state resulting from a past action. In the following examples, alternative forms are given in brackets.

अझ हाम्रा (हाम्रो) पाहुनाहरू आएका (आएको) छैनन्
So far our guests have not arrived

त्यस्लाई मैले चिनी किन्न पठाएको एक् घण्टा भयो तर अहिलेसम्म फर्केको छैन
I sent him to buy some sugar an hour ago, but he has not returned yet

Note that अझ **ajha** and अहिलेसम्म **ahilesamma** both mean 'yet', 'still'.

तपाईं कहिले भारत् जानुभएको छ ? अहँ । गएको छैन
Have you ever been ('gone') to India? No, I haven't

In questions of this type कहिले is translated 'ever'.

अ. तिमीले खोजेको किताब् पायौ ?
आ. अहँ । पाइनँ । तिमीले देखेको छौ ?
A. Did you find the book you were looking for?
B. No, I did not. Have you seen it?

मेरी बहिनीले भात् पकाएकी छैन
My little sister has not cooked the dinner

6. In short questions – usually containing interrogative adverbs like किन, कहाँ, कहिले, कता, को, कुन् etc., and in statements in which the adverb झण्डै **jhaṇḍəy** 'almost' is used, the First Perfect Participle may be used instead of a main verb:

तिमी कहाँबाट आएको ?
Where have you come from?

मकहाँ यतिका दिन्सम्म किन नआएको ?
Why haven't you been to see me for so long?

यतिका दिन्सम्म **yatikā dinsamma** 'up to so many days'

अस्तिको बिहिबार् आउन सक्तिन भनेर मलाई किन नभनेको ?
Why did you not tell me you could not come last Thursday?

ए बाबू, कता हिंड़ेको ?
Hey, boy. Where are you off to ('to where having set out?')?

उ चिसोले झण्डै मरेको ।
He almost died of the cold

त्यो कुकुरनजीक् नजाऊ है । हिजो त्यस्ले मलाई झण्डै टोकेको
Don't go near that dog. He almost bit me yesterday

टोक्नु **ṭoknu** 'to bite'

मोटरले केटीलाई झण्डै कुल्चेको
The car almost knocked the girl down

7. The First Perfect Participle, followed by त or तर may be translated by a concessive ('although') clause in English:

मैले उस्‌लाई भनेको तर मानेन
Although I told him, he did not obey ('I having told . . . but . . .')

मान्नु **mānnu** 'to obey', 'listen to', 'agree with'

मोल् घटाउन खोजेको त उस्‌ले मानेन
Although I tried to bring the price down, he would not agree

घटाउनु **ghaṭāunu** 'to make less'

भोलिपल्ट त्यहाँ जान ट्याक्सी खोजेको तर ड्राइभरहरूले बाटो राम्रो छैन भनेर जान मन् गरेनन्
The next day I looked for a taxi to go there but the taxi-drivers said that the road was not good and refused

(गर्न) मन् गर्नु **(garna) man garnu** 'to be willing to (do)'

मैले त्यस्‌लाई बाह्र बजे भेट्छु भनेको त फुर्सतै पाइनँ
I said I would meet him (I intended to meet him) at twelve, but I couldn't find the time

Note that 'to intend to', 'to mean to' etc. can often be translated by भन्नु . Thus, 'I intended to go but I did not' is rendered in Nepali as: म जान्छु भनेको त गइनँ .

8. The First Pluperfect Tense consists of the First Perfect Participle and some part of थियो which acts as an auxiliary. The subject of a transitive verb always takes -ले . Gender and number are distinguished in the participle (as with the First Perfect Tense) *and* in the auxiliary. Thus:

म गएको थिएँ	**ma gaeko thiẽ**
उ गएको थियो	**u gaeko thiyo**
उस्‌ले देखेको थिएन	**usle dekheko thiena**
हामीले गरेका थियौं	**hāmīle garekā thiyə̃w**
मेरी बहिनीले हेरेकी थिई	**merī bahinīle herekī thiī**
तपाईंले भन्नुभएको थियो	**tapāīle bhannubhaeko thiyo,** etc.

The same considerations for the distinction of gender and number and the alternative pronunciation of the participle apply to the Pluperfect as to the Perfect, discussed above. In speech, therefore, we often encounter forms such as:

उनीहरू गएको थियो (थिए)	**unīharū gaeko thiyo (*or* thie)**
मेरी बहिनीले गरेको थियो	**merī bahinīle gareko thiyo**
पाहुनाहरू आएको थियो (थिए)	**pāhunāharū āeko thiyo (*or* thie),** etc.

9. The First Pluperfect Tense often corresponds to the English pluperfect 'I had done', 'we had gone', etc.

त्यस्भन्दा अघि मैले काठ्माडौंमा कहिले बस्मा चढेको थिइनँ
Before that, I had never got into a bus in Kathmandu
उनी भर्खर् पहाड्बाट राज्धानीमा आइपुगेका थिए
He had just arrived in the capital from the hills
धेरै सन्तान् भएको हुनाले बल्बीर खत्रीले धेरै धन् कमाउन सकेको थिएन
Because he had so many children, Balbir Khatri had not been able to earn a large fortune

10. In many cases, however, the First Pluperfect Tense may be used in place of the Simple Past Tense, meaning 'I did', 'we came' etc. This is often so when the event referred to took place in the recent past or when the actual time is specified:

गएको हप्ता मैले एउटा राम्रो सिनेमा हेरेको थिएँ
Last week I saw a very good film
भानुभक्त आचार्यको जन्म पश्चिम् नेपाल्को एउटा सानो गाउँमा भएको थियो
Bhanubhakta Acharya was born in a small village in West Nepal ('B's birth came about')[1]
म लन्दन्मा जन्मेको थिएँ तर हिजोआज म फ्रान्स्मा बस्छु ।
I was born in London, but now I live in France
हिजो म तिमीकहाँ आएको थिएँ तर तिमी घर्मा थिएनौ
I came to see you yesterday, but you were not at home

11. With certain verbs and verbal expressions such as जान्नु **jānnu** 'to know (a fact)', चिन्नु **cinnu** 'to know (a person)', मन् लाग्नु **man lāgnu** 'to want to', मन् पर्नु 'to like' etc., the First Perfect Tense is used where the present tense would be used in English. The past of such expressions is made by the First Pluperfect Tense:

तिमीले घोडा चढ्न जानेको छौ ?
Do you know how to ride ('mount') a horse?

गर्न जान्नु, **garna jānnu** 'to know how to'

मेरो छोराले अंग्रेजी जानेको छ
My son knows English
तपाईंले नेपाली जान्नुभएको छ ?
Do you know Nepali?
तपाईंले प्रधान्ज्यूलाई चिन्नुभएको छ ?
Do you know Mr. Pradhan?

Occasionally the Simple Indefinite may also be used in such sentences, so that तपाईं......चिन्नुहुन्छ ? would also be possible.

[1]Bhānubhakta Ācharya – the famous nineteenth-century Nepali poet.

म काठ्माडौँमा दुइ महीना बस्छु होला । त्यस्पछि म पूर्बतिर जान्छु । त्यहाँ अलि दिन् घुम्न मन् लागेको छ
I shall probably stay in Kathmandu for about two months. After that I shall go to the east. I want to travel there for a little while

मन् लागेको छ **man lāgeko cha** 'I want to' ('at this particular time')
मन् लाग्छ **man lāgcha** would imply 'I usually want to'

हिजो पौडी खेल्न मन् लागेको थियो
Yesterday I wanted to go swimming
यो नयाँ उपन्यास् मन् परेको छ कि छैन ?
Do you like this new novel?
वहाँले लेख्नुभएको किताब् मलाई मन् परेको थिएन
I did not like the book he has written

Similarly, the First Perfect Tense of लाग्नु 'to begin to' and पर्नु 'must' (discussed in Lessons 11 and 12) is used to refer to a particular instance in present time. The First Pluperfect refers to a particular instance in the past:

म पनि उत्तै जान लागेको छु
I am also going ('I have begun to go') in that direction
उ सिनेमा हेर्न जान लागेको थियो
He was going to see a film
मलाई त अलि धेरै नै माल्ताल् किन्नुपरेको छ, साहूजी
I need to buy quite a lot of things (at this moment)
गएको हप्ता मलाई दिल्ली जानुपरेको थियो
Last week I had to go to Delhi

12. A variant form of the First Perfect Tense exists in which the auxiliary is हो rather than छ . 1st and 3rd person forms are those most commonly encountered:

मैले गरेको हुँ **məyle gareko hū**
उस्ले गरेको हो **usle gareko ho**
उनीहरूले गरेका हुन् **unīharūle garekā hun,** etc.

The two forms of the First Perfect Tense differ from each other in respect of emphasis.

मैले गरेको हुँ may be translated 'I am the one who did'
मैले गरेको छु is simply 'I have done'

मैले यो तस्वीर् खिंचेको हुँ
I am the one who painted this picture
यो मान्छे पहाड्बाट आएको हो
This is the man who has come from the hills
उस्ले यो काम् आफैले गरेको हो भन्छ
He says he did this by himself

आफै **āphəy** (the emphatic form of the reflexive pronoun आफू **āphū**) 'self', 'oneself'.

13. The Second Infinitive is used with the verbs खोज्नु **khojnu** 'to seek to/to try to', बिर्सनु **birsanu** 'to forget to' सम्झाउनु **samjhāunu** 'to remind to' लाउनु **lāunu** 'to force to'.

> उसले भनेको कुरा मैले बुझ्न खोजें, तर बुझ्न सकिनँ
> I tried to understand what he said, but I was unable to do so
> माफ् गर्नुहोला तर मैले तपाईंको चिठी खसाल्न बिर्सेको थिएँ
> I am sorry but I forgot to post your letter
> यसो गर्न नबिर्स है
> Don't forget to do it this way

Note that 'to remember' is often expressed as नबिर्सनु 'not to forget'.

> नबिर्सीकन गर है
> Be sure you remember to do it ('not having forgotten, do . . .')
> मैले उसलाई भीजा लिन सम्झाएको थिएँ
> I reminded him to get a visa
> आफ्नैलागि मात्रै साथीहरूलाई धेरै पैसा खर्च गर्न लाउन त भएन
> It is not right to force one's friends to spend a lot of money on oneself

आफ्नैलागि **āphnəy lāgi** 'for oneself'. आफ्नै is the emphatic form of आफ्नु.
गर्न त भएन **(garna) to bhaena** 'it is not right to (do)'

14. The numerals from 50-70 should be learnt at this stage. Remember that all numerals require appropriate classifiers:

पचपन्नजना मान्छे	fifty-five men
साठीवटा घर्	sixty houses
सत्तरी दिन्	seventy days, etc.

Vocabulary 13

अझ (अझै)	**ajha** (emph. **ajhəy**)	still, yet
अहँ	**ahā**	no
आफू (आफै)	**āphū** (emph. **āphəy**)	self, oneself
एक् न एक् दिन्	**ek na ek din**	one of these days
औलो	**əwlo**	malaria
औषधि	**əwṣadhi**	medicine, drugs
औषधि लेखिदिनु	**əwṣadhi lekhidinu**	to write a prescription
कम्	**kam**	less
कुकुर्	**kukur**	dog
कुखुरा	**kukhurā**	chicken
कुल्चनु	**kulcanu**	to knock down, trample
कुह्रनु (कुर्नु)	**kuhrnu (kurnu)**	to wait for

खसाल्नु	**khasālnu**	to post (a letter)
खिंच्नु	**khīcnu**	to draw, to pull
खोज्नु	**khojnu**	to seek, to try
खै	**khəy**	well, why, oh
गड्बड्	**gaṛbaṛ**	disorder[1]
घटाउनु	**ghaṭāunu**	to decrease, make less
घर्-बार्	**ghar-bār**	household, family
घर्-बार् बसाल्नु	**ghar-bār basālnu**	to start a family
जन्म	**janma**	birth
जन्मनु (जन्मिनु)	**janmanu (janminu)**	to be born
जरो	**jaro**	fever
जाँच्	**jā̃c**	examination
जाँच्नु	**jā̃cnu**	to examine
जाँचिहाल्नु	**jā̃cihālnu**	to examine (thoroughly)[2]
जान्नु	**jānnu**	to know (a fact)
जिभ्रो	**jibhro**	tongue
झण्डै	**jhaṇḍəy**	almost
टोक्नु	**ṭoknu**	to bite, sting
डाक्टर्	**ḍākṭar**	doctor
ड्राइभर्	**ḍrāibhar**	driver
तस्वीर्	**tasvīr**	picture, photograph
तस्वीर् खिंच्नु	**tasvīr khīcnu**	to draw a picture, to take a photo
तिर्नु	**tirnu**	to pay
थोक्	**thok**	thing, matter
दिसा	**disā**	diarrhoea
देखाउनु	**dekhāunu**	to show
धरान्	**dharān**	Dharan (town in East Nepal)
पकाउनु	**pakāunu**	to cook
पठाइदिनु	**paṭhāidinu**	to send for
फाइदा भयो	**phāidā bhayo**	got better, recovered
बनाउनु	**banāunu**	to make
भइहाल्यो	**bhaihālyo**	all right, don't mention it
-भन्दा बढ़ी	**-bhandā baṛhī**	greater than
भानुभक्त आचार्य	**bhānubhakta ācārya**	Bhanubhakta Acharya (famous nineteenth-century Nepali poet)
मन् गर्नु	**man garnu**	to be keen on
मान्नु	**mānnu**	to agree, obey
मोल्	**mol**	price
राम्ररी	**rāmrarī**	well, happily

[1]Note the phrase **peṭ gaṛbaṛ cha** 'my stomach is upset'.
[2]A compound verb, slightly more emphatic than **jācnu.**

लाउनु	**lāunu**	to cause to, to put on clothes, to shut
लेखिदिनु	**lekhidinu**	to write out
सम्झाउनु	**samjhāunu**	to remind
सन्तान्	**santān**	offspring, children
सफा	**saphā**	clean
समय्	**samay**	time, period
साबुन्	**sābun**	soap
हेरबिचार् गर्नु	**herbicār garnu**	to look after (oneself)

Reading Passage

डाक्टर्कहाँ

अ. नमस्कार्, डाक्टर् साहेब् । म आउन हुन्छ ?

आ. नमस्कार् । आउनुहोस् । बस्नुहोस् । तपाईंलाई के भयो, भन्नुहोस् ।[1]

अ. खै, दुइ तीन् दिन्देखि सन्चो छैन । मलाई जरो आएको जस्तो छ,[2] टाउको दुख्छ र केही खान सकेको छैन ।

आ. दिसा पनि लागेको छ ?

अ. दिसा त लागेको छैन, तर पेट् अलि गड्बड् छ ।

आ. खै त एक् फेरा जाँचूँ ?[3] जिभ्रो देखाउनुहोस् त । पेट् पनि दुख्छ ?

अ. अलि अलि दुख्छ । धेरै होइन ।

आ. तपाईं यहाँ खाना कहाँ खानुहुन्छ ?

अ. म त धेरैजसो शहर्को होटेल्हरूमा खान्छु, तर सफा ठाउँमा जान खोज्छु । यस्भन्दा अघि त केही पनि भएको छैन ।[4]

आ. पानी उमालेर पिउनुहुन्छ कि ?

अ. कहिले कहीं त उमालेको पानी खान्छु तर साथीहरूकहाँ गएको बेलामा त्यसो गर्न सकिंदैन नि ।[5] उनीहरूलाई आफ्नैलागि मात्रै पानी उमाल्न लाउन त भएन ।

आ. त्यो त हो, तर सकेसम्म सधैं उमालेको पानी पिउने गर्नुहोस् न ।[6] शहरको पानी उस्तो राम्रो छैन, र हामी नेपालीहरूको पनि कहिले कहीं पेट् खराब् हुन्छ । तपाईंलाई अरू थोक् त केही पनि भएको छ जस्तो छैन । म औषधि लेखिदिन्छु । बजार्मा किन्नुहोस् । पेट् दुखेको कम् भएन भने मकहाँ फेरि आउनुहोस् । म अस्पताल् पठाइदिन्छु ।[7] जरो त अलि अलि मात्रै छ । भोलि एक् दिन् आराम् गर्नुभयो भने कम् हुन्छ होला । अनि पानीचाहिं उमालेर खान नबिर्सनुहोस् ।

अ. धन्यवाद्, डाक्टर् साहेब् । कति तिर्ने त ?[8]

आ. ठीक् छ । भइहाल्यो । राम्रोसित हेर्बिचार् गर्नुहोला है ।

Notes

1. **tapāīlāī ke bhayo?** 'what has happened to you?', 'what's the matter with you?'
2. **malāi jaro āeko jasto cha**: 'I seem to have got a temperature.' Note the expression **jaro āunu** 'to have a fever'.
3. **ek pherā jācū?** 'let me have a look at you'. **jācū** – 1st sing. injunctive. cf. **ma jāū** 'let me go'.
4. **yasbhandā aghi**: 'before/prior to this'.

5. **tyaso garna sakīdəyna ni**: 'it is not always possible to do thus'.
6. **sakesamma sadhəỹ**: 'as often as possible'.
   piune garnuhos: 'keep on drinking'. The construction is discussed in Lesson 15.
7. **aspatāl paṭhāidinchu**: 'I'll send you to hospital'. **paṭhāidinu** (a compound of **paṭhāunu** and **dinu**) is rather more emphatic than the simple verb.
8. **kati tirne ta?** 'how much do I owe you?'

Exercise 13a

Translate into English

१. पानी परेको छ । छाता लान नबिर्स है ।
२. तपाईं कुन् देश्बाट आउनुभएको हजूर् ? म अंग्रेज् हुँ
३. तपाईं त नेपाली राम्रै बोल्नुहुन्छ । कहाँ सिक्नुभएको ? यहाँ आउनु अगाड़ी मैले बेलायत्बाट सिकेर् आएको ।
४. मेरो साथी निक्कै बिरामी परेको थियो । तर अहिले फाइदा भएको छ ।
५. एक् घण्टाभन्दा बढ़ी मैले तिमीलाई कुहें। तिमीले यति ढीलो किन गरेको ?
६. हाम्रो नोकर् दार्जीलिङ्मा जन्मेको थियो तर काठ्माड़ौंमा उस्ले धेरै समय् बिताएको छ ।
७. यो कुरा मलाई किन नसुनाएको त तिमीले ?
८. पोहोर् साल् मदेस् गईकन त्यो सिकिस्त बिरामी परेको थियो । औलोले झण्डै मरेको ।
९. भोलि बिहान उठेर म शहर् जाँदै छु । त्यहाँ मलाई धेरै नै सामान् किन्नुपरेको छ ।
१०. तपाईंको जन्म कहाँ भएको थियो ? म धरान्मा जन्मेको थिएँ । तर सानोमा म काठ्माड़ौं बस्न आएँ । यहीं बसेको बीस् बर्ष भयो ।
११. हामीहरू माथिको गाउँसम्म जान खोजेको तर बाटो नराम्रो भएको हुनाले फर्कनुपरेको थियो।
१२. म हिजो पौड़ी खेल्न गएको त झण्डै रुघा लाग्यो।
१३. म एक् न एक् दिन् बिहा त गर्छु तर अहिले नै घर्-बार् बसाल्न मन् लागेको छैन ।
१४. शहर् गएको बेलामा आफ्नो साथीसँग भेटेको थिएँ।
१५. तपाईं कहिले भारत् जानुभएको छ ? अहिलेसम्म त गएको छैन तर जान मन् लागेको छ ।

Exercise 13b

Translate into Nepali

1. Have you ever been to London? Yes, I was there six months ago.
2. I waited for him for over an hour, but he did not come. Therefore, I came by myself.
3. I tried to get a visa, but they said that foreigners were not allowed to go to Bhūṭān. Because it is on the borders of China, it is very difficult to get there.
4. He says he built this house all by himself.
5. I did not understand what your friend was saying. He doesn't speak Nepali very well, does he?
6. I'm sorry but I forgot to telephone you last night.
7. Do you know the man who has just arrived in our village?
8. How long have you been in Nepal? I haven't been here all that long. I arrived last November.

9. Gautama Buddha was born in a small town in the Terai called Lumbini. Have you ever seen his birth-place[1]?
10. These taxi drivers drive their cars far too quickly. The other day, I was almost knocked down.
11. If your head-ache does not get any better, come back to see me and I'll give you a prescription.
12. One can't very well make one's friends cook English food just for oneself.

Exercise 13c

In the following sentences, give the correct form of the First Perfect Participle, making agreement for gender and number

हामीहरू कहिले पनि काठ्माड़ौं (जानु) छैनौं
मेरी बहिनी मन्दिर्मा पूजा गर्न (जानु) छ
हिजो प्रधान्मन्त्रीले भाषण् (गर्नु) थियो
तपाईंले (लेख्नु) किताब् मलाई त मन् (पर्नु) थिएन
मैले आउन (खोज्नु) त आउन सकिनँ

[1]'birthplace' **जन्मस्थल् janmasthal.**

LESSON 14

1. *New conjunct consonants*

ट्व **ṭv**	as in	ट्वाल्ट्वाल्ती	**ṭvālṭvāltī**	staring
ठ्य **ṭhy**	as in	उठ्यो	**uṭhyo**	got up
म्घ **mgh**	as in	रम्घा	**ramghā**	Ramgha

2. The Infinitival Participle, of which we have already had a number of examples in earlier lessons, is formed by adding the suffix -ने to the Primary Base of the verb: गर्ने **garne,** खाने **khāne,** जाने **jāne,** आउने **āune.**

The negative is formed by adding the prefix न- to the positive form: नगर्ने **nagarne,** नखाने **nakhāne,** नजाने **najāne,** नआउने **naāune.**

HGH forms have -हुने added to the infinitive in **-nu**: गर्नुहुने **garnuhune,** नआउनुहुने **naāunuhune,** etc.

3. The Infinitival Participle has many functions. It is basically a verbal adjective, corresponding in some ways to the English participle 'coming', 'doing', etc.

आउने हप्ता
Next week ('the coming week')

खाने कुरा
Something to eat/food ('eating things')

काठ्माडौंलाई पोखरासँग जोड्ने बाटो
A road linking Kathmandu to Pokhara

पोखरा जाने बस् कहाँ पाइन्छ ?
Where can I get a bus going to Pokhara?

उताबाट नजाऊ है । त्यो बाहिर निस्कने ढोका हो । भित्र पस्ने ढोका यता छ
Don't go that way. That's the exit ('going out door'). The entrance ('coming in door') is over here

उता **utā** 'in that direction' यता **yatā** 'in this direction'

4. The Infinitival Participle may often be translated by a relative clause with reference to present or future time – 'who does', 'who will do'.

भोलि आउने मान्छे
The man who is coming tomorrow ('the tomorrow coming man')

Compare the use of the First Perfect Participle in Lesson 12, 6:

हिजो आएको मान्छे
The man who came yesterday
खाने कुरा बोक्ने भरिया कता गयो हँ ?
What's happened to the porter carrying the provisions?
पाटन् जाने बाटो कुन्चाहिं हो, दाइ ? त्यहाँ जाने बस् कहाँ पाइन्छ होला ?
Which is the road that goes to Patan? Where will I be able to find a bus going there?
तिमीले हेर्नुपर्ने किताब् त्यही हो
That's the book you ought to look at (lit. 'you having to look at book')

5. The Infinitival Participle followed by बेलामा can often be translated by a temporal 'when' clause, with reference to present or future time.

धान् रोप्ने बेलामा, धेरै काम् हुन्छ
When they plant paddy, there's a lot of work to do
रमेश सधैं भात् खाने बेलामा आउँछ
Ramesh always arrives at dinner time

If the verb in the main clause is in one of the past tenses, the Infinitival Participle has the sense of 'when one was about to . . .'

काठ्माडौंबाट हिंड्ने बेला, तिम्रो चिठी पाएँ
When I was about to leave Kathmandu, I received your letter

6. In short questions and statements, the Infinitival Participle may be used instead of a main verb. This function is very common in speech. Unless ambiguity is likely to arise, the personal pronouns may be omitted.

आज (हामी) के गर्ने ? ताश् खेल्ने ?
What shall we do today? Shall we play cards?
ए दाइ, कता जाने ? नेपाल् जाने
Where are you off to? I'm going to Kathmandu

Note that Kathmandu is often referred to as नेपाल् by people living outside the Valley.

उस्लाई भेट्न किन नजाने ?
Why not go and meet him?
आज पानी पर्ने रे
They say it's going to rain today

7. The Infinitival Participle is used in the following expressions which involve a noun or adjective and the verbs गर्नु or हुनु :

गर्ने विचार् गर्नु to think about doing, to decide to do
गर्ने कोशिश् गर्नु to attempt to do

गर्ने पक्का गर्नु to decide to do
गर्ने निश्चय गर्नु to be certain to do, to decide to do
गर्ने बन्दोबस्त गर्नु to make arrangements to do
गर्ने पक्का हुनु to be decided to do

मैले अर्को वर्ष भारत् जाने विचार् गरेको छु
I've decided to go to India next year
म आज आउन सक्तिन । भोलि आउने कोशिश् गर्छु
I can't come today. I'll endeavour to come tomorrow
रामेले सिनेमा हेर्न जाने पक्का गरेको थियो
Rame decided to go to the pictures
यहाँ जून्सम्म बस्ने पक्का भयो
It's settled that we shall stay here till June
हिजो हामीले फुल्चोक् चढ्ने निश्चय गरेका थियौं
Yesterday we made up our minds to climb Phulchok (a hill in the Kathmandu Valley)
नाम्चे बजार् जाने बन्दोबस्त गरेका थियौं
We had made arrangements to go to Namche Bazaar

8. The Infinitival Participle is used with the adverb बित्तिकै **bittikəy** 'as soon as'. The subject of a transitive verb takes -ले .

मैले पैसा पाउने बित्तिकै, तिमीलाई होटेल्मा लगेर खुवाउँछु
As soon as I get my money, I'll take you out to a hotel and buy you dinner

लग्नु **lagnu** 'to take away', 'to take along'
खुवाउनु **khuvâunu** 'to cause to eat', 'to feed'

गाई दुहुने बित्तिकै, उ भित्र गएर आगो ताप्न लाग्यो
As soon as he had milked the cow, he came inside and began to warm himself by the fire
पानी थामिने बित्तिकै, म कुकुर्लाई घुमाउन लैजान्छु
As soon as it stops raining, I'll take the dog out for a walk

थामिनु **thâminu** 'to stop' (esp. of rain, wind etc.)
घुमाउनु **ghumâunu** 'to cause to stroll', 'take for a walk'

9. भन्ने **bhanne** (the Infinitival Participle of भन्नु) is used to link a subordinate clause to verbal expressions which consist of a noun and a verb such as खबर् आउनु **khabar âunu** 'news to come that', थाहा हुनु **thâhâ hunu** 'to know that' कुरा उठ्नु **kurâ uṭhnu** 'the question to arise that', दावी गर्नु **dâvī garnu** 'to claim that', etc.

हाम्रो गाउँनजीक् पहिरो गयो भन्ने खबर् आयो
It was reported that there was a landslide near our village

के गर्ने भन्ने कुरा उठ्यो
The question arose as to what we should do
नयाँ बाटो खुलेको छ कि छैन भन्ने मलाई थाहा थिएन
I did not know whether the new road was open or not

Note that the words preceding भन्ने are reported as they were originally stated. Compare the section on reported speech in Lesson 10.

हिमाल्मुनिका गाउँहरूमा बस्ने शेर्पाहरू भन्छन् कि अग्ला चुचुराहरूमा 'यती' भन्ने अनौठो किसिम्का जनावर्हरू बस्छन् । कसैकसैलेचाहिं यी जनावरहरू देखेका छौं भन्ने पनि दावी गर्छन्
The Sherpas who live in the villages under the mountains say that (**ki**) in the high peaks strange kinds of animals, called 'yatis', live. Some of them even claim to have seen these animals

हिमाल्मुनिका गाउँहरू **himālmunikā gāũharū** 'the villages under (**-muni**) the mountains'

After a proper noun, भन्ने may be translated 'by name', 'called'

पश्चिम् नेपाल्मा जुम्ला भन्ने एउटा सानो शहर् छ
The small town called Jumla is in Western Nepal

10. In sentences like 'I have heard that', 'I understood that', where the main verb is past, भनेको introduces the subordinate clause.

तपाईं राम्ररी नेपाली बोल्नुहुन्छ भनेको सुनें
I have heard that you speak Nepali very well

In other words, one says 'I have heard (them) saying that . . .' In certain contexts भन्नु may imply 'to wonder', 'to think that', etc.

जोग्बनी पुग्ने बित्तिकै, सिलिगुड़ी जाने रेल् पाइन्छ कि भनेर खोज्न थाल्यौं र दिन्मा चार् पाँच्वटा रेल् जान्छ भनेको सुनेर हामीलाई धेरै खुशी लाग्यो
As soon as we arrived at Jogbani (a frontier town in Bihar), we enquired whether we might get a train for Siliguri ('we began to search having said "Can we get a train or not?"'),and when we heard that there were four or five trains a day, we were very happy

हामीलाई खुशी लाग्यो **hāmīlāī khuʃī lāgyo** 'we became happy'

11. *The Nepali calendar*

The Hindu calendar, which is in general use in Nepal, but used mainly for ritual purposes in India, is known as विक्रम् संवत् **vikram samvat** (abbreviated in writing to वि.सं.). It is named after King Vikramāditya of Ujjain, who founded the present era in the year corresponding to 57-58 B.C.

Each Nepali month corresponds roughly to the last half and the first half of two English months. The year begins with the month of वैशाख् **Vaiśākh** – mid-April to mid-May. In the following table, the names of the twelve Nepali months are given in both their written and colloquial forms. The written forms are always used in official contexts.

Spoken		*Written*		
बैसाख्	**bəysākh**	वैशाख्	**veyʃākh**	Apr.-May
जेठ्	**jeṭh**	ज्येष्ठ	**jyeṣṭha**	May-June
असार्	**asār**	आषाढ्	**āṣāṛh**	June-July
साउन्	**sāun**	श्रावण्	**ʃrāvaṇ**	July-Aug.
भदौ	**bhadəw**	भाद्र	**bhādra**	Aug.-Sept.
असोज्	**asoj**	आश्विन्	**āʃvin**	Sept.-Oct.
कार्तिक्	**kārtik**	कार्तिक्	**kārtik**	Oct.-Nov.
मंगसीर	**maŋgsīr**	मार्ग	**mārga**	Nov.-Dec.
पूस्	**pūs**	पौष्	**pəwṣ**	Dec.-Jan.
माघ्	**māgh**	माघ्	**māgh**	Jan.-Feb.
फागुन्	**phāgun**	फाल्गुन्	**phālgun**	Feb.-March
चैत्	**cəyt**	चैत्र	**cəytra**	March-Apr.

The *Vikram Samvat* year can be converted to the corresponding Christian year by subtracting 57 from the former, except in the case of the last three months, when 56 must be subtracted. Thus Śrāvaṇ 2029 V.S. corresponded to July-August 1972 A.D.

When referring to the Vikram calendar, the word गते **gate** is used with the number indicating the date: एक् गते 'the first', चौबीस् गते 'the twenty fourth' आज कति गते ? 'what is the date today?'

A date is fully written thus:

> बैसाख् एक् गते दुइ हजार् उनन्तीस् साल्
> **bəysākh ek gate dui hajār unantīs sāl**
> असोज् बाह्र गते उन्नाईस् सय् त्रिपन्न साल्
> **asoj bārha gate unnāīs say tripanna sāl**

The Christian era, which is generally used in India, but still rarely in Nepal, is termed ईसवी सन् **īsavī san** (ईसा **īsā** 'Jesus'). The names of the Christian months, which have all been adapted from English, are spelt in Nepali as follows:

जनवरी	**janvarī**	जूलाई	**jūlāī**
फेब्रुअरी	**februarī**	अगस्त्	**agast**
मार्च्	**mārc**	सितेम्बर्	**sitembar**
अप्रिल्	**april**	अक्टोबर्	**akṭobar**
मई	**maī**	नोभेम्बर्	**nobhembar**
जून्	**jūn**	डिसेम्बर्	**ḍisembar**

When the Christian calendar is used, the word तारीख् **tārīkh** is used in place of गते . तीन् तारीख् the third, दस् तारीख् the tenth, etc.

Vocabulary 14

अनौठो	**anəwṭho**	strange, curious
अन्त	**anta**	end, conclusion, finally
अलमल् गर्नु	**almal garnu**	to wait around, hang about
आखिरी	**ākhirī**	the end (of a month)
ईसवी	**īsavī**	Christian (era)
ईसा	**īsā**	Jesus
उता	**utā**	in that direction
कोशिश् गर्नु	**koʃiʃ garnu**	to try, attempt
कोसेली	**koselī**	a present, gift
खबर्	**khabar**	news
खुवाउनु	**khuvāunu**	to feed
खुशी	**khuʃī**	happiness
गते	**gate**	date (with Nepali months)
गार्ड्	**gārḍ**	guard (of a train)
घुमाउनु	**ghumāunu**	to take (for a walk, etc.)
घुम्फिर्	**ghumphir**	travelling, strolling
घूम्	**ghūm**	Ghum (a town near Darjeeling)
चुचुरा	**cucurā**	peak (of a mountain)
जँचाइहाल्नु	**jācāihālnu**	to get examined
जनावर्	**janāvar**	animal
जिउ	**jiu**	body
जोग्बनी	**jogbanī**	Jogbani (border town in Bihar)
जोम्सोम्	**jomsom**	Jomsom (name of a village in North Central Nepal)
ज्यान्	**jyān**	life, soul
ज्यापू	**jyāpū**	peasant
झैं	**jhəỹ**	like, as if (syn. **jasto**)
ट्वाल्ट्वाल्ती हेर्नु	**ṭvālṭvāltī hernu**	to stare
डाम्	**ḍām**	mark, bite
ड्राइभर्	**ḍrāibhar**	driver
तान्सेन्	**tānsen**	Tansen (town in central Nepal)
तापनि	**tāpani**	even so, however
तारीख्	**tārīkh**	date (of Christian calendar)
थामिनु	**thāminu**	to stop (of rain, etc.)
दावी गर्नु	**dāvī garnu**	to claim
दुलही	**dulahī**	bride
धान्	**dhān**	paddy (growing rice)
निश्चय गर्नु	**niʃcaya garnu**	to decide, to be sure of
पक्का गर्नु	**pakkā garnu**	to decide
पक्कै पनि	**pakkəy pani**	certainly, of course

प्रिय	**priya**	dear (in letters)
फुल्चोक्	**phulcok**	Phulchok (a hill near Kathmandu)
फोन् गर्नु	**phon garnu**	to telephone
बन्दोबस्त् गर्नु	**bandobast garnu**	to arrange to
बल्ल-बल्ल	**balla-balla**	at last, with difficulty
बानी	**bānī**	habit
बित्तिकै	**bittikəy**	as soon as
भरिया	**bhariyā**	porter
-भरि	**-bharī**	all over, all through
भीड्	**bhīɽ**	crowd
-मुनि	**-muni**	under
भैर्हवा	**bhəyrhavā**	Bhairava (town in Terai)
मान्नु	**mānnu**	to agree, obey, honour
राहदानी	**rāhadānī**	permit, passport
रोप्नु	**ropnu**	to plant
लग्नु	**lagnu**	to take away, take out
लाम्खुट्टे	**lāmkhuʈʈe**	mosquito
यता	**yatā**	in this direction
रिक्शा	**rikʃā**	rickshaw
रिक्शावाला	**rikʃāvālā**	rickshaw driver
लुम्बिनी	**lumbinī**	Lumbini (a village in the Terai, the site of the birthplace of the Buddha)
सजिलोसित	**sajilosita**	easily
सधैं झैं	**sadhəỹ jhəỹ**	as always
हिलो	**hilo**	mud
जिल्ला	**jillā**	(administrative) district
तनहुँ	**tanahū̃**	Tanahun (district of Central Nepal)
रम्घा	**ramghā**	Ramghā (village in Tanahun district, the birthplace of the poet, Bhānubhakta)

Reading Passage

पोखराबाट चिठी

पोखरा
असार् ८ गते २०२३ साल् ।

प्रिय श्याम्,

दुइ हप्ता अगाडि भैरहवा पुग्ने बित्तिकै, मैले तिम्रो लामो र चाख्लाग्दो चिठी पाएँ । गएको महीनाको अन्तातिर म आफ्नो साथी रमेश्सँग काठ्माड़ौंबाट हिंड़ेको तिमीलाई थाहा छँदै छ[1]। सधैं

झैं [2] हवाईजहाज् ढीलो भएको थियो, तर साँझ् पर्नु अगाड़ी, अगाड़ि हामी भैर्हवाको विमानस्थल्मा आइपुग्यौं । त्यसैले रिक्शा पाउन केही गाह्रो भएन[3]। विमानस्थल्बाट शहर्को केन्द्र धेरै टाढ़ा छैन । तापनि रिक्शावालाले पाँच् रुपियाँ नै लिन्छु भनेर भन्यो। हामीले मोल् घटाउन खोजेको त ज्यान गए मानेन[4]। शहर् आइपुग्ने बित्तिकै, हामीले बस्ने ठाउँ खोज्न शुरू गर्‍यौं । बल्ल बल्ल एउटा होटेल्मा सानो कोठा पायौं । थकाई लागेको हुनाले, हामी चाँड़ै सुत्न गयौं, तर कोठामा एक् दम् गर्मी थियो र लाम्खुट्टेले रात्भरी टोकेको हुनाले, हामी सुत्नै सकेनौं ।

भोलिपल्ट बिहान उठ्दा त, जिउभरी लाम्खुट्टेले टोकेका डाम् बसेका रहेछन्[5]। त्यसैले भैरहवाबाट सकेसम्म छिटो पहाड़्तिर जाने बन्दोबस्त गर्न थाल्यौं ।

तिमीलाई थाहा छँदै छ, हामी लुम्बिनी हेर्न मात्रै भैर्हवा आएका थियौं। भोलिपल्ट त्यहाँ जानलाई टचाक्सी खोजेको त ड्राइभरहरूले बाटोमा हिलो भएको हुनाले जान मन् गरेनन्। भैर्हवाबाट लुम्बिनी धेरै टाढ़ा भएकोले त्यहाँसम्म पैदल् जान सकेनौं।

हामीले भैर्हवामा जम्मा तीन् दिन् बितायौं र त्यहाँबाट हिंड़्ने बेलामा, मैले हुलाक्घर्मा तपाईंको चिठी पाएँ। भैर्हवाबाट तान्सेन् जाने बस् सजिलोसित फेला पर्‍यो,[6] र बाटो राम्रो भएको हुनाले, त्यहाँ पुग्न धेरै बेर् लागेन।

तान्सेन् पुग्ने बित्तिकै, पोखरा जाने बस् पाइन्छ कि भनेर खोज्न थाल्यौं र दिन्मा चार् पाँच्वटा बस् जान्छ भनेको सुनेर हामीलाई अतिनै खुशी लाग्यो। काठ्माड़ौंबाट हिंड़्नु अगाड़ी, नयाँ बाटो खुलेको छ कि छैन भन्ने मलाई थाहा थिएन। तान्सेन् त मलाई एक् दम् मन् पर्‍यो र अग्लो ठाउँ भएकोले अलि चिसो थियो। पोखरा जानु अगाड़ी, त्यहाँ दुइ तीन् दिन बस्ने विचार् गर्‍यौं।

यस् चिठीबाट तिमीले थाहा पायौ होला[7] कि हामी अहिले पोखरामा नै छौं। यहाँ आराम् गरेर, दुइ तीन् दिन्पछि हामी जोम्सोम्तिर जाँदै छौं। त्यहाँबाट मुस्ताङ्गसम्म जान खोजेको तर हामीले राहदानी पाएनौं, के गर्ने?

अबचाहिं हामीले भारी बोक्ने भरियाहरू मात्रै खोज्नुपरेको छ। जोम्सोम्बाट फर्केर त्यहाँको सबै कुरा म तिमिलाई लेख्छु।

तिम्रो साथी,

सूर्य प्रकाश्

Notes

This letter describes a journey made from Bhairava, a town in the Nepalese Terai, to Jomsom, a village near the border of Mustang. Bhairava is close to the site of Buddha's birthplace at the village of Lumbini. A bus goes from Bhairava, via the hill-town of Tansen, to Pokhara. From there the journey to Mustang is done on foot. For such journeys, it is usual to arrange for the services of a porter (**bhariyā**) who will cook and help with luggage. Trekking permits (**rāhadānī**) are usually required by foreigners who wish to travel in the Nepalese countryside.

1. **thāhā chādəy cha**: 'you are knowing', 'you must know'. **chādəy cha** is the present continuous tense of **cha** (cf. **gardəy cha,** etc.).
2. **sadhəỹ jhəỹ**: 'as always', 'as usual'.
3. **rikʃā pāunu kehī gāhro bhaena**: 'it did not prove at all difficult to get a rickshaw'.
4. **jyān gae mānena**: lit. 'even if his life went, he would not agree', i.e. 'he would not agree under any circumstances'.
5. **bholipalṭa uṭhdā . . . basekā rahechan**: lit. 'the next morning on getting up, all over the body the mosquito-having-bitten marks were (to our surprise – **rahechan**) having remained', i.e. 'When we got up the next day, we were horrified to find mosquito bites all over our bodies.'
   uṭhdā – the Imperfect Participle 'on getting up' (Lesson 19).
   -bharī – 'all over', 'all through', cf. **rātbharī** 'all night long'.
6. **bas phelā paryo**: 'a bus was caught', i.e. 'we got a bus'.
7. **timīle thāhā pāyəw holā**: 'you have probably found out'. Note the expression **thāhā pāunu** 'to find out', 'to acquire information'.

Exercise 14a

Translate into English

१ मेरो काम् सिद्धिने बित्तिकै, म तिमिलाई भेट्न आउँछु ।

२. काठ्माड़ौंमा बस्ने मान्छेहरूको धेरै घुम्फिर गर्ने बानी छैन ।

३. दुलही निस्कने बित्तिकै,सबैले ट्वाल्ट्वाल्टी हेर्न थाले।

४. अँध्यारो हुन लाग्यो ,अब के गर्ने भनेर उस्ले भन्यो ।

५. अहिलेसम्म म काठ्माड़ौं खाल्डोबाट बाहिर गएको छैन ।आघुँ त पूर्वतिर जाने बिचार् छ ।

६. पाँच बज्ने बित्तिकै,म घर् जान्छु। हाम्रो घर्मा पाहुनाहरू आउँछन् भन्ने खबर् आयो ।

७. अब फेरि यहाँ अल्मल् गर्‍यौं भने गाउँमा बास् बस्ने ठाउँ पाइँदैन भनेर मैले भनें ।

८. दार्जीलिङ्ग पुग्ने बित्तिकै मेरो दाइसित भेट्न जानुहोस् न । वहाँको घर् घूमतिर जाने बाटोमा छ नि ।

९. तपाईंको घर्मा बिजुली बत्ती छ भन्ने मलाई थाहा थिएन ।

१० सिलिगुड़ी जाने रेल् कति बजे आउँछ भनेर मैले गार्ड्लाई सोधेको त भोलि बिहान मात्रै आँउछ भन्यो ।

११ .लन्दन्बाट फर्कने बेलामा साथीहरूको लागि कोसेली किन्न नबिर्स है ।
१२ .भानुभक्त आचार्यको जन्म सं १८७१ साल्को आषाढ़ महिनामा नेपाल्को तनहुँ भन्ने जिल्लाको रम्घा गाउँमा भएको थियो ।
१३ .तपाईंको गाउँमा खाने कुरा पाइन्छ कि भनेर मैले ज्यापूलाई सोधें ।
१४ .अंग्रेजी सिक्नलाई तिमीले हेर्नुपर्ने किताब् त्यही हो ।
१५. त्यहाँबाट काठ्माडौं कसरी फर्कने भन्ने कुरा उठ्यो।

Exercise 14b

Translate into Nepali

1. Shall we have a game of cards? No, not now. I don't have the time.
2. What a strange man (**kasto mānche**)! He tried to leave by the entrance. I suppose he'll try to come in through the exit next time.
3. Excuse me. What time does the Patan bus leave from here? The Patan bus does not go from here. The bus stop is by that post-office.
4. As soon as we reach the next village, I'll try to find another porter. This one says he's not coming any farther (**aghi**).
5. If you wish to learn Nepali, this is the book you ought to read. That one is not so good.
6. The Sherpa who came today said that he will make all the arrangements for going to Namche Bazar. We'll have to give him 300 rupees.
7. As soon as you arrive in London, telephone me from the airport and I'll come and meet you. If I come by car, it only takes me twenty minutes to get there from my house, you know.
8. As usual the bus came late and was packed with people, but since there wasn't another, we just had to come by that.
9. As you will see from this letter, I am now in Delhi. If I can get an aeroplane, I shall arrive in Kathmandu the day after tomorrow.
10. I did not know that the road leading from Pokhara to Kathmandu was open.
11. I think that I shall stay in this hotel for two or three weeks. After that I shall try to find another place to live ('another living-place').
12. As soon as he came out of his house, everyone began to stare at him.

Exercise 14c

Translate into English

आउने हप्ता ; भोलि आउने पाहुनाहरू ; तिमीले गर्नुपर्ने काम् ; नेपाल् जाने विचार गर्नु ; काठ्माडौं पुग्ने बित्तिकै ; बस फेला पर्‍यो ; आउने महिनाको अन्तसम्म ; बैशाख् तीन् गते ; भदौ सात गते दुइ हजार् बीस साल ; जून् आठ् तारीख् उन्नाईस् सय् छहत्तर साल् .

LESSON 15

1. *New conjunct consonants*

प्य	**py**	as in	गोप्य	**gopya**	obscure
भ्य	**bhy**	as in	भ्याउनु	**bhyāunu**	to reach
ह्य	**hy**	as in	गुह्य	**guhya**	hidden, obscure

2. The Infinitival Participle, followed by the Conjunctive Participle गरी is the equivalent of a final ('so that . . ., in order that . . .') clause in English. Only the conjunctive participle in **-ī** may be used in this construction. The subject of the sentence, if expressed, takes -ले when the verb is transitive.

> अरूले बुझ्ने गरी , चिठी लेख है
> Write the letter so that others may understand it
> दुर्घट्ना नहुने गरी ,बिस्तारै मोटर् हाँक्नुहोला
> Drive the car slowly so that there may not be an accident
> त्यो औषधि नानीले नभ्याउने गरी दराजमा राख्नुहोला
> Put that medicine in the drawer so that the child cannot reach it
> कसैले नदेख्ने गरी रामे घर्बाट सुटुक्क गयो
> Rame crept out of the house so that no one would see him

सुटुक्क जानु **suṭukka jānu** 'to go stealthily'

3. The Infinitival Participle followed by गर्नु is frequentative (to keep on doing, etc.).

> उमालेको पानी पिउने गर्नुहोस्
> Keep on drinking boiled water
> त्यसो धेरैजसो हुने गर्दैन
> That never usually keeps happening
> स्वास्थ्य राम्रो राख्नलाई, बिहान बिहान खुला हावामा डुल्ने गर्नुहोस्
> To maintain your health, keep going for a walk every morning in the open air

4. Followed by हुनाले , the Infinitival Participle expresses a causal clause with reference to what is usually the case ('because it is usually the case that . . .', 'because I usually do . . .' etc.) Compare the following sentences:

नेपाल्मा थोरै दिन् मात्रै बस्ने हुनाले, पर्यटक्हरू काठ्माडौंबाट बाहिर जाँदैनन्
Because they (usually) stay only for a few days in Nepal, tourists do not go outside Kathmandu
नेपाल्मा थोरै दिन् मात्रै बसेको हुनाले म काठ्माडौंबाट बाहिर गइनँ
Because I stayed only for a few days in Nepal, I did not go outside Kathmandu
मदेस्मा चर्को घाम् लाग्ने हुनाले, जिमीन साह्रै सुक्खा हुन्छ
In the Terai, because the sun is very harsh, the ground becomes quite dry
मदेस्मा पानी नपरेको हुनाले, बाली-नाली नाश् भयो
Because it did not rain in the Terai, the crops failed

5. The Infinitival Participle may often function as a noun. For example:
ओढ्ने **oṛhne** (from ओढ्नु 'to wrap around') a wrap
माग्ने **māgne** (from माग्नु 'to ask, beg') a beggar

मार्ग महीनामा बेलुकातिर ओढ्ने ओढ्नुपर्छ
In the month of Marga, towards evening one has to wear a wrap
काठ्माडौंमा , खास् गरी मन्दिर्हरू वरिपरि , माग्नेहरू धेरै हुन्छन्
In Kathmandu, especially around the temples, there are many beggars
भनेको नमान्नेलाई सल्लाह दिएर के काम् ?
What's the use of giving advice to someone who does not listen to what you say?

6. The Infinitival Future Tense consists of the Infinitival Participle and the verb छ , usually written as one word:

म गर्नेछु	**garnechu**
तँ गर्नेछस्	**garnechas**
उ गर्नेछ	**garnecha**
हामी गर्नेछौं	**garnechəw̃**
तिमी गर्नेछौ	**garnechəw**
उनीहरू गर्नेछन्	**garnechan**
तपाईं / वहाँ } गर्नुहुनेछ	**garnuhunecha**

Negative: गर्नेछैन **garnechəyna,** गर्नेछैनस् **garnechəynas,** etc.
The feminine forms गर्नेछेस् **garneches,** गर्नेछे **garneche,** गर्नेछिन् **garnechin,** are occasionally found in the written language.

The Infinitival Future refers to future time ('I shall do', etc.) but tends to be more emphatic than the Simple Indefinite, and is therefore used with adverbs like जरूरै **jarūrəy** 'certainly', अवश्य **avaʃya** 'of course', etc. Note that अवश्य is often pronounced **abasse.**

Compare the following sentences:

Simp. Indef. त्यो बाह्र बजेभित्र आउँछ
He'll come by twelve o'clock today

Inf. Fut. त्यो आज अवश्य आउनेछ
Of course he will come today

Simp. Indef. खल्बल् नगर । बुवा रिसाउनुहुन्छ
Don't make a noise. Father will be angry

Inf. Fut. जाँच्मा फेल् भएँ भने ,बुवा पक्कै पनि रिसाउनुहुनेछ
If I fail the exam, father really will be angry

The Infinitival Future is therefore used in making predictions or forecasts:

काठ्माडौं उपत्यकामा आज पानी पर्ने सम्भावना छ । जल्स्रोत् तथा जल्वायु विज्ञान् विभाग्को अनुसार्, आज अधिक्तम् तापक्रम् १२ देखि १४ डिग्री सेन्टीग्रेड् रहनेछ
Today in the Kathmandu Valley there is a possibility of rain. According to the meteorological office, today the maximum temperature will remain between 12 and 14 degrees centigrade

जल् **jal** 'water' (a literary synonym of पानी), स्रोत **srot** 'current'
जल्वायु **jalvāyu** 'climate' (lit. 'water and wind'. cf. हावापानी)
विज्ञान् **vijnān** 'science'
तथा **tathā** 'and', a Sanskrit word commonly used in official Nepali.

त्यसरी हाँक्नुभयो भने दुर्घट्ना हुनेछ
If you drive like that, there will surely be an accident

त्यसरी **tyasarī** 'in that manner'

दक्षिण्-पूर्व एशियामा ठूलो लड़ाईं हुनेछ
In South East Asia, I predict there is going to be a great war

पहिरो जानेछ जोगीले भन्यो
The *jogi* predicted there would be a landslide

आज अवश्य पानी पर्नेछ
It will certainly rain today

7. The following construction, which is very common in spoken Nepali, consists of the Second Infinitive (in **-na**), followed by the particle त and some part of the verb followed by तर

गर्न त गर्ने तर he *will* do it but . . .
पानी पर्न त पऱ्यो तर it *did* rain but . . .

In colloquial speech, the Infinitival Participle is often used in place of the main verb:

जान त जाने तर I *shall* go but . . .
गर्न त गर्ने तर I *will* do it but . . .

काम् गर्न त गर्ने तर के काम् गर्ने भन त
I shall work but tell me what work am I to do

चिठी लेख्न त लेख्ने तर आज फुर्सद् छैन रे
He says he will write the letter, but he has no time today

उस्ले बिहा गर्न त गर्छ तर भनेको जस्तो केटी फेला पारेको छैन
He will get married but he has not found the right kind of girl

भनेको जस्तो केटी **bhaneko jasto keṭī** 'a girl fulfilling all the requirements'
फेला पार्नु **phelā pārnu** 'to find, to acquire' (the transitive form of फेला पर्नु 'to be acquired, to be found')

काठ्माड़ौंबाट पोखरा जाने बाटो खुल्यो ?
खुल्न त खुल्यो तर हवाई जहाज्मा जान फाइदा छ
Has the road from Kathmandu to Pokhara opened yet?
It *has* opened, but it's still better to go by air

The verb छ possesses a second infinitive छन **chana,** which is mainly employed in this construction:

छन त छ तर ... 'there is/are but ...'

जुम्ला जाने हवाईजहाज् पाउन त पाइन्छ,तर साउन्मा ठूलो पानी पर्ने हुनाले, कहिले कहीं चल्दैन
Well, there are aeroplanes going to Jumla, but in Śrāvaṇ it rains so heavily that they sometimes do not run

8. The Third Infinitive (really an inflected oblique form of the infinitive in **-nu**) is formed by changing the termination of the first infinitive to -ना **-nā**: गर्ना **garnā,** खाना **khānā,** आउना **āunā,** हुना **hunā,** etc. The Third Infinitive is used only with postpositions:

गर्नाको लागि	**garnāko lāgi**	for the sake of doing
आउनासाथ्	**āunāsāth**	along with coming ('as soon as I came')
गर्नाले	**garnāle**	by doing ('because I did')

साँझ् पर्नासाथ्,राम् शिकार् खेल्न बन्दूक् लिएर जङ्गल्तिर गयो
As evening was falling, Ram took his gun and went to the jungle to hunt

Note that हुनाले 'by being', 'because there is', etc., which we have met in constructions like गरेको हुनाले is the third infinitive of हुनु followed by -ले. हुनाले may often be used in the sense of भएको हुनाले 'because there is', 'since it was'.

हिमाल्मा धेरै चिसो हुनाले ,सधैं न्यानो लुगा लाउनुपर्छ
Because it is very cold in the mountains, you always have to put on warm clothes
हिन्दुस्तान्भन्दा नेपाल्मा माल्ताल् सस्तो पाइन्छ ।त्यसो हुनाले,धेरै हिन्दुस्तानीहरू नेपाल्मा किन्मेल् गर्न आउँछन्
Goods are cheaper in Nepal than in India. This being so, many Indians come to do their shopping in Nepal

किन्मेल् गर्नु **kinmel garnu** 'to do shopping'

अंग्रेज़हरू छुट्टी मनाउन दक्षिण् यूरप्‌तिर जानाको अर्को कारण् त्यहाँको राम्रो मौसम् पनि हो
Another reason for English people going to southern Europe to spend their holidays is the nice weather they have there.

With -को and compound postpositions containing -को, the infinitive in -नु may also be used. Thus:

जानुको कारण्	the reason for going
जानुका निमित्त	for the sake of going
गर्नुको साथै	along with doing, while doing

The use of the first or third infinitive in such constructions is a matter of personal preference. However, the infinitive in -नु is always used with अगाड़ि or भन्दा अगाड़ि

जानुभन्दा अगाड़ि	before going
काम् गर्नु अगाड़ि	before working

Vocabulary 15

अति	**ati**	very, exceedingly
अदृश्य	**adɹʃya**	unseen, invisible
अधिक्तम्	**adhiktam**	maximum
अधिराज्य	**adhirājya**	Kingdom (of Nepal)
(-का) अनुसार	**(-kā) anusār**	according to
अनेक्, अनेकौं	**anek, anekəw̃**	several, many
अवश्य	**avaʃya**	indeed, of course
आकार्	**ākār**	form, shape
आक्रमण्	**ākramaṇ**	attack
आजा	**ājā**	worship
उपत्यका	**upatyakā**	valley
उपाध्याय	**upādhyāya**	a class of Brahmins
किनभने	**kinabhane**	because
किन्मेल् गर्नु	**kinmel garnu**	to do shopping
कुखुरा	**kukhurā**	chicken
ख्याति	**khyāti**	fame
गर्म-महीना	**garm-mahīnā**	the warm months, summer
गहुँ	**gahũ**	wheat
गुह्य	**guhya**	dark, obscure
गोदावरी	**godāvarī**	Godavari (village near Kathmandu)
गोप्य	**gopya**	hidden, obscure
घट्ना	**ghaṭnā**	accident, event
चढ़ाउनु	**caṛhāunu**	to offer up
चर्को	**carko**	harsh (of the sun)

चलन्	**calan**	usage, use, operation
चोक्	**cok**	a square
छुट्टी	**chuṭṭī**	holiday
छुट्टी मनाउनु	**chuṭṭī manāunu**	to spend/celebrate a holiday
जतातते	**jatātatəy**	everywhere, all over
जनता	**janatā**	people, the public
जरूरै	**jarūrəy**	certainly
जल्	**jal**	water
जल्वायु	**jalvāyu**	climate
जल्स्रोत	**jalsrot**	stream of water, rainfall
जिल्ला	**jillā**	a district
जुन्	**jun**	whichever
जेल्	**jel**	jail
डर्	**ḍar**	fear
डर्लाग्दो	**ḍarlāgdo**	frightening
जुनसुकै	**junsukəy**	whichever
तथा	**tathā**	and
तला	**talā**	a storey, floor
तल्लो	**tallo**	bottom (adj.)
तान्सेन्	**tānsen**	Tansen (town in central Nepal)
तापक्रम्	**tāpkram**	temperature
तेर्सिनु	**tersinu**	to be spread out
त्यसरी	**tyasarī**	thus, in that manner
त्रिशूल्	**triʃūl**	trident
दर्शन्	**darʃan**	viewing (a holy place, etc.)
दुर्घट्ना	**durghaṭnā**	accident
देउता	**deutā**	a god
देखाइनु	**dekhāinu**	to be shown
देवस्थल्	**devasthal**	temple
दैनिक्	**dəynik**	daily
दुःखद्	**dukkhad**	painful
धर्मभीरु	**dharmabhīru**	a religious devotee
धातु	**dhātu**	metal
नवरात्री	**navarātrī**	Navaratri (see note to text)
नाथ्	**nāth**	lord, god (ref. esp. to Gorakhnāth)
निराश्	**nirāʃ**	disappointed
पक्कै पनि	**pakkəy pani**	certainly, for sure
पर्व	**parva**	festival
पिठो	**piṭho**	kind of rice cake
पुजारी	**pujārī**	priest, worshipper
प्यूठान्	**pyūṭhān**	Pyuthan (town in Terai)
प्रख्यात्	**prakhyāt**	celebrated, famous

प्रतिस्थ	**pratisthāpan**	set up, established
प्रथम्	**pratham**	first
प्रमुख्	**pramukh**	head, chief
प्राचीन्	**prācīn**	ancient
प्राप्त	**prāpta**	acquired
प्राप्त हुनु	**prāpta hunu**	to acquire
बड़ो	**baɽo**	big, great, very
बन्दूक्	**bandūk**	gun
बलि	**bali**	sacrifice
बाग्लुङ्ग	**bāgluŋg**	Baglung (town in central Nepal)
बोको	**boko**	he-goat
भक्त (-जन्हरू)	**bhakta (-janharū)**	devotee(s) (of religion)
भविष्य	**bhaviṣya**	the future
भाग्	**bhāg**	part, section, fortune
भेला	**bhelā**	crowd, throng
भैरव	**bhəyrava**	Bhairava
भ्याउनु	**bhyāunu**	to reach, to fit
मछिन्द्रनाथ्	**machindranāth**	Machindranath
मद्दत् गर्नु	**maddat garnu**	to help
-मध्ये	**-madhye**	among, in the midst of
मनाउनु	**manāunu**	to celebrate
मल्ल	**malla**	Malla
महन्त	**mahanta**	high priest
माग्ने	**māgne**	beggar
मानिनु	**māninu**	to be honoured, be agreed
मुकुन्द सेन्	**mukunda sen**	Mukunda Sen
मुख्य	**mukhya**	(most) important, main
मूर्ति	**mūrti**	statue
मृत्यु	**mɹtyu**	death
यात्रु	**yātru**	traveller, pilgrim
रहर्	**rahar**	desire, interest
राख्नु	**rākhnu**	to put, place, keep
राज्य गर्नु	**rājya garnu**	to rule
रूप्	**rūp**	shape, form, beauty
रोठ्	**roʈh**	a big loaf
लगाउनु	**lagāunu**	to put on clothes
लुट्नु	**luʈnu**	to rob, plunder
वंश	**vamʃa**	lineage, race
वंशावली	**vamʃāvalī**	traditional chronicle
(-को)वर्पर्, वरिपरि	**varpar, varipari**	around, about
वा	**vā**	or (syn. **athavā**)
वाहन्	**vāhan**	conveyance, carriage, car

विज्ञान्	**vijɲān**	science, study
विभिन्न	**vibhinna**	different, various
विस्तार्	**vistār**	extending, detail
विहार्	**vihār**	Buddhist shrine
व्यक्ति	**vyakti**	person, individual
शताब्दी	**ʃatābdī**	century
शिकार् खेल्नु	**ʃikār khelnu**	to hunt
शिव	**ʃiva**	Shiva
संख्या	**saŋkhyā**	number
संभव्	**sambhav**	possible
संभावना	**sambhāvanā**	possibility
सजिनु	**sajinu**	to be decorated
समय्	**samay**	time (syn. **belā**)
सल्लाह्	**sallāh**	advice
साथै	**sāthəy**	along with
-को साथ् साथै	**-ko sāth sāthəy**	along with, while, as
साधारण्तया	**sādhāraɳtayā**	usually
सामान्	**sāmān**	luggage, things
सुटुक्क जानु	**suʈukka jānu**	to creep away, go stealthily
स्थान्	**sthān**	place (syn. **ʈhāũ**)
स्थानीय	**sthānīya**	local
स्थित्	**sthit**	placed, located
स्वास्थ्य	**svāsthya**	health
हतियार्	**hatiyār**	weapon

Reading Passage

पाल्पा-भैरव एक् अदृश्य देउता

पश्चिम् नेपाल्का प्रमुख् जिल्लाहरूमध्ये पाल्पा एक् मानिन्छ ।ईसा को सोह्रौं शताब्दीमा पाल्पामा सेन् वंशका राजाहरू राज्य गर्थे[1]। वंशावलीहरू अनुसार् मुकुन्द सेन् प्रथम्ले आफ्नो राज्यको विस्तार गर्नुको साथ साथै काठ्माडौं उपत्यकाका मल्ल राजाहरूमाथि[2] आक्रमण गरेका थिए। उन्ले उपत्यकामा आक्रमण् गर्दा काठमाडौं केल्टोल् स्थित्[3] श्री मछिन्द्रनाथ्को विहार्मा रहेको अति ख्याति प्राप्त तथा प्राचीन भैरवको मूर्ति पनि लुटेका अरू अरू सामान्हरू साथै पाल्पा लगेका थिए[4]। शायद् पाल्पा स्थित् प्रख्यात् भैरव स्थान् भित्र प्रतिस्थापन् गरेको मूर्ति यो नै हुनु संभव छ ।

पश्चिमी नेपाल्का प्रमुख् देवस्थल्हरूमध्ये पाल्पा-भैरव-स्थान्लाई पनि एक् मानिन्छ । पाल्पा वर्पर्का मात्रै होइन,पश्चिम् नेपाल्का टाढ़ा टाढ़ाका जिल्लाहरू बाग्लुङ्ग , प्यूठान्, पोखरा

आदि ठाउँहरूबाट पनि धर्मभीरुहरू जनता भैरवको पूजा-आजा तथा दर्शन्[5] गर्न आउँछन्

भैरव्को मन्दिर्, पुजारीको घर्,यात्रुहरू बस्ने घर्-सबै एउटा ठूलो चोक् वरिपरि छन् । मन्दिर्को चोक् लामो आकार्को छ, र भक्तजन्हरूले चढ़ाएका धातुका ठूलो साना विभिन्न आकार्का घण्टाहरू, धातुकै कुकुरहरू[6]र त्रिशूल्हरूले सजिएका छन्[7]। भैरवको वाहन् कुकुर् भएको हुनाले, भक्तजन्हरूले कुकुरका मूर्तीहरू चढ़ाएको हुन सक्छ । साथै भैरवलाई शिवको अनेकौं रूप्हरूमध्ये एक् मानिन्छ, त्यसैले होला[8] शिवको हतियार् त्रिशूल् पनि मन्दिर् वर्पर् जतातत‍ै तेर्सिएका देखिन्छन् ।

वर्षमा दुइ पटक वैशाख् र मंग्सीर्मा खास् गरी,यहाँ भक्तजन्हरूको भेला हुने गर्छ ।नवरात्री[9] पर्वमा पनि यहाँ ठूलो संख्यामा मानिस्हरू पूजा-आजा, बलि आदि चढ़ाउन आँउछन् ।मन्दिर्का मुख्य पुजारी नाथ - सम्प्रदायका महन्त छन् र उन्लाई मद्दत् गर्न उपाध्याय ब्राह्मण्हरूले बोको, कुखुरा आदि बलि दिने काम् पनि गर्ने गर्छन्,जुन् साधारण्तया हुने गर्दैन[10]।

दैनिक् साधारण् पूजा-आजामा भने भक्तजन्हरूले गहुँ वा चामल्को पिठोको बाक्लो रोटी, जस्लाई स्थानीय मानिस्हरू 'रोठ्' भन्छन्,[11] त्यो चढ़ाउने गर्छन् ।भैरवलाई चामल्को रोठ् चढ़ाउने चलन् नेपाल्का अरू भाग्हरुमा देखिंदैन ।

पाल्पा-तान्सेन्सम्म पुग्ने जोसुकै मानिस्हरूलाई पनि भैरव स्थान्सम्म पुग्ने रहर् हुन्छ[12] किनभने यो भैरव स्थान् नेपाल् अधिराज्यभर प्रख्यात् छ। पहाड़्को बाटो बड़ो दुःख गरी भक्तजन्हरू भैरवनाथ्को दर्शन् गर्न जान्छन् तर त्यहाँ पुग्दा तिनीहरूलाई निराश् हुनुपर्छ,[13] किनभने मुख्य भैरवको मूर्ती कसैलाई पनि देखाईंदैन र त्यो मन्दिर् भित्र एउटा गुह्य कोठामा राखिएको छ।

भनिन्छ त्यहाँ भित्र रहेको भैरवको मूर्ति साह्रै डर्लाग्दो छ र केही व्यक्तिहरूको त्यो मूर्ति देखनासाथ् डर्ले मृत्यु भएथ्यो,[14] र भविष्यमा फेरि पनि यस्ता दुःखद् घट्नाहरू नहुने गरी भनी भैरवको मूर्तिलाई त्यस् समय्देखि मन्दिर्को तल्लो तलाको गोप्य कोठामा राखियो र त्यसै बेलादेखि पाल्पा-भैरव एक् अदृश्य देउताको रूप्मा रहन थाले ।

Notes

The passage has been adapted from an article by Sāphalya Amātya which appeared in the *Gorkhāpatra*, Nepal's leading Nepali language newspaper on the 30th of Vaiśākh 2035. It concerns a temple of Bhairava (one of the horrific forms of the god, Shiva) in the Palpa region of West Central Nepal. The style of the passage is literary and contains many Sanskrit words, most of which, however, would be easily understood by moderately educated people. Particularly notable is the consistent use of case and number, which is, of course, obligatory in the literary language.

1. **sen vamʃakā rājāharū rājya garthe**: 'the kings of the Sen dynasty used to rule'. **garthe** is 3rd person plural Past Habitual, discussed in Lesson 18. The **vamʃāvalī** are traditional chronicles, many of them written in Sanskrit.
2. The Malla kings ruled in the Kathmandu Valley until the late 18th century, when they were conquered by Prithvīnārāyan Shāh, the founder of the present ruling dynasty.
3. **keltol sthit**: 'situated in Keltol'. Keltol is a street in the centre of the old part of Kathmandu. Machindranath is the patron deity of the city.
4. **unle . . . gardā . . . luṭekā . . . lagekā thie**: 'by making an attack, he took away the statue of Bhairava . . . along with other things he had robbed, to Palpa'. **gardā**, the Imperfect Participle of **garnu** (Lesson 19) has the force of 'while doing', 'as he was doing'.
5. **darʃan**: 'viewing', 'visiting' – particularly the viewing of a statue of a deity in a temple.
6. **dhātukəy kukurharū**: 'even dogs of metal' **-kəy** is the emphatic form of **-ko.**
7. **triʃūl** – the trident which is the weapon of Shiva.
8. **tyasəyle holā**: 'for this reason perhaps'.
9. **navarātrī**: lit. 'nine nights' – the important Hindu festival in honour of the goddess, Durgā, which takes place during the first nine days of the month of Āśvin. Animal sacrifice (**bali**) is still common in Nepal.
   nāth-sampradāya: the sect of Hindu ascetics who are followers of the deity Gorakhnāth. **upādhyāya**: a class of Brahmins who traditionally teach the Vedas and other religious texts.
10. **jun . . . hune gardəyna**: 'which usually does not happen'. Brahmins do not usually sacrifice animals.
11. **jaslāī . . . bhanchan**: 'which the local people call **roṭh**'. **jas** is the oblique form of the relative pronoun **jo** 'who, which'. See Lesson 16.
12. **josukəy . . . rahar huncha**: lit. 'to whichever man arrives at Palpa-Tansen, there is a desire for arriving at the place of Bhairava', i.e. 'whoever arrives at Palpa-Tansen also desires to go to visit Bhairava'. Tansen is the main town in the Palpa region.
13. **tyahā pugdā . . . hunuparcha**: 'but on arriving there, they must be disappointed'.
14. **kehī . . . bhaethyo**: lit. 'along with seeing that statue, the death of several individuals had come about by fear'.
    bhaethyo the Second Pluperfect Tense of **hunu** (discussed in Lesson 16) which implies 'came about unexpectedly'.

Exercise 15a

Translate into English

१. सबैले सुन्ने गरी अलि ठूलो स्वरले कुरा गर त ।
२. बस् आउन त आउँछ तर हिजोआज अलि ढीलो आउँछ ।
३. काठ्माड़ौंबाट सगर्माथा देख्न त देखिन्छ तर धेरै नै टाढ़ा भएको हुनाले एक् दम् सानो देखिन्छ ।
४. यही औषधि खाने गर्नुहोस् । एक् दुइ दिन्मा नै निको हुनेछ ।
५. भोलि पानी पर्ने सम्भावना छ भनेको मैले रेडियोमा सुनें ।
६. यस् बर्ष पनि जाँच्मा फेल् भएँ भने मेरो बुवा पक्कै पनि रिसाउनुहुनेछ ।
७. मैले पोहोर् साल् भारत् जाने बिचार् गरेको थिएँ तर फुर्सत् पाइएन ।अब त यो बर्ष जाने कोशिश् गर्छु।
८. साँझ् पर्नासाथ् हामी माथिको गाउँमा पुग्यौं ।
९. जुम्लातिर हवाईजहाज् जान त जान्छ तर महीनाको एक् दुइ फेरा मात्रै जान्छ ।
१०. कति पानी परेको हेर ।यो बर्ष बाली-नाली पक्कै पनि बिग्रनेछ ।
११. आज बल्ल-बल्ल मैले तिम्रो भाइलाई फेला पारें ।
१२. हिजो बेलुका कसैले नदेख्ने गरी म घर्बाट सुटुक्क निस्केर साथीहरूसँग ताश् खेल्न गएँ ।
१३. यो किताब् पढ्न त पढ्ने तर कसरी पढ्ने? एक् दम् गाह्रो रहेछ।
१४. नेपाल्मा,खास् गरी पहाड़तिर, माग्नेहरू धेरै छैनन् । किसान्हरू माग्न लाज् मान्छन् नि ।
१५. जाँच्मा पास् भयौ भने सजिलैसित काम् पाउनेछौ ।

Exercise 15b

Translate into Nepali

1. I heard on the radio that there was a possibility of rain (falling) tomorrow.
2. Go and sit over there, so that you get a good view. (MGH).
3. When you go to Nepal, make a habit of drinking boiled water. If you do not drink boiled water, you will certainly have an upset stomach.
4. He says that he has made up his mind to go to India and look for work. If h goes to Calcutta, he will certainly find work.
5. There are aeroplanes going to Western Nepal, but they do not go every day.
6. That old man is very ill. If the doctor does not come quickly, he will certainly die.
7. He went quietly out of the office, so that no one would see him, but as soor as he arrived at the exit door, he had to come back.
8. You can get food in the villages, but it is better to buy your provisions in Kathmandu before going ('having taken . . . it is better to go').
9. One sees many beggars in the cities of India, but the people of the villages are ashamed to beg.
10. What you say is quite right. I shall certainly go and see ('meet') him in hospital.

11. In the 16th century A.D., the king of Palpa made an attack on the Kathmandu Valley.
12. In that temple, Brahmins are accustomed to sacrifice animals, something which usually does not happen.

LESSON 16

1. The Second Perfect Participle is formed by adding the suffix ए **-e** to the base of verbs belonging to groups (i) and (ii) and to the secondary base of verbs belonging to groups (iii), (iv) and (v).

गरे **gare,** खाए **khāe,** दिए **die,** बिर्से **birse,** दुहे **duhe**
धोए **dhoe,** आए **āe,** गए **gae,** भए **bhae,** etc.

The negative is formed by adding the prefix न **na-** to the positive form:

नगरे **nagare,** नखाए **nakhāe,** नआए **naāe,** नभए **nabhae,** etc.

The HGH forms have the suffix भए **-bhae** added to the infinitive in **-nu**:

गर्नुभए **garnubhae,** नखानुभए **nakhānubhae,** नआउनुभए **naāunubhae,** etc.

The subject word of the Second Perfect Participle (if expressed) always takes ले when the verb is transitive.

2. The Second Perfect Participle has many functions, some of which have been encountered in the reading passages of previous lessons. The participle may be used in the subordinate clause of an open conditional sentence instead of the Simple Past followed by भने (Lesson 9). It might be noted that भने itself is the Second Perfect Participle of the verb भन्नु . Both constructions are frequently used in both speech and writing, and may be regarded simply as alternatives. Thus त्यो आए म पनि जान्छु **tyo āe ma pani jānchu** means exactly the same thing as त्यो आयो भने म पनि जान्छु .

त्यो पाँच् बजेसम्म नआए , म घर् जान्छु
If he does not come by five o'clock, I'll go home
भोक् लागे फुल् पकाएर खानुहोस्
If you feel hungry, cook yourself an egg (and eat it)

In the above sentences त्यो . . . आएन भने and भोक लाग्यो भने would mean the same thing.

In the following idiomatic expressions, which all involve conditional clauses, the construction with the Second Perfect Participle is preferred:

अ. तिमीलाई कति पैसा चाहिन्छ ?
आ. दुइ रुपियाँ भए पुग्छ

A. How much money will you need?
B. Two rupees will be enough ('if there are two rupees, it is enough')
अ. के खाने?
आ. भात् र दाल् भए पुग्छ
A. What do you want to eat?
B. Rice and lentils will do
मोल् घटाउन खोजेको त ज्यान् गए मानेन।
I tried to bring the price down, but he would not agree at all

ज्यान गए **jyān gae** 'even if his life went'

यसो गरे हुँदैन। त्यसो गर्नुपर्छ
This is not the way to do it ('if you do it this way, it is not all right'). You must do it that way

यसो **yaso** 'in this way', त्यसो **tyaso** 'in that way'

यताबाट गए पनि हुन्छ। त्यताबाट गए पनि हुन्छ
If you go this way it will be all right. If you go that way it's all right

3. A remoter type of open condition ('if one happens to do . . .', etc.) consists of the Infinitival Participle followed by भए (the 2nd Perf. Part. of हुनु)

आज तिमी सिनेमा हेर्न जाने भए म पनि आउँछु
If you happen to be going to the cinema today, I'll come too
२५ तारीख्सम्म कल्कत्ता पुग्नुपर्ने भए, चाँडै टिकट् लिनुपर्छ नि
If it should be necessary to arrive in Calcutta on the 25th, you'll have to get your ticket soon

4. The Second Perfect Participle followed by पनि or तापनि **tāpani**[1], is translated by a concessive ('although', 'even though') clause in English. The tense of the verb in the English translation depends on the context:

मैले गरे पनि	**məyle gare pani**	although I do/did
त्यो आए तापनि	**tyo āe tāpani**	even though he comes/came

यो किताब् महँगो भए पनि म त किन्छु
Even though this book is expensive, I'll buy it
तपाईंले यसो भन्नुभए पनि मलाई विश्वास् लाग्दैन
Even though you say so, I don't believe it
ज्यादा अँध्यारो नभए तापनि हामीले गाउँमा बास् बस्ने फैसला गर्‍यौं
Although it was not very dark, we decided to spend the night in the village
गरीब् मुलुक् भए तापनि गत दस् वर्षमा नेपाल्मा निक्कै प्रगति हुन लागेको छ
Although Nepal is a poor country, in the last ten years, great progress has begun to be made there

[1] तापनि may also be used as an adverb in the sense of 'however', 'even so', etc.

उस्ले कहिले पनि काम् नगरे तापनि उस्को खल्तीमा पैसा सधैं हुन्छ नि ।
Although he never works, he always has money in his pocket

As in 3 above, the Infinitival Participle followed by भए तापनि indicates remoteness – 'even though it might be . . .'

बस्मा जहिले पनि भीड़ हुन्छ । त्यसैले पैसा अलि बढ़ता लाग्ने भए तापनि म सधैं टचाक्सीमा जान्छु
The buses are always crowded. Therefore, even though it might cost a bit more, I usually travel by taxi

अलि बढ़ता **ali baṛhtā** 'a bit more'

5. The Second Perfect Participle is used in the following constructions which involve a *relative* word such as जो **jo** 'whoever', जे **je** 'whatever', जहाँ **jahā̃** 'wherever', जस्तो **jasto** 'of whatever kind', जहिले **jahile** 'whenever'. The adverb पनि usually follows the participle:

जे भए पनि मलाई आज काठमाड़ौं नपुगी हुँदैन
Whatever happens, I really must get to Kathmandu today

नपुगी हुँदैन **napugī hū̃dəyna** 'not having arrived, it is not all right'

The particle -सुकै **sukəy** may be optionally added to the relative word (e.g. जेसुकै **jesukəy,** जहाँसुकै **jahā̃sukəy,** etc.).

जेसुकै भए पनि म घर् नगई छोड्दिन
Whatever happens, I shall definitely go home

नगई छोड्दिन **nagaī choṛdina** 'not having gone I shall not give up'

जुन् किताब् भए पनि हुन्छ
Any book will do (lit. 'whichever book there is . . .')
जो आए पनि हुन्छ
Anyone can come ('whoever comes it is all right')
जतिसुकै छिटो हिंड़े पनि बेलुकासम्म गाउँ पुग्न सकिंदैन
However quickly you walk, it is impossible to reach the village by evening
उस्लाई नचाहिने कुरा नगर् भनेर जति भने पनि मान्दैन
No matter how much you tell him not to say nasty things, he never listens

नचाहिने कुरा **nacāhine kurā** 'a thing which is not required'

जहाँसुकै गए पनि उस्ले स्वास्नीलाई सँगै लैजान्छ
Wherever he goes, he takes his wife with him
जहिलेसुकै उस्को घर् गए पनि उस्लाई कहिले पनि भेट् हुँदैन
Whenever you go to his house, you can never meet him

कसैलाई भेट् हुनु **kasəylāī bheṭ hunu** 'a meeting to come about with someone'

जस्तोसुकै राम्रो लुगा लगाए पनि त्यसै माग्ने जस्तो देखिन्छ
No matter how fine the clothes he puts on, he still looks like a beggar

त्यसै **tyasəy,** the emphatic form of त्यसो 'thus'. The second half of the sentence is literally 'he is thus seen like a beggar'.

6. In the above examples and in previous lessons, we have met a number of adjectives and adverbs which are derived from or connected with the demonstratives, the third person, interrogative and relative pronouns. For example, it is obvious that the interrogative adverb कसरी 'in what manner', bears the same relationship to the pronouns के 'what' and को 'who' as the relative adverb जसरी 'in the manner which' bears to the pronouns जे 'whatever' and जो 'whoever', and as त्यसरी 'in that manner' bears to the demonstrative त्यो, etc. The following is a complete list of the various forms in current use. Emphatic forms are given in brackets. It should be noted, however, that some of the emphatic forms are only formally emphatic and sometimes have special functions of their own.

(*i*) Forms derived from the demonstrative त्यो **tyo** (emph. त्यही **tyahī**)

त्यहाँ (त्यहीँ)	**tyahā̃** (emph. **tyahī̃**)	there, in that place
त्यता (त्यतै)	**tyatā** (emph. **tyatəy**)	to that place, thither
त्यसो (त्यसै)	**tyaso** (emph. **tyasəy**)	thus, in that way
त्यसरी	**tyasarī**	thus, in that way
तहिले	**tahile**	then, at that time
तब	**taba**	then, from that time onwards
त्यति	**tyati**	so, so much (adv.)
त्यस्तो (त्यस्तै)	**tyasto** (emph. **tyastəy**)	such, of that kind, thus
त्यत्रो (त्यत्रै)	**tyatro** (emph. **tyatrəy**)	so big, that big (adj.)
त्यतिको (त्यतिकै)	**tyatiko** (emph. **tyatikəy**)	so much, that much (adj.)[1]

(*ii*) Forms derived from the pronoun उ **u** (emph. उही **uhī**)[2]

उहाँ /वहाँ (उहीँ)	**uhā̃/vahā̃** (emph. **uhī̃**)	there, in that place
उता (उतै)	**utā** (emph. **utəy**)	to that place, there
उसो (उसै)	**uso** (emph. **usəy**)	thus, in that way
उसरी	**usarī**	thus, in that way
उहिले	**uhile**	then, at that time
उति	**uti**	so, so much (adv.)
उस्तो (उस्तै)	**usto** (emph. **ustəy**)	such, of that kind, thus
उत्रो (उत्रै)	**utro** (emph. **utrəy**)	so big, that big
उतिको (उतिकै)	**utiko** (emph. **utikəy**)	such, that much, so much

[1] The inflected plural form त्यतिका **tyatikā** 'so many', 'that many'. Similarly with उतिका **utikā** and यतिका **yatikā.**

[2] उ may occasionally be used as a demonstrative, like त्यो. E.g. उस् बखत् 'at that time'. The forms derived from **u** are in most cases interchangeable with those derived from **tyo.**

(*iii*) Forms derived from the demonstrative यो **yo** (emph. यही **yahī**)

यहाँ (यहीं)	**yahā̃** (emph. **yahī̃**)	here, in this place
यता (यतै)	**yatā** (emph. **yatəy**)	hither, to this place
यसो (यसै)	**yaso** (emph. **yasəy**)	thus, in this way
यसरी	**yasarī**	thus, in this way
अहिले	**ahile**	now, at this time
अब	**aba**	now, from now on
यति	**yati**	so, this much (adv.)
यस्तो (यस्तै)	**yasto** (emph. **yastəy**)	such, of this kind, thus
यत्रो (यत्रै)	**yatro** (emph. **yatrəy**)	so big, this big
यतिको (यतिकै)	**yatiko** (emph. **yatikəy**)	so much, this much (adj.)

(*iv*) Forms derived from the relative pronouns जो **jo** ('whoever') जे **je** ('whatever')[1]

जहाँ	**jahā̃**	where, wherever
जता (जतै)	**jatā** (emph. **jatəy**)	whither, whereso ever
जसो (जसै)	**jaso** (emph. **jasəy**)	as, in the way that
जसरी	**jasarī**	as, in the way that
जहिले	**jahile**	whenever
जब	**jaba**	whenever, from the time which
जति	**jati**	as much as, approximately
जस्तो (जस्तै)	**jasto** (emph. **jastəy**)	as, like, of the sort which
जत्रो (जत्रै)	**jatro** (emph. **jatrəy**)	as big as
जतिको (जतिकै)	**jatiko** (emph. **jatikəy**)	as much as

(*v*) Forms derived from the interrogative pronouns को **ko,** के **ke**

कहाँ	**kahā̃**	where? in which place?
कहीं	**kahī̃**	somewhere, in some place[2]
कता	**katā**	whither, to which place?
कतै	**katəy**	somewhere, to some place
कसो (कसै)	**kaso** (emph. **kasəy**)	in which way? how?
कसरी	**kasarī**	in which way? how?
कहिले	**kahile**	when? at what time?
कहिले कहीं	**kahile kahī̃**	sometimes
कति	**kati**	how much? how many?
कस्तो (कस्तै)	**kasto** (emph. **kastəy**)	how, of what kind
कत्रो (कत्रै)	**katro** (emph. **katrəy**)	how big?

[1]**jo** and **je** may occasionally function as proper relative pronouns in sentences like 'the man who came . . .', 'the book which I read . . .', etc. The construction (normally effected by means of participles) is rare and literary.

[2]**kahī̃** and **katəy**, though strictly speaking emphatic forms of **kahā** and **katā**, do not function as such.

Note that the adjectives in **-tro** (त्यत्रो, कत्रो etc.) are the equivalent of the corresponding adverb in **-ti** followed by ठूलो Thus:

यत्रो मान्छे	is the same as यति ठूलो मान्छे
कत्रो रूख्	is the same as कति ठूलो रूख्

7. The relative pronoun जो 'who', 'which', 'that' has an oblique from जस् **jas.** Thus जस्लाई **jaslāī** 'whom', 'to whom', जस्को **jasko** 'whose', 'of whom'. As we have seen above, जो is mainly used in the sense of 'whoever'. English relative clauses are most frequently rendered in Nepali by means of the First Perfect Participle (ref. to past time) and the Infinitival Participle (ref. to future or present time).

हिजो आएको मान्छे
The man who came yesterday . . .
मैले लेखेको चिठी
The letter which I wrote . . .
भोली आउने मान्छे
The man who will come tomorrow . . .
पाटन् जाने बस्
The bus which goes to Patan . . .

Occasionally, the relative pronoun जो may be used to introduce a relative clause. This is, however, largely a feature of the written language, where constructions tend to be more complicated and where a large number of participles would seem inelegant or be likely to obscure the meaning. The following sentence is from an essay by the famous Nepali poet, Lakshmī Prasād Devkoṭā;

नेपाल्का बन्हरूमा कति साहित्य छ जो लेखिएकै छैन, न लेखिनेछ ।
यहाँ कति सावित्रीहरू छन् जस्को कथा संसार्ले सुनेको छैन्
In the forests of Nepal, how much literature there is *which* has not been written, nor will ever be written. Here how many Sāvitrīs (*Sāvitrī* – a heroine of Hindu mythology) there are *whose* story the world has never heard

लेखिएकै **lekhiekəy** the emphatic First Perf. Part. of लेखिन् 'to be written'.
न लेखिनेछ **na lekhinecha** the Infinitival Future is used to make a prediction.
न . . . न **na . . . na . . .** 'neither . . . nor . . .'

8. In the following examples, the main clause begins with a word *correlative* to the word which introduces the relative clause:

जे जे . . . उही उही	whatsoever (things) . . . those very (things)
जहिले . . . तहिले	at the time which . . . at that time
जब . . . तब	whenever . . . then
जबसम्म . . . तबसम्म	as long as . . . till then
जुन् दिन् . . . त्यसै दिन्	on the day which . . . on that very day

Note that जुन् **jun** 'whichever' and कुन् **kun** 'which' are adjectives.

जुन् किताब्	**jun kitāb**	whichever book
कुन् किताब ?	**kun kitāb?**	which book?

The English translation of the following sentences should be carefully noted:

छोराले जे जे भन्छ,उही उही दिन्छ ।कस्तो मान्छे
He gives his son anything he asks for. What a stupid man!

खाना जहिले भन्नुहुन्छ, तहिले म लिएर आउँछु
I'll bring you your dinner when you ask for it

जब म विदेश्मा हुन्छु तब म बोल्चित्र र नाटक् हेर्न जान्छु
Whenever I'm abroad, (then) I go to see films and plays

जबसम्म म यहाँ काम् गर्छु तबसम्म पैसाको दु:ख हुँदैन
As long as I work here, I shall have no money troubles

नेपाली साहित्यको जन्म त्यसै दिन् भएको भन्नुपर्छ जुन् दिन् हाम्रा ग्रामीण्हरूले लोक्गीत्का सुरिला लय्हरू मुख्बाट उच्चारण् गर्न थाले
It must be admitted that Nepali literature was born on the day when ou villagers began to utter (from their mouths) the sweet tunes of folksongs

ग्रामीण **grāmīṇ** 'villager' a literary synonym of गाउँले
उच्चारण् गर्नु **uccāraṇ garnu** to utter, to pronounce

9. The Second Perfect Participle is used with the postpositions -पछि, -देखि, -सम्म

गरेपछि	**garepachi**	after doing/after I did
गरेदेखि	**garedekhi**	since doing/since I did
नगरेसम्म	**nagaresamma**	until I do/until I did

Note that 'until' clauses are rendered in Nepali by means of the *negative* secon perfect participle followed by -सम्म

यहाँ आएपछि एक् मिनेट् पनि फुर्सत् पाएको छैन
After coming here, I haven't had a minute's leisure

भात् खाएपछि रामे सुत्न गयो
After he had had his dinner, Rame went to bed

गर्मी सिद्धिएपछि बर्सात् शुरू हुन्छ
After the hot season finishes, the rainy season starts

बेलायत फर्केदेखि तपाईंसँग भेटेको छैन
Since I have returned to England, I have not met you

उ नआएसम्म यहाँ पर्खनुपर्‍यो
We shall have to wait until he comes

मेरो दाइ कलेज्बाट फर्केर साँझ् नपरेसम्म पढ्ने गर्नुहुन्छ
After returning from college, my brother goes on reading until nightfall

The construction with -देखि may sometimes be the equivalent of an ope conditional clause:

म भोलि भेट्न नगएदेखि वहाँ रिसाउनुहुनेछ
If I don't meet him tomorrow, he'll really be angry

10. *The Second Perfect Tense*

The Second Perfect Tense consists of the Second Perfect Participle and the verb छ written together as one word:

मैले गरेछु **məyle garechu** उ आएछ **u āecha** उसले बिर्सेछ **usle birsecha** तपाईं जानुभएछ **tapāī̃ jānubhaecha**

The negative is formed by infixing the negative particle न **-na-** between the participle and the auxiliary:

मैले गरेनछु **məyle garenachu** उ आएनछ **u āenacha** हामीले खाएनछौं **hāmīle khāenachəw̃,** etc.

Third person feminine forms, in which the participle suffix **-e** is changed to **ī** are in common use:

उसले गरीछ **usle garīcha** उनी भईछन् **unī bhaīchan**

In the following table the Second Perfect Tense of गर्नु is given in full. Feminine forms are given in brackets:

	Affirmative		*Negative*	
मैले	गरेछु	**garechu**	गरेनछु	**garenachu**
तैंले	गरेछस्	**garechas**	गरेनछस्	**garenachas**
त्यसले	गरेछ	**garecha**	गरेनछ	**garenacha**
(त्यसले	गरीछ)	**(garīcha)**	(गरीनछ)	**(garīnacha)**
हामीले	गरेछौं	**garechəw̃**	गरेनछौं	**garenachəw̃**
तिमीले	गरेछौ	**garechəw**	गरेनछौ	**garenachəw**
उनी (-हरू) ले	गरेछन्	**garechan**	गरेनछन्	**garenachan**
(उनी (-हरू) ले	गरीछन्)	**(garīchan)**	गरीनछन्	**(garīnachan)**
तपाईंले / वहाँले	गर्नुभएछ	**garnubhaecha**	गर्नुभएनछ	**garnubhaenacha**

11. The Second Perfect Tense is translated by the English perfect tense, 'I have done', etc., but implies that a fact has just been discovered or that it was contrary to what had previously been imagined. In English it may sometimes be rendered as, 'Oh, I see that . . . has done', etc.

उ भारत् गएछ
Why, he's gone to India
त्यसले आउन बिर्सेछ
I see that he's forgotten to come
मैले पैसा ल्याउन बिर्सेछु । मेरो खल्तीमा केही पनि रहेनछ
Oh, I've forgotten my money. I find that I've nothing in my pocket

Note that रहेछ is the Second Perfect Tense of रहन् 'to remain'.

> हेर न। झ्याल् थुन्न बिर्सेछौ
> Look now. You've forgotten to close the window
> ढोकामा को आएछ ?
> Who on earth can that be at the door?
> मेरो बहिनी बिरामी भएछ । डाक्टर्लाई बोलाउनुपर्छ क्यारे
> My sister is more ill than I expected. I'd better call the doctor
> नोकर्नीले मेरो कोठा राम्ररी सफा गरीछ
> Why, the chamber-maid has cleaned my room quite well
> मेरो दाज्यू दार्जीलिङ्ग बाट आउनुभएछ
> My brother has come (unexpectedly) from Darjeeling

12. रहेछ may be used with the First Perfect Participle instead of the auxiliary छ

उ आऐको रहेछ **u āeko rahecha**
तिमीले खाएको रहेछौ **timīle khāeko rahechaw,** etc.

The tense thus formed is the equivalent of the Second Perfect Tense, and is especially common in sentences containing the adverbs अझ, अहिलेसम्म .

> उसकी स्वास्ती अहिलेसम्म काठ्माडौं गएकी रहीनछ
> His wife hasn't yet gone to Kathmandu
> अहिलेसम्म तिमिले भात् खाएको रहेनछौ
> Why, you haven't eaten your dinner yet
> त्यो स्वास्नीमान्छे कता जान लागेकी रहीछ?
> Where on earth can that woman be going?

Note स्वास्नीमान्छे **svāsnīmānche** 'woman'
लोग्नेमान्छे **lognemānche** 'man'

13. *The Second Pluperfect Tense*

The Second Pluperfect Tense consists of the Second Perfect Participle and the following suffixes, which are, in fact, 'reduced' forms of the verb थियो .

म	-थें	**-thẽ**	हामी (हरू)	-थ्यौं	**-thyəw̃**
तँ	-थिस्	**-this**	तिमी (हरू)	-थ्यौ	**-thyəw**
उ	-थ्यो	**-thyo**	उनीहरू	-थे	**-the**
उ	-थी	**-thī** (f.)	उनी	-थिन्	**-thin** (f.)
तपाईं / वहाँ	- भएथ्यो	**bhaethyo**			

The negative is formed by infixing the negative particle न between the participle and the suffix. In 3rd person feminine forms (the most commonly used) the participle suffix **-e** is changed to **-ī.**

In the following table, the Second Pluperfect tense of गर्नु is given in full; 3rd person feminine forms are given in brackets. Transitive verbs require -ले .

	Affirmative		*Negative*	
मैले	गरेथें		गरेनथें	
तैंले	गरेथिस्		गरेनथिस्	
उस्ले	गरेथ्यो	(f. गरीथी)	गरेनथ्यो	(f. गरीनथी)
उन्ले	गरेथे	(f. गरीथिन्)	गरेनथे	(f. गरीनथिन्)
हामीले	गरेथ्यौं		गरेनथ्यौं	
तिमीले	गरेथ्यौ		गरेनथ्यौ	
उनीहरूले	गरेथे		गरेनथे	
तपाईं / वहाँ } -ले	गर्नुभएथ्यो		गर्नुभएनथ्यो	

14. The Second Pluperfect Tense is translated in English as 'I had done', 'I did', etc. (like the First Pluperfect Tense discussed in Lesson 13.6.), but usually implies suddenness of action, or that the action was unexpected:

उ भारत् गएथ्यो
He had gone/went (unexpectedly) to India
त्यस्ले आउन बिर्सीथी
She had forgotten to come
केही व्यक्तिहरूको त्यो मूर्ति देख्नासाथ् डर्ले मृत्यू भएथ्यो
Several people, as soon as they saw the statue, dropped dead from fright
उ काठ्माडौंबाट अचानक् आइपुगेथ्यो
He arrived (suddenly) from Kathmandu

15. The numerals from 71-100 should now be learnt. Remember that all numerals require the appropriate classifiers. After 100, the numerals proceed as follows:

एक् सय् एक्	**ek say ek**	101
दुइ सय् पचास्	**dui say pacās**	250
तीन् सय् उनन्सय्	**tīn say unansay,** etc.	399
एक हजार्	**ek hajār**	1000
दस् हजार्	**das hajār**	10,000
नब्बे हजार्	**nabbe hajār**	90,000
एक् लाख्	**ek lākh**	100,000
दस् लाख्	**das lākh**	1000,000
नब्बे लाख्	**nabbe lākh**	9,000,000
एक् कड़ोर्	**ek kaṛor**	10,000,000

Note especially the Nepali equivalents of 100,000, 1000,000, and 10,000,000.

Vocabulary 16

अचानक्	**acānak**	suddenly
अनुवाद्	**anuvād**	translation

अफसोच् (अफसोस्)	**aphsoc (aphsos)**	sorrow
अफसोच् मान्नु	**aphsoc mānnu**	to be sorry, to regret
अबेर्	**aber**	late
अभाग्यले	**abhāgyale**	unfortunately
अल्छी गर्नु	**alchī garnu**	to be lazy, waste time
असाद्धै	**asāddhəy**	extremely, very much
उच्चारण्	**uccāraṇ**	pronunciation, utterance
उच्चारण् गर्नु	**uccāraṇ garnu**	to pronounce, to utter
कक्षा	**kakṣā**	class
क्लास्	**klās**	class
कम्सेकम्	**kamsekam**	at least
खुशीसाथ्	**khuʃīsāth**	happily
खेर जानु	**khera jānu**	to be wasted, to be lost
ग्रामीण्	**grāmiṇ**	villager, rustic
चम्चा	**camcā**	spoon, spoonful
चाँडै	**cā̃ṛəy**	quickly, soon
जाँच्	**jā̃c**	examination
जेठो	**jeṭho**	eldest
ज्यादा	**jyādā**	more, most, very much
झैं	**jhəỹ**	as, as if, like
तापनि	**tāpani**	even so, although
थुन्नु	**thunnu**	to close, to fasten, to lock
दिन् प्रतिदिन्	**din pratidin**	every day
दुवै	**duvəy**[1]	both
नाटक्	**nāṭak**	play, drama
नोकर्नी	**nokarnī**	female servant
पछाड़ि	**pachāṛi**	behind, at the back
परिश्रम् गर्नु	**pariʃram garnu**	to make an effort
प्रगति	**pragati**	progress, advance
प्रतिदिन्	**pratidin**	daily
फुर्ती	**phurtī**	smartness
फुर्तीसाथ्	**phurtīsāth**	smartly
फैसला गर्नु	**phəyslā garnu**	to decide
बढ़ी	**baṛhī**	more, increasingly (adv.)
बढ़ता	**baṛhtā**	more, greater (adj.)
बढ़्नु	**baṛhnu**	to increase, to grow
बन्, (वन्)	**ban (van)**	forest
बर्सात्	**barsāt**	rain, rainy season
बिग्रनु	**bigranu**	to be spoilt, to break down
बिचरा	**bicarā**	poor, unfortunate
बिन्ती (विन्ती)	**bintī (vintī)**	request
बोलाउनु	**bolāunu**	to call
बोल्चित्र	**bolcitra**	film, 'talky'
भाग्यले	**bhāgyale**	fortunately

[1]**v** pronounced as English **w**.

भीड़्	**bhīṛ**	crowd
भेट्	**bheṭ**	meeting, encounter
महँगी	**mahãgī**	expense, cost of living
माथिल्लो	**māthillo**	upper
(-को) मान् गर्नु	**(ko) mān garnu**	to give respect to
मुलुक्	**muluk**	country (syn. **deʃ**)
मेहनत्	**mehnat**	effort
रमाइलो गर्नु	**ramāilo garnu**	to enjoy oneself
रोकिनु	**rokinu**	to be stopped
लय्	**lay**	tune
लोक्गीत्	**lokgīt**	folksong
लोग्नेमान्छे	**lognemānche**	man (as opposed to woman)
विश्वास्	**viʃvās**	trust, belief
विश्वास् लाग्नु	**(lāī) viʃvās lāgnu**	to believe in
संसार्	**samsār**	world
सफल्	**saphal**	successful
सफा	**saphā**	clean
सफा गर्नु	**saphā garnu**	to clean
समस्या	**samasyā**	problem
सवारी	**savārī**	conveyance, means of transport
सापट् दिनु	**sāpaṭ dinu**	to lend
सुरिलो	**surilo**	sweet, tuneful
स्वागत् गर्नु	**svāgat garnu**[1]	to welcome
स्वास्नीमान्छे	**svāsnīmānche**	woman
हराउनु	**harāunu**	to lose, to be lost
हिउँद्	**hiũd**	winter (syn. **jāṛo**)

Reading Passage

दाइ र भाइका समस्याहरू

मेरो दाइ मभन्दा तीन् वर्ष जेठो हुनुहुन्छ,तर हामी दुवैजना एउटै क्लास्मा पढ़्छौं ।हाम्रो बुवा धेरै धनी नहुनुभए तापनि हामीलाई कलेज्मा पठाउन आमाद्धैं मेहनत् गर्नुहुन्छ । मेरो दाइ पढ़्नलाई धेरै परिश्रम् गर्नुहुन्छ र कलेज्बाट घर फर्केपछि साँझ् नपरेसम्म पढ़्ने गर्नुहुन्छ। मचाहिं दिन् प्रतिदिन् साथीहरूलाई भेट्न शहर् जान्छु र राति अबेरसम्म त्यहाँ रमाइलो गर्छु ।मैले यस्तै गर्ने गरेकोले,[1] दाइ रिसाउनुहुन्छ ।वहाँ भन्नुहुन्छः

हेर, हामी गरीब् छौं । त्यसैले तिमीले अलि बढ़ी मेहनत् गर्नुपर्छ। अर्को महीना जाँच् आउँदै छ नि, र तिमीचाहिं खाली साथीहरूसँग चियापसल्मा बस्ने गर्छौ। तिमी पक्कै पनि फेल् हुनेछौ। बुवाले खर्च गर्नुभएको पैसा खेर मात्रै जानेछ ।

[1]**v** pronounced like English **w**.

हो ,दाइले भनुभएको कुरा ठीकै हो ।दुइ वर्ष अगाडि पनि वहाँले मलाई यसै भन्नुभएको थियो । तर भाग्यले म जाँच्मा पास् भएँ, र अभाग्यले वहाँ फेल् हुनुभयो। फेरि पनि उही क्लास्मा बस्नुपरेकोले, दाइले अफसोच् मान्नुभयो [2] ।

हिउँद्मा एक् दिन् साँझ्को बेला , म अँग्रेजीबाट नेपालीमा अनुवाद् गर्दै थिएँ । मैले गरेको अनुवाद् ठीक् छ कि छैन भनी हेर्न दाइ पाल्नुभयो [3]। पछाडिबाट हेर्दै [4] वहाँले भन्नुभयो:

के लेखेको त्यस्तो तिमीले ? कम्सेकम् नेपाली लेख्दा बुझ्ने गरी त लेख ।तिमीले यस्तै गर्‍यौ भने पोहोर्को जाँच्मा पास् गरे झैं, [5] अर्को जाँच्मा सफल् हुनेछैनौ । गाह्रो हुन्छ नि ।

तर अर्को वर्ष पनि म पास् भएँ र बिचरा दाइ फेल् हुनुभयो ।के गर्ने ? मचाहिं माथिल्लो कक्षामा गएँ, र वहाँलाईचाहिं उही कक्षामा नै बस्नुपरेकोले, हामी दुवैजना अहिले एउटै क्लास्मा छौं।

मैले बढ़ी मेहनत् गर्नुपर्छ भन्ने मलाई थाहा छ । तिमीले अल्छी गर्‍यौ भनेर दाइले गाली गर्नुभएको पनि ठीकै हो [6]। हामी एउटै क्लास्मा भए तापनि वहाँ मभन्दा जेठो हुनहुन्छ । त्यस् कारण्ले , म सधैं दाइको मान् गर्छु।

Notes

This passage tells the story of a careless young brother who is constantly being given advice by his hard-working elder brother. The elder brother, by failing his exams and thus being kept in the same class year after year, eventually finds himself in the same standard as his young brother, who manages to get himself promoted. The elder brother, however, by virtue of his years, is still considered wiser, even though the facts indicate the contrary. In a family children are often referred to by a term indicating the order of their birth. The terms, which are often used instead of the personal name, are as follows:

जेठो	**jeṭho**	the eldest	माहिंलो	**māhĩlo**	the second
साहिंलो	**sāhĩlo**	the third	काहिंलो	**kāhĩlo**	the fourth
थाहिंलो	**thāhĩlo**	the fifth	काँछो	**kā̃cho**	the youngest

Feminine forms (used for girls) are: जेठी, माहिंली, साहिंली, काहिंली, थाहिंली, काँछी

1. **məyle yasto garne garekole**: 'because I keep acting in this way'.
2. **aphsoc mānnu**: 'to feel sorry for oneself'.
3. **bhanī herna . . . pālnubhayo**: 'he came to see whether my translation was all right or not'. Note the use of the conjunctive participle **bhanī** in this construction.
4. **herdəy**: 'looking over my shoulder'. **herdəy** is the imperfect participle of **hernu** discussed in Lesson 19.

5. **pās gare jhəȳ**: 'as you passed in the last exam'. Note the use of the Second Perf. Part. with **jhəȳ.**
6. **timīle alchī . . . ṭhīkəy ho**: lit. 'having said "you wasted your time" my elder brother having scolded me, it is quite all right', i.e. my brother was of course quite right to have scolded me for wasting my time.

Exercise 16a

Translate into English

१. बाटो त्यति उकालो नभए तापनि , गाउँ पुग्न हामीलाई पाँच् घण्टा जति लाग्यो ।
२ . मैले पैसा ल्याउन बिर्सेछु । दस् रुपियाँ सापट् देऊ। म भोलि फिर्ता दिन्छु ।
३ . नेपालीहरू गरीब् भए तापनि उनीहरू खुशीसाथ् पाहुनाहरूको स्वागत् गर्छन्।
४ . मलाई वहाँको घर् समय्मा नपुगी हुँदैन । अलि पैसा धेरै लाग्ने भए तापनि ,ट्याक्सीमा जान्छु
५ . जे जे भन्यो उही उही दिएर तिमीले स्वास्नीलाई बिगार्‍यौ।
६ . हेर त त्यो लाले होइन? त्यस्तो फुर्तीसाथ् कहाँ जान लागेको रहेछ ?
७ . पाँच् रुपियाँ दिएको त रिक्शावालाले ज्यान् गए लिएन। आजकाल् नेपाल्मा पनि कस्तो महँगी बढ़ेको ।
८ . मलाई जतिसुकै बिन्ती गरे पनि तिमीलाई सिनेमा हेर्न जान दिँदिन।
९ . कति चिनी चाहिन्छ? दुइ चम्चा भए पुग्छ ।
१० . मेरो काम् नसिद्धिएसम्म काठ्माड़ौंमा बस्नुपर्छ। सिद्धिने बित्तिकै म पहाड़तिर जानेछु।
११ . मेरो कलम् हराएछ । चिठी कसरी लेख्ने ?
१२ . यो बाटोबाट गए पनि ,त्यो बाटोबाट गए पनि ,एउटै हो ।
१३ . हिउँद्मा पहाड़का वरिपरि गाउँहरूमा हिउँ धेरै पर्छ ।
१४ . पानी परेको बेलामा ,पहिरो जाने सम्भावना हुन्छ । त्यसो भए,बाटोहरू दुइ तीन् हप्तासम्म बन्द हुन्छन् र सबै सवारी जहाँको तहाँ रोकिन्छन् ।
१५ . म अड्डा गएर साँझ् नपरेसम्म काम् गर्छु । काम् सिद्ध्याएपछि घर्तिर फर्कन्छु।

Exercise 16b

Translate into Nepali

1. Although many of the countries of Asia are poor, over the next ten years, they will make much progress.
2. Even though it was dark, he decided to go as far as the next village.
3. What time shall I come? Come any time you wish.
4. However much money it costs, I shall definitely go to Nepal next year.
5. As long as he was in Kathmandu, he was perfectly well. When he went to the mountains he fell ill.
6. We shall have to wait here until the bus comes. We can't walk.
7. After I returned home, I read the newspaper, and went to bed at about half past eleven.
8. Who is that at the door? Why it's Rāme! Why has he come so late?
9. How many (elder) brothers do you have? I have one elder brother. He is two years older than I. I am the second one in the family.
10. My son has made much progress at school. This year he's even gone up to the higher standard.

11. My wife always wants to buy everything she sees in the shops.
12. How expensive it is in Nepal these days. I had to pay three rupees for a cup of tea this morning.
13. Although my home is quite far away from the city, I like living there. But in the morning, if I come by car, it takes me nearly half an hour to arrive at my office.
14. How much milk do you want in your tea? Just a little will be enough.
15. I'll work in the library until my work is finished. After that, I intend to spend three months in the hills.

Exercise 16c

Translate into Nepali

The minister's death came about suddenly; we intend to go to England; what's the use of giving him advice?; he happened to arrive before nightfall; can I get lodgings for the night?; we called the doctor; who told you to do that?; I have a headache; whether you go by bus or train, it amounts to the same thing; whatever you say, he will not listen; the temple was decorated with metal statues; after failing the exam my eldest brother felt sorry; where can that man be going?

Exercise 16d

Give the correct form of the verb in brackets:

१. किसान्ले एउटा राम्रो नेपाली लोक्गीत् (गाउनु)थियो ।
२. अंग्रेज् (हुनु) तापनि, उस्को उच्चारण् राम्रो (रहनु)।
३. आज काठ्माडौं उपत्यकामा मौसम् सफा (रहनु)
४. रामे त फुर्तीसाथ् (आउनु)। कहाँ जान (लाग्नु)
५. उ जाँच्मा सफल् पो (हुनु) ।
६. तिमीले बिन्ती (गर्नु) पनि ,(नगर्नु) पनि म जान दिन्न ।
७. पट्ना भएर (जानु) पनि ,बनारस् भएर (जानु)पनि, दुइ घण्टा त लाग्छ।
८. जेसुकै (गर्नु)पनि ,साँझ् (पर्नु) अगाड़ी पुग्न सक्नेछैनौं
९. काम् (सिद्धिनु) पछि , म शहर् (जानु) रमाइलो गर्छु ।

LESSON 17

1. *The Injunctive*

The personal suffixes of the Injunctive are as follows:

म	-ऊँ	**-ũ**	हामी	-औं	**-əw̃**
तँ	-एस्	**-es**	तिमी	-ए	**-e**
त्यो	-ओस्	**-os**	उनी (-हरू)	-ऊन्	**-ūn**

The suffixes are added directly to the base of verbs belonging to groups (i) and (ii) and to the secondary base of verbs belonging to groups (iii), (iv) and (v).

म गरूँ **ma garũ**	म खाऊँ **ma khāũ**	म दिऊँ **ma diũ**
म बिर्सूँ **ma birsũ**	म धोऊँ **ma dhoũ**	म आऊँ **ma āũ**

The Injunctive of हुनु is formed from the base हो **ho-**. Thus म होऊँ **ma hoũ,** etc. However, the 2nd person LGH and MGH suffixes are added to the base भ- **bha-**. Thus: तँ भएस् **ta bhaes,** तिमी भए **timī bhae.**

Similarly, the Injunctive of जानु is formed from the primary base **jā-** except in the case of the 2nd person LGH and MGH forms, which are formed from the secondary base: म जाऊँ **ma jāũ,** *but* तँ गएस् **ta gaes,** तिमी गए **timī gae.**

The affirmative forms of the injunctive of the verbs गर्नु, हुनु and जानु are as follows:

म	गरूँ	होऊँ	जाऊँ
तँ	गरेस्	भएस्	गएस्
त्यो	गरोस्	होओस्	जाओस्
हामी	गरौं	होऔं	जाऔं
तिमी	गरे	भए	गए
उनी (-हरू)	गरून्	होऊन्	जाऊन्

The negative injunctive is formed by adding the negative prefix न- **na-** to the positive forms: नगरूँ **nagarũ,** नखाऊँ **nakhāũ,** नजाऊँ **najāũ,** नहोऊँ **nahoũ.**

The HGH is formed by adding the termination -होस् **-hos** to the infinitive in **-nu:** गर्नुहोस् **garnuhos,** नगर्नुहोस् **nagarnuhos.**

It will be noted that the HGH injunctive is the same as the HGH imperative.

2. The Injunctive is most commonly used to express a wish or desire ('let me do', 'let him come', etc.) or in questions of the type 'may I do?', 'shall I do?'. In earlier lessons we have already met one or two examples:

म जाऊँ है त ?
May I go now?
हवाईजहाज्मा ठाउँ छ कि छैन म एक् चोटी हेरूँ
Let me see if there is any room or not in the aeroplane
अ. चियामा कति चिनी हालूँ ?
आ. दुइ चम्चा भए पुग्छ
A. How much sugar shall I put in your tea?
B. Two spoons are enough
मेरो पैसा हराएको जस्तो छ । अब के गरूँ?
I seem to have lost my money. Now what shall I do?
त्यो काम् भोलिसम्म रहोस्
Let that work remain till tomorrow
उस्को घर् नाश् भयो । अब के गरोस् गरीब् बिचरा?
His house has been ruined. Now what can the poor fellow do?
खाने बेला भयो ।जाऔं त
It's time for dinner. Let's go

Note that जाऔं is often pronounced **jām,** especially in phrases like हिंड् जाऔं **hīṛa jām** 'let's be off'.

The second person forms of the Injunctive are rather infrequent. They may be translated into English as 'make sure that you do', etc. The subject of 3rd and 2nd person forms of the Injunctive of transitive verbs sometimes takes -ले

त्यो काम् तैंले राम्ररी गरेस् ।सुनिस् तैंले?
Make sure that you do that well. Did you hear me?
धेरै पढ़ेर भोलि पर्सी तँ ठूलो मान्छे भएस्
Study hard and you'll become a great man ('having studied, make sure you become')

3. Sentences of the type: 'whether he goes or not . . .' are rendered in Nepali by means of the Injunctive. In this case, the subject of a transitive verb usually takes -ले :

त्यो आओस् कि नआओस् 'whether he comes or not . . .'
उस्ले गरोस् कि नगरोस् 'whether he does or not . . .'

उ जाओस् कि नजाओस् म त पक्कै जानेछु
Whether he goes or not, I am certainly going
उस्ले भनोस् कि नभनोस् हामी त जरूरै भित्र जानेछौं
Whether he says so or not, we're going in just the same
पानी परोस् कि नपरोस् बाहिर जानैपर्छ
Whether it rains or not, we'll have to go out

4. The Injunctive may express the idea of 'hoping' and is used with expressions like आशा गर्नु **aʃā garnu** (or आस् गर्नु **ās garnu**) 'to hope':

उस्को कुरा साँचो होस् भन्ने म आशा गर्छु
I hope what he says is true ('Let what he says be true . . .')
भोलि पानी नपरोस् बा भनेर उस्ले भन्यो
He said that he hoped it would not rain the next day. ('Let it not rain tomorrow, having said, he said')

5. Used with the conjunctive participles भनेर or भनी , the injunctive expresses purpose, when the subject of the verb in the main clause is different from that of the verb in the subordinate clause:

उस्ले तिमीलाई ठीक् सुनोस् भनी ठूलो स्वरले बोल त
Speak louder so that he might hear you well

Alternatively उस्ले ठीक् सुन्ने गरी . . . (the construction discussed in Lesson 15) may be used.

उस्लाई थाहा होस् भनी मैले उस्लाई बताएँ
I told him so that he might know

This sentence may be literally translated: 'Having said/thought "Let him know", I told him'.

सन्तान् होस् भन्नाका निमित्त उन्ले हरेक् उपाय गरे
He did all he could to have children ('for the sake of saying, "Let there be offspring," he made every plan')

6. Sentences like: 'I was going to do something, but could not . . .' are translated by the Injunctive and the phrase कि जस्तो लागेको थियो तर

तिमिलाई भनूँ कि जस्तो लागेको थियो तर भन्न पाइनँ
I was going to tell you, but I didn't manage it
उस्लाई भेट्न जाऊँ कि जस्तो लागेको थियो तर फुर्सत् पाइएन
I was going to meet him, but I couldn't find the time

7. *The Future Tense*

As the name suggests, the Future Tense refers to future time, but also expresses the idea of doubt or uncertainty. In English it can usually be translated: 'I shall probably do', 'I may do', 'perhaps I'll do', etc.

The positive suffixes are as follows:

म	-उँला	**-ũlā**		
तँ	–लास्	**-lās**	(f. -लिस्	**-lis**)
त्यो	–ला	**-lā**	(f. -ली	**-lī**)
हामी	-औँला	**-əw̃lā**		
तिमी	-औला	**-əwlā**	(f. -औली	**-əwlī**)
उनी(-हरू)	-लान्	**-lān**	(f. -लिन्	**-lin**)

The negative suffixes are as follows:

म	-ओइन	**-oina**
तँ	- ओइनस्	**-oinas**
त्यो	-ओइन	**-oina**
हामी	-ओइनौं	**-oinəw̃**
तिमी	-ओइनौ	**-oinəw**
उनी(हरू)	-ओइनन्	**-oinan**

The positive suffixes are added to the base of verbs belonging to group (i) and to the base of verbs belonging to group (ii) which have the base vowel **-ā** (e.g. खान्).

म	गरूँला	**garūlā**	
तँ	गर्लास्	**garlās**	(f. गर्लिस् **garlis**)
त्यो	गर्ला	**garlā**	(f. गर्ली **garlī**)
हामी	गरौंला	**garəw̃lā**	
तिमी	गरौला	**garəwlā**	(f. गरौली **garəwlī**)
उनी (-हरू)	गर्लान्	**garlān**	(f. गर्लिन् **garlin**)
	खाउँला	**khāūlā**	
	खालास्	**khālās**	
	खाला	**khālā**, etc.	

Verbs of group (ii) with the base vowel **-i** (e.g. उभिन् 'to stand') have the vowel **-e-** infixed between the base vowel and the 2nd and 3rd sing., and the 3rd pl. suffixes:

उभिउँला	**ubhiūlā**	
उभिएलास्	**ubhielās**	(f. अभिएलिस् **ubhielis**)
उभिएला	**ubhielā**	(f. अभिएली **ubhielī**)
उभिऔंला	**ubhiəw̃lā**	
अभिऔला	**ubhiəwlā**	(f. अभिऔली **ubhiəwlī**)
अभिएलान्	**ubhielān**	(f. अभिएलिन् **ubhielin**)

Verbs belonging to group (iii) have the suffixes added directly to the secondary base: धोउँला **dhoūlā,** धोला **dholā,** धोली **dholī,** etc.

Verbs belonging to group (iv) have the suffixes added to the secondary base. The vowel **-e-** is infixed between the base and the 2nd and 3rd sing., and 3rd pl. suffixes:

बिर्सूंला	**birsūlā**	
बिर्सेलास्	**birselās**	(f. बिर्सेलिस् **birselis**)
बिर्सेला	**birselā**	(f. बिर्सेली **birselī**)
बिर्सौंला	**birsəw̃lā**	
बिर्सौला	**birsəwlā**	(f. बिर्सौली **birsəwlī**)
बिर्सेलान्	**birselān**	(f. बिर्सेलिन् **birselin**)

Verbs belonging to group (v) have the suffixes added to the secondary base. The vowel **-u-** is infixed before the 2nd and 3rd sing., and 3rd pl. suffixes:

आउँला	**āũlā**	
आउलास्	**āulās**	(f. आउलिस् **āulis**)
आउला	**āulā**	(f. आउली **āulī**)
आऔंला	**āəw̃lā**	
आऔला	**āəwlā**	(f. आऔली **āəwlī**)
आउलान्	**āulān**	(f. आउलिन् **āulin**)

There are commonly used alternative forms for the 2nd person pl. (तिमी) and 3rd person pl. (उनी / उनीहरू). They are as follows:

Group		2nd pl.		3rd pl.	
(i)	m.	गर्लाउ	**garlāu**	गर्नन्	**garnan**
	f.	गर्लेउ	**garleu**	गर्निन्	**garnin**
(ii)	m.	उभिएलाउ	**ubhielāu**	उभिनन्	**ubhinan**
	f.	उभिएलेउ	**ubhieleu**	उभिनिन्	**ubhinin**
(iii)	m.	धोलाउ	**dholāu**	धुनन्	**dhunan**[1]
	f.	धोलेउ	**dholeu**	धुनिन्	**dhunin**
(iv)	m.	बिर्सेलाउ	**birselāu**	बिर्सनन्	**birsanan**[1]
	f.	बिर्सेलेउ	**birseleu**	बिर्सनिन्	**birsanin**
(v)	m.	आउलान्	**āulān**	आउनन्	**āunan**[1]
	f.	आउलेउ	**āuleu**	आउनिन्	**āunin**

The forms of हुनु and दिनु are slightly irregular:

हुँला	**hũlā**	दिउँला	**diũlā**
होलास्	**holās**	देलास्	**delās**
होला	**holā**	देला	**delā**
होऔंला	**hoəw̃lā**	दिऔंला	**diəw̃lā**
होऔला	**hoəwlā**	दिऔला	**diəwlā**
होलान्	**holān**	देलान्	**delān**

The negative suffixes are added to the base of vowels belonging to groups (i) and (ii) and to the secondary base of verbs belonging to groups (iii), (iv) and (v).

गरोइन **garoina**	खाओइन **khāoina**	धोओइन **dhooina**
बिर्सोइन **birsoina**	आओइन **āoina**	होओइन **hooina**

Alternatively, the negative may be formed by adding the prefix न- **na-** to the positive form: नगरूँला **nagarũlā,** नआउँला **naāũlā,** etc. These forms are by far the most common in speech.

HGH forms consist of the **-nu** infinitive followed by गर्नुहोला **garnuholā,** नगर्नुहोला **nagarnuholā.**

The subject of the future tense of a transitive verb often takes -ले . This is frequently the case with 2nd and 3rd person forms.

[1]Note that the alternative 3rd pl. suffixes are added to the Primary Base.

तिमीले पाउलाउ (पाऔला)	you will find
उस्ले के भन्ला?	what will he say?
उन्ले गर्लान्	he will probably do
बुवाले के भन्नुहोला?	what will father say?

However, -ले is often omitted from the subject of 1st person forms: मैले गरुँला or म गरुँला 'I shall probably do'.

8. As we have seen, the future tense expresses doubt or uncertainty. We have met one example in previous lessons:

भोलि फेरि भेटौंला
We'll (probably) meet tomorrow

Here the future tense indicates that the appointment is a probability, but not altogether fixed.

Compare the following examples:

म शायद् आउने साल् नेपाल् जाउँला
I shall probably be going to Nepal next year

शायद् **ʃāyad** 'perhaps', 'probably'

अ. त्यहाँ जानलाई कति बेर् लाग्ला ?
आ. आधा घण्टा जति लाग्ला
A. Roughly how long will it take to go there?
B. It'll take about half an hour
त्यहाँ पुग्नलाई कति बेर् लाग्ला ?
How long do you think it will take us to arrive there?

Note that the future tense may often be translated 'I think that . . .', 'I suppose . . .'

यो कुरा उस्लाई कस्तो लाग्ला ?
How do you think he'll take it?
बाटोको लागि के के चाहिएला ?
What things do you think we shall need for the journey?
आज मलाई सन्चो छैन । एक् दिन् आराम् गरें भने भोलि त निको होला ।
I'm not feeling well today. If I have a day's rest, it should be all right tomorrow
कलेज्का विद्यार्थीहरू भोलि हड्ताल् गर्लान्
It looks as if the college students will go on strike tomorrow

हड्ताल् **haṛtāl** 'a strike'

भात् पाकेको रहेनछ भने नखाउँला।
If the food isn't cooked, I don't think I'll eat

पाक्नु **pāknu** 'to be cooked'

The future tense is frequently used with the phrase जस्तो छ 'it looks as if'. (Lesson 7).

अ. तिमीलाइ रुघा लाग्यो ?
आ. लाग्ला लाग्ला जस्तो छ
A. Do you have a cold?
B. It looks as if I'm going to have one
आज पानी पर्ला जस्तो छ
It looks as if it's going to rain today
अर्को बर्ष म भारत् जाउँला जस्तो लागेको छ
It looks as if I shall be going to India next year
हामी आज पुगौंला जस्तो छैन
It doesn't look as if we shall arrive today

9. As we have seen in previous lessons, होला **holā** (the 3rd sing. future of हुनु) following a verb in the Simple Indefinite, is the equivalent of the future tense. Thus म जान्छु होला **ma jānchu holā** means the same as म जाउँला 'I shall probably go'. This is extremely common in speech, especially where a negative form of the future is required. Thus म जाँदिन होला **ma jādina hola** frequently replaces the form म जाओइन

अ. ट्याक्सीमा जान कति पर्छ होला ?
आ. कम्सेकम् छ रुपियाँ लाग्ला
A. How much do you think it will cost to go by taxi?
B. It will probably cost at least six rupees
अ. ए दाइ, हवाईजहाज्मा ठाउँ छ कि छैन ?
आ. छ होला। म एक् चोटी हेर्छु
A. Is there any room in the aeroplane?
B. I think there is. I'll go and have a look
त्यो आज आउँदैन होला। घर्मा पाहुनाहरू आएका छन् रे
He probably won't come today. He has guests to stay

Similarly, the Simple Past may be followed by the future tense of हुनु. This is translated in English as 'I must have done', 'I probably have done'.

मैले गरें हुँला **məyle garẽ hūlā** I must have done, etc.
उसले गर्‍यो होला **usle garyo holā** he must have done

Note that both verbs have the appropriate personal form:

उ हिजो यहाँ आयो होला। उस्को टोपी टेबुल्मा रहेछ
He must have come here yesterday. His hat is on the table
बाटो बन्द छ रे। पहिरो गयो होला
They say the road's closed. There must have been a landslide
भोलि बिदा हुन्छ। तपाईंले सुन्नुभयो होला
There's a holiday tomorrow. You must have heard about it

The First Perfect Participle may also be followed by the future of हुनु . Again the meaning is 'I must have done', etc.

> तिमीले अहिलेसम्म त्यो काम् सिद्ध्याएको होऔला
> You must have finished that work by now
> वहाँ त नेपाल्मा धेरै दिन् बस्नुभएको होला
> He must have lived in Nepal for a long time

Vocabulary 17

अक्सर	**aksar**	generally, mostly
अच्छा	**acchā**	very well, I see
अभ्यास्	**abhyās**	practice
आँसु	**ā̃su**	tears
आँसु झार्नु	**ā̃su jhārnu**	to shed tears
आशा गर्नु	**āʃā garnu**	to hope
आस् गर्नु	**ās garnu**[1]	to hope
इष्ट-मित्र	**iṣṭa-mitra**	friends
कमाउनु	**kamāunu**	to earn, to win
कागत्	**kāgat**	paper
कुन्नि	**kunni**	I don't know (colloq.)
केन्द्र	**kendra**	centre
खूबै	**khūbəy**	well, fine
चिनी	**cinī**	sugar
(एक्) चोटी	**(ek) coṭī**	(one) time
छर्-छिमेकी	**char-chimekī**	neighbours
झार्नु	**jhārnu**	to shed, to pour
झुम्का	**jhumkā**	tassel, ear ring
झुम्के-शाल्	**jhumke-ʃāl**	tasselled shawl
टोपी	**ṭopī**	hat
ठेगाना	**ṭhegānā**	address, a place to stay
थुप्रै	**thūprəy**	loads of (colloq.)
देखाउनु	**dekhāunu**	to show
धन्यवाद्	**dhanyavād**	thank you
धावा	**dhāvā**[2]	campaign, battle
नाम्	**nām**[3]	name, glory
नाम् कमाउनु	**nām kamāunu**	to win fame
निको	**niko**	well, in good health
-नेर, -निर	**-nera, -nira**	near, by
पशुपतिनाथ्	**paʃupatināth**	Pashupatinath Temple
पहिला	**pahilā**	first of all

[1]An alternative colloquial form for **āʃā.**
[2]**v** pronounced like English **w.**
[3]A common alternative of **nāū.**

पाउन्ड	**pāunḍ**	pound (money)
पाक्नु	**pāknu**	to be cooked
पाली	**pālī**	time, turn
पुऱ्याउनु	**puryāunu**	to make arrive, to take along
पुऱ्याईदिनु	**puryāidinu**	to take along
पोको	**poko**	bundle
पौड़ी खेल्नु	**pəwṛī khelnu**	to swim
प्रशस्त	**praʃasta**	enough, much, many
प्यारो	**pyāro**	beloved
बताउनु	**batāunu**	to tell
बन्नु	**bannu**	to be made, to become
बस्तु (वस्तु)	**bastu (vastu)**	property, cattle
बाख्रो	**bākhro**	goat
बाबु	**bābu**	father
बिदा दिनु	**bidā dinu**	to give leave to
बीर् (वीर्)	**bīr (vīr)**	brave, brave man
भनाई	**bhanāī**	saying
भनाईको मतलब्	**bhanāīko matlab**	what I mean is . . .
मान्मनीतो	**mānmanīto**	honouring, honourable treatment
माल्-सामान्	**māl-sāmān**	luggage
माया	**māyā**	love
युरोपियन्	**yuropiyan**	European
रक्षक्	**rakṣak**	guardian, keeper
राज्दूतावास्	**rājdūtāvās**	embassy
लोग्ने	**logne**	husband, man
लौ लौ	**ləw ləw**	there now!
ल्याईदिनु	**lyāidinu**	to bring back
सन्तान्	**santān**	offspring, children
साट्नु	**sāṭnu**	to change, to exchange
सामान्	**sāmān**	goods
सूट्केस्	**sūṭkes**	suitcase
स्याहार् गर्नु	**syāhār garnu**	to look after
हड्ताल्	**haṛtāl**	a strike
हड्ताल् गर्नु	**haṛtāl garnu**	to go on strike
हवस्	**havas**	very well
हाल	**hāl**	hall
हाल्नु	**hālnu**	to put in, to tell (a tale)
हेर्-बिचार् गर्नु	**her-bicār garnu**	to look after, to take care of

Reading Passage

विमान्स्थल्मा

(काठ्माड़ौंको अन्तर्राष्ट्रीय विमानस्थल्मा पुगेपछि, माल्-सामान्को हालमा ।)

अ. नमस्कार्, दाज्यू म अहिले दिल्लीबाट आएको छु। मेरो हवाईजहाज् भर्खर् आइपुग्यो। त्यो भन्नुहोस्। मेरो माल्-सामान् कतातिर् होला?

आ. यताबाट आउनुहोला। म अहिले बताउँला। पहिला, तपाईंको राहदानी देखाउनुहोस्। म एक् चोटी हेरूँ। खै ठीक् जस्तो छ। तपाईंले आफ्नो भीजा लन्दन्को राज्दूतावास्मा लिनुभयो होला। तपाईं बेलायत्बाट आउनुभएको रहेछ, होइन त? यस्भन्दा पहिला पनि नेपाल् आउनुभएको छ कि यो पहिलो पाली हो?

अ. यो पहिलो पटक् हो।

आ. त्यसो भए नेपाली कहाँ सिक्नुभएको नि?

अ. यहाँ आउनु अगाड़ि मैले बेलायत्मै सिकेको, लन्दन्मा मेरो दुइ तीन्जना नेपाली साथी बस्छन्। यिनीहरूसँग मैले सिक्न थालें। अहिले अभ्यास् गर्नलाई म नेपाल् आएको छु।

आ. अच्छा। नेपाल्मा कति बस्ने बिचार् छ त?

अ. मेरो बिचार्ले, छ महीना जति बस्छु होला। त्रिभुवन् विश्वविद्यालयमा अलिकति काम् छ।

आ. काठ्माड़ौंमा कहाँ बस्नुहुन्छ त?

आ. अहिलेसम्म त केही ठेगाना भएको छैन, तर दुइ तीन् हप्ताको लागि कुनै होटेल्मा गएर बस्नुपर्ला । तपाईं मलाई अलिकति सल्लाह दिनुहोस्, होटेल्मा कोठा सजिलैसँग पाइएला?

आ. गाह्रो हुँदैन होला। शहर्मा प्रशस्त होटेल्हरू छन् ।

अ. साधारण् होटेल्मा एक् रात्को कति तिर्नुपर्ला? म त धेरै महँगो होटेल्मा बस्न सक्दिन।

आ. दिन्को चालीस् रुपियाँ जतिमा कोठा पाउन सक्नुहुन्छ होला। अक्सर् नेपालीहरूको लागि त्यो त अलि महँगो पर्छ तर युरोपियन्हरूको लागि त्यति महँगो होइन। भनाइको मतलब्, दुइ पाउन्ड भन्दा अलि बढ़ता पर्न आउँछ।

अ. केही दिन्को लागि त ठीकै होला। त्यस्पछि हेरूँला। खै, मेरो माल्-सामान् अहिलेसम्म आइपुगेको छैन?

आ. आयो होला कि? शायद् अर्को कोठामा छ। एक् चोटी गएर हेर्नुहोस् न।

अ. हो। ऊ त्यहीं छ मेरो सूट्केस्। खोल्नुपर्छ कि पर्दैन?

आ. भैगो। खोल्नुपर्दैन। जानुहोस् त।

अ. ट्याक्सी कहाँ पाइएला?

आ. यहाँबाट बाहिर निस्कनुभएपछि, थुप्रै ट्याक्सीहरू पाउनुहुन्छ।

अ. यहाँबाट शहर्सम्म जान कति रुपियाँ लाग्ला?

आ. बीस् रुपियाँभन्दा बढ़ी लाग्दैन होला। धेरै टाढ़ा छैन नि। ट्याक्सी-ड्राइभर्ले तपाईंको होटेल्सम्म पुऱ्याइदिन्छ।

अ. ट्याक्सी लिनु अगाड़ि, मलाई अलिकति पैसा साट्नुपर्छ। कहाँ जाऊँ?

आ. हो। बाहिर निस्कने ढोकानेर पैसा साट्ने ठाउँ छ। त्यहीं गएर साट्नुहोस् न।

अ. हवस्। धेरै धेरै धन्यवाद्। म जाऊँ है त। फेरि भेटौंला।

एउटा नेपाली लोकगीत्

१ . नरोऊ नरोऊ मेरी साहिंली
बिदा देऊ न, आँसु नझारी ।
जाँदै छु म धावैमा लौ लौ ।
फर्की आउँला नाम् कमाई।[1]

२ . बूढ़ी-बूढ़ा आमा-बाबुलाई
हेर्-बिचार् राम्ररी गर्नु ।
एउटा छोरो मायाको पोको
छाड़ी राखें स्याहार् गर्नु ।[2]

३ .कुखुरा बाख्रो गाई बस्तु
हेर्–बिचार् राम्ररी गर्नु ।
इष्ट-मित्र,छर्-छिमेकीको
मान्मनीतो खूबै गर्नु ।

४ . नाम् कमाई फर्की आउँदा[3]
झुमके-शाल् ल्याइदेउँला,
प्यारो देश्को रक्षक् बनी
संसारमा म बीर बनुँला ।

This folk song from Sikkim was sung by a woman. The words are addressed by a soldier departing for a campaign **(dhāvā)** to his wife whom he calls **sāhīlī,** probably the name by which she is known at home.

Notes

1. lit. 'having returned, I shall come, having earned a name.' **nām** is a common alternative form of **nāũ.**
2. lit. 'having left (him) I have put (him). Look after (him)', i.e., I am leaving him with you to look after him. Note that the infinitive is frequently used as an imperative.
3. **āũdā** 'while coming'. The Imperfect Participle of **āunu.**

Exercise 17a

Translate into English

१. पानी पर्ला जस्तो छ । बाहिर जानु अघि छाता लिन नबिर्सनुहोला ।
२. यहाँबाट पशुपतिनाथ् जान कति बेर् लाग्ला? पैदल् जानुभयो भने कम्सेकम् आधा घण्टा लाग्ला टचाक्सीमा जानुहोस् न ।
३. प्रधानमन्त्रीको मृत्यु भएपछि उन्को ठाउँ कस्ले लेला? कुन्नि ।
४. तिमीलाई चिठी लेखूँ कि जस्तो लागेको थियो तर घर्मा कागत् नभएर लेख्न पाइनँ ।
५. मलाई त रुघा लाग्न लागेको जस्तो छ ।आज पौड़ी खेल्न नजाऊँ क्यारे ?
६. छोरा होस् भनेर सकेसम्म कोशिश् गऱ्यो,तर छोरी छोरी मात्र भयो ।के गरोस् बिचरा ?
७. मैले साथीलाई टेलिफोन् गर्नुपरेको छ ।तपाईंको फोन्बाट गरूँ ?
८. छुट्टीमा पाँच् हप्तासम्म होटेल्मा काम् गरें भने कम्सेकम् तीन् सय् रुपियाँ कमाउँला ।
९. भारत् जाऊँ कि जस्तो लागेको थियो तर अहिले धेरै नै गर्मी हुन्छ भनेर जान मन् लागेन ।
१०. सकेसम्म छिटो हिंड़चौं भने साँझ् पर्नु अगाड़ी पुगिएला ।
११. पानी परोस् कि नपरोस् अब त मलाई नगई हुँदैन । एघार बज्नु अगाड़ी विमान्स्थल् पुग्नैपर्छ
१२. चियामा कति दूध् हालूँ? अलिकति मात्रै भए पुग्छ ।
१३. बस् त आइपुग्यो होला । कति बजे यहाँबाट जान्छ म गएर एक चोटी सोधेर आऊँ ।
१४. तिमीले मेरो चिठी बेलामा पाउलाउ भन्ने म आस् गर्छु
१५. रामे कता गयो ? कुन्नि ।बाहिर गयो होला ।
१६. लोग्ने मरेपछि के गर्ली बिचरीले ? उस्को अरू कोही पनि छैन ।

Exercise 17b

Translate into Nepali

1. It will probably take us about three hours to walk to the village and back. Shall we go?
2. Do you have a cold? I think I'm going to have one. I have a nasty headache.
3. How much sugar shall I put in your tea? Two spoons will be enough.
4. It's quite late already. I'd better go. When shall I see you again?
5. I hope you receive my letter before you leave London.
6. What's the time? I don't know. I haven't got a watch. I suppose it must be five o'clock.
7. I could not finish all this work today. There's a lot left to do. Never mind, leave it ('let it remain') till tomorrow.
8. Where is the servant? I don't know. He must have gone to the bazar. He'll probably be back in an hour.
9. I learnt Nepali in London University, before going to Nepal.
10. You'll probably get a hotel room in Kathmandu for thirty rupees a day.
11. Where shall I change my money? You can change it at the airport.
12. Roughly how much will it cost me to get from the hotel to the centre (**kendra**) of the city? If you go by taxi, it will probably cost five rupees. If you go by bus it will only cost you twenty paisa.
13. It's started to rain and I don't have an umbrella. Now what shall I do?

14. After arriving in Kathmandu, go and meet my elder brother. Shall I give you his address?
15. Whatever happens, I really must be home at six o'clock. Our guests will have arrived by then.

Exercise 17c

Translate into English

धेरै धन्यवाद्; फेरि भेटौंला तिमी कता जान लाग्यौ?; पहिरो गयो होला; म तपाईंलाई पुऱ्याइदिन्छु; कति पैसा कमाउँछौ?; पानी पर्ला जस्तो लाग्छ; मेहनत् गर्नैपर्छ;अर्को वर्ष म जाँच्मा सफल् हुनेछु; त्यसो भए म पनि आउँछु; उस्ले ज्यान् गए मानेन; दिन् प्रतिदिन्; सबै पैसा खेर जानेछ; उ नआएसम्म म यहीं बस्छु; कसरी जाने? जो आए पनि हुन्छ; माफ् गर्नुहोला

LESSON 18

1. *The Past Habitual Tense*

The Personal suffixes of the Past Habitual Tense are as follows:

Positive		*Negative*	
-थें	**-thẽ**	-दिनथें	**-dinathẽ**
-थिस्	**-this**	-दैनथिस्	**-dəynathis**
-थ्यो	**-thyo**	-दैनथ्यो	**-dəynathyo**
-थ्यौं	**-thyəw̃**	-दैनथ्यौं	**-dəynathyəw̃**
-थ्यौ	**-thyəw**	-दैनथ्यौ	**-deynathyəw**
-थे	**-the**	-दैनथे	**-deynathe**

The suffixes are added to the Primary Base, like the suffixes of the Simple Indefinite Tense. Verbs belonging to groups (ii), (iii), (iv) have **-n-** infixed between the primary base vowel and the positive suffixes. Verbs belonging to group (v) have the last vowel of the primary base nasalised before the positive suffixes. Thus:

म गर्थें	**ma garthẽ**	उ दिन्थ्यो	**u dinthyo**
हामी खान्थ्यौं	**hāmī khānthyəw̃**	तिमी बिर्सन्थ्यौ	**timī birsanthyəw**
उनी धुन्थे	**unī dhunthe**	म आउँथें	**ma āũthẽ**
तँ पिउँथिस्	**tã piũthis**	उ हुन्थ्यो	**u hunthyo**

Bases ending in a vowel (groups ii, iii, iv, v) have the final vowel nasalised before negative suffixes:

म गर्दिनथें	**ma gardinathẽ**	उ खाँदैनथ्यो	**u khā̃dəynathyo**
हामी आउँदैनथ्यौं	**hāmī āũdəynathyəw̃**	उनी जाँदैनथे	**unī jā̃dəynathe**

When a base of a group (i) verb ends in an unvoiced consonant (See Lesson 6.3), the negative suffix may be written -तिनथें **-tinathẽ,** etc.

उ बस्तैनथ्यो	**u bastəynathyo**
हामी हाँक्तैनथ्यौं	**hāmī hā̃ktəynathyəw̃**

The HGH is formed with the suffixes -हुन्थ्यो **-hunthyo** (pos.) and -हुन्नथ्यो **-hunnathyo** (neg.), added to the **-nu** infinitive:

गर्नुहुन्थ्यो	**garnuhunthyo**	गर्नुहुन्नथ्यो	**garnuhunnathyo**

Verbs belonging to groups (ii), (iii), (iv), (v) have alternative negative forms of which the suffixes are:

-न्नथें	**-nnathẽ**	-न्नथ्यौं	**-nnathyə̃w̃**
-न्नथिस्	**-nnathis**	-न्नथ्यौ	**-nnathyəw**
-न्नथ्यो	**-nnathyo**	-न्नथे	**-nnathe**

These suffixes are added directly to the Primary Base:

खान्नथें	**khānnathẽ**	दिन्नथें	**dinnathẽ**	धुन्नथें	**dhunnathẽ**
बिर्सन्नथें	**birsannathẽ**	आउन्नथें	**āunnathẽ**	हुन्नथें	**hunnathẽ**

The only feminine forms in common use are those of the 3rd person sing. and pl. positive. The suffixes are: -थी **-thī** (3 sing.), -थिन् **-thin** (3 pl.). उ आउँथी **u āũthī,** उनी आउँथिन् **unī āũthin,** etc.

2. The Past Habitual is used to express action or a state which continued over a period of time. It can often be translated in English as 'I used to do', 'I would do', '(for some time) I did', etc.

म सिनेमा हेर्न जान्थें,तर हिजोआज म जान्न
I used to go to the cinema, but nowadays I don't go
उहिले नेपाल्मा माल्ताल् अलि सस्तो हुन्थ्यो
At that time in Nepal things used to be quite cheap
पहिले म काठ्माड़ौंमा बस्थें, तर आज्काल् धरान्मा बस्छु
At first, I used to live in Kathmandu, but nowadays I live in Dharan
होटेल् धेरै महँगो भएकोले मैले एक्जना साथीको घरमा दुइटा कोठा बहाल्मा लिएँ । मैले उस्लाई महिनाको चालीस् रुपियाँ मात्रै दिनुपर्थ्यो
Because the hotel was very expensive, I rented ('took on rent') two rooms in a friend's house. I used to have to give him only forty rupees a month

जोतिषीहरू देवीरमण्लाई अर्को विवाह गर्ने सल्लाह् दिन्थे, परन्तु सुभद्राको आदेश् बिना उनी अर्को विवाह गर्न सक्दैनथे। सुभद्रा बहुतै पतिपरायणा रमणी थिइन्, आजसम्म कहिले उन्ले देवीरमण्को चित्त दुखाइनन्, मन्को कुरा जानेर सेवा गर्थिन्
The astrologers used to advise Deviraman to marry again, but without Subhadra's consent he could not remarry. Subhadra was a woman greatly devoted to her husband (and) to that day had never given Deviraman any anxiety (but) would serve him completely

परन्तु	**parantu** but (a literary word)
बिना	**binā** without (usually written separately from the word it follows)
चित्त दुखाउनु	**citta dukhāunu** (lit. 'to give pain to the heart/feelings')
मन्को कुरा जानेर	**manko kurā jānera** knowing the things of the heart

3. Another important use of the Past Habitual Tense is in the main clause of

'impossible' conditional sentences of the type: 'If I had come, you would have gone.' The verb in the subordinate 'if'-clause is the First Perfect Participle followed by भए . The verb in the main clause is in the Past Habitual Tense:

म आएको भए तिमी जान्थ्यौ
If I had come, you would have gone
हिजो पानी नपरेको भए म तपाईंकहाँ आउँथें
If it had not rained yesterday, I would have come to see you

Alternatively, the verb in the subordinate clause may be the Second Perfect Participle followed by the particle त .

म आए त तिमी जान्थ्यौ
If I had come, you would have gone
हिजो पानी नपरे त म तपाईंकहाँ आउँथें
If it had not rained yesterday, I would have come to see you

Both constructions are equally common.

अलि चाँडै आउनुभए त हुन्थ्यो
If you had come a bit earlier, it would have been better
त्यो बाटोबाट गए त हुन्थ्यो
It would have been better if we had gone by that road
तिमी सिनेमा हेर्न जान्छौ भनेर थाहा पाएको भए म पनि आउँथें
If I had known you were going to the cinema, I should have come too
मसँग पैसा भएको भए त म हिंड्रै आउन्नथें
If I had had some money on me, I wouldn't have walked
हामी बेलामा नआइपुगेको भए बा रिसाउनुहुन्थ्यो
If we hadn't arrived on time, father would have been angry

4. In the main clause of 'impossible' conditional sentences the Past Habitual may be replaced by a compound tense, consisting of the Infinitival Participle and the verb थियो . The tense is known as the Infinitival Conditional Tense. The subject of a transitive verb takes -ले .

म जाने थिएँ	I would have gone
उसले गर्ने थियो	he would have done
हामी आउने थिएनौं	we would not have come
तिमीले देख्ने थियौ	you would have seen

In such sentences, the Infinitival Conditional is in free variation with the Past Habitual:

म आएको भए तिमी जाने थियौ
If I had come, you would have gone
त्यतिका पिपि नखाएको भए पेट् दुख्ने थिएन
If you hadn't eaten so many sweets, you would not have stomach-ache

पानी पर्छ भनेर थाहा पाएको भए यति टाढासम्म आउने थिइनँ
If I'd known it was going to rain, I shouldn't have come so far

Note that गर्नुपर्ने थियो **garnuparne thiyo** is translated 'ought to have done'.

तिमीले यो किताब् हेर्नुपर्ने थियो नि
This is the book you ought to have looked at
मलाई त त्यस्सँग भेट्न जानुपर्ने थियो
I really ought to have gone to visit him

5. *A note on causative verbs*

Causative Verbs (i.e. verbs meaning 'to cause someone to do', 'to cause something to happen') are formed from other verbs, in many cases, by the addition of the stem suffix **-āu/-ā.** for example गराउनु **garāunu** 'to cause to do' from गर्नु 'to do', चलाउनु **calāunu** 'to cause to move', from चल्नु 'to move'. Some causative verbs are formed by a modification of the verbal root. For example, मार्नु **mārnu** 'to cause to die/to kill' from मर्नु 'to die', खोल्नु **kholnu** 'to cause to come open/to open' (trans.), from खुल्नु 'to come open'.

The causative of an intransitive verb is usually the corresponding transitive form of the verb. For example उठ्नु 'to rise', उठाउनु 'to raise', 'to cause to rise'.

In many cases, the Nepali causative verb is translated by a completely different verb in English. For example, पढ्नु 'to read/study' पढाउनु 'to teach' ('to cause to read'). In practice causative verbs are best learnt as separate items of vocabulary, and it must be remembered that not all verbs have corresponding causative forms.

In the following list a number of the most common causative verbs are given. Many of them have been encountered in previous lessons.

(*a*) *Causative verbs formed with the stem suffix* **-āu/ā** (*Group v*)

उठ्नु	to rise, to get up
उठाउनु	to raise, to make get up
उड्नु	to fly (intrans.)
उड़ाउनु	to fly (trans.), to cause to fly
गर्नु	to do
गराउनु	to cause to do
चल्नु	to move, to go, to proceed
चलाउनु	to move (trans.), to operate, to drive
दुख्नु	to ache
दुखाउनु	to give pain to
देख्नु	to see
देखाउनु	to show, to cause to see

सम्झनु	to remember
सम्झाउनु	to remind
सुन्नु	to hear
सुनाउनु	to relate, to cause to hear
बोल्नु	to speak
बोलाउनु	to call
बुझ्नु	to understand
बुझाउनु	to explain, to return, to give back

(*b*) *Causative verbs of I-Stem Verbs add the suffix* **-yāu/-yā**

छुट्टिनु	to be separated
छुट्ट्याउनु	to separate
सिद्धिनु	to be ended, to come to an end
सिद्ध्याउनु	to end, to finish (something)
पुगिनु	to be reached, be arrived at
पुऱ्याउनु	to cause to arrive, to deliver
टुँगिनु	to end (intrans.)
टुँग्याउनु	to finish (something)

(*c*) *Causatives formed by some modification of the verbal root*

खस्नु	to fall
खसाल्नु	to drop, to post (a letter)
बस्नु	to sit
बसाल्नु	to make sit, to settle
खुल्नु	to come open
खोल्नु	to open, to cause to come open
छुट्नु	to be abandoned, to be missed
छोड्नु	to abandon
पर्नु	to fall, to happen
पार्नु	to make happen, to bring about, to lay (eggs)
मर्नु	to die
मार्नु	to kill
निस्कनु	to go out
निकाल्नु	to bring out
पिउनु	to drink
पिलाउनु ,पिवाउनु	to cause to drink, to give a drink

खानु	to eat
खुवाउनु	to cause to eat, to feed
बिग्रनु	to be spoilt
बिगार्नु	to spoil

Causative verbs may all (theoretically at least) have I-Stem passive counterparts. Thus गराइनु **garāinu** 'to cause to be done', बोलाइनु **bolāinu** 'to cause to be called', etc. Some verbs have a complete range of forms:

खुल्नु	to come open
खलिनु	to be opened
खोल्नु	to open (trans.)
खोलाउनु	to cause to open
खोलाइनु	to cause to be opened

With the majority of verbs, however, *all* the possible forms exist only in the dictionary, and it is advisable to use only those forms you have actually seen or heard used by Nepali speakers.
Note the following phrases involving causative verbs:

कसैबाट काम् गराउनु	to get someone to do a job
कसैलाई सिफारिश् गराउनु	to have someone recommended
मोटर चलाउनु	to start/operate a car
कसैको चित्त दुखाउनु	to give someone mental pain
गीत् सुनाउनु	to sing a song
किताब बुझाउनु	to return a book
छुट्ट्याएर लेख्नु	to write clearly (separating the letters)
कसैलाई (स्टेशन्सम्म) पुऱ्याउनु	to take someone (to a station, etc.)
घर्-बार् बसाल्नु	to start a family, set up house
कसैलाई पागल् तुल्याउनु	to make someone mad

त्यो काम् मैले राम्बाट गराउनुपर्छ
I'll have to get that work done by Ram
मैले राष्ट्र बैंकमा जागीर् खान अध्यापक्को सिफारिश् गराएँ
I had myself recommended by my teacher for a position in the Rashtra Bank

जागीर खानु **jāgīr khānu** to get (official) employment

मैले आफ्नो मोटर् चलाउन खोजें तर बिग्रेको थियो
I tried to start my car, but it had gone wrong
आजसम्म स्वास्नीले पतिको चित्त दुखाइनन्
To this day the wife had never hurt her husband
म पुस्तकालयमा यो किताब् बुझाउन जान्छु
I'm going to return this book to the library

अरूहरूले पढ्न सक्ने गरी छुट्टयाएर लेख न
Write clearly so that others will be able to read it
म वहाँलाई स्टेशन्सम्म पुऱ्याएर आउँछु
I'll just take him to the station
एक् न एक् दिन् त घर्-बार् बसाल्नैपर्छ
Some day or another, one just *has* to start a family
उसले त मलाई पागलै तुल्याइदियो
He really made me mad

Vocabulary 18

अचम्मा	**acammā**	surprise
अचम्मा मान्नु	**accamā mānnu**	to become surprised
अनुसरण् गर्नु	**anusaraṇ garnu**	to follow
अवस्था	**avasthā**	state, condition
अहंकार्	**ahaŋkār**	vanity, boasting
आज्काल्	**ājkāl**	nowadays
आदेश्	**ādeʃ**	permission
आनन्द्	**ānand**	joy, happiness
उत्तर्	**uttar**	answer
उत्पन्न गराउनु	**utpanna garāunu**	to cause to arise, to give rise to
उदेक्	**udek**	amazement
उद्देश्	**uddeʃ**	purpose, plan
उपाय	**upaya**	plan
एक् न एक् दिन्	**ek na ek din**	one of these days
एक्कासी	**ekkāsī**	all of a sudden
कदापि	**kadāpi**	ever
कार्यरूप्मा ल्याउनु	**kāryarūpmā lyāunu**	to bring into practice
कृपा	**kɹpā**	kindness
कृपादृष्टि	**kɹpādɹṣṭi**	a look of kindness
गहिरो	**gahiro**	deep
घटीमा	**ghaṭīmā**	at least
घर्-बार्	**ghar-bār**	household, family
घर्-बार् बसालनु	**ghar-bār basālnu**	to set up house, to start a family
घमण्ड्	**ghamaṇḍ**	pride
चलाउनु	**calāunu**	to move, to operate
चित्त	**citta**	heart, feelings
चिप्लो	**ciplo**	slippery
छेउ	**cheu**	side, flank
जङ्गल्	**jaŋgal**	jungle
जागीर्	**jāgīr**	(official) employment
जोतिषी	**jotiṣī**	astrologer
ज्ञानी	**jɲānī**	wise
तुल्याउनु	**tulyāunu**	to cause, to bring about

दण्डवत्	**daṇḍavat**	respectful salutation
दशा	**daʃā**	plight
दह	**daha**	hole, pit
दीन्	**dīn**	miserable, humble
दुखाउनु	**dukhāunu**	to give pain to
दुष्ट्	**duṣṭ**	wicked
दु:खी	**dukkhī**	pained, miserable
धूर्त	**dhūrta**	cunning
नम्र	**namra**	coaxing
नामक्	**nāmak**	by name
निधो गर्नु	**nidho garnu**	to decide
निवेदन्	**nivedan**	request
पक्रनु	**pakranu**	to catch hold of
पछि पछि जानु	**pachi pachi jānu**	to follow
पति	**pati**	husband, master
पतिपारायणा	**patipārāyaṇā**	dutiful (towards one's husband)
परन्तु	**parantu**	but (literary)
पशु	**paʃu**	animal, cattle
पागल्	**pāgal**	mad
पिपि	**pipi**	sweets (a children's word)
पुच्छर्	**pucchar**	tail
पूर्ण हुनु	**pūrṇa hunu**	to be fulfilled
पेट्	**peṭ**	stomach
प्रतिनिधि	**pratinidhi**	representative
प्रभाव्	**prabhāv**	effect
प्रसन्न	**prasanna**	happy
प्राप्त गर्नु	**prāpta garnu**	to acquire
फल्	**phal**	result
बचन्, (वचन्)	**bacan (vacan)**	saying, words, speech
बड़ो	**baṛo**	very
बल्	**bal**	strength
बल्वान्	**balvān**	strong
बहाल्	**bahāl**	rent
बहाल्मा लिनु	**bahālmā linu**	to rent, to hire
बहुतै	**bahutəy**	very much
बाठो	**bāṭho**	cunning
बिना	**binā**	without
बिन्ती चढाउनु	**bintī carhāunu**	to make a humble request
बुझाउनु	**bujhāunu**	to make understand, to return
बुद्धि	**buddhi**	intelligence
ब्रम्हा-देश्	**bramhā-deʃ**	Burma (a literary word)
भरिनु	**bharinu**	to be filled
भाइहो	**bhāiho**	oh brothers
भाव्	**bhāv**	feeling, effect, rate

भासिन् **bhāsinu** to be sucked into, to fall
भेला हुन् **bhelā hunu** to crowd around
भोज् **bhoj** feast
मन्परी **manparī** at will, as one pleases
महान् **mahān** great, enormous
माल्ताल् **māltāl** goods, luggage
मित्र **mitra** friend
मुसुक्क हाँस्नु **musukka hãsnu** to smile
मोज्ले **mojle** with gusto, happily
रक्षा गर्नु **rakṣā garnu** to protect
रमणी **ramaṇī** woman
योग्य **yogya** worthy of, suitable
लोभ् **lobh** greed
वश् **vaʃ** power, subjugation
विदेशी **videʃī** foreigner
विपत **vipat** trouble, difficulty
व्याङ्ग **vyāŋga** sarcastic
समस्त **samasta** all, entire
समीप् **samīp** presence
सम्पूर्ण **sampūrṇa** entire
सर्नु **sarnu** to move forward
सहायता **sahāyatā** help, aid
सिफारिश् **siphāriʃ** recommendation
सेवा **sevā** service, serving
स्याल् **syāl** jackal
स्वरूप् **svarūp**[1] like, as, in the form of
स्वीकार गर्नु **svīkār garnu**[1] to accept
हतार् हतार् **hatār hatār** slowly
हात्ती **hāttī** elephant
हिंड्डुल् गर्नु **hĩṛḍūl garnu** to walk around, to stroll

Reading Passage

हात्ती र स्याल्

एउटा कपूर्टीके[1] नाउँ भएको हात्ती ब्रम्हा-देश्को कुनै ठूलो जङ्गल्मा मन्परी हिंड्डूल् गर्थ्यो । त्यस्लाई देखेर जङ्गल्का समस्त स्यालहरू लोभ्का वश्मा परी,'यस्लाई कुनै उपायले मार्न पाए यस्को मासुले हाम्रा पेट् भरिने थिए' भन्ने बिचार् गर्न लागे । यस् बिचार्लाई कार्यरूपमा ल्याउनलाई एउटा बूढो स्याल्ले अघि सरेर यसो भन्यो ।

'हेर भाइहो । बुद्धिले जुन् काम् हुन सक्छ, त्यो खाली बल्ले कदापि हुन सक्दैन । यो हात्ती बड़ो

[1]v pronounced like English **w**.

बल्वान् छ, तापनि हामी आफ्ना बुद्धिका प्रभाव्ले यस्लाई अवश्य पनि मार्न सक्नेछौं' ।

बूढो स्याल्का यस्ता कुरा सुनेर सबैले उदेक् र अचम्म माने । त्यस्पछि त्यस् बाठो स्याल्ले हात्तीका समीप्मा गएर, बड़ो नम्र भाव्ले दण्डवत् गरेर भन्यो[2]।

'महाराज् । यस् दीन्, दुःखीमाथि कृपादृष्टि राखिबक्सियोस्'[3]।

'स्याल्को यस्तो नम्र बचन्ले हात्तीका मन्मा केही घमण्ड् उत्पन्न गरायो । उस्ले बड़ो अहंकार् गरी सोध्यो

'भन्, तँ को होस्? किन आइस्? के माग्छस्?'

बूढो स्याल्ले पनि नम्र भई बिन्ती चढ़ायो ।

म जम्बुमन्त्री नामक् स्याल् हुँ, हजूर । मलाई सम्पूर्ण जङ्गल्मा पशुहरूले प्रतिनिधि स्वरूप्[4] हजूर्का समीप्मा पठाएका छन् । हजूर ज्ञानी होइबक्सन्छ। हामीहरू सबै राजा बिना बड़ो दुःख पाएर दिन् काटिरहेछौं[5]। समस्त जङ्गलमा राजा हुने योग्य कुनै पशु निस्केन । यस् कारण् म हजूर्का समीप्मा बिन्ती चढ़ाउन आएको हुँ । हजूरले हाम्रा राजा भई हाम्रो रक्षा गरिबक्सिनुपर्छ ।'

धूर्त स्याल्को यस्तो बचन् सुनेर हात्तीलाई हुनसम्मको आनन्द्[6] लाग्यो ।यस्पछि हात्तीले उत्तर् दियो ।

'हुन्छ, तिमीहरूको निवेदन् म स्वीकार् गर्छु । लौ, अब कुन् बाटोबाट कहाँ जानुपर्ने हो[7], भन् ।

बाठो स्याल् आफ्नो उद्देश पूर्ण हुन लागेको देखेर बड़ो प्रसन्न भयो ।

'महाराज्, मेरो अनुसरण् गरिबक्सियोस्[8]। म हजूरलाई बाटो देखाउँछु' भनी स्याल् अघि अघि बाटो देखाउँदै हिंड्न[9] लाग्यो ।हात्ती पनि धूर्त स्याल्को पछि पछि जान लाग्यो । राज्य प्राप्त गर्ने आशाले स्याल्ले देखाएको बाटो हतार् हतार् हिंड्दा[10] हात्ती एक्कासी हिलोका एउटा गहिरो दह्मा भासियो । आफ्नो त्यस्तो दशा भएको देखेर हात्तीले भन्यो ।

'मित्र जम्बुमन्त्री ।म त महान् विपत्मा परें । सहायता गर ।हेर म त यो गहिरो दह्मा भासिएँ'।

हात्तीको त्यो अवस्था देखेर स्याल् मुसुक्क हाँस्यो । अनि त्यस्ले हात्तीको छेउमा गएर, 'हजूर्, मेरो पुच्छर् पक्रेर निस्किबक्सियोस्' भनेर भन्यो ।

यति भएपछि,'म जस्तो धूर्त्का बचन्मा विश्वास् गर्नाले यस्तै फल् हुन्छ' भन्ने व्याङ्ग बचन् सुनाएर दुष्ट् स्याल् त्यस् ठाउँबाट आफ्ना मित्रहरू भएका ठाउँमा गयो। त्यस्पछि,सबै स्याल्हरूले भेला भई त्यो हात्तीलाई मारेर मोज्ले भोज् लाए [11]।

Notes

This Nepali rendering of the fable (नीति कथा) of the elephant and the jackal has been slightly adapted from the version given in *Nepālī Sāhitya*, vol. 4 (Macmillan, 1968). The language is fairly typical of the literary style adopted by most modern Nepali writers.

1. **kapūrṭīke**: lit. 'with a "forehead-spot" of camphor'. The name is given to the elephant.
2. **daṇḍāvat**: a respectful salutation made by touching the ground at the other's feet.
3. **kɹpādɹṣṭi rākhibaksiyos**: lit. 'keep a look of compassion on this poor unfortunate one'.
   rākhibaksiyos is the imperative of the 'Royal Honorific' form of the verb **rākhnu.** The Royal Honorific is formed by adding the verb **baksanu** 'to bestow' to the Absolutive Participle of the simple verb. This form is used mainly when addressing royalty. It is fully discussed in Lesson 20.
4. **pratinidhi svarūp**: 'as a representative'.
5. **din kāṭirahechəw̃**: 'we are spending our days'. The form of the verb is discussed in Lesson 20.
6. **hunasammako ānand**: 'the greatest possible pleasure'.
7. **kahā̃ jānuparne ho?** 'where is it that I am to go?' Note the use of the Infinitival Participle with **ho.**
8. **mero anusaraṇ garibaksiyos**: 'follow me' – a very respectful phrase. An equivalent would be **pachi pachi āunuhos.**
9. **bāṭo dekhāũdəy**: 'while showing the road'.
10. **hĩṛdā**; 'walking along'.
11. **mojle bhoj lāunu**: 'to enjoy oneself having a feast'.

Exercise 18a

Translate into English

१ . उमालेको पानी खाएको भए तिमी बिरामी हुने थिएनौ ।

२ . पाकिस्तान्का हवाईजहाज्हरू ढाका भएर काठ्माडौंसम्म आउँथे तर भारत्सँग लड़ाई शुरू भएपछि आउन छाड़ेका छन् ।

३ . अर्को बाटोबाट गएको भए हुन्थ्यो ।योचाहिं त एक् दम् उकालो र चिप्लो पो रहेछ।

४ . लन्दन्मा बसेको बेला त्यो हरेक् हप्ता सिनेमा हेर्न जान्थ्यो ।

५ . पाँच् बर्ष अगाडि काठ्माडौंमा सबै माल्ताल् सस्तो थियो,तर हिजोआज धेरै पर्यटक्हरू आउने भएकोले भारत्भन्दा नेपाल्मा महँगी बढ़ेको छ ।

६. तपाईं भारत् कहिले जान चाहनुहुन्छ? सकेसम्म छिटो जान पाए हुन्थ्यो ।
७. तपाईंले आफ्नो दाइको ठेगाना दिनुभएको भए म वहाँलाई भेट्न जान्थें ।
८. मलाई फुर्सत् भएको भए तिमीलाई भेट्न आउँथें तर साँझ् अबेलासम्म मेरो साथीसित कुरा गरेको हुनाले आउन सकिनँ ।
९. यहाँ तिमी हुँदैनौ भन्ने थाहा पाएको भए म आउने थिइनँ।
१०. शुरूमा म बिहानदेखि बेलुकासम्म काम् गर्थें ,तर आजकाल् म त्यतिको काम् गर्न सक्तिन ।
११. १९५०-भन्दा अगाडि विदेशीहरूलाई नेपाल्मा घुम्न निक्कै गाह्रो हुन्थ्यो ।
१२. मैले घर् फर्कने निधो गरें ।आउने महीना बेलायत् छाड्छु होला ।
१३. दुइ बर्ष पहिले थ्याङ्बोचे जान मन् लागेको भए त्यहाँसम्म हिंड्रेरै जानुपर्थ्यो ।काठ्माडौंबाट त्यहाँ पुग्न घटीमा दुइ हप्ता लाग्थ्यो। तर अहिले त्यहाँ जाने विमान्सेवा छ रे ।

Exercise 18b

Translate into Nepali

1. If you had gone by the road I showed you, you would have arrived sooner.
2. I used to smoke twenty cigarettes a day, but I gave up smoking last year. Now I don't smoke.
3. If he had worked harder, he would have easily passed the exam. Now he will have to try again next year.
4. My father used to live in an old house near Hanumān Ḍhokā.
5. If you (MGH) had listened to what I said, you would not be ill now.
6. We used to go into the temples in the centre of the city to watch the **pūjā**.
7. Once, I used to be able to speak Newārī well, but because I have not lived in Kathmandu for a long time, I have forgotten everything.
8. In the beginning I used to work from morning till evening, but these days I cannot do so much work.
9. Did you find the book you lost? No, I did not. It must have got mislaid.
10. Thirty years ago there were many elephants in the Terai, but now, since much of the jungle has been destroyed, there are not so many elephants there.
11. That coat was very expensive. The shopkeeper should have let (you) have it for a hundred rupees.
12. If I had had the time, I should have gone to India sooner. But now whether it rains or not, I really must go. I have a lot of work there, you know.

Exercise 18c

Translate into English

राजा मरेपछि उनका छोराले राज्य प्राप्त गरे ; यस् विचार्लाई कार्यरूप्मा कसरी ल्याउने?; उनी प्रतिनिधि स्वरूप् महाराजाको दर्बार्मा पठाइएका थिए ; त्यो कुरा सुनेर उस्लाई अतिनै आनन्द लाग्यो । मेरो निवेदन् स्वीकार् गर्नुहोस्,हजूर :त्यति अनौठो कुरा सुनेर उ मुसुक्क हाँस्न लाग्यो ;मैले एउटा राम्रो कोठा बहाल्मा लिएँ ; तपाईं यस्भन्दा पहिला नेपाल् आउनुभएको छ कि छैन ?; त्यो

पसल्‌मा थुप्रै माल्‌ताल्‌ पाइन्छ ; उस्‌ले मलाई पागलै तुल्याउँछ; वहाँले सिंह दर्‌बार्‌मा जागीर्‌ खानुभएको थियो ; तिमीले हेर्नुपर्ने किताब्‌ त्यही हो नि ; मेरो कलम्‌ हराएको जस्तो छ ; मलाई रुघा लाग्ला लाग्ला जस्तो छ ; त्यो बेलामा आओस्‌ भनी मैले खूब्‌ झाँटें ;जीविका चलाउनलाई म होटेल्‌मा काम्‌ गर्छु ; ठूलो लड़ाईंमा सिपाहीले नाम्‌ कमायो; म दुइ दिन्‌भित्र फर्की आउँला

LESSON 19

1. *The Imperfect Participle*

The Imperfect Participle has four suffixes. They are as follows: (1) -द **-da,** (2) -दो **-do,** (3) -दा **-dā,** (4) -दै **-dəy.** These suffixes are added directly to the base of verbs belonging to group (i), to the nasalised base of verbs belonging to group (ii), and to the nasalised primary base of verbs belonging to other groups.

	1	2	3	4
(i)	गर्द **garda**	गर्दो **gardo**	गर्दा **gardā**	गर्दै **gardəy**
(ii)	खाँद **khā̃da**	खाँदो **khā̃do**	खाँदा **khā̃dā**	खाँदै **khā̃dəy**
(iii)	धुँद **dhū̃da**	धुँदो **dhū̃do**	धुँदा **dhū̃dā**	धुँदै **dhū̃dəy**
(iv)	बिर्सँद **birsā̃da**	बिर्सँदो **birsā̃do**	बिर्सँदा **birsā̃dā**	बिर्सँदै **birsā̃dəy**
(v)	आउँद **āū̃da**	आउँदो **āū̃do**	आउँदा **āū̃dā**	आउँदै **āū̃dəy**
हुनु	हुँद **hū̃da**	हुँदो **hū̃do**	हुँदा **hū̃dā**	हुँदै **hū̃dəy**

In verbs belonging to group (i) of which the base ends in an unvoiced consonant, the द of the suffix may be changed to त . बस्त **basta,** बस्तो **basto,** बस्ता **bastā,** बस्तै **bastəy.** Nowadays, however, there is a tendency to generalise the suffixes in -द and write बस्द **basda,** सुत्दो **sutdo,** etc. (Cf. Lesson 6.3).

HGH forms consist of the infinitive in -नु followed by the Imperfect Participles of हो :

गर्नुहुँदो **garnuhū̃do**	जानुहुँदा **jānuhū̃dā**	आउनुहुँदै **āunuhū̃dəy**

The negative is formed with the prefix -न

नगर्दो **nagardo**	नजाँदा **najā̃dā**	नखानुहुँदै **nakhānuhū̃dəy**

The verb छ possesses the Imperfect Participles:

छँदा **chãdā** and छँदै **chãdəy**

2. In previous lessons we have already met a number of examples of the imperfect participles in -दा and -दै , the two forms which are most commonly used.

The Imperfect Participle in -दा may often correspond to the English present participle 'doing', 'eating', etc., or sometimes a temporal participle phrase like 'while doing', or a clause like 'when I was doing', 'as I was going', etc. The English translation will of course depend on the context.

पहाड़बाट ओर्लदा लड़ेर उस्को खुट्टा भाँचियो
As he was coming down the hill, he slipped and his leg broke
शहर् जाँदा मलाई यो चिठी खसाल्न सम्झाऊ है
When we're on our way to town, remind me to post this letter
त्यो लन्दन्मा छँदा, हरेक् हप्ता सिनेमा हेर्न जान्थ्यो
When he was in London, he used to go to the pictures every week
सूर्य अस्ताउन लाग्दा, हामी त्यहाँ पुग्यौं
We arrived there, just as the sun began to set
हिजो घर् आउन लाग्दा,मैले सबै पैसा हरायो कि भन्ठानेको थिएँ, तर घर् आएर हेर्दा त खल्तीमै रहेछ
Yesterday, as I was coming home, I thought that I had lost all my money, but when I arrived I had a look and found that it was in my pocket the whole time

In colloquial speech, the particle -खेरि **-kheri** is often added to the participle in -दा when it has temporal force:

शहर् जाँदाखेरि when we were going to town
वहाँसित क्रा गर्दाखेरि while talking to him
काठ्माड़ौंमा बस्दाखेरि when living in Kathmandu

3. The postposition -ले followed by the Imperfect Participle गर्दा means 'because of', 'by reason of' and is the equivalent of the phrase को कारण्ले

झरीले गर्दा, म आउन सकिनँ
I couldn't come because of the rain
त्यसैले गर्दा मैले तिम्रो चिठी पढ्न पाइनँ
For that reason, I could not read your letter

4. The participle in -दै is morphologically an emphatic form. When it follows the participle in -दा (e.g. गर्दा गर्दै , आउँदा आउँदै), the participle phrase is temporal, but more emphatic than those in the construction discussed in 2 above. In English, such phrases may be translated as 'just as I was doing', 'at the very moment of doing', etc. More often, however, गर्दा गर्दै is simply the equivalent of गर्दा

सिनेमा हेर्दा हेर्दै, म त भुसुक्कै निंदाएछु
I fell asleep right in the middle of the film
यस् प्रकारले विचार् गर्दा गर्दै, भानुभक्तले यही श्लोक् बनाए
With these very thoughts in mind, Bhanubhakta wrote this verse
नेपालीहरूसँग कुराकानी गर्दा गर्दै, मैले नेपाली सिकें
I learnt Nepali, simply by talking to Nepalis

The Imperfect Participle in -दै may be used by itself as an alternative to the participle in -दा. Thus तिम्रो घर् आउँदै or तिम्रो घर् आउँदै आउँदै mean more or less the same as तिम्रो घर् आउँदा (-खेरि). हुँदा and हुँदै are frequently used as an alternative of भएर in the sense of 'via'.

म बेलायत्बाट दिल्ली हुँदा काठ्माडौं जाउँला
I shall probably go from England to Kathmandu via Delhi

5. The participle in -दै followed by the postposition -मा has the sense of 'just because one does'. The subject word of a transitive verb in this construction requires -ले

तिमीले मलाई चोर् भन्दैमा, म चोर् हुन्छु र?
Just because you say I'm a thief, does that make me one then?
उस्ले गर भन्दैमा तिमीलाई गर्नुपर्थ्यो र?
Just because he told you to do it, did you have to do it then?

6. The construction त्यो गर्दै गर्दैन is emphatic and may be translated 'he absolutely refuses to do'.

त्यो केटा काम् गर्दै गर्दैन । एक् दम् अल्छी छ
That boy just refuses to work. He's really lazy
मैले भनेको त्यो मान्दै मान्दैन । तपाईं नै भन्नुहोस् न
He absolutely refuses to listen to what I tell him. *You* talk to him

7. The Imperfect Participle in -दै is used to form two continuous tenses:
(*a*) Present Continuous (discussed in Lesson 5.11) formed by the participle in -दै followed by the verb छ: म गर्दै छु 'I am doing' म गर्दै छैन 'I am not doing'.
(*b*) Past Continuous, formed by the participle in -दै followed by the verb थियो. म गर्दै थिइन 'I was not doing', म गर्दै थिएँ 'I was doing'.

The HGH forms are: गर्दै हुनुहुन्छ गर्दै हुनुहुन्थ्यो, etc.

तिमी के गर्दै छौ? म किताब् पढ्दै छु
What are you doing? I'm reading a book
उ काम् गर्दै, गीत् गाउँदै थियो
As he was working, he was singing a song
तपाईं रेडियो नेपाल्बाट समाचार् सुन्दै हुनुहुन्थ्यो
You were listening to the news from Radio Nepal

As we have already seen, the Present Continuous Tense is frequently used in speech with reference to future action, like the English continuous tense 'I am going next week'. The Simple Indefinite may be used in the same way, while the Future Tense (गरुँला) expresses doubt and the Infinitival Future Tense (गर्नेछु) expresses great certainty. Compare the following sentences:

म आउने हप्ता भारत् जान्छु
म आउने हप्ता भारत् जाँदै छु
I'm going to India next week
म आउने हप्ता भारत् जाउँला
I'll probably go to India next week
म आउने हप्ता पक्कै पनि भारत् जानेछु
I am definitely going to India next week

The continuous tenses of छ– छँदै छ, छँदै थिएँ have the force of 'it still is', 'it still was', 'it obviously is', etc.

मैले गएको महीनाको आखिरीतिर काठ्माडौंबाट हिंड़ेको तिमीलाई थाहा छँदै छ
As you must know, I left Kathmandu towards the end of last month
आज दिउँसो पानी पर्ने कुरा हामीलाई थाहा छँदै थियो
We knew of course that it would rain this afternoon

8. The Imperfect Participle in -दो is a verbal adjective, and like other adjectives in **-o** has a feminine singular form in **-ī** (गर्दी **gardī**), and a plural form in **-ā** (गर्दा **gardā**). As in the case of other adjectives agreement for gender and number is made mainly in writing.

Examples of its purely adjectival use are:

चाख्लाग्दो interesting (चाख् 'taste', 'interest')
डर्लाग्दो frightening (डर् 'fear')
आउँदो हप्ता the coming week, next week (an alternative for आउने हप्ता)

9. The Imperfect Participle in -दो is used to form three tenses with the verbs छ, रहेछ, हो acting as auxiliaries:

1. म गर्दो छु, etc.
2. म गर्दो रहेछु, etc.
3. म गर्दो हुँ, etc.

All three tenses possess feminine and plural forms:

उ गर्दी छे, उनी गर्दी छिन्, हामी गर्दा छौं,
उनीहरू गर्दा छन्, etc.
उ गर्दी रहीछ, उनी गर्दी रहीछन्, हामी गर्दा रहेछौं
उनीहरू गर्दा रहेछन्, etc.
उ गर्दी हो, उनी गर्दी हुन्, हामी गर्दा हौं
उनीहरू गर्दा हुन्, etc.

The first of these tenses (म गदो छु) is an alternative to the Simple Indefinite गर्छु, but is almost entirely restricted to writing and especially poetry. Note the following verse from a poem by the modern Nepali poet, Dharaṇīdhar Koirālā;

नेपाल् तिम्रो मुहुडा हँसिलो
देखेर मर्छु कि यसै म मर्छु?
चिन्ता यही चित्त सताउँदो छ ।
आशा निराशातिर धाउँदो छ

'Oh Nepal, do I die seeing your laughing face or do I just die (for no reason)? This very grief vexes my heart. Hope turns often to despair'

धाउनु 'to come frequently'

This tense is rarely found in spoken Nepali.

The second tense (गर्दो रहेछ) indicates surprise, and may be translated 'I see that I am doing', etc. As we have seen this is the usual implication of the Second Perfect form रहेछ .

त्यो मान्छे प्रधान्मन्त्रीको घर्मा पनि जाँदो रहेछ
Why, that man even goes to the Prime Minister's house
ट्याक्सीमा घुम्न अलि महँगो पर्दो रहेछ
I see that it is quite expensive to travel by taxi
नेपाली त राम्रै बोल्नुहुँदो रहेछ । कहाँ सिक्नुभएको नि?
Why, you speak Nepali quite well. Where did you learn it?

The third tense (म जाँदो हुँ) is conditional, and is used in the subordinate ('if') clause of impossible conditional sentences:

उ आउँदो हो त म जान्नथें
If he had come, I would not have gone

This construction is the equivalent of those discussed in Lesson 18.3.

उ काम् गर्दो हो त बाटोमा मागेर हिंड्ने नै थिएन
If he had worked, he would not have had to walk the streets begging
उहिले म सिंह -दर्बार्मा जागीर् खाँदो हुँ त अहिले मलाई पैसाको दुःख हुने नै थिएन
If I had taken a post in the Singha Darbar, I would not have any money troubles now

जागीर् खानु 'to receive (official) employment'

10. The Imperfect Participle in -द is used only in the formation of two tenses which are merely alternative forms of the Simple Indefinite (गर्छु) and the Past Habitual (गर्थें). These alternative forms consist of the participle in -द followed by the positive suffixes of those tenses. The participle and suffixes are written together as one word:

म गर्दछु **ma gardachu**
त्यो जाँदछ **tyo jā̃dacha**
म खाँदथें **ma khā̃dathẽ**
उनी बस्दथे **unī basdathe,** etc.

The alternative forms are in every respect synonymous with the two tenses introduced in earlier lessons (viz. गर्छु and गर्थें), but are almost entirely restricted to the written language, being particularly common in newspaper Nepali.

Vocabulary 19

अन्तमा	**antamā**	finally, in the end
अल्छी	**alchī**	lazy
आउँदो	**āũdo**	coming, next
इतिहास्	**itihās**	history
ओर्लनु	**orlanu**	to descend, to come down
कट्वाल्	**kaṭvāl**	Katval (place name)
कमल्	**kamal**	lotus
कर्कोटक्	**karkoṭak**	Karkotak (name of a Naga)
कात्नु	**kātnu**	to twine thread, make a lamp
किनकि	**kinaki**	because (syn. **kinabhane**)
घसिदिनु	**ghasidinu**	to rub in
किराँत्	**kirā̃t**	the Kirant people
खुट्टा	**khuṭṭā**	leg, foot
-खेरि	**-kheri**	temporal particle used with the imperfect participle
चलन्	**calan**	usage, use, custom
चिन्ता	**cintā**	worry, care
चिर्नु	**cirnu**	to cleave, to cut through
चोभार	**cobhār**	Chobhar (place name)
चोर्	**cor**	thief
जागीर् खानु	**jāgīr khānu**	to get official employment
जाति	**jāti**	caste, class, clan
झरी	**jharī**	rain, shower
टुप्पा	**ṭuppā**	top, summit
टौदह	**ṭəwdaha**	Taudaha (name of a lake)
तपस्वी	**tapasvī**	ascetic, pilgrim
थरी	**tharī**	sect, group
देवल्	**deval**	temple (syn. **mandir**)
धाउनु	**dhāunu**	to come repeatedly
धागो	**dhāgo**	thread
नाग्	**nāg**	a Naga (serpent god), cobra

निंदाउनु	**nīdāunu**	to go to sleep
निकाल्नु	**nikālnu**	to take out
निक्लनु	**niklanu**	to go out (syn. **niskanu**)
निराशा	**nirāʃā**	disappointment
न्हसिकाप्	**nhasikāp**	Nhasikap (place name)
पंचमी	**paɲcamī**	period of five days (see note to text)
पछिल्तिर	**pachiltira**	towards the back, behind
पल्ट	**palʈa**	time, turn, occasion
पोखरी	**pokharī**	lake
प्रकार्	**prakār**	sort, kind
प्रचलन	**pracalan**	current, generally accepted
यस् प्रकारले	**yas prakārle**	in this way
बुद्ध -धर्म	**buddha-dharma**	Buddhism
भक्तिपूर्वक्	**bhaktipūrvak**	devotedly
भनठान्नु	**bhanʈhānnu**	to assume, to think
भाँचिनु	**bhā̃cinu**	to be broken
भादगाँउ	**bhādgāũ**	Bhadgaon (town in Kathmandu Valley, also called Bhaktapūr)
भिक्षु	**bhikṣu**	beggar, religious mendicant
भुसुक्कै निंदाउनु	**bhusukkəy nīdāunu**	to fall asleep (suddenly)
मञ्जुश्री	**maɲjuʃrī**	Manjushri
मुहुड़ा	**muhuɽā**	face, countenance
मेला	**melā**	fair, festival
मोक्षदा	**mokṣadā**	Mokshada (name of goddess)
वरदा	**varadā**	Varada (name of goddess)
विपश्वी बुद्ध	**vipaʃvi buddha**	Vipashvi Buddha (name of an ascetic)
विवरण्	**vivaraɳ**	description, account
वेग् (बेग्)	**veg (beg)**	speed, force
शाखा	**ʃākhā**	branch
श्लोक	**ʃloka**	a verse
सताउनु	**satāunu**	to trouble, vex
समाचार्	**samācār**	news
सम्मान् गर्नु	**sammān garnu**	to honour greatly
सरस्वती	**sarasvatī**	Sarasvati (name of goddess)
साँच्चै	**sā̃ccəy**	really, truly
सूझ	**sūjha**	recalling, recollection
सोच्नु	**socnu**	to think, to consider
स्वयंभू	**svayambhū**	Svayambhu
हँसिलो	**hāsilo**	laughing, humorous

Reading Passage

श्री मञ्जुश्री

स्वयंभू डाँड़ाको पछिल्तिरको मन्दिर 'मञ्जुश्री 'को हो । यहाँ श्रीपंचमीको दिन्[1] मेला लाग्छ । यस् देवल्लाई एक् थरी सरस्वतीको मन्दिर् भनी पूजा गर्छन्, अर्को थरी मञ्जुश्रीको देवल् भनी सम्मान् गर्छन्। बुद्ध-धर्म मान्नेहरू यस्लाई मञ्जुश्री मान्दछन्[2]। शिव-धर्म मान्ने हिन्दुहरू सरस्वती भन्छन्। श्रीपंचमीको दिन् यहाँ दुवै थरीका मान्छेहरू पुग्छन्। एक् थरी मञ्जुश्री अर्को थरी सरस्वती मानी , दुवै थरी नै त्यतिकै भक्तिपूर्वक् पूजा गर्दछन् । साँच्चै नै यो अनौठोलाग्दो कुरा हो किनकि मञ्जुश्री लोग्नेमान्छे र सरस्वती स्वास्नीमान्छे हुन् ।नेपाल्को इतिहास्मा मञ्जुश्रीको खूब् मान् छ । यिनी सबभन्दा पहिले चीन्बाट आएका हुन् ।यिन्ले नै आएर नेपाल् -खाल्डो बनाएका हुन् भन्ने प्रचलन् छ । त्यो कथाको विवरण् यस् प्रकारको छ ।

नेपाल्-खाल्डो पहिले एउटा ठूलो पोखरी रहेछ।यस् पोखरीलाई नाग्पोखरी भन्दछन् । यहाँ विपश्वी बुद्ध भन्ने भिक्षुले आएर कमल् रोपेछन् । यस् कमल्मा स्वयंभू खड़ा भएछन्[3]। अनि स्वयंभूको दर्शन् गर्न धेरै तपस्वीहरू यहाँ आइपुगे। यो खाल्डो पोखरी छँदा पनि स्वयंभू पहाड़्को टुप्पा पानीको माथि नै पर्थ्यो । यस्लाई देवता भनी दर्शन् गर्न आएका होलान्।

यिनै[4] 'स्वयंभू' को दर्शन् गर्न चीन्बाट मंञ्जुश्री पनि यहाँ आए ।स्वयंभूको दर्शन् गरेपछि उन्ले खाल्डोको पानीलाई बाहिर निकाल्ने सूझ गरे ।यस्भन्दा पहिले उनी चीन्बाट आएर भाद्गाउँतिरको एउटा डाँड़ामा बसेका थिए। यहींबाट उन्ले पोखरीको पानी निकाल्ने विचार् गरेका हुन् रे।

पोखरीको पानी बाहिर निकाल्ने विचार् गरी मञ्जुश्रीले दुइवटा पहाड़मा अग्लो 'वरदा' र 'मोक्षदा' भन्ने देवीहरू खड़ा गरे। आजसम्म पनि देवीहरूको पूजा गर्न त्यही पहाड़्हरूमा मेला लाग्छ।

त्यस्पछि मञ्जुश्री आफ्नो विचार् अनुसार् पोखरीबाट पानी बाहिर पठाउने काम्मा लागे। कुन् ठाउँमा पानी निकाल्न सकिन्छ भनी सोचे। अन्तमा उन्ले 'कट्वाल्' भन्ने ठाउँलाई चिरेर त्यहाँबाट पानी निकाल्न लगाए। त्यो ठाउँलाई 'न्हसिकाप्' पनि भन्दछन्। यो चोभार् डाँड़ामा पर्छ।

मञ्जुश्रीले पहाड़्लाई चिरेपछि यहाँको पानी ठूलो वेग्ले बाहिरतिर बग्न थाल्यो। सबै नाग्हरू[5] निक्लन लागे। 'कर्कोटक्' भन्ने नाग् पनि निस्कन लाग्यो। मञ्जुश्रीले उस्लाई रोकेर 'टौदह' भन्ने पोखरीमा लगी राखे।

यसरी पोखरीको पानी निस्केपछि यो खाल्डो एउटा ठूलो ठाउँ बन्यो। अनि मञ्जुश्रीले यो ठाउँमा ठूलो शहर् बसाले। उन्को नाम्बाट यस्को नाम् पनि 'मञ्जुपत्तन्' हुन गयो[6] । त्यस्पछि उन्ले यस् शहर्मा मानिस्हरू बसाई एक्जनालाई राजा बनाए र आफू चीन्मै फर्केर गए।

यिनै[4] मञ्जुश्रीको नाम्मा पछि एउटा मन्दिर् स्वयंभूको पछाड़ी बन्यो। यहाँ साल्को एक् पल्ट श्री पंचमीको दिन् मेला लाग्छ। त्यस् दिन् मञ्जुश्रीको पूजा गर्दा नेवार् स्वास्नीमान्छेहरू आफूले कातेको बत्ती, धागो आदि चढ़ाउँछन् र तेल् पनि घसिदिने चलन् छ।

मञ्जुश्रीले पहाड़ काटी पानी निकालेर बनाएको खाल्डोको यो शहर्लाई पहिले मञ्जुपत्तन् भनिन्थ्यो। पछि यहाँ किराँत्हरूको[7] एक् शाखा 'नेपार्' जातिका मान्छेहरू रहन थाले। यिनै नेपार्बाट यस् ठाउँको नाउँ 'नेपाल्' भएको भन्ने कुरा त लेखिसकिएको छ।

Notes

This short passage in which the legend of Manjushri and the naming of Nepal is recounted, has been slightly adapted from an article written by Chittaranjan Nepālī in *Nepalī Itihās Paricaya,* published by Ratna Pustak Bhanḍār. The Boddhisatva Manjushri is said to have come from China, and to have drained the Nepal Valley by cutting the gorge of Chobhar. A temple dedicated both to Manjushri and the Hindu goddess, Sarasvati, was erected near the hill of Svayambhunath, which now houses the vast stupa.

1. **ʃrīpaɲcamī**: the spring festival (**vasant-paɲcamī**) which takes place in Phālgun. Sarasvatī is worshipped on this day.
2. **ʃiva-dharma**: i.e. the branch of Hindus who regard the god Shiva as the most important deity.
3. **svayambhū**: the name given to several deities, including Bramha, Shiva and Vishnu, and also the Buddha. The Svayambhu stupa is one of the famous landmarks of the Kathmandu Valley.
4. **yinəy**: the plural of the demonstrative is used for respect.
5. **nāg**: the serpent gods. **nāg** is now used in the sense of 'cobra'.
6. **maɲjupattan**: **pattan** 'city, town'.
   nām . . . huna gayo 'its name came to be', i.e. 'it was named'.
7. **kirā̃t**: the Kirant people are often considered to be the oldest inhabitants of Nepal. This is one of the many theories about the etymology of 'Nepal', which still remains obscure.

Exercise 19a

Translate into English

१. मेरो साथीको घर्मा बस्दा बस्दै मलाई जरो आयो ।

२. तिमीले ठीक् हो भन्दैमा,ठीक् हुन्छ र ?

३. त्यो मान्छे के भन्दै छ? अलि ठूलो स्वरले सबैले सुन्ने गरी भने पो हुन्छ ।
४. उस्ले राजदूतावास्मा काम् गर्दा गर्दै धेरै पैसा कमाएको होला ।
५. दुइ हप्ता अगाडि भैरहवामा हुँदा मैले तिम्रो चिठी पाएको थिएँ ।
६. हाम्रो घर्मा कोठा खाली छँदै छ । जहिले मन् लाग्छ उहिले आऊ ।
७. तपाईं लन्दन्मा के गर्दै हुनुहुन्छ त अहिले? म विश्वविद्यालयमा काम् गर्दै छु ।
८. ए दाइ ,अबेला हुँदै छ । अहिले जान बेस् होला नि ।
९. उस्ले पढ्दो हो त जाँच्मा फेल् हुने नै थिएन ।
१०. काठ्माडौंमा एक् दुइ पटक् ट्याक्सीमा घुमेको छु, तर अलि महँगो पर्दो रहेछ ।
११. म सुत्न जाँदाखेरि,तलबाट आवाज् आएको सुनें । मैले चोर् घर्भित्र पस्यो भन्ठानी तल हेर्न जाँदा, ढोका लगाएर आउन बिर्सेको रहेछु ।
१२. उमेर् छँदा त म कोसौं हिंड्थें तर अहिले त घरै बस्न मन् लाग्छ ।
१३. बीसौं शताब्दीको आरम्भ भएपछि नेपाली साहित्यले अनेकौं विघ्नवाधाहरू पार् गर्दै विकास्को क्षेत्रमा प्रवेश गर्‍यो[1] ।
१४. उस्ले एक्लै जाऊ भन्दैमा तिमीलाई जानुपर्थो र?
१५. यस्तो गर्मी हुन्छ भनेर थाहा पाएको भए त आज दिउँसो पौड़ी खेल्न जाने थिएँ ।
१६. त्यो मान्छे के भन्दै छ? म यहाँबाट सुन्न सक्दिन ।
१७. तिम्रो घर् आउँदा, म कुन् बाटोबाट आऊँ?
१८. रामे छ महीनाको लागि बेलायत् आएको थियो र अहिलेसम्म यहाँ छँदै छ ।

Exercise 19b

Translate into Nepali

1. While in Kathmandu, he used to go to the University Library every day.
2. Because of the rain, there was a landslide. After that the road was closed for three days.
3. How did you learn Nepali? I learnt it by sitting in teashops and talking to Nepalis.
4. Just because he told you to go home early, did you have to go?
5. That boy just refuses to work. If he does not learn to read and write English, he certainly will not get a job.
6. As I was going to my office this morning, I met your young brother. I see he's working in the State Bank these days.
7. While working in India, he must have earnt a lot of money. I want to go there too.
8. When I was young, I used to be able to get to my village in two hours. Now as I walk along the road, I have to rest. For that reason, it now takes me three hours.
9. Just because he told you to buy this book, did you have to buy it?
10. While I was listening to the Prime Minister's speech, I dropped off to sleep.

[1]**ārambha** 'beginning', **vighnavādhā** 'obstacle', **pār garnu** 'to cross', **vikāsko kṣetra** 'the field of progress'..

Exercise 19c

Translate into English

उनी घर् बनाउने काम्मा लागे ; मञ्जुश्रीले नेपाल्-खाल्डो बनाएका हुन् भन्ने प्रचलन् छ; बुवाले भन्नुभएको त्यो मान्दै मान्दैन ; पहिरो जाने कुरा यिनीहरूलाई थाहा छँदै थियो ; त्यसैले गर्दा ,म जान सकिनँ ; लन्दन्मा बसेको बेला वहाँले धेरै काम् गर्नुभयो ; धूर्त मान्छेको कुरामा विश्वास् गर्नुपर्दैन ; अलि चाँड़ै जानुभए त हुन्थयो ; मैले उस्लाई नेपाली पढ्ने सल्लाह दिएँ ; हामीले एउटा सानो कोठा बहाल्मा लियौं ; मलाई बिदा देऊ न ; उस्ले काम् गरोस् कि नगरोस् , जाँच्मा सफल् हुनेछ; उस्ले ज्यान् गए मानेन ।

LESSON 20

1. *The Absolutive Participle*

The Absolutive Participle, which is used in the formation of compound verbs and certain compound tenses, is formed by adding the suffix -इ to the base of verbs belonging to groups (i) and (ii) and to the secondary base of verbs belonging to other groups:

गरि-	खाइ-	दिइ-	धोइ-	बिर्सि-	आइ-
gari-	**khāi-**	**dii-**	**dhoi-**	**birsi-**	**āi-**

The verbs हुनु and जानु have two absolutive participles:

1. जाइ- **jāi-** 2. गइ- **gai-**
1. होइ- **hoi-** 2. भइ- **bhai-**

The Absolutive Participle, the suffix of which is written with a short **-i,** should be distinguished from the Conjunctive Participle, the suffix of which is written with a long **ī.**

Conj. Part. गरी **garī** Absol. Part. गरि **gari-**

The Absolutive Participle is always compounded with another verb. It can never stand alone. It therefore has no negative or HGH forms.

2. The Absolutive Participle is used in the formation of a number of continuous ('I am doing', 'I was doing', etc.) tenses, and frequentative ('I keep on doing', 'I kept on doing') tenses and participles. These are all formed by the Absolutive Participle followed by the various tenses of the verb रहनु **rahanu** 'to remain'. The most commonly encountered forms are given in the following list:

(*a*) Present Frequentative (Abs. Part. and Simple Indef. of रहनु)

म गरिरहन्छु **ma garirahanchu**

I keep/shall keep on doing

(*b*) Past Habitual Frequentative (Abs. Part. and Past Hab. of रहनु)

म गरिरहन्थें **ma garirahanthē**

I used to keep on doing

(*c*) Past Frequentative (Abs. Part. and Past of रहनु)
म गरिरहें **ma garirahẽ**
I kept on doing

(*d*) Present Continuous (1) (Abs. Part. and 1st Perf. of रहनु)
म गरिरहेको छु **ma gariraheko chu**
I am doing

(*e*) Present Continuous (2) (Abs. Part. and 2nd Perf. of रहनु)
म गरिरहेछु **ma garirahechu**
I am doing

(*f*) Past Continuous (Abs. Part. and 1st Plup. of रहनु)
ma gariraheko thiẽ
म गरिरहेको थिएँ I was doing

(*g*) Future Continuous (Abs. Part. and Future Perf. of रहनु)
म गरिरहेको हुँला **ma gariraheko hũlā**
I (probably) shall be doing

(*h*) Continuous Participle (1)
गरिरहँदो **garirahãndo**
while doing/as I am/was doing

(*i*) Continuous Participle (2)
गरिरहेको **gariraheko**
while doing/as I am/was doing

Tenses (*d*) and (*e*) are in free variation with each other. There is no difference in the meaning.

3. The continuous tenses (*d*), (*e*) and (*f*) express continuous action like the English tenses 'I am doing', 'I was doing', etc., and may be used in place of the continuous tenses म गर्दै छु and म गर्दै थिएँ which were discussed in Lesson 19. The use of one set of tenses or the other is a matter of personal choice, and both are equally common. Thus म किताब् पढ़िरहेको छु or म किताब् पढ़िरहेछु mean exactly the same thing as म किताब पढ़्दै छु Similarly उ गीत् गाइरहेको थियो means exactly the same thing as उ गीत गाउँदै थियो .

Feminine and Plural forms of the continuous tenses are commonly used in the written language and are optional in the spoken language. The rules are the same as those for the First Perfect and Pluperfect Tenses (Lesson 13) and the Second Perfect Tense (Lesson 16). Thus:

मेरी बहिनी लुगा सिइरहेकी छे
My sister is sewing her clothes

सिउनु **siunu** 'to sew' is a group (v) verb like पिउनु

मेरी दिदी भात् पकाइरहेकी थिइन्
My elder sister was cooking dinner

किसान्हरू धान् रोपिरहेका थिए
The peasants were planting paddy in the fields

4. The HGH forms of all the tenses listed above are as follows:

(*a*) गरिरहनुहुन्छ **garirahanuhuncha**
(*b*) गरिरहनुहुन्थ्यो **garirahanuhunthyo**
(*c*) गरिरहनुभयो **garirahanubhayo**
(*d*) गरिरहनुभएको छ **garirahanubhaeko cha**
(*e*) गरिरहनुभएछ **garirahanubhaecha**
(*f*) गरिरहनुभएको थियो **garirahanubhaeko thiyo**
(*g*) गरिरहनुभएको होला **garirahanubhaeko holā**

मेरो बुवा थकाई मारिरहनुभएको छ
My father is resting
तपाईं के गरिरहनुभएको थियो
What were you doing?

5. In the above tenses and participles, the verb राख्नु **rākhnu** is sometimes used as an auxiliary in place of रहनु

म गरिराखेको छु	**ma garirākheko chu**	I am doing
गरिराखेको	**garirākheko**	while doing

This is largely a feature of the spoken language and is rarely found in written Nepali.

6. The tenses discussed above are illustrated in the following sentences. Note that -ले is sometimes used with 3rd person forms of transitive verbs:

बस नआएसम्म म यहीं बसिरहन्छु
I'll keep sitting here until the bus comes
उ जहिले पनि जुवा खेलिरहन्थ्यो
He always used to keep on gambling
घर् आउने बित्तिकै मैले उपन्यास् पढ्न शुरू गरें,र नसिद्धिएसम्म पढिरहें
As soon as I got home, I started reading the novel and went on reading it until it was finished
डाक्टर्ले मलाई औषधि खाइराख्नु भनेका थिए
The doctor told me to keep taking the medicine
आज बस्-चालक्हरूले हड्ताल् गरिरहेका छन्
The bus drivers are on strike ('are striking') today
रामे कहाँ छ? ऊ त्यहाँ उभिरहेछ
Where is Rame? He's standing over there
आज मेरो टाउको एक् दम् नराम्रोसित दुखिरहेको छ
I've got a terrible headache today ('my head is aching')
दिन्भरि हावा चलिरहेको थियो र साँझ् पर्नासाथ् पानी पर्न थाल्यो
The wind was blowing all day long and as evening fell it began to rain

छानाबाट झण्डा फर्‌फराइरहेको थियो
The flag was flying from the roof

7. The continuous participles are illustrated in the following sentences:

म बाटो काटिरहँदा, ट्रक्ले मलाई झण्डै कुल्चेको
As I was crossing the road, a truck almost knocked me over
नदी तर्नलाग्दा, त्यो अचानक् चिप्लेर लड्‌यो
Just as he was crossing the river, he slipped and fell
डाँड़ाको टुप्पाबाट हाम्रा साथीहरूले नदी तरिरहेका हामीले देख्यौं
From the top of the ridge, we could see our friends crossing the stream

8. In earlier lessons, we have met a number of compound verbs like लाइहेर्नु **lāihernu** 'to try on (clothes)', आइपुग्नु **āipugnu** 'to arrive', etc., which are made up of two verbs, the first of which is in the form of the Absolutive Participle. The two verbs compounded in this way convey a single idea. Such verbs must be learnt as separate items of vocabulary.

Other types of compound verbs, in which the first element is the Absolutive Participle, are as follows:

(*a*) those of which the second element is the verb दिनु implying that the action is performed on behalf of someone else, or that the action is sudden or final. For example:

लेखिदिनु	**lekhidinu**	to write for someone
खसालिदिनु	**khasālidinu**	to post (a letter) for someone
गरिदिनु	**garidinu**	to do for someone
खाइदिनु	**khāidinu**	to eat up

शहर् जाँदाखेरि, मेरो चिठी खसालिदेऊ न
When you go to town, post my letter for me
डाक्टर् साहेब्ले औषधि लेखिदिए
The doctor wrote me out a prescription
तिम्रो काम् मै गरिदिन्छु
I'll do the work for you
धेरै भोकाएको हुनाले, केटाले सबै भात् खाइदियो
The little boy was so hungry that he ate up all the rice

(*b*) those of which the second element is the verb हाल्नु **hālnu** 'to put in, to pour', which adds a certain amount of emphasis. In colloquial speech, there is in fact little difference in the meaning of the simple verb and that of the verb compounded with हाल्नु

लुगा मैलो भयो। भोलि म धोइहाल्छु
The clothes are dirty. I'll wash them through tomorrow
वहाँलाई थाहा छैन होला । वहाँको अड्डा गएर म भनिहाल्छु
Perhaps he doesn't know. I'll go to his office and tell him

म एक् छिन्मा आइहाल्छु
I'll come in just a moment

Note also the expression भइहाल्यो **bhaihālyo** (often written and pronounced भैहाल्यो **bhəyhālyo**) which means 'never mind', 'let it pass'.

(*c*) those of which the second element is the verb सक्नु (e.g., गइसक्नु **gaisaknu,** मरिसक्नु **marisaknu,** etc.), which implies that the action is completed once and for all. In general, only the Simple Past and the Perfect tenses are used.

सिनेमा शुरू भइसक्यो
The film has already started
हाम्रो बूढो नोकर् मरिसक्यो
Our old servant has (just) died
काम् त सिद्धिसक्यो, म जाऊँ अहिले त?
All the work is finished, sir. May I go home now?
म नेपाल्मा हुँदो हुँ त अहिले सुतिसकेको हुँन्थें
If I were in Nepal now, I would be (already) fast asleep

The I-Stem verb सकिनु **sakinu** is frequently used in the sense of 'to be finished', 'to be over'.

त्यो काम् त सकियो
Well, that job's over

Note also the expression बजिसक्यो **bajisakyo** 'it's already . . . o'clock':

चार् बजिसक्यो। मलाई त जानुपर्‍यो
It's already four o'clock. I must be off now

(*d*) two verbs of which the second element is लाग्नु

जाइलाग्नु	**jāilāgnu**	'to go for, to attack'
आइलाग्नु	**āilāgnu**	'to come for, to attack'

Note that the Absolutive Participle जाइ- (and not गइ-) is used in this compound.

आइलाग्नेमाथि जाइलाग्नुपर्छ
One has to go for one's attacker (a proverb)

9. *The 'royal honorific'*

As the name implies, the 'royal honorific' forms are used mainly when addressing or talking about royalty, especially the royalty of Nepal. The second person forms may also be used for people to whom particular respect is due, but nowadays the HGH is preferred in this case. In historical works, the MGH (उनी , यिनी , तिनी) is often used for dead royalty, but it is now the practice in Nepal to use the 'royal honorific' forms for all the ancestors of the Nepalese royal family.

The 'royal honorific' consists of the absolutive participle followed by the auxiliary verb बक्सनु **baksanu** (or in some cases बक्सिनु **baksinu**).[1] The same form is used for both second and third persons. The honorific word हजूर् **hajūr** acts as a 2nd and 3rd person pronoun.

The following forms of the 'royal honorific' are in common use. Note that -ले is added to the subject of transitive verbs:

Infinitive	गरिबक्सनु	**garibaksanu**
Simp. Indef. Aff.	गरिबक्सन्छ	**garibaksancha**
Simp. Indef. Neg.	गरिबक्सन्न	**garibaksanna**
Simp. Past	गरिबक्स्यो	**garibaksyo**
Simp. Past Neg.	गरिबक्सेन	**garibaksena**
Habit. Past Aff.	गरिबक्सन्थ्यो	**garibaksanthyo**
Habit. Past Neg.	गरिबक्सन्नथ्यो	**garibaksannathyo**
Imperative/Injunctive	गरिबक्सियोस्	**garibaksiyos**
Infinit. Part.	गरिबक्सिने	**garibaksine**
1st Perf. Part.	गरिबक्सेको	**garibakseko**
2nd Perf. Part.	गरिबक्से	**garibakse**

The 'royal honorific' of हुनु is formed with the absolutive participle होइ . Thus: होइबक्सनु **hoibaksanu,** होइबक्सन्छ **hoibaksancha,** etc. A number of special honorific words and phrases are used in the context of the 'royal honorific', such as:

सवारी होइबक्सनु	**savārī hoibaksanu**	to go
ज्युनार् गरिबक्सनु	**jyunār garibaksanu**	to eat/drink
अनुसरण् गरिबक्सनु	**anusaraṇ garibaksanu**	to follow

The King of Nepal is often referred to as मौसूफ् **məwsūph** or मौसूफ सर्कार् **məwsūph sarkār,** or simply as श्री ५ **ʃrī pāc** ('five times lord'). The latter term is used before the titles of all the members of the Nepalese royal family:

श्री ५ महाराजाधिराज्	the King of Nepal
श्री ५ बड़ा महारानी	the Queen of Nepal
श्री ५ युवराजाधिराज्	the Crown Prince of Nepal

For example, the present King of Nepal has the following title:

श्री ५ महाराजाधिराज् बिरेन्द्र वीर् विक्रम् शाह देव्
ʃrī pāc mahārājādhirāj birendra vīr vikram ʃāh dev

Formerly, the Rāṇā Prime Ministers of Nepal took the title श्री ३ **ʃrī tīn.** The kingdom of Nepal is referred to as अधिराज्य **adhirājya.**

[1] बक्सनु is derived from the Persian verb **bakhshīdan** 'to bestow'. The language of the Nepalese court and the jargon of the law courts abound in words of Persian origin, inherited from the Indian Mughal administration.

हजूरले चिया ज्युनार् गरिबक्सन्छ?
Will you have some tea, Your Majesty?
श्री ५ बाट हुकुम् भयो (lit. 'an order came about from . . .')
An ordinance was issued by the King
महाराज्, मेरो अनुसरण् गरिबक्सियोस्
My lord, please follow me
श्री ५ दुइ हप्ताका लागि पोखरा सवारी होइबक्सन्छ
His Majesty is going to Pokhara for two weeks
आज श्री ५ महाराजाधिराज् बाउन्नौं वर्ष प्रवेश् गरिबक्स्यो
Today His Majesty entered his fifty second year
श्री ५ को सर्कारले यो घोषणा गरेको छ
His Majesty's government has made the following announcement

10. *The construction with* -जेल् **-jel** *'as long as', 'until'*

The particle -जेल् **jel** 'as long as', 'while' is added to the secondary base of the verb which is extended by the syllable ऊञ् **-ūɲ** (or rarely इञ् **-iɲ**). The form of the verb is invariable. Transitive verbs in this form require -ले .

मैले गरूञ्जेल्	**məyle garūɲjel**	as long as I do/did
तिमी बसूञ्जेल्	**timī basūɲjel**	as long as you stayed/stay
उस्ले धोऊञ्जेल्	**usle dhoūɲjel**	as long as he washes/washed
हामी आऊञ्जेल्	**hāmī āūɲjel**	as long as we come/came

The negative is formed with the negative prefix न- and has the sense of 'until I do/did', etc.

उस्ले नगरूञ्जेल्	**usle nagarūɲjel**	until he does/did
म नआऊञ्जेल्	**ma naāūɲjel**	until I come/came

The tense of the verb in the English translation depends on the context.

मैले यहाँ काम् गरूञ्जेल, राम्रो तलब् पाउँछु
As long as I am working here, I'll earn a good salary
म पानी लिन जान्छु । म फर्केर नआऊञ्जेल् यहीं बसिराख्नु
I'm going to get some water. Sit here till I come back
किताब् नलेखिसकूञ्जेल् लेखक्लाई संतोष् भएन
The writer was not content until he had finished writing his book

Note also यतिञ्जेल् **yatiɲjel** 'during this time', 'meanwhile', and त्यतिञ्जेल् **tyatiɲjel** 'during that time', 'meanwhile'.

The construction with -जेल् is exactly the equivalent of that involving the Second Perfect Participle followed by -सम्म (Lesson 16), the latter being by far the most common. The above sentences could be equally well written:

मैले यहाँ काम् गरेसम्म राम्रो तलब् पाउँछु ।
म फर्केर नआएसम्म यहीं बसिराख्नु ।
किताब् नलेखिसकेसम्म लेखक्लाई संतोष् भएन ।

The construction with जेल् is now used rather infrequently, the one with -सम्म being preferred.

Vocabulary 20

अध्यक्ष	**adhyakṣa**	chairman, leader
अपरान्ह	**aparānha**	afternoon (literary)
अभिनन्दन्	**abhinandan**	greeting, welcome
अभिवादन्	**abhivādan**	greeting, salute
अरुणोदय	**aruṇodaya**	daybreak
अवसर्	**avasar**	interval, time, occasion
आयोजना	**āyojanā**	plan, function
आरोग्य	**ārogya**	good health, freedom from disease
आस्था	**āsthā**	devotion
आस्थापूर्ण	**āsthāpūrṇa**	devoted(ly)
उच्च-पदस्थ	**ucca-padastha**	high-class, top
उड्नु	**uṛnu**	to fly
उल्लास्	**ullās**	joy, delight
उल्लास्मय	**ullāsmaya**	joyful
कतै कतै	**katəy katəy**	here and there, everywhere
कर्मचारी	**karmacārī**	civil servant
कामना	**kāmanā**	good wishes, congratulations
क्षेत्र	**kṣetra**	field (of study, etc.), area
घाँस्	**ghā̃s**	grass
घाँसी	**ghā̃sī**	grass-cutter
घोषणा	**ghoṣaṇā**	announcement
चढाइनु	**caṛhāinu**	to be offered up
चर्को	**carko**	harsh (of sun)
चालक्	**cālak**	driver
छहारी	**chahārī**	shade
छाना	**chānā**	roof
जंगी	**jaŋgī**	military (adj.)
जता तते	**jatā tatəy**	here and there, everywhere
जुवा खेल्नु	**juvā khelnu**[1]	to gamble
जुनाफ्	**junāph**	presence (royal hon. word)
झण्डा	**jhaṇḍā**	flag
झींगा	**jhīŋgā**	a fly
टक्र्याउनु	**ṭakryāunu**	to present
डुल्नु	**ḍulnu**	to stroll, walk
तलब्	**talab**	wages
तयार्	**tayār**	ready
तिब्बत्	**tibbat**	Tibet (syn. **bhoṭ**)

[1]v pronounced like English **w.**

तोप्	**top**	cannon, gun
दिवस्	**divas**	day, a special day
दीर्घायु	**dīrghāyu**	long life
धुलो	**dhulo**	dust
ध्वनित् गर्नु	**dhvanit garnu**	to sound, be sounded
नत्र	**natra**	otherwise, if not
नदी	**nadī**	river
नर्-नारी	**nar-nārī**	men and women
निजामती	**nijāmatī**	civil, civilian
न्यायाधीश्	**nyāyādhīʃ**	justice, magistrate
पंच्	**paɲc**	member of a **panchayat**
परेवा	**parevā**	dove, pigeon
पुनीत्	**punīt**	sacred, auspicious
पुष्प	**puṣpa**	flower
पुष्प-गुच्छा	**puṣpa-gucchā**	bunch of flowers
प्रति	**prati**	before, by, *per*
प्रधान्	**pradhān**	chief, main, head
प्रवेश् गर्नु	**praveʃ garnu**	to enter
प्रहरी	**praharī**	guard
बजाउनु	**bajāunu**	to make sound, to strike
बाउन्नौँ	**bāunnəw̃**	fifty-second
भक्ति	**bhakti**	devotion
भक्तिपूर्ण	**bhaktipūrɳa**	devotedly
भक्तिभावना	**bhaktibhāvana**	sentiments of devotion
-भर्	**-bhar**	throughout (syn. **bharī**)
भाग्	**bhāg**	part, region (of a country)
भूमि	**bhūmi**	land
भेग्	**bheg**	nearby, neighbouring
भेग् र विश्व	**bheg ra viʃva**	near and far
मंच	**maɲc**	stage
मज़्दूर	**majdūr**	labourer
मन्त्रीगण्	**mantrīgaɳ**	ministers
महाकाली नदी	**mahākālī nadī**	Mahakali River
माल्यार्पन्	**mālyārpan**	garlanding
मेची नदी	**mecī nadī**	Mechi River
मैदान्	**məydān**	plain, the plains
राज्सभा	**rājsabhā**	Royal Council, State Council
राष्ट्नायक्	**rāṣtranāyak**	head of state
रिभ्याली	**ribhyālī**	reveille
वर्गीय	**vargīya**	class (adj.)
विशेष्	**viʃeṣ**	special
विशेष्-आस्था	**viʃeṣ-āsthā**	special devotion
विश्व	**viʃva**	universe, world

शाही	**ʃāhī**	royal
संगठन्	**saŋgaṭhan**	assembly, organisation
संपन्न	**sampanna**	completed, accomplished
सदस्य	**sadasya**	member
समारोह्	**samāroh**	celebration
समिति	**samiti**	committee
सम्मान्	**sammān**	honour, respect
सर्कार्	**sarkār**	government
सलामी	**salāmī**	a salute
सिउनु	**siunu**	to sew
सुख्नु	**sukhnu**	to dry up
सेना	**senā**	army
सोल्लास्	**sollās**	with great pleasure
सैनिक्	**səynik**	military (adj.), soldier (noun)
स्थायी	**sthāyī**	standing, acting
हार्दिक	**hārdik**	heartfelt

Reading Passage

श्री ५ को बाउन्नौं शुभजन्मोत्सव

सोल्लास् संपन्न

अधिराज्यभर् भक्ति-र आस्थापूर्ण अभिनन्दन् समारोह

कार्यालय प्रतिनिधि [1]। काठ्माड़ौं ज्येष्ठ, ३० गते

राष्ट्रनायक् श्री ५ महाराजाधिराज् महेन्द्र वीर विक्रम् शाह देव एकाउन्नौं वर्ष पूर्ण गरी बाउन्नौं वर्ष प्रवेश् गरिबक्सेको पुनीत् उपलक्ष्यमा आज नेपाल् अधिराज्य भर् मौसूफ् सर्कार्को शुभजन्मोत्सव विशेष्आस्था र भक्तिभावनाका साथ् विभिन्न कार्यक्रमहरूको आयोजना गरी मनाइयो [2]।

आजको उल्लास्मय दिवस्मा [3] देश्का समस्त भेग् र विश्वका विभिन्न भाग्मा बस्ने राजभक्त नेपालीहरूले राष्टनायक् श्री ५ महेन्द्रको् दीर्घायु र आरोग्य कामनाका साथ् मौसूफ्का तस्वीर्मा माल्यार्पण र अभिवादन् गरे ।

आज बिहान अरुणोदयका साथ् भीम्सेन् स्तम्भबाट[4] शाही सेनाले रिभ्याली बजाएर शुभजन्मोत्सवको हार्दिक् उल्लास् ध्वनित् गऱ्यो ।

रासस् [5] अनुसार् श्री ५ महाराजाधिराज् सर्कार्को ५२ औं शुभजन्मोत्सवको उपलक्ष्यमा आज अपरान्ह शाही सैनिक् मंच्मा एक् विशेष् समारोह्का बीच् मौसूफ सर्कार्को तस्वीरमा माल्र्यापण्

तथा पुष्प-गुच्छाहरू चढ़ाइयो ।

सो अवसर्मा[6] श्री ५ महाराजाधिराज् सर्कार्को सम्मान्मा शाही सलामी चढ़ाउनाका साथै ३१ तोप्को सलामी पनि टक्र्याइएको थियो ।

सो अवसर्मा ५२ सेता परेवाहरू पनि उड़ाइएका थिए ।साथै श्री ५ महाराजाधिराज् सर्कार्को जुनाफ्मा मौसूफ् सर्कार्को ५२ औं शुभजन्मोत्सवको उपलक्ष्यमा तयार् गरिएको अभिनन्दन् पत्र[7] र उपहार्हरू नारायणहिटी राजदर्बार्मा[8] चढ़ाउन पठाइयो ।

सो अवसर्मा प्रधान्मन्त्री श्री कीर्तिनिधि बिष्ट, प्रधान्न्यायाधीश् श्री रत्नबहादुर बिष्ट, मन्त्रीगण्, समारोह समितिका अध्यक्ष् श्री रंगनाथ् शर्मा, राज्सभा स्थायी समिति तथा राष्ट्रीय पञ्चायत्का सदस्यहरू निजामती, जंगी, तथा प्रहरीका उच्च-पदस्थ कर्मचारीहरूले मौसूफ् सर्कार्को तस्वीरमा माल्यार्पण् तथा पुष्प-गुच्छाहरू चढ़ाउनुभएको थियो ।

साथै मौसूफ् सर्कार् प्रति[10] अभिवादन् टक्र्याउन शाही सैनिक् मंच् अगाड़ी पञ्च तथा वर्गीय संगठन्हरूका सदस्यहरू, विद्यार्थीहरू, स्काउट् तथा नर-नारीहरू भेला भएका थिए ।

Notes

This passage, taken from the Gorkhapatra, is a fairly straightforward account of the celebrations held for the late King Mahendra's 52nd birthday. The language, which is highly Sanskritised, is typical of many articles in modern Nepali newspapers, and although it would be difficult for uneducated villagers to understand, most of the words (that one hears constantly repeated on Radio Nepal) would be familiar to moderately educated Nepalis. The events described in the article took place in 1971 A.D.

1. **kāryālaya pratinidhi**: 'staff-reporter'. **kāryālaya** is a commonly used 'official' term for 'office' (syn. **aḍḍā**).
2. **ʃubhajanmotsava . . . manāiyo**: 'having done a project of various programmes, the birthday was celebrated', i.e. it was celebrated with a number of arranged programmes.
   kā sāth: 'with', 'along with'.
3. **divas**: a special day on which a particular event is celebrated.
4. **bhīmsen stambha**: 'the Bhimsen Column', popularly referred to as धरहरा **dharahrā** – a prominent landmark of Kathmandu.
5. **rāsas**: an abbreviation for राष्ट्रीय समाचार् समिति **rāṣṭrīya samācār samiti** 'the National News Agency'.
6. **so avasarmā**: 'on that occasion'. **so** in certain phrases may be used as a demonstrative (syn. **tyo**) or as an adverb meaning 'thus'.
7. **abhinandan patra**: 'letters of greeting'. **patra** is a literary synonym of **ciṭhī.**

8. The Narayanhiti Palace in the centre of the old town of Kathmandu is the traditional residence of the Nepalese Royal Family.
9. **rāṣṭrīya pañcāyat**: 'the state panchayat'. Nepal is governed by a 'partyless panchayat system'.
10. **prati**: a Sanskrit word, used as a postposition in literary Nepali, in the sense of 'towards', 'in front of', 'for the sake of'. As a prefix it denotes 'per', e.g. **प्रति घण्टा** 'per hour', **प्रति दिन्** 'per day', **दिन् प्रतिदिन्** 'every day'.

Reading Passage 2

The following passage is an extract from a short story, entitled *Bihā*, by Paṇḍit Vishveshvar Prasād Koirālā. When he hears that the elderly Subbā Kaṭak Bahādur is to marry a young, fourteen-year-old girl, the author reflects upon the subject of marriage. Supplementary vocabulary is given at the end of the passage.

बिहा

सुब्बा कटक् बहादुर्ले १४ वर्षकीलाई [1] बिहा गरेर घर् लिएर आए ।

भन्नुपर्ने कुरा यत्ति हो, र कटक् बहादुरलाई नचिन्ने मानिस् योभन्दा धेरै कुरा सुन्न पनि चाहँदैनन् । तर मलाई १४ वर्षकी भन्नासाथ्,केटीको विषयमा जान्ने रहर् लाग्छ । सुब्बा कटक् बहादुर् निश्चय नै छिपिएका होलान्[2]। मैले सानो उमेर्को सुब्बा देखेको छैन। भर्सक् यो उन्को अर्को बिहा हो । पहिलेकी दुलहीबाट दुइवटा छोरा होलान्, र उस्को मृत्यु भएपछि, यिन्ले १४ वर्षकीलाई बिहा गर्ने विचार् गरेका होलान्। कटक् बहादुरलाई त के छ? बिहाको क्षेत्रमा खग्गु र निपुण् भइसकेका मानिस्लाई दिन्भरी कलम् घस्दा [3] र अड्डाका साथी -भाइसँग खेल्-ठट्टा गर्दा, शायद् नै १४ बर्षकी हरिमतिको [4] ध्यान् आउँदो हो । तर हरिमति,भर्खरै १४ वर्षकी, बिहाको अर्थ बुझ्न नसक्ने उमेरमै बिहाको अनुभव गर्न थालेकी हरिमतिको कुरा नै भिन्नै होला ।

मैले एउटा बिहा देखेको छु ।म जन्तीपट्टि [5] थिएँ । हामीहरूलाई चार् बजेको निम्ता थियो, तर जन्ती सात् बजेभन्दा पहिले निस्केनन् ।हामीहरू बाहिर बसी बसी जन्ती निकाल्ने उद्योग्मा थियौं तर दुलहाले नै अबेर लगाए।उनी सिंगार [6] पारिरहेका छन् रे। विहाको अवसरमा एक् चोटि सिंगारिने मौका पाइन्छ भनी हामीहरू चुप्प लागी उन्को प्रतीक्षा गरिरहेका थियौं । मैले दुलहालाई देखेको थिइनँ कस्ता होलान् ।गाउँका स्वास्नीमानिस्हरू पनि आएर उभिरहेका थिए । तिनिहरू पनि दुलहालाई हेर्छन् रे कस्ता होलान् ।दुलहा भन्नासाथ्,[7] २० ,२२ वर्षको युवक्को कल्पना हुन

थाल्दछ, र ती ग्रामीण् रमणीहरू पनि यस्तै दुलहाको कल्पना गरी ,हेर्न उभिरहेका होलान् ।धेरै बेरपछि ढोकातिर खल्बली भयो ।'दुलहा आए,दुलहा आए 'भनेर,सब् उतातिर ओइरिन लागे,तर मैले चिन्न सकिनँ कुन्चाहिने[8] दुलहा हुन् । सब् छिपिएका उमेरका मानिस्हरू ढोकाबाट बाहिर निस्के । तेसो ठम्याउन नसके पनि पहिरन्ले ती कालो कोट् लाउने नै दुलहा हुन् भनिठानें[9]। नभन्दै तिनी रहेछन्[10], अफ्नो खुशी र सुख्लाई नदेखाऊँ भन्दा भन्दै पनि,[11] उन्को चलाई र बोलाईले नै तिनी दुनियाँको सबै भन्दा सुखी मानिस् जस्ता देखिन्थे। ठीक् आठ् बजे जन्ती घर्बाट बाहिर निस्क्यो । दुलहा हात्तीमा चढ़े औ हामीहरू पैदल् हिंडचौं । मलाई दुलहा देख्नासाथ् दुलहीको ध्यान् आउन् थाल्यो । दुलही पनि त्यस्तै ३५ ,४० की ढोकाबाट निस्की भने मेरो सारा उत्साह् व्यर्थ हुनेछ। तर सानी १४ वर्ष निस्की भने? मैले त्यो हात्तीमा चढ़ेको दुलहातिर हेरें र म नजीकै हिंड्ने एउटा भद्र मानिस्लाई सोधें 'दुलहाको यो पहिलो बिहा हो?

उन्ले उत्तर दिए ।'अहँ' ।

पैलेकी दुलही नि?[11]

'उ मरेर त ई अर्को बिहा गर्न हिंडे़का। इन्की पैलेकी दुलहीबाट, दुइऔटा छोरा छन्। घर्मा स्वास्नीमानिस् नभएर, घर् नचल्ने, तेस्मा पनि छोराहरूलाई हेरिदिने कोई नहुँदा, इन्ले बिहा गर्नुपरेको।'

दुलहापट्टिबाट निश्चिन्त भई, म दुलहीको कल्पना गर्न थालें। दुलहाको त घर् चलाउन् थियो[12] र ती साना साना केटाकेटीहरूलाई हेरिदिने मानिस् ल्याउन् थियो र बिहा गरे। तर यिन्को घर् चलाउने र यिन्का छोराछोरीलाई हेरिदिने आउने दुलही कस्ती होलिन्? ती निश्चय नै बढ़ेकी होलिन्[13] नत्र कसरी घर् चलाउलिन्,कसरी छोराछोरीलाई हेर्लिन? म दुलहीको विषयमा पनि निश्चिन्त भएँ र दुलहीको घर्मा पुग्ने बखत्मा[14] मलाई फेरि उत्साह आउन थाल्यो । नाच्गान्मा र वहाँको उत्साहमा म पनि खूब् शामिल् भएँ र दुलही निस्क्ने बखत्मा हत्पताई मण्डप्मा आएँ । गाउँका स्वास्नीमानिस्हरूले मण्डप् घेरिएको थियो ।तिनीहरू कस्ती दुलहीको कल्पना गरिरहेका होलान्? २५,३० वर्षकी,घर्को काम् चलाउन निपुण्,दुलहाको सारा व्यवहार्लाई थाम्ने दुलहीको कल्पना गरिरहेका होलान्? म त यस्तै दुलहीको कल्पना गरिरहेको थिएँ,तलदेखि माथिसम्म रातो लुगाले छोपिएकी एउटी सानी बालिकालाई डोरचाउँदै ठेल्दै दुइ तीन् स्वास्नीमानिस् मण्डप्मा पुगे ।यहाँ पनि मेरो कल्पनाले मलाई धोका दियो ।म वहाँको उत्साहदेखि विरक्त भएँ । मैले विचार् गर्न सकिनँ

कसरी यी १४ वर्षकी कलिली बालिकाले दुलहाको घर् थाम्लिन् र उन्का छोराहरूको हेर्-विचार् गर्न सक्लिन् । म यी बालिकाका विषयमा गम्न थालें, यिनी दुलहाको घर्मा कसरी बस्लिन्,यिन्को र दुलहाको कस्तो संबन्ध रहला? अहिले यिनी के सोच्न थालेका होलिन् इत्यादि । त्यस्पछि मैले कुनै बिहामा जाने साहस् गरिनँ । मलाई अब पनि बिहा हेर्ने रहर् लाग्दैन ।

Supplementary vocabulary for Reading Passage 2

अनुभव्	**anubhav**	experience, feeling
अबेर लगाउनु	**aber lagāunu**	to delay, hang around
इत्यादि	**ityādi**	et cetera
उत्तर्	**uttar**	answer
उत्साह्	**utsāh**	joy, peace of mind
उद्योग्	**udyog**	effort, industry
ओइरिनु	**oirinu**	fall headlong, drop
औ	**au**	and, but
कलिलो	**kalilo**	unripe, slender
खग्गु	**khaggu**	clever, smart
खलबली	**khalbalī**	noise, fuss
गम्नु	**gamnu**	to ponder
ग्रामीण्	**grāmīṇ**	village (adj.), rustic
घस्नु	**ghasnu**	to drag, push (a pen)
घेरिनु	**gherinu**	be surrounded
चलाई	**calāī**	actions, behaviour
चुप्प लाग्नु	**cuppa lāgnu**	to be silent
छिपिनु	**chipinu**	to be getting on (in years)
जन्ती	**jantī**	wedding party (of groom)
ठट्टा	**ṭhaṭṭā**	joke
ठम्याउनु	**ṭhamyāunu**	to make up one's mind
ठेल्नु	**ṭhelnu**	to push, shove
डोर्याउनु	**ḍoryāunu**	to lead (by a rope)
त्यस्माथि पनि	**tyasmāthi pani**	on top of that, in addition
थाम्नु	**thāmnu**	to support, sustain
धोका दिनु	**dhokā dinu**	to deceive
ध्यान्	**dhyān**	attention
नाच्गान्	**nācgān**	dancing and singing
निपुण्	**nipuṇ**	experienced
निम्ता (निम्तो)	**nimtā (nimto)**	invitation
निश्चिन्त्	**niʃcint**	unworried, carefree
-पट्टि	**-paṭṭi**	on the side of
पहिरन्	**pahiran**	clothes, dress

प्रतीक्षा गर्नु	**pratīkṣā garnu**	to wait for
बखत्	**bakhat**	time
बढ़ेको उमेर्	**baṛheko umer**	advanced years
बालिका	**bālikā**	young girl
भद्र	**bhadra**	kind, gentle
भनिठान्नु	**bhaniṭhānnu**[1]	to surmise, conclude
भरसक्	**bharsak**	probably, as much as possible
भिन्न	**bhinna**	different, other
मण्डप्	**maṇḍap**	canopy
मौका	**maukā**	opportunity
युवक्	**yuvak**	a youth
रमणी	**ramaṇī**	woman
रहर	**rahar**	interest, desire
विरक्त	**virakta**	detached, indifferent
व्यर्थ	**vyartha**	in vain
व्यवहार	**vyavahār**	business, trade, practice
शामिल्	**ʃāmil**	included
संबन्ध	**sambandha**	connection
सारा	**sārā**	whole, entire
साहस्	**sāhas**	courage, resolve
सिंगार पार्नु	**siŋgār pārnu**	to make up, decorate oneself
सिंगारिनु	**siŋgārinu**	to be made up
सुख्	**sukh**	peace, relief
सुखी	**sukhī**	at ease, happy
सोच्नु	**socnu**	to think, ponder
हत्पताउनु	**hatpatāunu**	to hurry, jostle
हेरिदिनु	**heridinu**[2]	to look after

Notes

1. **cəwdha varṣakī**: 'a fourteen-year-old girl'.
2. **chipinu**: 'to become ripe', hence **chipieko** – a colloquial term for 'getting on in years'.
3. **kalam ghasnu**: 'to push a pen', 'to do an office job'.
4. Harimatī – the name of his new bride.
5. **jantī**: 'a wedding party', especially the guests on the groom's side. **-paṭṭi** 'on the side of' cf. **arkopaṭṭi** 'on the other side'.
6. **siŋgār**: 'make up', 'dressing up'.
7. **dulahā bhannāsāth:** 'as soon as anyone mentions (the word) bridegroom'.
8. **kuncāhine**: an alternative form of **kuncāhī** 'which one'.

[1]A compound of भन्नु and ठान्नु **ṭhānnu** 'to decide'. The word is frequently pronounced and written भन्ठान्नु **bhanṭhānnu.**
[2]A compound of हेर्नु and दिनु .

9. **pahiranle**: 'from his dress, I imagined that the one wearing the black coat must be the bridegroom'.
   bhaniṭhānnu: a compound of **bhannu** and **ṭhānnu** 'to decide'.
10. **nabhandəy tinī rahechan**: 'it went without saying he was (the bridegroom)'.
    nadekhāū bhandā bhandəy pani: 'he did not have to say in so many words how happy he was', lit. 'although saying let me not show . . .'
11. In the answer the spelling of the words **ī (yī), inkī (yinkī), pəyle (pahile), duiəwṭā (duivaṭā), tesmā (tyasmā), koī (kohī), inle (yinle)** reflect the colloquial pronunciation. This device is often used in novels and plays where speech is portrayed.
12. **ghar calāunu thiyo**: 'it was necessary to manage the house'.
13. **baṛhekī**: 'advanced (in years)'.
14. **bakhat**: 'time', a synonym of **belā.**

Exercise 20a

Translate into English

१. श्री ५ महाराजाधिराज् आउँदो महीना पश्चिम् नेपाल्को भ्रमण गरिबक्सिनेछ ।
२. साँझ् नपरेसम्म म यहाँ बसी काम् गरिरहन्छु । काम् सिद्धिएपछि म तपाईंकहाँ आइहाल्छु ।
३. मेरी बहिनी घर्मा छे ।उ मेलाको लागि लुगा सिइरहेकी छ ।
४. मदेस्तिर विशेष् गरी जेठ र असार् महीनामा अतिनै गर्मी पर्छ । चर्को घाम् लाग्ने हुनाले, जमीन् सुखेर जान्छ । त्यसैले गर्दा , जता ततै धुलो उड़िरहन्छ
५. ओहो, नौ बजिसक्यो ।मलाई त जानुपर्‍यो नत्र स्वास्नी रिसाउनेछ ।
६. नेपाल्को सीमाना यस् प्रकार छ ।पूर्वमा मेची नदी,पश्चिम्मा महाकाली नदी,दक्षिणमा तराईको मैदान् र उत्तरमा सेतो हिमाल् ।हिमाल्पछिल्तिर पनि कतै कतै नेपाल्को भूमि पर्छ र त्यस्भन्दा उत्तर चीन्को तिब्बत् क्षेत्र पर्दछ ।
७. एक् दिन् भानुभक्त जंगल्मा डुल्दा डुल्दै थकाई लागेर एउटा रुख्को छहारीमा बसेछन् । त्यहाँ एउटा घाँसीलाई घाँस् काट्न लागेको देखी,उनी समय् काट्नलाई त्यस्सँग कुरा गर्नु लागेछन् ।
८. मेरो टाउको नराम्रोसित दुखिरहेको छ । बजार् गएर अलिकति औषधि ल्याइदिनुहोस् न ।
९. आज पनि विद्यार्थीहरू हड्ताल् गरिरहेका छन् । हिजोआज विश्वविद्यालयहरूमा त्यो सधैं भइरहन्छ नि ।
१०. तपाईंको पेट्मा अलिकति गड्बड् रहेछ । ठीक् नभएसम्म औषधि खाइराख्नुहोस् ।
११. रामे बहिनी आउँछे कि भनेर बाटो हेरिरहेको थियो ।
१२. यो कोट् एक् दम् बाक्लो छ , हजूर्। एक् फेरा लाइहेर्नुहोस् त ।

Exercise 20b

Translate into Nepali

1. What were you doing in the library? I was reading a book on the subject of Nepali history.
2. We shall go on sitting in the tea-bar until the aeroplane arrives.
3. As we walked to Jomsom, the wind was blowing and it was raining very hard.

4. I tried on the coat that the shopkeeper showed me, but because it was too big, I did not buy it.
5. If you have got stomach trouble, go and see the doctor. He will write you out a prescription.
6. It is already six o'clock. I must be going now. You will have to wait here until Mr. Pradhān arrives.
7. His Majesty will go to India on the 1st of Phālgun.
8. The staff-correspondent of the Gorkhā Patra was talking on the radio last night. Did you hear what he said?
9. What are you doing? I am trying to translate this Nepali letter into English. I wish my friend would write clearly.
10. The women of the village were all standing around the house and imagining what the bride would be like.
11. Because there was no one in the house to look after the children he had to get married again.
12. The girl was covered from head to foot in yellow clothes.

Exercise 20c

Give the correct form of the verb in brackets

१. शहर् (जानु) बस् कुनचाहिं(हुनु) दाइ?
२. काठ्माड़ौं(पुग्नु) बित्तिकै, म उस्लाई (भेट्नु)गएँ ।
३. भोलिपल्ट (उठ्नु)नुहाउन गएँ ।
४. यस् चिठीबाट तिमीलेथाहा (पाउनु) होला कि म नेपाल्मा (हुनु) ।
५. के(गर्नु)भनेर उस्ले (सोध्नु) ।
६. साँझ् (पर्नु)साथ् हामी गाउँसम्म(पुग्नु) ।
७. जो (आउनु)पनि हुन्छ ।
८. मैले उस्ले गीत् (गाउनु)सुनें ।
९. उ गरीब्(हुनु)तापनि कहिले पनि (माग्नु) ।
१०. त्यो काम् भोलिसम्म (रह्नु) ।

Exercise 20d

Translate into English

जेसुकै भए पनि आज नपुगी हुँदैन ।
सधैं झैं बस् ढीलो आयो ।
म त्यहाँसम्म पैदल् जान सकिनँ ।
आज पानी अवश्य पर्नेछ ।
मेरो साथी सिक्स्त बिरामी थियो ।
पानीले गर्दा म बाहिर जान सकिनँ ।
उस्ले त्यता जाऊ भन्दैमा,तिमीलाई जानुपर्थो र?
त्यो त्यस् होटेल्मा पनि जाँदो रहेछ ।
श्री पंचमीको दिन् सरस्वतीको मन्दिर्मा मेला लाग्छ ।
त्यो नेपाली पढ्ने काम्मा लाग्यो ।

APPENDIX 1

The Nepali Numerals

At first sight, the Nepali numerals look bewildering, since there is no obvious pattern running through the system, as, for instance, there is in English. You are advised to learn them gradually at the places suggested in the lessons. Note that whereas the English system is divided into hundreds, thousands and millions, the Nepali system is divided into hundreds (सय्), thousands (हजार्), hundred thousands (लाख्), and ten millions (करोड्).

Nepali numerals (0-99)

०	शून्य	२५	पच्चीस्	५०	पचास्	७५	पच्हत्तर्
१	एक्	२६	छब्बीस्	५१	एकाउन्न	७६	छयहत्तर्
२	दुइ	२७	सत्ताईस्	५२	बाउन्न	७७	सत्हत्तर्
३	तीन्	२८	अट्ठाईस	५३	त्रिपन्न	७८	अठ्हत्तर्
४	चार्	२९	उनन्तीस्	५४	चौवन्न	७९	उनासी
५	पाँच्	३०	तीस्	५५	पच्पन्न	८०	असी
६	छ	३१	एक्तीस्	५६	छपन्न्	८१	एकासी
७	सात्	३२	बत्तीस्	५७	सताउन्न	८२	बयासी
८	आठ्	३३	तेत्तीस्	५८	अठाउन्न	८३	त्रियासी
९	नौ	३४	चौंतीस्	५९	उन्सट्ठी	८४	चौरासी
१०	दस्	३५	पैंतीस्	६०	साठी	४५	पचासी
११	एघार	३६	छत्तीस्	६१	एक्सट्ठी	८६	छयासी
१२	बाह्र	३७	सैंतीस्	६२	बयसट्ठी	८७	सतासी
१३	तेह्र	३८	अठ्तीस्	६३	त्रिसट्ठी	८८	अठासी
१४	चौध	३९	उनन्चालीस्	६४	चौसट्ठी	८९	उनान्नब्बे
१५	पन्ध्र	४०	चालीस्	६५	पैंसट्ठी	९०	नब्बे
१६	सोह्र	४१	एक्तालीस्	६६	छयसट्ठी	९१	एकान्नब्बे
१७	सत्र	४२	बयालीस्	६७	सतसट्ठी	९२	बयान्नब्बे
१८	अठार	४३	त्रिचालीस्	६८	अठ्सट्ठी	९३	त्रियान्नब्बे
१९	उन्नाईस्	४४	चौवालीस्	६९	उन्हत्तर्	९४	चौरान्नब्बे
२०	बीस्	४५	पैंतालीस्	७०	सत्तरी	९५	पंचान्नब्बे
२१	एक्काईस्	४६	छयालीस्	७१	एक्हत्तर्	९६	छयान्नब्बे
२२	बाईस्	४७	सत्चालीस्	७२	बहत्तर्	९७	सन्तान्नब्बे
२३	तेईस्	४८	अठ्चालीस्	७३	त्रिहत्तर्	९८	अन्ठान्नब्बे
२४	चौबीस्	४९	उनन्चास्	७४	चौहत्तर्	९९	उनान्सय्

Nepali numerals (100 onwards)

१००	एक् सय्	१०.०००	दस् हजार्
१०१	एक् सय् एक्	२०.०००	बीस् हजार्
१०२	एक् सय् दुइ	१००.०००	एक् लाख्
२००	दुइ सय्	२००.०००	बीस् लाख्
३००	तीन् सय्	१०००.०००	दस् लाख्
९००	नौ सय्	१०. ०००. ०००	एक् करोड़्
१०००	एक् हजार्		
२०००	दुइ हजार्		

Ordinal numbers

The first four ordinal numbers are formed irregularly. Thereafter, the ordinal is formed by adding the suffix **əw̃** to the cardinal. The first four ordinal behave like other adjectives in **-o**, and may have feminine and plural forms:

पहिलो,-ली,-ला	first
दोस्रो-स्री,-स्रा	second
तेस्रो,-स्री, स्रा	third
चौथो,-थी,-था	fourth
पाँचौं	fifth
छटौं	sixth
दसौं	tenth
बीसौं	twentieth

In spoken Nepali, the numerals have a number of dialectal variants, and in some cases alternative spellings in the written language. The most commonly found alternatives are as follows:

०	सून्य, सून्ने
६	छ:
१५	पन्द्र
४३	त्रितालीस्
५९	उनन्साठी
६९	उनान्सत्तर्

The numeral 10 is often found written as दश् (still the case on banknotes), and the numeral 100 as शय् .

All Nepali numerals may take the classifiers -जना and -वटा . The first two are slightly irregular:

१ एउटा

२ दुइटा *or* दुइवटा

३ तीन्वटा, *or* तीनटा, ४ चारवटा etc.

Note that -वटा is pronounced **-əwṭā** and is sometimes written -औटा , e.g तीन्वटा *or* तीनौटा , etc.

APPENDIX 2

Names of countries and cities

The Nepali names for most countries and cities outside the subcontinent have been adapted from English, either directly or through Hindi. Here are some of the most important:

अफ्गानिस्तान्	Afghanistan
अफ्रिका	Africa
अम्लेख्गंज	Amlekhganj
अमेरिका	America
अरब्	Arabia
अस्ट्रेलिया	Australia
आइरलैंड्	Ireland
इँग्लैंड्	England
इण्डोनीश्या	Indonesia
इज़्राइल्	Israel
इटली	Italy
इलाम्	Ilam
इस्लामाबाद्	Islamabad
ईरान्	Iran
एम्स्टर्डम्	Amsterdam
ओखल्ढुङ्गा	Okhaldhunga
कनडा	Canada
कपिल्वस्तु	Kapilvastu
कल्कत्ता	Calcutta
कान्तिपूर्	Kantipur (Kathmandu)
काठ्माड़ौं	Kathmandu
काबुल्	Kabul
काशमीर्	Kashmir
काहिरा	Cairo
कुआला-लुम्पूर्	Kuala-Lumpur
गान्तोक्	Gantok
गोर्खा	Gorkha
चित्वन्	Chitwan
चीन्	China

चीन् जनवादी गणतंत्र	Chinese People's Republic
जनक्पूर्	Janakpur
जुम्ला	Jumla
जर्मनी	Germany
जापान्	Japan
जेनेवा	Geneva
टर्की	Turkey
टोकियो	Tokyo
डोल्पा	Dolpa
ढाका	Dacca
ताश्कन्द्	Tashkent
तिब्बत्	Tibet
तिब्रिकोट्	Tibrikot
तेह्रान	Tehran
थाइलैंड् (थाइल्यान्ड्)	Thailand
दार्जीलिङ्ग	Darjeeling
दिल्ली	Delhi
दैलेख्	Dailekh
धन्कुटा	Dhankuta
धरान्	Dharan
नाम्चे-बजार	Namche Bazar
नुवाकोट्	Nuvakot
नेपाल्	Nepal
न्यू यार्क	New York
नयू जिलैंड्	New Zealand
पट्ना	Patna
पाकिस्तान्	Pakistan
पाटन्	Patan
पाल्पा	Palpa
पीकिङ्ग (पेकिङ्ग)	Peking
पेरिस्	Paris
पोखरा	Pokhara
फ्रान्स्	France
बंग्लादेश्	Bangladesh
बनारस् (वाराणसी)	Benares (Varanasi)
बर्मा	Burma
बर्लिन्	Berlin
बिराट्नगर् (विराट्नगर्)	Biratnagar
बिहार्	Bihar
बीरगंज्	Birganj
बेलायत्	U.K.
बेल्जियम्	Belgium
ब्याँकक् (बैंकाक्)	Bangkok

बोन्	Bonn
भक्तपूर	Bhaktapur (Bhadgaun)
भाद्गाउँ	Bhadgaun
भारत्	India
भियत्नाम्	Vietnam
भैर्हवा	Bhairava
भोज्पूर	Bhojpur
भोट्	Tibet
मद्रास्	Madras
मनाङ	Manang
मर्स्याङ्डी	Marsyandi
मालेशिया	Malaysia
मास्को	Moscow
मिस्र	Egypt
यूनान्	Greece
रूस्	Russia
रोम्	Rome
लन्दन (लन्डन्)	London
ललित्पुर्	Lalitpur (Patan)
ल्हासा	Lhasa
वाराणसी	Benares (Varanasi)
श्री लंका	Sri Lanka (Ceylon)
संयुक्त अरब् गणतन्त्र	United Arab Republic
सिक्किम्	Sikkim
सुर्खेत्	Surkhet
सोभियत् संघ्	Soviet Union
स्पेन्	Spain
हर्लैंड्	Holland
हिन्दुस्तान्	India
हुम्ला	Humla

APPENDIX 3

Nepali relationship terms

Nepali possesses many more relationship terms than English. Here are the most important:

बुवा, बा, बाबु, पिता	Father
आमा, माता, महतारी, जननी	Mother
बाजे	Grandfather
बज्यै	Grandmother
बराज्यू	Great grandfather
जिज्यू आमा	Great grandmother
दाइ, दाज्यू	Elder brother
भाइ	Younger brother
भाउज्यू	Elder brother's wife
बुहारी	Younger brother's wife
सोल्टी	Brother's wife's sister
भतीजो	Brother's son
भतीजी	Brother's daughter
दिदी	Elder sister
बहिनी	Younger sister
भिना (-ज्यू)	Elder sister's husband
जुवाई	Younger sister's husband
भान्जो,(भानिज्)	Sister's son
भान्जी	Sister's daughter
छोरा	Son
बुहारी	Son's wife
नाति	Grandson
नातिनी	Granddaughter
छोरी	Daughter
ठूलो बा	Father's elder brother
ठूली आमा	Father's elder brother's wife
काका	Father's younger brother
काकी	Father's younger brother's wife
फुपु,	Father's sister
फुफा, (फुपा)	Father's sister's husband

मामा	Mother's brother
लोग्ने,पोइ, पति, खसम्	Husband
स्वास्नी, जोइ, पत्नी, जहान्	Wife
ससुरा	Father-in-law
सासू	Mother-in-law
जेठान्	Husband's elder brother
जेठानी	Husband's elder brother's wife
देवर्	Husband's younger brother
देवरानी	Husband's younger brother's wife
आमाज्यू	Husband's elder sister
नन्द	Husband's younger sister
जेठान्	Wife's elder brother
सालो	Wife's younger brother
जेठी सासू	Wife's elder sister
साली	Wife's younger sister

Terms for uncles and aunts (**ṭhūlo bā, kākā**) are often qualified by an adjective like **jeṭho, kāncho**, etc., indicating the exact position in the family. Cousins are simply 'brothers' and 'sisters' (**dāi, didī, bhāi,** etc.) There are no special terms in common use. All elder relations require the HGH forms of the verb and, in writing, plural adjectival concord.

The above list is by no means exhaustive and there are many local variants.

KEY TO EXERCISES

The translations from Nepali into English in the Key have been done as literally as possible in order to help you understand the Nepali construction. In the translations from English into Nepali, where one may have the choice of several constructions, only one (usually that which has been dealt with in the lesson preceding the exercise) has been used. Admittedly, many English sentences can have several different Nepali renderings.

If you require further practice in translating, you will find it useful to translate back from the Key, comparing your version with that in the lesson.

Lesson 1

1a

1. Where is my book? It is on the table. 2. Who is that man? He is our servant. 3. Where is Rām? He is at school. 4. That temple is very old. 5. Mt. Everest is in Nepal. 6. Where is Kathmandu? It is in Nepal. 7. Where is your house? It is there. 8. Kathmandu is a big town, but Pokharā is very small. 9. What is your name? My name is Rām. 10. Where is the washerman? He is in my house. 11. Who is at the door? It is my son. 12. Who is that man? He is the washerman.

1b

१. हाम्रो घर् पोखरामा छ । २. मेरो साइकल् कहाँ छ? ३. नोकर् ढोकामा छ । ४. यो किताब् धेरै राम्रो हो / छ। ५. काठ्माड़ौं नेपाल्मा छ धेरै ठूलो शहर् छ । ६. तिम्रो नाउँ के हो? ७. तिम्रो घर्मा को छ? ८. मेरो शहर् काठ्माड़ौं हो। ९. यो मन्दिर् धेरै पुरानो हो / छ। १०. मेरो छोरा नोकरसँग छ।

1c

१.छ, २.हो ३.छ, ४.छ, ५.हो / छ, ६.हो ७.छ, ८.छ.

1d

घर्मा; टेबुल्मा; राम्सँग; यो देश् नेपाल् हो; त्यो धोबी हो; त्यो को हो? त्यो नेपाल्मा छ; ठीक् छ; काठ्माड़ौं कहाँ छ? त्यो मन्दिर्मा छ; सानो केटासँग.

Lesson 2

Reading Passage

A. Hello (lit. 'elder brother, hello')

B. Hello.
A. How far is Gorkha from here?
B. It is not very far, sir. It is over there. Above.
A. How is the road? Is it steep?
B. It is rather steep, sir.
A. How is the town? Is it big (or not)?
B. It is not very big, but in the market there are many shops.
A. What else is there in the town? Are there (any) temples?
B. There are, sir. The old court of Prithvinarayan is also there. My village is here. I'll take my leave now, sir. Goodbye.
A. Goodbye.

2a

1. In that shop there are all sorts of goods. 2. What is your son's name? It is Ganesh, sir. 3. Who are those men? Those men are soldiers. 4. Is there tea in your shop or not? There is, sir, but there is no milk. 5. What is the capital of India? It is Delhi. 6. Hello (elder brother), how are you? Quite well. 7. In which country is Kathmandu? It is in Nepal. 8. Are those vegetables nice tasting or not? They are very good. 9. Gorkhā is rather far from Kathmandu. 10. In Kathmandu there are many old temples. 11. How far is it from the town to the University? It is not very far. 12. My sons are students. They are at the university. 13. How is that big hotel? It's all right. 14. That man has been in Nepal for two months. 15. Where is your village? It is right over there, sir. 16. In Rām's shop there are all sorts of good quality things. 17. That old man does not come from here. He's from Gorkhā. 18. What things have you got in your pocket? 19. My younger brother is in Pokharā. 20. The cities of Nepal are not large.

2b

१. यहाँबाट होटेल् कति टाढ़ा छ? २. राम्‌को पसल् कहाँ छ? शहर्‌मा छ। ३. पसल्‌मा दूध् छ कि छैन? ४. नेपाल्‌को राजधानी के हो? काठ्‌माड़ौं हो। ५. त्यो मान्छे दुइ साल्‌देखि काठ्‌माड़ौंमा छ। ६. मेरो (मेरा) बहिनीहरू विश्वविद्यालयमा छन्। ७. यो मन्दिर् पुरानो हो कि होइन? हो, धेरै पुरानो हो। ८. ए दाइ, यहाँबाट पुस्तकालय कति टाढ़ा छ? ९. भात् कस्तो छ? धेरै मीठो छ। १०. मेरो छोराको नाउँ गणेश् हो। ११. नमस्ते, हजूर्। कस्तो छ? धेरै राम्रो छ। १२. भारत्‌मा ठूलठूला शहर्‌हरू छन्।

2c

मेरा किताब्‌हरू; आठ् रुपियाँ; धेरै ठूला शहर्‌हरू; हाम्रा नोकरहरू; पाँच दिन्; ठूला राजाहरू; तिम्रो लुगा; ती गाउँहरू; तीन् कोस्।

2d

शहर्‌हरू; स्वास्नीहरू; छेत्रीहरू; विद्यार्थीहरू; यी किताब्‌हरू; ती घोड़ाहरू; ठूला मान्छेहरू; पुराना मन्दिरहरू; तिम्रा छोराहरू; मेरा भाइहरू; साना खेत्‌हरू।

2e

नोकर्को घर; भारत्को राजधानी ; गणेश्को स्वास्नी ; काठ्माड़ौं को विश्वविद्यालय; यो बूढ़ो यहाँको होइन; त्यो गोर्खाको हो ; भारत्का गाउँहरू; पाकिस्तान्का ठूला शहरहरू ।

2f

1. There are many villages in Nepal. 2. Rām's sister's name is Sītā. 3. Hello, Mr. Ganesh. How are you? I'm quite well. 4. How far is your house away from here, child? It is not very far, sir. It is over there. 5. Where is Pokharā? It is in Nepal. 6. Where is Delhi? Delhi is in India. Delhi is the capital of India. 7. In Kathmandu, there are many old temples. 8. In the Himalayas there are many big rivers. 9. These vegetables do not taste good. What else do you have in your shop? 10. My brother has been in India for three months.

Lesson 3

Reading Passage

A. Hello, how are you?
B. Well.
A. Where are you these days?
B. I am at the university. And you?
A. I'm in an office. My young brother is in the university. In the English department.
B. Where is he today?
A. He's at home. The university is closed today, isn't it?
B. Yes, there's a holiday, today.
A. Where is your elder brother nowadays?
B. He is in India. In the army.
A. I see. My bus is coming. I'll be off now. Today, I've got some work (to do) at home. Goodbye.
B. Goodbye.

3a

1. What about that big hotel? Is it cheap? It is not cheap. In fact it is expensive. 2. There's no one at all in our house today. 3. Who are those men? They are Brahmins. 4. My father is a lecturer. 5. In Nepal there are not many big cities. Kathmandu is the biggest city in Nepal. 6. This road is better than that road. 7. What is your caste? I am a Chetri, sir. 8. Mt. Everest is the highest mountain in the world, isn't it? Yes. 9. We are Nepalis, sir. We are not Indians. 10. My elder brother is in Darjeeling. 11. What sort of goods do they have in that shop? Cloth and clothes. 12. We are poor, sir. There is no electricity in our house. 13. There is nothing at all in that room. 14. The President of America is in China these days. 15. Ram's sons are very well behaved. 16. My sister is at home. She is not at school today. 17. Today, there's a holiday. Every shop is

closed. 18. The border of Nepal is not far from Darjeeling. 19. That book is not yours. It is mine, I tell you. 20. That road is terribly steep, sir. This is the best road.

3b

१. मेरो खल्तीमा केही पनि छैन। २. कलकत्ता भारत्को सब्भन्दा ठूलो शहर् हो। ३. मेरी दिदी दार्जीलिङ्मा हुनुहुन्छ। ४. तपाईंको जात् के हो? म बाहुन् हुँ हजूर्। ५. दिल्ली कुन् देश्मा छ? भारत्को राजधानी हो। ६. त्यो होटेल् नि। राम्रो छ? ७. आज बिदा छ। कलेज् बन्द छ, होइन त? ८. मेरो दाइ विश्वविद्यालयमा अध्यापक् हुनुहुन्छ। वहाँ नेपाली विभाग्मा हुनुहुन्छ। ९. प्रधान्मन्त्री हिजोआज भारत्मा हुनुहुन्छ। १०. टोक्यो दुनियाँको सब्भन्दा ठूलो शहर् हो नि। ११. तिम्रो गाँउ यहाँबाट कति टाढ़ा छ? धेरै टाढ़ा छैन, हजूर। १२. प्रधान्ज्यूको पसल् काठ्माडौंमा छ। त्यो धेरै धनि हो नि।

3c

सब् पसल्; सबभन्दा ठूलो मन्दिर्; उनी नेपाली हुन्; त्यो त मेरो किताब् होइन त? त्यहाँ कोही छ? म जाउँ है त। तिम्री बहिनी कहाँ छे? मेरो आमा बजार्मा हुनुहुन्छ। उनी यहाँकी होइनन्; उनी बेलायत्की हुन्।

3d

छैन, होइन, छैन, छैन, होइनौं, छैन, हुनुहुन्न

Lesson 4

Reading Passage

A. Hello, how are you?
B. Very well, sir. And you?
A. Fine. How far is your village from here?
B. It's not very far. It's up there.
A. Is there a teashop in the village or not?
B. Yes, sir. There's a good teashop. You can get both tea and food.
A. What is your name?
B. My name is Raṇ Bahādur.
A. And your caste?
B. I am a Chetri, sir.
A. How many children do you have?
B. Two sons and one girl. Where do you come from?
A. I am English. My country is England, you know. But nowadays I am in Nepal.
B. Do you have a cigarette, sir?
A. Yes. I have a lot. Take two cigarettes. I'll be off now. Goodbye.
B. Goodbye.

4a

1. What's the time by your watch? It is now 4 o'clock.
2. That man is very rich. He has two shops in the city.
3. How far is Patan from here? It's a very long way away.
4. Have you got any money on you or not? I haven't got much. I've only two rupees in my pocket.
5. How many children has Dhane got? He has two boys and one girl.
6. Why, this road is not good. In places there is a lot of mud.
7. Excuse me, what's the time? I don't know. I haven't got a watch on me.
8. Those people are very poor. There is nothing at all in their village.
9. How many students are there in Kathmandu University?
10. What about the food in that hotel? Is it cheap? It is not cheap. Indeed, it is expensive.
11. Your house is bigger than his.
12. Where is Rām's shop? Do you know? I do know, sir. You see that post-office? Well, it's just there.
13. How old are you, little boy? I am twelve, sir.
14. At this time, there are many foreigners in Kathmandu.
15. Where does your teacher come from? He is from India.
16. My wife is in Darjeeling these days. Her home is there, you know.
17. The Prime Minister's speech is (surprisingly) very interesting, isn't it?
18. Is Tokyo bigger than London? Yes. It's the biggest city in the world.

4b

१. धनेका तीन्जना छोरा र दुइजना छोरी छन् ।
२. तिम्री छोरी कति बर्षको हो।? उ पाँच् बर्षको हो ।(तिम्री की)
३. यस् शब्दको माने के हो? मलाई थाहा छैन ।
४. अहिले कति बज्यो ? सात् बज्यो।
५. त्यस् (त्यो) खोलाको पानी असल् हो कि होइन?
६. तपाईंको घर्मा बिजुली रहेछ ।
७. मेरी बहिनी दुइ हप्तादेखि बिरामी छे ।उस्लाई रुचि छैन ।
८. प्रधान्ज्यूको घर् कहाँ छ? ऊ त्यहीं छ,हजूर ।
९. शहर्बाट विश्वविद्यालय टाढ़ा छ कि छैन? छ,हजूर।छ मील् टाढ़ा छ ।
१०. तपाईंको (-का) कतिजना छोराछोरी छन्? मेरो (मेरा) छोराछोरी छैन (न्) हजूर्।

4c

तपाईंसँग; उस्लाई; वहाँलाई थाहा छ; हाम्रा किताबहरू; मेरा छोराहरू: त्यस्का खेत्हरू; तपाईंलाई थाहा छ? वहाँको छोरासँग; रामकहाँ; उन्को उमेर् कति हो? मलाई निश्चय छैन; पाँच्जना मान्छे; कतिवटा किताब्; छ बजे; तपाईंको घडी़मा कति बज्यो? दुइ कप् चिया ; चार्जना राजा, तपाईंसँग चुरोट् छ कि छैन? तपाईंसँग पैसा रहेनछ ।

4d

हुनहुन्छ; छ, छ; छौ; छिन् छ, हुनहुन्छ; छ; हुनहुन्छ ।

4e

मेरा दुइजना छोरा छन् ; उस्को खल्तीमा केही पनि छैन ; तिमीसँग चुरोट् छ कि छैन ? तिन्सँग चार् रुपियाँ छ; मेरो घर् काठ्माडौंमा छ। वहाँहरूको पुस्तकालय धेरै राम्रो हो ; उनीहरूका तीन्वटा खेत् छन् ।

Lesson 5

Reading Passage

A. Hello.
B. Hello, sir.
A. Where do you come from?
B. I'm from Pālpā, sir. But nowadays I live in Kathmandu.
A. What work do you do here?
B. I work as a waiter in a hotel.
A. Do you go home sometimes?
B. I go only occasionally, sir. Pālpā is a long way from here, sir. Where do you come from then?
A. I'm English. I live in London. Do you know where London is?
B. I do, sir. It's in England, isn't it? Which place are you staying at here?
A. I'm staying with a friend in Bāneshvar.
B. How long will you stay in Nepal?
A. I'll stay here for six months. After that I'll go to India. I have a bit of work to do in Calcutta.
B. What work do you do in England?
A. I'm a student. I study at London University.
B. What's the time by your watch, sir?
A. According to my watch, it's four o'clock.
B. I see. My shift starts at five. I'd better be going.
A. Goodbye.

5a

1. Do you smoke? I only smoke occasionally, sir. What about you? *I* smoke a lot.
2. What hotel do you stay at? You see that big hotel? I stay there.
3. Excuse me (big sister), where does that road go to? Do you know? It goes to Darjeeling.
4. My father goes to town every day. His office is there.
5. Many people in Nepal eat only lentils and boiled rice.
6. What time will you come to my place tomorrow? I'll come at seven in the evening.
7. Do you go to school, little boy? Yes, sir.
8. My elder brother goes to Calcutta twice a month.

9. What work do those men do? They work as waiters.
10. I shall go to London in six months' time. How are you going? By air.
11. Why, that man is an Indian. He's not a Nepali after all.
12. He will go by air to Delhi next Thursday.
13. I'll stay in Kathmandu for a fortnight. After that I'll go to Pokharā.
14. In that shop the rice is terribly dear.
15. My friend is going to Darjeeling next week.
16. What are you doing (elder brother)? I am reading a book.

5b

१. ए दाइ,यो बाटो कता जान्छ? पाटन्सम्म जान्छ ।
२. तपाईंको कतिजना छोराछोरी छन्? मेरो एक्जना छोरा र दुइजना छोरी छन् ।
३. आउने हप्ता म पोखरा जान्छु। केमा जानुहुन्छ ? हवाईजहाज्मा जान्छु ।
४. तपाईं दार्जीलिङ्मा कति बस्नुहुन्छ? दुइ हप्ता मात्रै बस्छु।
५. तपाईं हामीकहाँ कति बजे आउनुहुन्छ? म पाँच् बजे आउँछु ।
६. ए,घरमा कोही पनि रहेनछ ।
७. कतिवटा चुरोट् खानुहुन्छ? दस्वटा खान्छु।
८. बिष्टज्यू हिजोआज भारत्मा बस्नुहुन्छ ।वहाँ कहिले कहीं मात्रै नेपाल् आउनुहुन्छ।
९. तपाईंको घड़ीमा कति बज्यो ? अहिले बाह्र बज्यो ।
१०. वहाँको छोरा पाटन् महाविद्यालयमा पढ्छ? मलाई थाहा छैन ।
११. हिजोआज नेपाल्मा धेरै विदेशीहरू छन् ।
१२. मेरो अड्डा आज बन्द छ । बिदा छ नि ।

5c

बस्नुहुन्छ; गर्छन ; गर्नुहुन्छ ; आउनुहुन्छ ; पढ्छे ; हुनुहुन्छ ; बस्छौं ; खान्छु ; जान्छु

5d

१. छेत्री हो ।
२. वहाँको दुइजना छोरा र एक्जना छोरी छन् ।
३. हिंड़ेरै जानुहुन्छ ।
४. हिजोआज काठ्माड़ौंमा बस्नुहुन्छ ।
५. घर्मा बस्नुहुन्छ ।

Lesson 6

Reading Passage

A. Hello.
B. Hello.
A. Where is your house?
B. My house is in Dilli Bazar
A. What do you do?
B. I am a student. I study in Tribhuvan University.
A. Which department are you in?

B. I am in the English department.
A. How many students study in your class?
B. Twenty-five.
A. How far is the University from your home?
B. It isn't very far. It is two miles away from our house.
A. How do you go? By bus?
B. Usually I go by bus. Sometimes I also go on foot.
A. Do you go to the University every day?
B. I don't go *every* day. I go only five times a week. Saturday is a holiday, you know.
A. What work does your father do?
B. My father works in an office in the city.
A. What about your mother?
B. Mother just stays at home. She never goes out at all.

6a

1. We are coming to your place tomorrow morning at nine sharp.
2. In my opinion, it will rain today. *I* shall not go out.
3. My father will not go to the office today. There's a holiday, you know.
4. We never eat beef at all.
5. The Prime Minister will give a speech in Patan today at three o'clock, won't he?
6. Brahmins do not eat meat. They only eat lentils, rice and vegetables.
7. It does not rain in the winter, but in summer it rains a great deal.
8. How will you go to Namche Bazar? I'll go on foot.
9. Where does this road lead to (elder brother)? Do you know? Yes, sir. It leads to Gorkha.
10. It is (usually) very hot in the Terai, but it is never so hot in Kathmandu.
11. In the winter, thousands of American tourists go to Nepal.
12. Saturday is a holiday in Nepal. Sunday is not a holiday.
13. Next week father will give me a nice present.
14. Will you go to town today? I shall not go today. There's a lot of work (to do) at home.
15. I am going to Delhi next week. How are you going? I shall go by air as far as Patna, then after that I shall go by train.
16. What time will you come to see me? I'll come around eight this evening.
17. Excuse me, what do you make the time? I make it eleven o'clock.
18. This book is mine, I tell you. I shall not give it to you.
19. I won't eat today. I have no appetite.
20. Next month my elder brother is going to India. But I shall stay here.

6b

१. आउने महीना मेरी दिदी बेलायत जानुहुन्छ । केमा जानुहुन्छ ? हवाईजहाज्मा जानुहुन्छ ।
२. आज पानी पर्छ कि पर्दैन ? मलाई थाहा छैन ।

३. तपाईं विश्वविद्यालय कति बजे जानुहुन्छ? आज त म जान्न ।बिदा छ नि ।
४. त्यो बाटोले कहाँ कहाँ लान्छ?/ कता जान्छ?/हाम्रो गाउँसम्म जान्छ तर धेरै नै लामो बाटो हो नि ।
५. गर्मीमा धेरैजसो पर्यटकहरू मदेसतिर जाँदैनन् ।त्यस् बेला त्यहाँ धेरै गर्मी हुन्छ ।
६. बाहुन्हरू गाईको मासु कहिले पनि खाँदैनन् । धेरैजसो तर्कारी मात्रै खान्छन् ।
७. ए, मेरो खल्तीमा पैसा रहेनछ ।म हिंड़ेरै जान्छु ।
८. लन्दनका बस्हरू पाँच बजे सधैं भरीभराउ हुन्छन।
९. यो हप्ता उस्ले मलाई केही पनि दिंदैन । आउने हप्ता उस्ले मलाई दस् रुपियाँ दिन्छ ।
१० छोरालाई किन पिटनुहुन्छ ? त्यो त धेरै ज्ञानी हो ।
११. हिजोआज तिमी कहाँ पढ्छौ? म त पढ्दिन। म अड्डामा छु नि ।मेरो भाइ त विश्वविद्यालयको अंग्रेजी विभाग्मा छ।
१२. अहिले त म खान्न ।रुचि छैन ।

6c

म जाँदिन/जान्न; उनी खाँदैन/खान्न; हामी (हरू) पठाउँदैनौं; तपाईं पिउनुहुन्न, उनीहरू **लिंदैनन्/लिन्नन;उ गाई दुहन्छ ; तपाईं त्यस् मान्छेलाई चिन्नुहुन्छ?** म त्यस्लाई चिन्दिन ; वहाँहरू **ठूलो स्वरले कहिले पनि बोल्दैनन्; हामी कहिले कहीं काठ्माड़ौं जान्छौं; कल्कत्तामा संधैं गर्मी हुन्छ; नेपाली केटीहरू राम्रो /राम्रा /हुन्छन्;सिनेमा ठीक् दुइ बजे शुरू हुन्छ ।**

Lesson 7

Reading Passage

In the heart of the Himalayas is a small kingdom called Nepal. The capital of Nepal is Kathmandu. In Kathmandu there is an international airport. From several cities in India aeroplanes come and go, and aeroplanes come also from the other cities of Asia like Dacca, Bangkok and Rangoon. Apart from Kathmandu there are also one or two other big towns in Nepal. In the Terai, big towns like Birganj and Biratnagar are industrial towns. For this reason, these towns have great importance in the economy of Nepal.

There are two roads linking Kathmandu with India. The oldest of these is the Rajpath. This road leads to a small town in India called Raksaul. There is also a road now open which links Kathmandu to the Chinese border.

In Nepal, there is also a small but very beautiful town called Pokhara. An air-service operates between Kathmandu and Pokhara and every day aeroplanes make the round trip. Nowadays large numbers of tourists come to Nepal. In the winter season, all the hotels of Kathmandu are filled with tourists.

7a

1. Next week, I am going to Nepal for two months.
2. What's the hurry (elder brother)? Sit down for a while, won't you?
3. Many people read the speeches of His Majesty.
4. There's a lot of mud on this road. Drive the car carefully.

5. The most expensive hotel in Kathmandu is that one, isn't it?
6. There is a small temple near our house. My young sisters worship there every day.
7. Don't go by that road. It is terribly steep.
8. In the winter season the climate of Nepal is usually good. In the hot season, however, it is not so good.
9. In honour of the birthday of His Majesty the Prime Minister will make a speech on Tundikhel at two o'clock in the afternoon.
10. Please come in, sir. Won't you take a seat for a minute?
11. They say that Rām is getting married next week.
12. My son will not go to school today. He says there is a holiday.
13. My mother always stays at home. She never goes outside at all.
14. What time does the evening plane arrive? They say it arrives at five o'clock.
15. With whom do you stay in Nepal? I usually stay in the house of a friend of mine.
16. My little sister will not eat today. She says she has no appetite.
17. Chetris will usually eat anything. As for Brahmins, they only eat vegetables.
18. In that village, which one is the best teashop? Rām's (one).
19. What your servant says does not seem true.
20. It does not look as if it will rain today. I'll go out. I'll be back at five o'clock.

7b

१. काठ्माडौंको सब्भन्दा राम्रो सिनेमा कुनचाहिं हो? मेरो विचार्ले सबभन्दा राम्रो त्योचाहिं हो । पाटन्कोचाहिं पनि धेरै राम्रो हो ।
२. भरे कति बजे घर् फर्कन्छौ? म साढ़े सात बजेतिर फर्कन्छु ।
३. पाकिस्तान्का राष्ट्रपति आउने महीना श्रीमती गान्धीलाई भेट्नुहुन्छ रे ।
४. हिजोआज काठ्माड़ौं र जुम्ला बीच् हवाई सेवा चालु छ। हवाईजहाज्हरू महीनाको दुइ पटक् ओहोर् दोहोर् गर्छन् ।
५. बाटो धेरै राम्रो छैन रे। बिस्तारै हाँक्नुहोस् न ।
६. ए दाइ ।होटेल्बाट विमान्स्थल् कति टाढ़ा छ? धेरै टाढ़ा छैन ।बस् हरेक् घण्टामा जान्छ ।
७. तपाईंको बिहा कहिले हुन्छ? मेरो बिहा आउने महीना हुन्छ ।
८. बेलायत्को हावापानी कस्तो हुन्छ? बेलायत्को हावापानी धेरैजसो राम्रो हुन्छ ।
९. तपाईंको कलम् मेरो जस्तो रहेछ ।मलाई एक छिन दिनुहोस् न?
१०. भोलि शहर्को सब् पसल् बन्द हुन्छ रे ।साँचो हो कि होइन? हो बिदा हुन्छ नि ।
११. केको हतपत?बस्नुहोस् त ।अहँ,हामी सिनेमा जाँदै छौं र फिल्म् दस् मिनेट्पछि शुरू हुन्छ ।
१२. श्री ५ महाराजाधिराज्को शुभजन्मोत्सवको उपलक्ष्यमा, काठ्माड़ौमा धेरै पर्यटक्हरू आउँछन् । त्यस् बेला सबै होटेल् मान्छेहरूले भरिभराउ हुन्छ ।

7c

कतिजना मान्छे; पच्चीस् दिन्; साढ़े तीन् घण्टा ; आधा किलो : दिन्को दुइ पटक्: तीन् महीनापछि; साढ़े पाँच मील्; एक् कप् चिया; दुइजना छोरा र एक्जना छोरी ; पन्ध्र दिन्को चार् पटक्, नौजना मान्छे ।

7d

1. We are coming to your place at two o'clock. 2. They say that the train goes from Patnā to Raksaul every hour. 3. The film will start at exactly six o'clock. 4. At what time does the bus come here? It comes on the half hour, sir. 5. What is the time by your watch? According to my watch, it is ten minutes to eight. 6. What is the time now, please? It is now exactly quarter past nine.

7e

बस्छौं; गर्नुहुन्छ; दुहुन्छ; सुत्नुहुन्छ; बस्नुहुन्छ गर्छु ;

Lesson 8

Reading Passage

A. Hello. How are you? Are you well?
B. Yes, I am. What about you?
A. I'm all right. Have you heard? Next year, I'm going to Nepal for six months. You have been to Nepal, as well, haven't you?
B. Yes. I was in Nepal last year. How nice it was. Tell me. When are you going.
A. I am not certain. I think I shall go at the end of June.
B. What places will you go to there?
A. First of all, I shall go to Kathmandu to get a visa. After that, I shall go towards Okaldhunga. Tell me, do planes also go there from Kathmandu?
B. There are aeroplanes but it rains heavily in June, you know. Sometimes, the plane does not go.
A. Where did you go in Nepal? Did you also go outside Kathmandu?
B. Yes. I travelled to many places. I spent the first two months in Kathmandu. After that, I went towards Khumbu.
A. What did you go by?
B. I mostly went on foot. That's the only way to get about in Nepal.
A. Did you go alone, or did others go along with you?
B. No. A friend was also with me.
A. What was the road to Khumbu like?
B. Here and there the road was very bad. In places it was terribly steep. But the weather was splendid.
A. Who did you stay with in Khumbu?
B. I stayed in the house of a Sherpa, in a village called Khumjung. From there, we went twice to Thyangboche. That's a very lovely place.
A. Thyangboche is near Khumjung, isn't it? How far is it from there?
B. Not very far. But the road proved to be rather steep.

8a

1. I went to the market today, but every shop was closed.
2. When did you come from town? I have just come.
3. I did not sleep last night. It was extremely hot.
4. Did you hear the radio last night? No, I didn't. We had guests in our house.
5. My friend was gravely ill. Now he is in good health.
6. I am sorry (excuse me), but I have forgotten your name.
7. I did not understand your question. Would you mind repeating it?
8. I met him for the first time the other day (lit. 'day before yesterday').
9. Where did Rām go? I sent him to the shop. There were no vegetables in the house.
10. Two weeks ago, my wife went to Darjeeling. Her parents' home is there, you know.
11. Why didn't you come yesterday? I am sorry. I had a lot of work (to do) at home.
12. Excuse me, what is the time? I make it nine twenty-five. But according to the Clock Tower it is half past nine. My watch seems to be slow.
13. My clothes are (have become) very dirty. I'll give them to the washerman tomorrow.
14. Have a little (cooked) rice, won't you? No, I've had enough. I can't eat any more now.
15. Where did you travel in Nepal? I travelled to a lot of places.
16. It did not rain last year. Therefore, there was great loss in the fields.
17. Mr. Bista has been appointed minister, so they say. Do you know? I know, I read it in the newspaper today.
18. He says he spent two months in Khumjung last year.

8b

१. वहाँले के भन्नुभयो? मैले वहाँको प्रश्न बुझिनँ ।

२. तपाईंले कहाँ पढ्नुभयो? मैले लन्दन्मा पढें ।

३. मेरो बुवा जून्को आखिरीमा कल्कत्ता जानुभयो ।केमा जानुभयो? पहिले हवाईजहाज्मा दिल्लीसम्म जानुभयो त्यस्पछि रेल्मा कल्कत्ता जानुभयो ।

४. तिमी हिजो कहाँ थियौ? मकहाँ किन आएनौ? हिजो म घरै थिएँ ।धेरै काम् थियो

५. तीन् साल् अघि अमेरिकाका राष्ट्रपति, पीकिङ्ग जानुभयो ।

६. माफ् गर्नुहोला,तर मैले तपाईंको प्रश्न बुझिनँ ।एक् फेरा फेरि दोहऱ्याउनुहोला कि?

७. पसल् बन्द भयो ।म भोलि बिहान बजार जान्छु।

८. उस्को कलम् मेरो जस्तो थियो ।

९. तिमीले मेरो लुगा धोयौ? अहँ,धोइनँ ।भोलि धुन्छु ।

१०. पोहोर् साल् मदेस्मा पानी परेन रे ।

११. तपाई हिजो राति कति बजे सुत्नुभयो ? म दस् बजेतिर सुतें ।

१२. तिमीले यो नयाँ सिनेमा हेरेनौ? एक् दम् राम्रो थियो ।

१३. मेरी स्वास्नी दुइ साल् अघि भारत् गइन् ।उन्ले दिल्लीमा तीन् महीना बिताइन् ।उन्को माइती त्यहीं छ नि ।

१४. बिराट्‌नगर्‌मा अतिनै गर्मी थियो । म गएको हप्ता त्यहाँ थिएँ ।

१५. उनी काठ्‌माड़ौं कहिले आए? उनी गएको महीना पुगे,र एक्‌ बर्ष यहाँ बिताउँछन्‌ रे, त्यस्‌पछि उनी बेलायत्‌ फर्कन्छन्‌ ।

8c

हामीले खायौं; उस्‌ले काम्‌ गरेन; मेरो अध्यापक्‌ले भन्नुभयो ; नोकर्‌ आएन; कस्‌ले भन्छ? तपाई चुरोट्‌ खानुहुन्छ? उन्‌ले चिया खाए; उनीहरूले बिर्से;मेरो साथी बिरामी भयो; गएको महीना पानी परेन,बिस्तारै हाँक्नुहोला: हामीले गाउँमा दुइ दिन्‌ बितायौं: मेरी बहिनी सिकिस्त बिरामी छे: त्यो बिरामी भई: नरिसाउनुहोला।

Lesson 9

Reading Passage

A. Tell me, sir. What do you require?

B. May I look at the coats please, shopkeeper? What sort of coats do you stock? I need a fairly heavy woollen coat. Next week, I am going to the hills on foot.

A. I have all sorts of coats, sir. I'll give you just the sort you need.

B. Is this coat woollen or not?

A. Yes. It's good quality cloth, sir.

B. Well, how much is this coat?

A. I'll let you have it for 120 (rupees).

B. Really, shopkeeper. That won't do at all. It's far too expensive.

A. What do you mean – dear? You won't find it for less money anywhere else.

B. This one is white. What other colours do you stock?

A. Look. Here's a red one. For this one, 100 rupees, sir.

B. Yes. The red one is rather nice, but 100 rupees is a bit dear. Let me have it for 70 rupees, won't you?

A. There. 90 rupees and it's yours. I can't make it any cheaper than that. Just try it on, won't you?

B. Yes. It's all right. There, I'll take it (lit. 'I took') for 85 rupees.

A. Very well. Have it for that.

B. I also need a pair of shoes, shopkeeper. Do you have any or not?

A. I don't stock shoes. There's a shoe-shop over there, you know. Look. Here, take your change.

B. Thank you, shopkeeper, goodbye.

A. Goodbye.

9a

1. If it does not rain tomorrow, I'll meet you around ten o'clock. If it rains, I'll stay at home.
2. If we walk quickly, they say we shall manage to arrive by evening.

3. Very many Hindi words are used in Nepali.
4. These days in Nepal Chinese goods are found extremely cheaply. Just yesterday I bought a nice raincoat for ten rupees.
5. In Kathmandu the shops usually open at half past eight in the morning.
6. If you go by this road, you will arrive very soon.
7. Be good, little boy. Don't make such a noise.
8. I'm sorry. I have come late. What time does the film start?
9. If you take (buy) this one, it will cost you 45 rupees.
10. If you climb this hill, they say you will get a good view of Mt. Everest.
11. A. How much money do you earn a month?
    B. I earn 120 rupees, sir.
    A. That seems rather a little. Is that much enough?
    B. It is not enough, sir.
12. That (thing) does not sound right. Say it again, will you?
13. In Nepali Mt. Everest is called 'Sagarmatha'. The Tibetans call it 'Chomolongmo'.
14. Excuse me, can I have a lodging in your house (or not)? You can, sir. Please come in.
15. Put on the light then. I can't see anything here.
16. I need a pair of shoes, shopkeeper. What sorts of shoes do you stock?

9b

१. सुन्तलाको कति? एउटाको एक् सुका,हजूर् ।
२. आज पानी पर्छ जस्तो लाग्छ । तपाईंसँग बर्सादी छ?
३. हवाईजहाज्बाट जानुभयो भने, एक् घण्टामा जति पुगिन्छ।
४. त्यो घड़ी एक् दम् राम्रो रहेछ।नेपाल्मा त्यति राम्रोचाहिं पाइँदैन ।
५. त्यो ऊनी कप्ड़ा धेरै राम्रो छ, तर गज्को सोह्र रुपियाँ पर्छ ।
६. हिजोआज रेडियो नेपाल्मा धेरै संस्कृत् शब्द (हरू)प्रयोग् गरिन्छन्
७. यहाँबाट गोर्खा कति टाढ़ा छ? बेलुकासम्म पुगिन्छ कि पुगिंदैन ?
८. काठ्माडौंको पसल्हरूमा जे पनि पाइन्छ ।पहाड़्को गाउँहरूमा पाउन अलि गाह्रो हुन्छ ।
९. हिजोआज मेरो दाइ दार्जीलिङ्गमा हुनहुन्छ ।अस्ति नै मैले वहाँको चिठी पाएँ ।
१०. ए दाइ,तपाईंको गाउँमा बास् पाइन्छ कि पाईंदैन?
११. यस्(यो) बर्सादीलाई कति पर्छ त? पच्चीस् रुपियाँ मात्रै पर्छ ,हजूर्।त्यो त धेरै नै भयो ।बीस् रुपियाँ लिनुहोस् त ।ल भैगो,म तपाईंलाई बाईस् रुपियाँमा दिन्छु ।
१२. विश्वविद्यालय्को पुस्तकालय ध्रैजसो साढ़े छ बजेसम्म खुला रहन्छ, तर सञ्चर्बार् एक् बजे बन्द हुन्छ ।
१३. यहाँ अँध्यारो भयो ।केही पनि देखिन्न ।बत्ती बाल त ।
१४. यो बाटोबाट जानुभयो भने दार्जीलिङ्ग पुग्नुहुन्छ त्योचाहिंबाट जानुभयो भने कालिम्पोङ्गसम्म पुग्नुहुन्छ ।
१५. त्यो घड़ी कतिमा लिनुभयो? मैले सस्तोमा किनें ।एक् सय् पैंतालीस् रुपियाँमा मात्रै लिएँ ।

9c

आउनुहोस् आऊ; लिनुहोस्, लेऊ पठाउनुहोस् पठाऊ;धुनुहोस् धोऊ; दोहऱ्याउनुहोस्

दोहऱ्याऊ; भन्नुहोस् भन; जानुहोस् जाऊ; पढ्नुहोस् पढ,खोल्नुहोस् खोलः सुन्नुहोस् सुन : उभिनुहोस् उभिऊः

9d

यो शब्द दार्जिलिङ्गको नेपालीमा मात्रै प्रयोग् गरिन्छः शेर्पालाई आठ् रुपियाँले पुग्दैन रे :पँखा खोल त ;भो भो,अब म खान्न; नेपाली चुरोट्लाई चार् पाँच् रुपियाँ पर्छ;त्यो रातो टोपी कतिमा दिन्छ रे? माफ् गर्नुहोला,म ढीलो आएँ; बाटोको लागि तीन् सय् रुपियाँ चाहिन्छ ;यस्/यो/कोठामा गर्मी छ; मेरो घड़ी ढीलो रहेछ; हामीले पोखरामा पाँच् दिन् बितायौंःउ ठीक् छ बजे पुग्यो ;केको हत्पत् त? अलिकति चिया खानुहोस् न? पोहोर साल् पानी परेन ; यस्को सट्टा अर्को नोकर् आउँदै छ ।

Lesson 10

Reading Passage

A. Hello, Padma. You are a student at London University, aren't you? Where do you come from?

B. I come from Kathmandu. But nowadays, I am living in London. I have been doing research into (the subject of) Nepali literature in this University for two years.

A. How do you find London? Do you like it or not?

B. I like it very much. Compared to Kathmandu, the city of London is very big, you know. From one point of view, life in London seems easy, but sometimes for us Nepalis, it is also difficult. I have many friends. For that reason, I find it pleasant.

A. What do you usually do on weekdays?

B. Usually, I get up about seven in the morning, I have a wash, or sometimes I have a bath, and at eight o'clock, I rush off to the bus-stop. From there it only takes me ten minutes to get to the station. Then, I catch the underground and go to my office.

A. Do you work in an office in the morning?

B. Yes. These days, the condition of students is not all that good. What can we do about it? Therefore, in order to make both ends meet (lit. 'in order to run my livelihood'), I am working in an office, and earning a bit of money.

A. What do you do there?

B. The work in the office is not very difficult. I sort out the morning post, and distribute it to the different departments.

A. What time do you work there till?

B. I work only till 12 o'clock. After that, I have lunch in the office canteen, and go to the University. When I arrive there, from two o'clock onwards, I read in the library. Twice a week I meet my supervisor. Sometimes, if there is a lecture about some interesting subject, I go and listen to it.

B. Saturday and Sunday are holidays, aren't they? What sort of things do you do on holidays?

A. On holidays, I meet my friends and enjoy myself. If it is sunny, we rest in some London park. If it rains, we go to see a film. Otherwise, we sit at home and listen to the radio. In the summer, we sometimes go out of London and go for a walk at the seaside. That is a very nice experience, you know.

A. When you return to Nepal, what do you plan to do?

B. So far, I don't know. But if I get the chance, I hope to teach Nepali literature in Kathmandu University.

10a

1. If it is sunny tomorrow, I shall get up early and come to your house.
2. My elder brother came to Kathmandu via Paṭnā.
3. Drive carefully, won't you? These days the road is very bad.
4. We got to Raxaul late, but easily found a hotel. The next morning we got up early, had our breakfast and walked to the station.
5. Who told you to go into my room?
6. The Subedar ordered the soldier to stand there.
7. He asked where the road led to.
8. How do you like our country? I like it very much.
9. Wait a moment. I'll have a quick bath and come.
10. Do you like Nepali sweets or not? I don't care for them all that much. They are too sweet for me.
11. How old is your young brother? He must be ten.
12. How did you find this novel? Did you like it or not? I did not like it all that much.
13. In South India, especially in cities like Madras, it is never cold. But in North India in the winter months, it is very cold.
14. This tea has become absolutely cold. Bring some hot water, please.
15. He carried and brought that heavy package by himself.
16. You told me that this hotel was good, but I find it terrible.
17. The morning plane goes directly to Pokhara, but the evening one goes via Gorkha.
18. Last year, as soon as I got to the Terai, I fell gravely ill.

10b

१. त्यो (त्यस्)केटाको उमेर् कति भयो? पन्ध्र साल लाग्यो रे ।

२. मलाई तिर्खा लाग्यो । अलिकति पानी दिनुहोस् न

३. हिन्दुस्तानी खाना मन् पर्दैन रे । तपाईंलाई मन् पर्छ नि? मलाई त मन् पर्छ, तर कहिले कहीं मलाई धेरै पिरो लाग्छ ।

४. भोली बिहान म सवेरै उठेर शहर् जान्छु । पसल्हरू कति बजे खुल्छन? तपाईंलाई थाहा छ?

५. भारत् र नेपाल् जस्ता देशहरुमा, धेरैजसो मान्छेहरू भात् र दाल् मात्रै खान्छन् । सधैं नै मासु महँगो पाइन्छ ।

६. यहाँबाट हवाईजहाज् सोझै मद्रास् जान्छ? होइन,दिल्ली भएर जान्छ ।
७. म छिटो नुहाएर आउँछु ।एक् छिन् पर्खनुहोस् न ।
८. सुबेदारले तिम्रो उमेर् कति भयो भनेर सिपाहीलाई सोधे ।सिपाहीले म तीस् बर्ष लागें क्यारे भनेर भन्यो ।
९. हिजो बिदा थियो ।मेरी दिदी सवेरै उठी छिटो नुहाई सोझै मन्दिर्मा जानुभयो ।मचाहिं बाह्र बजेसम्म सुतें ।
१०. यो पोको धेरै गह्रुँगो रहेछ ।होश् गरेर बोक है ।
११. काठ्माडौं तपाईंलाई कस्तो लाग्यो? धेरै चाख्लाग्दो रहेछ ।
१२. अचेल् धेरैजसो देश्का विद्यार्थीहरूको हालत् उस्तो राम्रो छैन । तर गाली गरेर के काम्?

10c

कस्ले भन्छ? कुन्चाहिं? त्यतिका गाउँहरू; म कसैलाई पनि भन्दिन; केमा जानुहुन्छ? उस्को बिहा आउने हप्ता हुन्छ; मेरो साइकल् उस्को जस्तो रहेछ; तर्कारी मिठो छैन; होश् गरी हाँक्नुहोस्; हामीलाई तिर्खा लाग्यो ;पोहोर् साल् धेरै पानी परेन; त्यो पच्चीस् वर्ष लाग्यो; त्यो कहाँको हो? आज अलि गर्मी छ; अलिकति चिया ल्याऊ;

10d

उठेर आउँछु; भयो सोध्नुभयो; खाएर निस्क्यो; जान्न; नगर भन्नुभयो; पर्खनुहोस् नुहाएर आउँछु :

Lesson 11

Reading Passage

On the road

A. Excuse me. How far is the next village from here? How much time do you think it will take us to get there?
B. It is far away. From here it will take you at least two hours.
A. Can we arrive there before nightfall or not?
B. No, sir. The road is rather steep, you know. Our village is nearby. Stay there today. Get up early tomorrow morning and go.
A. Very well. Can we get a lodging for the night in your village?
B. Yes, sir. Why don't you come and stay in my house? How many of you are there?
A. Just the two of us.

A little later, after reaching the village

B. There, my house is this one. Come in. I'll be back in a moment.
A. Can we also get something to eat? We're very hungry.
B. Yes, sir. I can give you lentils, rice and vegetables.
A. How much will you charge us for the lodging then?

B. One and a half rupees for the food, one rupee for the firewood – altogether two and a half rupees I suppose.
A. Very well. That's all right.

The peasant goes to milk the cow and to get firewood. We go into the house, undo our shoes and sit down on the ground. In 15 minutes the peasant comes into the house.

B. Will you have tea now?
A. Very well. Have you got biscuits as well?
B. I don't have any, but I'll probably be able to get them from the shop. I'll send my son to get them. How many do you want?
A. Just one packet. Here, take one rupee. It's a bit cold today, isn't it?
B. Yes. In the hills it is always a little cold after nightfall. Sit there and warm yourselves by the fire.

The peasant calls his boy

B. Hey, boy. Go (somewhere for me). Buy a packet of biscuits from over there and bring them back. Do you want anything else from the shop, sir?
A. If they sell cigarettes. send (him) to get two packets of *Asha*. We'll go to the watering place, wash our hands and faces, and be back in a moment.
B. Very well. The watering place is down there.

11a

1. How many days does it take to get from Kathmandu to Namche Bazar? If you walk quickly, it takes about ten days.
2. Thinking that I was late going home, I went to get a bus (lit. 'to get up on a bus').
3. It's late. I must go now. We'll meet tomorrow. Very well. If you come to my place around ten o'clock, I'll meet you.
4. Who told you to take my book out of the drawer?
5. In the winter, it is very pleasant to go and stay in the Terai. It is always sunny, and it is never as cold as it is in Kathmandu.
6. Aren't you ashamed to beg, little boy?
7. I've got mud on my clothes. I'll have to give them to the washerman tomorrow.
8. Nepalis think ('say') that it is a sin to eat beef.
9. Before nightfall if we do not arrive, they say we shall not find lodgings in the village.
10. How much does the return trip to Calcutta by air cost? It costs 350 rupees.
11. You can get a lodging for the night on the road quite easily, but it is a bit difficult to find food in the villages. As far as food is concerned, buy it in Kathmandu and take it (with you).
12. In order to see Mt. Everest well, you have to go to Khumbu.

13. In comparison with the cities of Europe, you must say that Kathmandu is small, but there are many big hotels there, and you can find all you require in the market.
14. They only allow Hindus to go into Pashupatinath temple.
15. How long will it take to finish this work? It will take at least two hours.
16. Don't make a noise. Let the baby sleep. Did you hear me?
17. I don't know whether it will rain today or not. But it will be best to go with ('taking') an umbrella.
18. Will it be all right if I come at five this evening? Yes.

11b

१. सिपाहीले हामीलाई मन्दिरमा जान हुन्न भनेर भन्यो। खाली हिन्दुहरूलाई मात्रै जान दिन्छन् क्यारे?

२. अब मलाई जन्नुपर्‍यो भोलि भेटौंला ।हवस् ।साढे दस् बजेतिर मकहाँ आउनुहोस्। घाम् लाग्यो भने शहर्बाट बाहिर गएर घुम्न जान्छौं ।

३. तपाईंलाई ताश् खेल्न मन् लाग्छ?हो, कहिले कहीं मन् लाग्छ ।

४. कति बजे आउन हुन्छ? जहिले पनि आउनुहोस्।

५. लन्दन्बाट काठ्माडौंसम्म हवाईजहाज्मा जान कति बेर् लाग्छ? हवाईजहाज्मा जानुभयो भने, चौबीस् घण्टा जति लाग्छ ।

६. तपाईंले त्यो जुत्ता कतिमा किन्नुभयो? मैले अठाईस् रुपियाँमा किनें।

७. नेपाल्का गाउँहरूमा बास् धेरैजसो सजिलै पाइन्छ ।

८. हिमालय राम्ररी हेर्नलाई खुम्बुतिर जानुपर्छ । त्यहाँबाट सगर्माथा एक् दम् राम्रो देखिन्छ नि ।

९. बिहान उठेर,मुख हात् धोई साढे सात् बजेतिर जल्पान् गर्छु।

१०. आज धेरै जाडो छ ।यहाँ बसेर आगो ताप्नुहोस् न ।

११. तपाईंलाई नेपाल् कस्तो लाग्यो? मलाई धेरै राम्रो लाग्यो ।काठ्माडौं धेरै सुन्दर शहर् हो ।यहाँबाट हिमालय पनि देखिन्छ । आउनु अगाडि मलाई थाहै थिएन ।

१२. मन्दिर्मा जानुभन्दा अगाडि, जुत्ता खोल्नुपर्छ ।

१३. अलिकति पैसा कमाउनलाई मैले बिहान अड्डामा काम् गर्नुपर्छ तर म बाह्र बजेसम्म मात्रै काम् गर्छु र काम् धेरै गाह्रो छैन।

१४. हप्तामा,सबेरै उठी र जल्पान् गरी म घर्बाट निस्कन्छु। धेरैजसो बेलुका दस् बजेपछि घर् फर्कन्छु। सञ्चर्बार् र आइत्बार मैले आराम् गर्नैपर्छ ।

१५. भारत्का ठूला शहरहरूको दाँजोमा,नेपाल्का शहरहरू अलि साना छन् ।तर पोखरा र गोर्खा जस्ता शहरहरू धेरै सुन्दर छन्।

Lesson 12

Reading Passage

In the Sanskrit language, *him* means 'snow' and *ālaya* means 'home'. For that very reason, the mountains situated in the north of the Indian subcontinent are called the 'Himalayas'. The highest peaks of the Himalayas are Mt. Everest, Makalu, Annapurna and Dhaulagiri. These Himalayas divide the border of Nepal and Tibet. Among these, the highest mountain is Mt. Everest. Its height is more than 29,000 feet above sea-level. Because they are so high above the level of the sea, the summits of the Himalayas are always covered with snow. In the summer, when the snow there melts, rivers are formed. The Ganges, the Jamna, the Bramhaputra, the Indus and many other great rivers rise from there. It is possible to see the peaks of the mountains well from the ridge in the Kathmandu Valley, called Nagarkot. From there both evening and early morning, extremely ravishing views can be seen. When ('at the time of') the rays of the yellow sunlight fall on the white snow, these mountains seem to be made of gold. In order to see such a sight (as this) foreign tourists from many far off (lands) go there. But as far as seeing Mt. Everest well is concerned, one has to go to Namche Bazar. Namche Bazar is the largest village of the Sherpas of Nepal. This village is about 100 miles distant from Kathmandu. Small aircraft go from Kathmandu as far as a place called Lukla quite near to Namche Bazar. But it is very expensive to go like this in an aeroplane. As far as ordinary men are concerned, they have to make the journey on foot.

In Western Nepal, there is another small but extremely beautiful town called Pokhara. This town is in the lap of Annapurna and Dhaulagiri. Because its height above sea-level is only 2000 feet, it is warm and cosy there even in the winter, and every day tourists come to see the peaks of the mountains, which are covered with snow.

12a

1. How long is it since you came to Nepal? It is only three weeks since I came here.
2. When it rains, if you go out without ('not having taken') an umbrella, you will get a cold.
3. In the Terai there is a small industrial town called Biratnagar.
4. The water for the tea has not boiled yet. Wait five minutes and I'll bring it.
5. When you have stomach-ache, you just have to take medicine.
6. Because it rained yesterday, I did not manage to come and see you. Will it be all right if I come today?
7. I cannot come to meet you tomorrow. I've got a bit of work at home.
8. Hey, where are you off to? I'm going to do some work in the fields, sir.
9. It seems just like yesterday since I came to London. I like it here very much.
10. We walked as fast as possible, but it was impossible to reach home before nightfall.
11. He has been in Nepal for ages. He knows Nepali and Newari.
12. Because it did not rain last year, the entire crop failed.
13. I seem to have lost my glasses. Look and see if they are in the next room.
14. It is rather difficult to read Nepali newspapers. There is a great difference between the spoken and the written language, isn't there?
15. Excuse me (elder sister), I'm thirsty. Can I get a little water to drink, please.

16. He says he started to learn Nepali six months ago.
17. *I* didn't understand what he said. Can you understand him?
18. Because Namche Bazar is 11,000 feet above sea-level, in the winter months, a lot of snow falls there.

12b

१. तपाईं लन्दन् आउनुभएको कति दिन् भयो? म यहाँ आएको दुइ वर्ष भयो ।
२. पोहोर साल् पानी नपरेकोले, गाउँका मानिस्हरूलाई खाने कुरा अहिले पाइँदैन
३. काठ्माडौँको उँचाई समुद्रको तट्बाट चार् हजार् पाँच् सय् फुट् छ ।
४. नगरकोट्को डाँड़ो त्यति अग्लो भएको हुनाले, त्यहाँबाट हिमालयका धेरै टाकुराहरू देखिन्छन्। बिहान बेलुका, अत्यन्त मनोहर् दृश्य देखिन्छन्।
५. यो ऊनी कोट्को लागि साहूजीले एक् सय बीस् रुपियाँ लिए । त्यो त धेरै नै भयो नि ।
६. नेपाली सिक्नलाई छ महीना लाग्यो, तर अहिलेसम्म छापा पढ्न मलाई गाह्रो लाग्छ । त्यतिका संस्कृत् शब्द प्रयोग् गरिन्छन् ।
७. अचेल् साना हवाईजहाज् लुक्लासम्म त जान्छन् । त्यहाँबाट नाम्चे बजार्सम्म हिंड़ेरै जानुपर्छ । साधारण मानिसहरूलेचाहिं काठ्माडौँबाट पैदल् नै जानुपर्छ।
८. भारतीय उपमहाद्वीप्का ठूला नदीहरू सब् हिमालयबाट उत्पन्न हुन्छन् ।
९. ए दाइ कता जान लाग्नुभएको ? दाउरा काट्न जान लागें
१०. छिटो हिंड्नुभयो भने तीन् बज्नु अगाड़ि गाउँ पुग्नुहुन्छ ।
११. म नेपाल्मा बसेको धेरै वर्ष भयो तर मलाई नेवारी आउँदैन । धेरै नै गाह्रो भाषा हो नि ।
१२. हाम्रो घरमा पाहुनाहरू आएका हुनाले म तपाईंकहाँ आउन पाइनँ । आज बेलुका (भरे)आउन हुन्छ कि?
१३. ए भाइ, चिया लिएर आऊ /ल्याऊ/। चिया छैन हजूर् । अहिलेसम्म पानी उम्लेको छैन ।
१४. मलाई भोक् लाग्यो। यहाँ भात् खान पाइँछ?
१५. त्यो नेपाली राम्ररी बोल्न सक्छ, तर लेखाईको भाषामा त्यतिका संस्कृत् शब्द प्रयोग् गरिएका हुनाले, छापा पढ्न सक्तैन रे ।

12c

before coming; well, that job's done; may I come in; we'll meet tomorrow; I like to see a film; I did not like this book; he always plays cards; he is about five-years-old; come here; can I get a night's lodging?; very well, I'll let you have it for that much; how much a yard is this cloth?; there was a landslide.

12d

उसिनेको फुल्; करीब् दुइ सय् मील् ; तपाईं घोड़ा चढ्न सक्नुहुन्छ? सकेसम्म छिटो; पानी परेको छ; गाउँ नाश् भयो; उ अस्ति आयो ; त्यो कोठामा बसेको थियो ; मेरो टाउको दुखेको छ; गाउँ लुक्ला नाउँ गरेको ; रङ्गून र कलकत्ता जस्ता शहरहरू; ए भाइ , चिया ल्याऊ; निस्कनुभन्दा अगाड़ि म मुख् हात धुन्छु; दिल्लीको दाँजोमा नेपाल्को राज्धानी सानो छ

Lesson 13

Reading Passage

At the doctor's

A. Good morning, doctor. May I come in?

B. Good morning. Come in. Take a seat. Tell me, what's the matter with you?

A. Well, for two or three days, I have not been feeling right. I seem to have a temperature. My head aches, and I have not been able to eat anything.

B. Do you also have diarrhoea?

A. No, I don't, but my stomach is a bit upset.

B. Well, let me have a look at you. Show me your tongue. Do you also have stomach-ache?

A. A little, but not very much.

B. Where do you have your meals here?

A. I usually eat in the hotels in the city. But I try to go to clean places. I've never had anything like this before.

B. Do you drink boiled water?

A. I sometimes drink boiled water. But when one goes to see friends it is not always possible to do that, you know. It is not right to make them boil the water just for oneself.

B. That's true, but drink boiled water as far as possible. The city water supply is not all that good, and we Nepalis sometimes get an upset stomach. It doesn't look as if there is anything else wrong with you. I'll write you a prescription. Get it in the market. If your stomach ache does not get any better, come and see me again, and I'll send you to the hospital. You have only got a slight temperature. If you have rest for one day tomorrow, it will probably go down. And don't forget to drink boiled water.

A. Thank you, doctor. How much do I owe you?

B. That's all right. Never mind. Look after yourself, now.

13a

1. It's raining. Don't forget to take your umbrella, now.
2. Which country have you come from, sir? I am English.
3. You speak good Nepali. Where did you learn it? I learnt it before coming here from England.
4. My friend fell very ill. But he has got better now.
5. I waited for you for over an hour. Why were you so late?
6. Our servant was born in Darjeeling, but he has spent a long time in Kathmandu.
7. Why didn't you tell me this?
8. Last year, when he went to the Terai, he fell gravely ill. He almost died of malaria.
9. I'm getting up tomorrow morning and going to town. I have to do a lot of shopping there.

10. Where were you born? I was born in Dharan.
11. We tried to go to the village above, but because the road was bad, we had to turn back.
12. Yesterday I went swimming and almost caught a cold.
13. I shall get married one of these days, but I don't feel like settling down just yet.
14. When I went to town, I met my friend.
15. Have you ever been to India? I have not been yet, but I want to go.

13b

१. तपाईं लन्दन् जानुभएको छ? गएँ, म छ महीना अघि त्यहाँ थिएँ ।

२. मैले एक् घण्टाभन्दा बढ़ी उस्‌लाई कुर्हें ,तर उ आएन।त्यसैले म आफै आएँ ।

३. मैले भीजा लिन खोजेको तर विदेशीहरूलाई भूटान् जान दिंदैन (न्) रे ।चीन्‌को सीमानामा भएकोले,त्यहाँ पुग्न धेरै नै गाह्रो हुन्छ ।

४. उस्‌ले यो घर् आफैले बनाएको हो रे ।

५. तपाईंको साथीले भनेको मैले बुझिनँ ।त्यस्‌लाई नेपाली राम्ररी आउँदैन,होइन त ?

६. माफ् गर्नुहोला,हिजो राति मैले तपाईंलाई फोन् गर्न बिर्सें ।

७. हाम्रो गाउँमा भर्खर् आएको मान्छेलाई तपाईंले चिन्नुभएको छ?

८. तपाईं नेपाल् आउनुभएको कति दिन् भयो ? धेरै त भएन। म गएको नोभेम्बर् आएको थिएँ ।

९. गौतम् बुद्ध लुम्बिनी नाउँ गरेको तराईको सानो शहर्‌मा जन्मेका थिए ।तपाईंले उन्‌को जन्मस्थल् कहिले देख्नुभएको छ ?

१०. यी टचाक्सी ड्राइभरहरू धेरै नै छिटो मोटर हाँक्छन् ।अस्ति मोटरले मलाई झण्डै कुल्चेको ।

११. टाउको कम् दुखेको भएन भने मकहाँ फेरि आउनुहोस् ।म औषधि लेखिदिन्छु ।

१२. साथीहरूलाई आफ्नैलागि मात्रै अंग्रेजी खाना पकाउन लाउन त भएन ।

13c

गएका; गएकी; गर्नुभएको; लेख्नुभएको परेको; खोजेको

Lesson 14

Reading Passage

A letter from Pokhara

Pokhara Asar 8, 2023 V.S.

Dear Shyam,

Two weeks ago, as soon as I arrived at Bhairava, I received your long and interesting letter. As you know, I left Kathmandu with my friend, Ramesh, towards the end of last month. As always, the plane was late, but we arrived at Bhairava airport before nightfall. Therefore, there was no difficulty in finding a rickshaw. The city centre is not very far away from the airport. Even so, the rickshaw driver insisted upon having five rupees. We tried to bring down the price, but they would not agree under any circumstances. As soon as we reached the town, we began to look for a place to spend the night. Finally, we got a small room in a hotel. Because we were tired, we went to bed early. But it was very hot in the room, and because the mosquitoes were biting all night long, we could not get to sleep. When we got up the next morning, we found to our surprise that we had mosquito-bites all over our body. For that reason, we began to make arrangements to go from Bhairava to the hills as soon as possible.

As you know, we came to Bhairava just to see Lumbini. The next day, we looked for a taxi to go there, but because there was mud on the road, the drivers were not inclined to go. Because Lumbini is a long way from Bhairava, we could not go there on foot.

Altogether we spent three days in Bhairava and as we were leaving, I got your letter in the post-office. We easily got a bus going from Bhairava to Tansen, and since the road was good, it did not take us much time to arrive there.

As soon as we arrived in Tansen, we looked to see if we could get a bus going to Pokhara, and were very relieved to find that there were four or five buses a day. Before leaving Kathmandu, I did not know whether the new road was open or not. I enjoyed Tansen immensely. And since it is high up, it was quite cold. Before going to Pokhara, we decided to stay there for two or three days.

From this letter, you will gather that we are now in Pokhara. We'll have a rest here, and set off for Jomsom in two or three days' time. We tried to go to Mustāng from there, but we could not get a permit. What to do?

Now all we have to do is to look for porters to carry our luggage. When we get back from there, I'll write you all the news of Jomsom.

Your friend,
Surya Prakash.

14a

1. As soon as my work is finished, I shall come and meet you.
2. The people who live in Kathmandu are not accustomed to travel around very much.
3. As soon as the bride came out, everybody began to stare.
4. 'It is getting dark. Now what shall we do?' he said.
5. So far I have not been outside the Kathmandu Valley. But later I intend to go to the east.
6. I am going home sharp at five ('as soon as it is . . .'). I have had news that guests are coming to our house.
7. 'If we hang around here again, we won't be able to find a lodging for the night in the village,' I said.
8. As soon as you arrive in Darjeeling, go and meet my elder brother. His

house is on the road that goes in the direction of Ghūm.

9. I did not know that you had the electric light in your house.
10. I asked the guard what time the train going to Siliguri arrived, but he said it would not come before ('it only comes') the next day.
11. When you return from London, don't forget to buy presents for your friends.
12. Bhānubhakta Acharya was born in 1871 V.S. in the month of Āṣāṛh in the village of Ramgha in the district called Tanahun.
13. I asked the *jyapu* (Newar peasant) whether I could get food in his village.
14. That is the book you ought to read if you want to learn English.
15. The matter arose as to how we might get back to Kathmandu from there.

14b

१. ताश् खेल्ने? अहँ,अहिले नखेल्ने।मलाई फुर्सत् छैन ।

२. कस्तो मान्छे ।भित्र आउने ढोकाबाट निस्कन खोज्यो । अघि त निस्कने ढोकाबाट भित्र आउने कोशिश् गर्छ क्यारे ?

३. ए दाइ, पाटन् जाने बस् यहाँबाट कति बजे जान्छ?पाटन् जाने बस् यहाँबाट त जाँदैन । बस्-बिसौनी त्यो हुलाक्घरनेर छ नि ।

४ पल्लो गाउँ पुग्ने बित्तिकै,अर्को भरिया खोज्ने कोशिश् गर्छु ।योचाहिं अघि जाँदैन रे ।

५. नेपाली सिक्नलाई हेर्नुपर्ने किताब् यही हो ।त्योचाहिं उस्तो राम्रो छैन ।

६. आज आएको शेर्पाले नाम्चे बजार् जाने सबै बन्दोबस्त गर्छ रे ।उस्लाई तीन सय् रुपियाँ दिनुपर्छ रे ।

७. लन्दन् पुग्ने बित्तिकै,हवाईघाट्बाट मलाई फोन् गर्नुहोस् ।म तपाईंलाई भेटन् आउँछु ।म मोटर्मा आएँ भने, मेरो घर्बाट त्यहाँ पुग्न बीस् मिनेट् मात्रै लाग्छ नि ।

८. सधैं झैं बस् ढीलो आयो र मान्छेहरूले भरिभराउ थियो ।तर अर्को बस् नभएकोले,त्यसैमा आउनुपर्‍यो ।

९. यस् चिठीबाट तिमीले थाहा पायौ होला कि म अहिले दिल्लीमा छु ।हवाईजहाज् पाइयो भने,म काठ्माड़ौं पर्सी पुग्छु ।

१०. काठमाड़ौंबाट पोखरा जाने बाटो खुलेको छ भन्ने मलाई थाहा थिएन ।

११. मेरो विचार्ले म दुइ तीन् हप्तासम्म यस् होटेल्मा बस्छु ।त्यस्पछि अर्को बस्ने ठाउँ खोज्ने कोशिश् गर्छु ।

१२. उ घर्बाट निस्कने बित्तिकै,सब मान्छेहरूले ट्वाल्ट्वाल्ती हेर्न थाले ।

14c

next week; the guests who are coming tomorrow; the work you ought to do; to decide to go to Nepal; as soon as we reached Kathmandu; I got a bus; up to the end of next month; the third of Vaishākh; the seventh of Bhadau 2020 V.S.; the eighth of June 1976.

Lesson 15

Reading Passage

Pālpā Bhairava — an invisible god

Pālpā is considered to be one of the important districts (*jillā*) of Western Nepal. In the 16th century A.D., the Sen dynasty of kings ruled in Pālpā. According to the *Vamshāvalīs* ('chronicles'), Mukunda Sen I, while extending his kingdom, made an attack upon the Malla kings of the Kathmandu Valley. While making this attack on the Valley, along with the other goods he stole, he took back to Pālpā, as well, the extremely famous and ancient statue of Bhairavā which was ('remained') in the *Vihāra* of Lord Macchindranāth, situated in Kathmandu's Keltol. Perhaps it is possible that the statue set up inside the famous Bhairava temple, situated in Pālpā, is this very one.

The Pālpā Bhairava temple is also considered to be one of the most important temples of Western Nepal. Not only from (the places) around Pālpā, but also from the far-off districts of Western Nepal, (such as) Bāglung, Pyūṭhān and Pokhara, etc., religious-minded people come (there) to worship Bhairava and to look at (the deity).

The Bhairava temple, the house of the officiating priest, the houses where the pilgrims stay – are all around a large square. The temple-square is long in shape, and large and small metal bells of various shapes which the devotees have offered are decorated even with metal dogs and tridents. Since the conveyance of Bhairava is a dog, it is possible that the devotees have offered statues of dogs. Along with this, Bhairava is recognised as one of Shiva's many forms. It may be for this reason, the weapons of Shiva, the tridents are seen scattered all over the place around the temple.

Twice a year, especially in Vaishākh and Mangsir, a gathering of devotees is accustomed to take place here. On the festival of Navarātrī also, great numbers of people worship here and offer up sacrifice. The main officiant of the temple is the high priest of the *Nāth-Sampradāya* (the sect of the followers of Gorakhnāth), and to help him, the Upadhyāya Brahmins are also accustomed to fulfil the function of making sacrifices of he-goats, chickens, etc., which usually does not happen.

However, in the day-to-day, ordinary worship, the devotees are accustomed to offer thick bread made of the dough of wheat or rice, which the local people call *roṭh*. The practice of offering rice-bread to Bhairava is not found in other regions of Nepal.

Any people who come as far as Pālpā-Tānsen, also desire to go to the Bhairava temple, because this Bhairava temple is renowned throughout the whole of the Kingdom of Nepal. The devotees, suffering the great trouble of the mountain road, go to view Bhairava, but when they arrive there, they must be disappointed, because the main statue of Bhairava is shown to no one at all, and is placed inside that temple in a secret room.

It is said that the statue of Bhairava (remaining) inside there is extremely frightening, and several individuals, upon seeing that statue, died from fright, and to avoid such painful events occurring again in the future, from that time onwards, the statue of Bhairava was put in a dark room on the lower floor of that temple, and from that very time the Pālpā Bhairāva began to assume (lit. 'remain in') the form of an invisible god.

15a

1. In order that everyone may hear, speak loudly, will you?
2. The bus will come, but these days it comes a bit late.
3. You can see Mt. Everest from Kathmandu, but because it is very far away, it looks quite small.
4. Keep taking this medicine. You will certainly be better in a couple of days.
5. I heard on the radio that there was a possibility of rain tomorrow.
6. If I fail in the exam again this year, my father will certainly be angry.
7. I planned to go to India last year, but could not find the time. I shall try to go this year now.
8. We reached the village above just as night fell.
9. Aeroplanes do go towards Jumlā, but they only go once or twice a month.
10. Look how it is raining. This year the crops will certainly be spoilt.
11. Today I just managed to meet your young brother.
12. Last night, without anyone seeing, I crept out of the house and went to play cards with friends.
13. I should read this book, but how can I read it? I find it too difficult.
14. In Nepal, especially in the hills, there are not many beggars. The peasants are ashamed to beg, you know.
15. If you pass the exam, you will easily find a job.

15b

१ भोलि पानी पर्ने संभावना छ भनेको मैले रेडियोमा सुनें ।
२ . राम्ररी हेर्ने गरी उता गएर बस त ।
३ . नेपाल् पुगेर, उमालेको पानी पिउने गर्नुहोस्। उमालेको पानी पिउनुभएन भने पेट् पक्कै पनि गड़्बड़् हुनेछ।
४ . उस्ले भारत् गएर काम् खोज्ने पक्का गर्‍यो।भन्छ ।कलकत्ता गयो भने,त्यहाँ काम् अवश्य पाउनेछ।
५ . पश्चिम् नेपाल् जाने हवाईजहाज् छन त छ,तर दिन्हुँ भने जान्न।
६ . त्यो बूढ़ो सिकिस्त बिरामी छ । डाक्टर् छिटो आएन भने,उ अवश्य मर्नेछ ।
७ . कसैले नदेख्ने गरी त्यो अड्डाबाट सुटुक्क निस्क्यो ,तर भित्र आउने ढोकासम्म पुग्ने बित्तिकै, फर्कनुपरेको थियो ।
८ . गाउँतिर खाने कुरा पाइन त पाइन्छ, तर काठ्माड़ौंबाट सामान् लिएर जानु बेस् हुन्छ।
९ . भारत्का शहर्हरूमा धेरै माग्नेहरू देखिन्छन्,तर गाउँका मान्छेहरू माग्न लाज् मान्छन् ।
१० तपाईंले भन्नुभएको ठीकै हो ।म अस्पताल् गएर उस्लाई पक्कै पनि भेट्नेछु ।

११. ईसाको सोह्रौं शताब्दीमा,पाल्पाका राजाले काठ्माडौंको उपत्यकामा आक्रमण गरेका थिए।
१२. त्यस् मन्दिरमा ब्राहमणहरूले जनावरहरूको बलि दिने काम् गर्ने गर्छन् जुन् साधारणतया हुने गर्दैन ।

Lesson 16

Reading Passage

The problems of a younger and elder brother

My elder brother is three years older than I, but both of us are in the same class. Although our father is not very rich, he works extremely hard to send us to college. My elder brother makes a great effort to study, and when he returns home from college he makes a habit of reading until nightfall. As for me, I go every day to town to meet my friends, and till late at night, I enjoy myself there. Because I keep doing that, my elder brother gets angry. He says:

'Look here. We are poor people. Therefore you should work a little harder. There is an exam coming next month, you know, and all you do is to sit with your friends in the tea-shop. You will certainly fail, and all the money father has spent will be wasted.'

Indeed, what my elder brother says is quite right. He told me just the same thing two years ago as well. But fortunately, I passed the exam, and unfortunately, he failed. Because he had to stay down in the same class, my elder brother was sorry.

One evening in the winter, I was doing a translation from English into Nepali. My elder brother came to see whether the translation I had written was right or not and looking over my shoulder, said:

'What on earth is that you have written? At least when you write Nepali, write something (others) can understand. If you go on like that, you won't be successful in the next exam, as you passed in last year's exam. It is difficult, you know.'

But the next year, I passed and my poor brother failed. What to do? I went up a class, and he had to stay down in the same class. We are now both in the same class.

I know that I have to work harder. My elder brother is quite right to scold me and tell me I have been lazy. Although we are in the same class, he is older than I. For that reason, I always respect my elder brother.

16a

1. Although the road was not all that steep, it took us almost five hours to reach the village.
2. I have forgotten to bring any money. Lend me ten rupees. I'll pay you back tomorrow.

3. Although Nepalis are poor, they are happy to welcome guests.
4. I simply must reach his house on time. Even though it might cost a bit more money, I'll go by taxi.
5. By giving her everything she asked for, you spoilt your wife.
6. Look, that's Lāle, isn't it? Where on earth can he be off to, looking so smart?
7. I offered five rupees, but the rickshaw driver would not accept it under any circumstances. How the cost of living has gone up these days, even in Nepal.
8. No matter how much you plead with me, I shall not let you go and see the film.
9. How much sugar do you want? Two spoons will be enough.
10. I shall have to stay in Kathmandu until my work is finished. As soon as it is finished, I shall definitely go travelling in the hills.
11. I seem to have lost my pen. How can I write the letter?
12. Whether you go by this road, or go by that road, it's the same.
13. In the winter, a lot of snow falls in the villages around the mountains.
14. When it rains, there is a possibility of landslides. In that case, the roads are closed for two or three weeks, and all transport is stopped everywhere.
15. I'll go to my office and work till nightfall. I'll come back home as soon as my work is finished.

16b

१. एशियाका धेरै देश्हरू गरीब् भए तापनि ,आउने दस् साल्भित्र धेरै प्रगति गर्नेछन् ।

२. अँध्यारो भए तापनि,उस्ले पल्लो गाँउसम्म जाने फैस्ला गऱ्यो।

३. म कति बजे आउन हुन्छ? जहिले पनि आउनुहोस् ।

४. जति खर्च लागे पनि म आउने वर्ष नेपाल जानेछु।

५. त्यो काठ्माड़ौंमा बसेसम्म एक् दम् संचो थियो ।पहाड़तिर गएपछि,बिरामी पऱ्यो।

६. बस् नआएसम्म, हामीलाई यहाँ पर्खनुपर्छ ।हिंड़ेरै जान त हुँदैन ।

७. घर फर्केपछि,छापा पढ़्न लागें र साढ़े एघार बजेतिर सुत्न गएँ ।

८. ढोकामा को आएछ? ए,रामे रहेछ ।किन यति ढीलो आएको?

९. तपाईंका कतिजना दाइहरू छन्? मेरो एक्जना दाइ छ ।वहाँ मभन्दा दुइ बर्ष जेठो हुनुहुन्छ । म माहिलो छु ।

१०. मेरो छोराले स्कूल्मा धेरै प्रगति गरेको छ ।यो साल् माथिल्लो कक्षामा गयो नि ।

११. पस्ल्मा जे जे देखिन्छ स्वास्नीलाई उही उही चाहिन्छ ।

१२. हिजोआज नेपाल्मा महँगी कस्तो बढ़ेको ।आज बिहान मैले एक् कप् चियाको लागि तीन् रुपियाँ दिनुपरेको थियो।

१३. मेरो घर् शहर्बाट अलि टाढ़ा भए तापनि त्यहाँ बस्न मलाई मन् लाग्छ ।तर बिहानचाहिं मोटर्मा आएँ भने, अड्डासम्म पुग्नलाई आधा घण्टा जति लाग्छ नि ।

१४. चियामा कति दूध चाहियो?अलिकति मात्रै भए पुग्छ ।

१५. मेरो काम् नसिद्धिएसम्म म पुस्तकालयमा काम् गर्छु ।त्यस्पछि पहाड़तिर तीन् महीना बिताउने विचार् छ।

16c

मन्त्रीको मृत्यु अचानक् भएथ्यो; बेलायत् जाने विचार छ; उसलाई सल्लाह दिएर के फाइदा? साँझ पर्नु अगाडि पुगेथ्यो; मलाई बास् पाइन्छ? हामीले डाक्टर्लाई बोलायौं; कसले भनेर तिमीले त्यसो गऱ्यौ। मेरो टाउको दुखेको छ बस्मा गए पनि, रेल्मा गए पनि, एउटै हो; जे भने पनि, त्यो त मान्नेछैन। धातुका मूर्तिहरूले मन्दिर् सजिएको थियो; जाँच्मा फेल् भएपछि, मेरो दाइले अफ्सोच् मान्नुभयो, त्यो मान्छे कता जान लागेको रहेछ?

16d

गाएको; भए रहेछ; रहनेछ; आएछ लागेको; भएथ्यो;
गरे नगरे; गए; गरे पर्नु; सिद्धिए, गएर।

Lesson 17

Reading Passage

At the airport

(After arrival in Kathmandu International Airport, in the baggage lounge)

A. Excuse me. I have just come from Delhi. My aeroplane landed a little while ago. Tell me. Where do you think my luggage will be?

B. Come this way, please. I'll show you now. First of all, let me see your passport. Let me just have a look at it. Well, it seems in order. You must have got your visa from the London embassy. You've come from England, haven't you? Have you ever been in Nepal before, or is this your first visit?

A. This is the first time.

B. In that case, where did you learn Nepali?

A. I learnt it in England, before coming here. Two or three Nepali friends of mine live in London. I began to learn it with them. Now I have come to Nepal to practise.

B. I see. How many days do you intend to spend in Nepal, then?

A. I think I shall stay for six months probably. I have a bit of work in Tribhuvan University.

B. Where will you stay in Kathmandu?

A. So far, I have no fixed address, but for two or three weeks, I shall probably have to go in a hotel and stay there. You give me a little advice. Will I easily get a room in a hotel?

B. It shouldn't be difficult. There are many hotels in town.

A. How much do you think I shall have to pay for a night in an ordinary hotel? I can't stay in a very expensive hotel.

B. You will probably be able to find a room for about 40 rupees a day. For most Nepalis that is a bit expensive, but it is not so expensive for Europeans. What I mean to say is that it comes to a little more than two pounds.

A. That will be all right for a few days. I'll look around after that. Well, hasn't my luggage arrived yet?

B. It must have. It is probably in the next room. Just go and have a look.

A. Yes. My suitcase is over there. Do I have to open it or not?

B. That's all right. No need to open it. Go on.

A. Where do you think I can get a taxi?

B. After you go out from here, you will find lots of taxis.

A. How much roughly will it cost to go to town from here?

B. It shouldn't cost more than 20 rupees. It's not very far, you know. The taxi driver will take you up to your hotel.

A. Before I take a taxi, I shall have to change some money. Where shall I go?

B. Yes. There's a place to change money near the way-out. Go there and change it.

A. Very well. Thank you very much. I'll be going now. I hope we shall meet again.

A Nepali folksong

1. Do not cry, my darling. Give me leave without shedding tears. See, I am going to war. I shall return, when I have won my reputation.
2. The old ones, mother and father – look after them well. I have left behind a son, a bundle of love, keep him safe.
3. The chickens, the goat, the cow and cattle – look after them well. Do honour to our friends and neighbours.
4. When I have made my name and come back, I shall bring you a tasselled shawl. Becoming the defender of my dear land, I shall be a hero in the world.

17a

1. It looks as if it is going to rain. Don't forget to take an umbrella, before you go out.
2. How long do you think it will take to get to Pashupatinath from here? It will take at least half an hour. Why don't you go by taxi?
3. After the Prime Minister's death, who do you think will take his place? I don't know.
4. I was going to write you a letter, but since there was no paper in the house, I didn't manage to.
5. I think I've got a cold coming on. Perhaps I'd better not go swimming today.
6. He did his best to have a son, but all he had was daughters. What can he do, the poor fellow?
7. I have to telephone a friend. Can I use your phone?
8. If I work in a hotel for five weeks in the vacation, I'll earn at least 300 rupees.

9. I was going to go to India, but thinking it would be so hot there now, I did not feel like going.
10. If we walk as quickly as possible, we ought to arrive before the evening.
11. Whether it rains or not, I simply must go. I have to arrive at the airport before eleven.
12. How much milk shall I pour into your tea? Just a little will do.
13. The bus must have arrived. Let me come back when I've been to ask at what time it leaves.
14. I hope you receive my letter on time.
15. Where is Rame? I don't know. He must have gone out.
16. What will the poor woman do, now her husband is dead? She has no one else at all.

17b

१. गाउँसम्म आउन जान तीन् घण्टा जति लाग्ला ।हामी जाऔं कि नजाऔं?
२. तपाईंलाई रुघा लाग्यो? लाग्ला लाग्ला जस्तो छ ।टाउको नराम्रोसित दुखेको छ ।
३. तपाईंको चियामा कति चिनी हालूँ? दुइ चम्चा भए पुग्छ ।
४. अलि अबेर् भयो ।म जाऊँ त ।फेरी कहिले भेटौंला?
५. तपाईं लन्दन्बाट जानुभन्दा अगाड़ि मेरो चिठी पाउनुहोला भन्ने मलाई आशा छ ।
६. कति बज्यो? कुन्नि,मसँग घड़ी छैन ।पाँच् बज्यो होला ।
७. यो सब् काम् आज सिद्ध्याउन सकिनँ ।धेरै नै बाँकी छ ।भैगो,केही छैन। भोलिसम्म रहोस्।
८. नोकर् कता गयो? कुन्नि ।बजार् गयो होला। एक घण्टामा फर्केला/फर्कन्छ होला।
९. मैले नेपाल् जानुभन्दा अगाड़ि नै लन्दन्को विश्वविद्यालयमा नेपाली् सिकेको थिएँ।
१०. काठ्माडौंमा होटेल्को कोठा तीस् रुपियाँमा पाइएला ।
११. म पैसा कहाँ साटूँ? हवाईघाट्मा साट्न सुक्नुहुन्छ ।
१२. होटेल्बाट शहर्को केन्द्रसम्म जान कति खर्च लाग्ला? टच्याक्सीबाट गयौ भने ५ रुपियाँ लाग्ला । बस्मा गए,बीस् पैसा मात्रै लाग्छ ।
१३. पानी पर्न लाग्यो र मसँग छाता छैन ।अब के गरूँ?
१४. काठ्माडौंमा पुगेपछि,मेरो दाइसँग भेट्न जानुहोस् । वहाँको ठेगाना देऊँ ?
१५. जे भए पनि,छ बजेसम्म घर नपुगी हुँदैन ।यस् बेलासम्म हाम्रा पाहुनाहरू आइपगेका होलान् ।

17c

thank you very much; we'll meet again; where are you going? there must have been a landslide; I shall take you along; how much money do you earn?; it looks as if it is going to rain; one must work hard; next year I will be successful in the exam; in that case, I shall come as well; he would not agree under any circumstances; every day; all the money will be wasted; I shall sit here until he comes; how does one go?; anyone may come; excuse me.

Lesson 18

Reading Passage

An elephant, called Kapurṭike, used to stroll, just as he pleased, in some big jungle in Burma. Seeing him, all the jackals of the jungle, overcome by envy, began to think that if they could kill him by some means, their stomachs would be filled with meat. In order to bring this idea into practice, an old jackal, moving forward, spoke in this way:

'Look, brothers. Work that can be accomplished by intelligence, can never be accomplished merely by strength. This elephant is very strong. Even so, we can certainly kill him by the force of our own intelligence.'

Hearing the words of the old jackal, all of them expressed amazement and surprise. Afterwards, the cunning jackal, going into the presence of the elephant, greeted him in a very coaxing manner, and said:

'Your Majesty, look with kindness upon this poor, miserable creature.'

Such coaxing words of the jackal gave rise to some pride in the elephant's heart. With great vanity he asked:

'Tell me. Who are you? Why have you come? What do you want?'

Then, the old jackal, becoming even more coaxing, made this request:

'I am the jackal called Jambumantri, sir. In the whole of the jungle, the animals have sent me into Your Majesty's presence as a representative. Your Majesty is wise. All of us have found great trouble and spend our days without a king. In the whole jungle, no animal has turned out worthy of being king. For this reason, it is I who have come to Your Majesty's presence to make a request. Your Majesty must become our king and protect us.

Hearing the speech of the cunning jackal, the elephant was overjoyed. After this, the elephant answered:

'Very well. I accept your request. Now, tell me by what road and where I must go.'

The cunning jackal, seeing that his purpose was being fulfilled, became very happy.

'Your Majesty, be good enough to follow me. I shall show you the way,' said the jackal, and going ahead to show the way, began to proceed. The elephant also began to go behind the cunning jackal. In the hope of gaining a kingdom, as the elephant walked quickly along the road the jackal showed him, he suddenly fell into a deep pit of mud. Seeing the misfortune that had befallen him, the elephant said:

'My friend, Jambumantri, I am in great difficulty. Assist me. Look, I am stuck in this deep pit.'

Seeing the plight of the elephant, the jackal smiled. Then going to the side of the elephant, said:

'Your Honour, catch hold of my tail and come out.'

After this had happened, the evil jackal said sarcastically, 'By trusting the words of someone as sly as I, this is the result', and he went from that place to the place where his friends were. After that, all the jackals crowded around, and killing the elephant, enjoyed themselves by having a feast.

18a

1. If you had drunk boiled water, you would not have been ill.
2. Pakistan's aeroplanes used to come to Kathmandu via Dacca, but after the beginning of the war with India, they have stopped coming.
3. It would have been better to go by the other road. This one has turned out to be very steep and slippery.
4. When he was living in London, he used to go and see a film every week.
5. Five years ago, all the goods in Kathmandu were cheap. But these days since so many tourists come, the cost of living in Nepal is higher than in India.
6. When do you want to go to India? It would be better to go as soon as possible.
7. If you had given me your brother's address, I should have gone to meet him.
8. If I had had the time, I should have come to meet you, but since I was talking to my friends till late in the evening, I could not come.
9. If I had known that you were not here, I would not have come.
10. In the beginning, I used to work from morning till evening, but these days I am not capable of doing so much work.
11. Before 1950 it was very difficult for foreigners to travel in Nepal.
12. I have decided to go home. I shall probably leave England next month.
13. If you had wanted to go to Thyangboche two years ago, you would have had to go on foot. It used to take at least two weeks to get there from Kathmandu. But now they say there is an air-service that goes there.

18b

१. मैले देखाएको बाटोबाटा जानुभएको भए, चाँड़ै पुग्नुहुन्थ्यो।
२. म हरेक् दिन् बीस्वटा चुरोट् खान्थें, तर पोहोर् साल् मैले खान छोड़ें। अहिले त म खाँदिन।
३. उस्ले बढ़ता मेहनत् गरेको भए, जाँच्मा सजिलै नै सफल् हुने थियो। अब त अर्को साल् फेरि कोशिश् गर्नुपर्छ।
४. मेरो बुवा हनुमान् ढोकानेर एउटा पुरानो घरमा बस्नुहुन्थ्यो ।
५. तिमीले मेरो कुरा सुनेको भए, अहिले बिरामी हुने थिएनौ।
६. पूजा हेर्नलाई हामी शहर्को केन्द्रमा भएका मन्दिरहरूमा जान्थ्यौं ।
७. पहिले म नेवारी भाषा राम्ररी बोल्न सक्थें,तर धेरै दिन्देखि काठ्माडौंमा नबसेकोले मैले सब् बिर्सेको छु ।
८. शुरूमा म बिहानदेखि बेलुकासम्म काम् गर्थें,तर हिजोआज म त्यतिको काम् गर्न सक्दिन ।
९. तिमीले खोजेको किताब् पाइयो? अहँ,पाइएन। हराएको होला ।
१०. तीस् बर्ष अधि मदेस्मा धेरै हाथी थिए,तर अहिले जंगल्को ठूलो भाग् काटिएको हुनाले,त्यतिका हाथी छैनन् ।
११. त्यो कोट् धेरै नै महँगो भयो,।साहूजीले सय् रुपियाँमा दिएको भए त हुन्थ्यो ।

१२. मलाई फुर्सत् भए त म चाँड़ै नै भारत् जान्थें। अहिले त पानी परोस् कि नपरोस् मलाई जानैपर्छ। त्यहाँ धेरै काम् छ नि।

18c

After the king died, his son acquired the kingdom; how to bring this idea into practice?; he was sent to the Maharaja's court as a representative; hearing this, he was overjoyed; please accept my request, sir; hearing such a strange thing, he began to smile; I have rented a nice room; have you been to Nepal before this or not?; you can get lots of things in that shop; he makes me mad; he had found official employment in the Singha Darbar; this is the book you ought to look at, you know; it seems that I have lost my pen; I think I am about to get a cold; I scolded him and told him to come on time; I work in a hotel to earn my living; the soldier made his name in the great war; I'll probably come back in two days' time.

Lesson 19

Reading Passage

The temple behind the Svayambhu Ridge belongs to Manjushri. Here, on the day of Shrīpanchamī, a fair is held. One sect holds this temple to belong to Sarasvatī and worships her. Another sect, holding it to belong to Manjushrī, honours him. The Buddhists hold it to belong to Manjushrī. Those Hindus who follow the Shiva religion, hold it to belong to Sarasvatī. On the day of Shrīpanchamī people of both sects come there. Both sects – one followers of Manjushrī and the other followers of Sarasvatī – worship in an equally devoted manner. Indeed, this is a surprising thing, because Manjushrī is male, and Saraṣvatī is female. In the history of Nepal, Manjushrī is greatly honoured. He first came from China. It is traditionally accepted that after coming (to Nepal), it was he who made the Nepal Valley. The account of the tale goes like this.

The Nepal Valley was first of all a great lake. This lake was called Nāgpokharī. Coming here, an ascetic called Vipashvī Buddha planted a lotus. Svayambhū stood up (appeared) on this lotus, and then many pilgrims arrived here to gaze upon Svayambhū. As long as this valley was a lake, the peak of the Svayambhū hill was above the water. Imagining it (to be) a god, they must have come to gaze upon it.

Manjushrī also came here from China to gaze upon this very Svayambhū. After gazing on Svayambhū, he recalled (his plan) to take the water out of the valley. Before this, he had come from China, and had sat on a ridge near Bhādgāon. They say that it was from here that he decided to take out the water from the valley.

Having decided to take the water out of the valley, Manjushrī stood the goddesses named Varada and Mokṣada high up on two hills. To this day, a festival takes place on those very hills to worship the goddesses.

After that, in accordance with his decision, Manjushrī set about sending the water out of the lake. He thought in which place it would be possible to take the water out. Finally, cleaving the place called Kaṭvāl, he made the water come out from there. They also call that place Nhasikāp. It is on the ridge of Chobhār.

After Manjushrī had cut the hill, the water here began to flow out with great force. All the Nāgas began to emerge. The Nāga known as Karkoṭak also came out. Manjushrī stopped him and, taking him away, put him in the lake, called Ṭaudaha.

After the water of the lake had come out in this way, a great place was made in the valley. And then, Manjushrī founded a great city in this place. From his name, its name also came to be Manjupattan. After that, he set men in this city, made one of them king, and went back, himself, to China.

In the name of this very Manjushrī, afterwards, a temple was built behind Svayambhū. Here, once a year, a fair takes place on the day of Shrīpanchamī. On that day, while worshipping Manjushrī, the Newar women, offer up lamps they have made themselves, thread, and so on, and it is also customary to rub in oil.

When Manjushrī cut the hill and took out the water, the town in the valley he made was first named Manjupattan. Afterwards, a branch of the Kirānts, the men of the Nepar caste, began to live here. It has been written that from these Nepars the name of the place became Nepal.

19a

1. While I was sitting in my friend's house, I got a fever.
2. Just because you say it is all right, does it become all right?
3. What is that man saying? If he speaks louder so that everyone can hear, it will be better.
4. He must have earnt a lot of money, when he was working in the embassy.
5. I received your letter two weeks ago when I was in Bhairava.
6. There's a room empty in our house. Come whenever you like.
7. What are you doing in London now? I am working in the university.
8. It is getting late. It will probably be better to go now, you know.
9. If he had studied, he would simply not have failed the exam.
10. I have travelled once or twice in a taxi in Kathmandu, but now I find it rather expensive.
11. As I was going to sleep, I heard a noise coming from downstairs. I thought that a thief had come into the house, and on going downstairs to look, I found that I had forgotten to close the door.
12. When I was young, I could walk for miles, but now I like to stay at home.
13. After the beginning of the twentieth century, Nepali literature crossing countless obstacles, entered the field of progress.

14. Did you have to go alone, just because he told you to?
15. If I had known that it was going to be as hot as this, I would have gone swimming this afternoon.
16. What is that man saying. I can't hear from here.
17. When I come to your place, by what road shall I come?
18. Rāme came to London for six months and is still here.

19b

१. काठ्माड़ौंमा हुँदा,त्यो दिनहुँ विश्वविद्यालयको पुस्तकालयमा जान्थ्यो ।

२. पानीले गर्दा पहिरो गयो ।त्यस्पछि बाटो तीन् दिन्सम्म बन्द थियो ।

३. तपाईंले नेपाली कसरी सिक्नुभएको थियो? चियापसल्हरूमा बसेर नेपालीहरूसँग कुराकानी गर्दा गर्दै मैले सिकें ।

४. उस्ले छिटो घर जाऊ भन्दैमा,तिमीलाई जानुपर्थ्यो र?

५. त्यो केटा काम् गर्दै गर्दैन ।अंग्रेजी पढ्न र लेख्न सिकेन भने,काम् पाउनेछैन ।

६. आज बिहान अड्डामा जाँदाखेरि,तपाईंको भाईसँग भेटें ।हिजोआज राष्ट्र बैंक्मा काम् गर्दो रहेछ ।

७. उस्ले भारत्मा काम गर्दा गर्दै धेरै पैसा कमायो होला ।मलाई पनि त्यहाँ जान मन् लाग्छ ।

८. उमेर छँदा म आफ्नो गाउँसम्म दुइ घण्टामा पुग्न सक्थें।अहिले बाटोमा हिंड्दा हिंड्दै मलाई आराम् गर्नुपर्छ। त्यसैले गर्दा हिजोआज तीन् घण्टा लाग्छ ।

९. उस्ले यो किताब् किन भन्दैमा,तिमीले किन्नुपर्थ्यो र?

१०. प्रधान्मन्त्रीको भाषण् सुन्दा सुन्दै म त भुसुक्कै निंदाएछु ।

19c

he set about building the house; there is a tradition that Manjushrī was the one who made the Nepal Valley; he just refuses to accept what his father says; of course, he must have known there would be a landslide; for that reason, I could not go; when he lived in London, he did a lot of work; one must not trust the word of a cunning man; it would have been better to go sooner; I advised him to study Nepali; we rented a small room; give me leave (to go) please; whether he works or not, he will pass the exam; he would not agree under any circumstances.

Lesson 20

Reading Passage

The 52nd birthday of His Majesty accomplished
with great pleasure

Throughout the Kingdom celebrations welcomed with devotion

Staff Reporter: Kathmandu, Jyestha 30

On the auspicious occasion of the Leader of the State, His Majesty King Mahendra's completing his 51st year and entering his 52nd year, today, throughout the Kingdom of Nepal, his Majesty's birthday was celebrated with special respect and sentiments of devotion in a number of different arranged programmes.

On this joyful day, loyal Nepalis, living near and far in different parts of the entire country, along with wishes of long life and good health to King Mahendra, garlanded his Majesty's picture and greeted it.

This morning, at the crack of dawn, the Royal Army sounded the reveille from the Bhīmsen tower and gave voice to the heart-felt happiness of the birthday.

According to RSS, on the occasion of His Majesty's 52nd birthday, this afternoon, on the royal military platform, in the course of a special celebration, His Majesty's picture was garlanded and bunches of flowers were offered.

On that occasion, along with the offering of a royal salute, in honour of His Majesty, a 31 gun salute was also fired.

On that occasion, 52 white doves were also released. In addition, letters of greeting and gifts, prepared in honour of His Majesty's 52nd birthday, were sent to the Narayanhiti Palace to be offered to His Majesty the King.

On that occasion, the Prime Minister, Mr. Kīrtinidhi Bista, the Chief Justice, Mr. Ratnabahādur Bista, the ministers, the chairman of the celebrations committee, Mr. Rangnāth Sharmā, members of the Rājsabhā standing committee and the State Panchayat, civilians and military, and high ranking civil servants of the guard, garlanded His Majesty's picture and offered bunches of flowers.

At the same time, in front of the royal military platform, members of the panchayat and class organisation, students, scouts and men and women gathered to offer greetings to His Majesty.

Reading Passage 2

A wedding

Subbā Kaṭak Bahādur married a 14-year-old girl and brought her home.

This is all there is to say, and someone who does not know Kaṭak Bahādur, does not even want to hear much more than this. But as soon as you tell me she is 14 years old, I get a desire to know about the girl. Subbā Katak Bahādur will certainly be getting on. I never saw Subbā when he was young. This is probably his second marriage. He probably has a couple of children from his first wife, and after her death, he must have decided to marry a 14-year-old girl. What does it matter to Kaṭak Bahādur? A man who has already become clever and experienced in the field of marriage, pushing his pen all day and playing around and joking with his mates in the office – it is very probable that he started thinking about the 14-year-old Harimati. But as for Harimati, only just 14, at an age when she could not understand the meaning of marriage and when she had just begun to sense (the idea of) marriage, Harimati's case is quite different.

I have seen one wedding. I was on the side of the groom's guests. We were invited for four o'clock, but the procession did not come out before seven. We were all sitting outside, occupied with getting the procession out, but the bridegroom delayed. We heard that he was getting himself dressed up. Thinking that you only get one chance to dress up, on the occasion of a wedding, we stayed silent and were waiting for him. I had not seen the groom (and did not know) what he would look like. The women of the village had also come and were standing there. They were also watching to see how the groom would be, so we heard. As soon as anyone says 'bridegroom' you start to imagine a young man of 20 to 22 years old, and these village ladies, imagining such a bridegroom as this, were probably standing there to watch. After a long time, there was a commotion near the door. Calling out 'The bridegroom's come, the bridegroom's come', all of them started to tumble in that direction, but I could not recognise which one was the groom. All the elderly men emerged from the door. Although I could not be absolutely certain, from the dress I reckoned that the one wearing the black coat must be the bridegroom. It went without saying it was him. He did not have to say how happy and joyful he was, his actions and speech were enough to make him seem the happiest man in the world.

The procession came out of the house on the dot of eight. The bridegroom got up onto his elephant, and we went on foot. As soon as I saw the bridegroom, I began to turn my attention towards the bride. If a 35 to 40-year-old bride also comes out of the door, all my enthusiasm will be for nothing. But what if a little 14-year-old steps out? I looked towards the bridegroom on that elephant, and I enquired of one gentleman, who was walking nearby,

'Is this the bridegroom's first marriage?'

'No,' he replied.

'What about the first bride then?'

'When she died, he took steps to marry again. He's got two sons from his first wife. Without a woman at home, the house couldn't be run. On top of that, since there was no one to look after the boys, he had to get married again.'

Having satisfied myself about the groom, I started to wonder about the bride. The bridegroom had to run his house and had to get someone to look after those little children, and so he got married. But how would the bride be who was coming to run the house and look after his little children? She'll certainly be getting on, otherwise, how will she run the house, how will she look after the children? I was also satisfied about the bride, and by the time I got to the bride's house, my enthusiasm began to return to me. I wholeheartedly joined in the singing and dancing and the excitement (going on) there, and as the bride was coming out, hurried off to the pavilion. The pavilion was surrounded by the village women. How must they have imagined the bride? Would they have imagined the bride as a 25 to 30-year-old, clever at managing the house work, able to run all the bridegroom's business? That's the kind of bride I imagined when, two or three women arrived in the pavilion, tugging and pushing a little girl covered from head to foot in red clothes. Here as well my imagination had deceived me. I removed myself from the merry-making going on there. I could not think how that 14-year-old, unripe girl could manage the groom's house and look after his children. I began to think about that girl – what sort of relationship will she have with the groom? What must she be starting to think now? And so on. After that I never had the courage to go to a wedding. Even now, I have no desire to see a marriage.

20a

1. His Majesty will make a tour of Western Nepal next month.
2. I shall continue to sit here and work till evening. When my work is finished, I'll come over to your place.
3. My little sister is at home. She is sewing clothes for the fair.
4. In the Terai, especially in the months of Jeth and Asār, it is extremely hot. Because of the harsh sun, the ground dries up. For that reason, dust keeps flying all over the place.
5. Oh, it is already nine o'clock. I must go, otherwise my wife will be angry.
6. The frontier of Nepal is like this: In the east, the river Mechī, in the west, the river Mahākālī, in the south, the plains of the Terai, in the north, the white mountains. The territory of Nepal in places, lies behind the Himalayas, and farther north than that, lies the area of Chinese Tibet.
7. One day, while wandering in the jungle, Bhanubhakta felt tired and happened to sit down in the shade of a tree. There, seeing a grasscutter cutting grass, he started to talk to him.
8. I have an awful headache. Go to the market and bring some medicine, will you?
9. The students are striking today as well. That's always happening in the universities these days, you know.
10. You seem to have a bit of trouble with your stomach. Keep taking the medicine until it gets better.
11. Rāme was looking to see if his sister was coming.
12. This coat is very thick, sir. Try it on, won't you?

20b

१. तपाईं पुस्तकालयमा के गरिरहनुभएको थियो? म नेपाल्को इतिहास्को विषयमा किताब् पढ़िरहेको थिएँ ।

२. हवाईजहाज् नपुगेसम्म/नपुगून्जेल्/हामी चियापसल्मा बसिरहनेछौं ।

३. हामी जोमसोम्तिर हिंड़्दाखेरि,हावा चलिरहेको थियो र धेरै पानी परिरहेको थियो ।

४. पसलेले देखाएको कोट् मैले लाइहेरें,तर धेरै नै ठूलो भएकोले, मैले किनिनँ।

५ पेट् गड्बड् भयो भने डाक्टरकहाँ जानुहोस् ।वहाँ औषधि लेखिदिनुहुन्छ ।

६. छ बजिसक्यो ।मलाई त जानुपर्‍यो । प्रधान्‌ज्यू नआउनुभएसम्म तपाईलाई यहाँ पर्खनुपर्छ ।

७. फाल्‌गुन एक् गते श्री ५ महाराजाधिराज् भारत् सवारी होइबक्सिनेछ ।

८. गोर्‌खापत्रका कार्यालय-प्रतिनिधि हिजो राति रेडियोमा बोल्दै हुनुहुन्थ्यो/बोलिरहनुभएको थियो/वहाँले के भन्नुभएको तपाईंले सुन्नुभयो?

९. के गरिरहेछौ त? म यस् नेपाली चिठीको अनुवाद् अंग्रेजीमा गर्ने कोशिश् गरिरहेको छु ।मेरो साथीले छुट्टयाएर लेखेको भए त हुन्थ्यो ।

१०. गाँउका आइमाईहरू दुलही कस्तो होली भनेर घर्‌नेर उभिरहेका थिए ।

११. घर्‌मा छोराहरूलाई हेरिदिने कोही नहुँदा,उस्‌ले अर्को बिहा गर्नुपरेको थियो ।

१२. केटी तलदेखि माथिसम्म पहेंलो लुगाले छोपिएकी थिई ।

20c

जाने हो; पुग्ने भेट्‌न ; उठेर: पायौ छु; गर्ने साध्यो; पर्ना पुग्यौं;
आए; गाएको; भए माग्दैन; रहोस्

20d

whatever happens, we just must arrive today; as usual, the bus came late; I could not go there on foot; it will certainly rain today; my friend was gravely ill; because of the rain, I could not go out; just because he told you to go there, did you have to go?; why, he even goes into that hotel; on the day of Shrī Panchamī, a fair takes place in the temple of Sarasvatī; he set about studying Nepali.

NEPALI-ENGLISH VOCABULARY

अ

अँ	yes
अँध्यारो	darkness
अँध्यारो भयो	it is dark
अँहँ	no
अंग	limb (see अङ्ग)
अंग्रेज	Englishman
अंग्रेजी	English (language)
अकल्	intelligence (see अक्कल्)
अक्सर (अक्सर्)	frequently
अकस्मात्	suddenly
अक्कल्	intelligence
अक्षर्	letter of the alphabet
अख्बार्	newspaper
अगाडि	before, in front of
जानुभन्दा अगाडि	before going
अग्लो	high
अघि	before, ago
दुइ हप्ता अघि	two weeks ago
अघि जानु	to go on, proceed
अङ्ग	limb, member
अङ्ग्रेज	see अंग्रेज
अङ्ग्रेजी	see अंग्रेजी
अचम्म	surprise
अचम्म मान्नु	to be surprised
अचानक्	suddenly

अचेल्	nowadays
अच्छा	very well, I see, O.K.
अञ्चल्	(administrative) district
अञ्जुलि	cupped hands
अझ	yet, still
अझै	yet (emph. of अझ)
अड्डा	office, (bus) station
अढाई	two and a half
अति	very, too much
अतिनै	extremely
अत्यन्त	very, extremely
अथवा	or, otherwise
अदृश्य	invisible, unseen
अधिक्	much, many, very
अधिक्तम्	maximum
अधिकार्	right, authority
अधिराज्य	kingdom, the Kingdom of Nepal
अध्यक्ष	chairman, leader
अध्यक्षता	chairmanship
अध्यापक्	teacher, lecturer
अनि	and, and then, and so
अनुभव	feeling, experience
अनुवाद्	translation
(-को) अनुवाद् गर्नु	to translate
अनुसन्धान्	research
अनुसरण् गर्नु	to follow
(को) अनुसार्	according to
अनुस्वार्	**anusvār**, the sign of nasalisation
अनुहार्	face, countenance
अनेक्	much, many
अनेकौं	many, several
अनौठो	strange, unique
अन्त	end, finish
अन्तमा	at last, in the end
अन्तर्	difference
अन्तर्राष्ट्रीय	international
अन्तिम्	last, final
अन्दाजी	roughly, at a guess
अन्नपूर्णा	Annapurna
अपरान्ह	afternoon
अप्ठ्यारो	difficult, awkward
अफसोच्	sorrow
अफसोच्को कुरा हो	it's a pity

अफ्सोच् मान्नु	to feel sorry, regret
अफ्सोस्	see अफ्सोच
अब	from now on, now
अबदेखि	from now on
अबेर्	late(ness)
अबेर् भयो	it's late
अबेर् लगाउनु	to delay
अबेला	late, untimely
अबेलासम्म	till late
अभाग्यले	unfortunately
अभिनन्दन	greeting, welcome
अभ्यास्	practice
अभ्यास् गर्नु	to practise
अमेरिका	America
अमेरिकाली	American
अरुणोदय	dawn
अरू	other (of several), else, more
अरू के?	what else?
अरू चिया	more tea
अरूहरू	others, other people
अर्को	other (of two), next, another
अर्को हप्ता	next week
अर्थ	meaning, economy
अर्थ व्यवस्था	economy
अलग्ग	separate(ly)
अलग्ग गर्नु	to separate, to sort out
अल्मल् गर्नु	to wait around, delay
अलि	a little bit, rather
अलिकति	a little, some
अल्छी गर्नु	to be lazy, waste time
अवश्य	certainly
अवसर्	period, occasion, time
त्यस् अवसरमा	on that occasion
अवस्था	state, condition
अवाज्	voice (see आवाज्)
असजिलो	difficult, not easy
असल्	good, of good quality
असल् मान्छे	a good man
असाध्य, असाध्यै	very, extremely
अस्ताउनु	to set (of the sun)
अस्ति	the day before yesterday
अस्पताल्	hospital
अहँ	no

अहँकार्	boasting
अहिले	now
अहिल्यै	emph. of अहिले
अह्राउनु	to order, command

आ

आँखा	eye
आँखा नदेख्ने	blind
आँप्	mango
आँसु	tear
आँसु झार्नु	to shed tears
आइत्बार्	Sunday
आइपुग्नु	to arrive
आइलाग्नु	to attack
आइमाई	woman
आउँदो	next
आउँदो महीना	next month
आउनु	to come
आउने	next
आउने हप्ता	next week
आकार्	shape
आकाश्	sky
आक्रमण्	attack
आक्रमण् गर्नु	to attack
आखिरी	last, the end (of a month)
आगो	fire
आगो ताप्नु	to warm oneself by a fire
आगो लाग्नु	to catch fire
आचार्य	Acharya (a Brahmin name)
आज	today
आज्कल्, आज्काल्	nowadays
आजभोलि	nowadays
आजा	worship
आदि	et cetera, and so on
आदेश्	command, order
आधा	half
आधुनिक्	modern
आनन्द	joy
आनन्दपूर्वक्	joyfully
आफुस्मा	together, amongst oneselves
आफू, आफै	self, one's self, by one's self
आफ्नो	one's own (reflexive pronominal adj.)

आमा	mother
आयोजना	plan
आरम्भ	beginning
आराम्	rest, ease
आरामै	restfully, slowly
आराम् गर्नु	to rest
आरोग्य	healthy, free from disease
आलु	potato
आवाज्	voice
आशा	hope
आशा गर्नु	to hope
आस्	see आशा
आस्था	faith, devotion

इ

इच्छा	wish, desire
इतिहास्	history
इत्यादि	et cetera
इनार्	a well
इन्, इनी	see यिन्, यिनी
इनीहरू	see यिनीहरू
इष्टमित्र	friends and relations

ई

ई	see यी
ई	oh, I see
ईश्वर्	God
ईसवी	Christian, Christian era
ईसा	Jesus

उ

उ	he, she
उँग्	drowsiness
उँग लाग्नु	to feel drowsy
उँचाई	height, altitude
उखान्	proverb
उकालो	steep
उच्च-पदस्थ	high ranking
उच्चारण्	pronunciation
उठ्नु	to rise, get up

उठाउनु	to lift
उड्नु	to fly
उड़ाउनु	to make fly
उता	there, in that direction
उतापट्टि	over there
उत्तर्	north
उत्तर	answer
उत्पति	rise, origin, source
उत्पन्न हुनु	to rise (of rivers)
उत्साह्	enthusiasm, joy
उदेक्	surprise
उदेश्	desire
उद्योग्	industry
उनी	he, she
उपत्यका	valley
उपमहाद्वीप्	subcontinent
-को उपलक्ष्यमा	in honour of
उपहार्	gift
उपाय	means, way
उभिनु	to stand
उमाल्नु	to boil (trans.)
उमालेको पानी	boiled water
उमेर्	age
उम्लनु	to boil (intrans.)
उल्लास्	joy, pleasure
उल्लास्मय	joyful
उसिन्नु	to boil (food)
उसिनेको फुल्	boiled egg
उस्तो	such, like that
उहाँ	see वहाँ

ऊ

ऊ त्यहाँ	over there
ऊ माथि	up there
ऊँट्	camel
ऊन्	wool
ऊनी	woollen

ऋ

ऋण्	debt
ऋतु	weather

ए

ए	eh, oh
एक्	one, a
एउटा	one
एक्जना	one (person)
एक् दम् एक्दम्	absolutely
एक् न एक्	one or other
एक्कासी	suddenly
एक्लो	alone
एक्लै	emph. of एक्लो
एशिया	Asia एक्लो
एस्तो	see यस्तो

ऐ

ऐन्	constitution
ऐना	mirror
ऐले	see अहिले
ऐश्	pleasure, enjoyment

ओ

ओइरिनु	fall forward, rush forward
ओखती	medicine, drug
ओछ्यान्	bedding
ओढ्नु	to wrap around, cover
ओढ्ने	a wrap, quilt
ओर्लनु	to descend, come down
ओस्	dew
ओहो	oh, aha
ओहोर् दोहोर् गर्नु	to come and go, make a round trip

औ

औ	and, so
औंलो	finger
औद्योगिक्	industrial
औलो	malaria
औषधालय	druggist's, chemist's shop
औषधि	medicine
औषधि लेखिदिनु	to write a prescription

क

कक्षा	class (in school)
कड़ोर्	crore, 10,000,000
कता	to where?
कति	how much, how many?
कति टाढ़ा?	how far?
कति पर्छ?	how much does it cost?
कतै	somewhere, (neg.) nowhere
कत्रो?	how big?
कथा	story
कथा हाल्नु	to tell a story
कदापि	ever
कप्	cup
कप्ड़ा	cloth
कपाल्	hair, head
कपाल् दुख्नु	to have a headache
कफी	coffee
कम्	less, a little
कमल्	lotus
कम्सेकम्	at least
कमाई	earnings
कमाउनु	to earn, to make one's name
कम्ती	less, a little
कम्पनी	company, Indian rupees
करीब्	almost, approximately
करोड्	a hundred **lākhs**, 10,000,000
कर्मचारी	civil servant
कलम्	pen
कला	art
कलाकार्	artist
कलिलो	slender, young, tender
कलेज्	college
कल्पना	imagination
कल्पना गर्नु	to imagine
कवि	poet
कविता	poetry
कसरी	how? in what manner?
कसो	how? in what manner?
कस्तो	what sort of? how?
कहाँ	where?
-कहाँ	at the house of
कहिले	when, ever
कहिले कहीं	sometimes

कहिल्यै	emph. of कहिले
कहीं	somewhere, anywhere
का	obl. and pl. of को
काका	paternal (younger) uncle
काकी	wife of काका
काख्	lap, side
कागत्	paper
काट्नु	to cut
काठ्माडौं	Kathmandu
कात्नु	to thread
कान्	ear
कान्छो	youngest (in a family)
कान्तिपूर	Kantipur, Kathmandu
काम्	work, employment
काम् गर्नु	to work
कामना	good wishes, congratulations
कारण्	reason
त्यस् कारण्	for that reason
कार्यरूप्मा ल्याउनु	to put into practice
काल्	period, age, time
कालिम्पोङ्ग	Kalimpong
कालो	black
काष्ठमण्डप्	'the wooden pavilion', Kathmandu
कि	(i) or (ii) interrogative particle (iii) that (in reported speech)
किताब्	book
किन	why?
किनकि	because
किनभने	because
किन्मेल् गर्नु	to go shopping
किन्नु	to buy
किलो	kilo(gram)
किलोमीटर्	kilometre
किसान्	peasant, farmer
किसिम्	sort, kind
कुन् किसिम्को	of what kind?
कुकुर्	dog
कुखुरा	chicken
कुन्	which?
कुन्चाहिं	which one?
कुन्नि	I don't know
कुरा	thing, something said, speech

कुरा गर्नु	to converse
कुराकानी	conversation
कुर्सी	chair
कुल्चनु	to trample, knock over
कुर्नु	to wait for
कृपा	kindness
कृपादृष्टि राख्नु	to look kindly on
कृषि	agriculture
कृष्ण-पक्ष	the dark half of the lunar month
के?	what?
केको?	of what, what for?
केटा	boy
केटाकेटी	children, childhood
केटी	girl
केन्द्र	centre
केन्द्रीय	central
केवल्	only
केही	something, anything
केही छैन	it does not matter
कैयन्	several
को	who?
-को (-की, -का)	of
कोट्	coat
कोठा	room
कोशिश्	attempt
कोशश् गर्नु	to try
कोस्	**kos** (distance of approx. 2 miles)
कोसेली	present, gift
कोही	someone (neg.) no one
कोहीकोही	some people
क्या?	what?
क्यारे	why? what do you think?
क्लास्	class
क्षत्रिय	Kshatriya (see छेत्री)
क्षमा	forgiveness
क्षेत्र	field (of study, etc.), aspect

ख

खड़ा हुनु	to stand up
खतम्	end, finish
खतम् गर्नु	to finish
खतम् हुनु	to be finished

खबर्	news
खबर आउनु	news to come, to be reported
खराब्	bad, spoilt
खर्च	expense
खर्च गर्नु	to spend
खर्च लाग्नु	to cost
जान कति खर्च लाग्छ?	how much does it cost to go?
खल्बल् गर्नु	to make a fuss, noise
खल्ती	pocket
खस् कुरा	Khas Kura (a form of the Nepali language)
खसम्	husband
खसाल्नु	to drop, to post
खस्नु	to fall
खाना	food
खानु	to eat
खाने कुरा	food-stuff
खाली	empty, only
खाली मात्रै	only
खाल्डो	valley
खास्	special
खास् गरेर	especially
खिंच्नु	to draw, to take a photo
खुकुरी	**khukuri** (a Nepalese knife)
खुट्टा	leg
खुम्बु	Khumbu
खुला	open
खुल्नु	to be opened, to come open
खुवाउनु	to feed
खुशी (खुसी)	happy, happiness
मलाई खुशी भयो	I am glad
खुसी	see खुशी
खूब् (खूप्)	well, very, extremely
खूबै	emph. of खूब
खेत्	field (cultivated)
खेतीकमाई	farming, agriculture
खेर जानु	to be wasted
-खेरि	while (particle added to imperf. part.)
खेल्	game
खेल्नु	to play
खै	well, why, so
खोइ	where is? where are you?
खोज्नु	to search for, to try
खोला	stream, river

खोलिनु	to be opened
खोल्नु	to open
ख्याति	fame, renown

ग

गंगा	Ganges
गएको	past, last
गएको हप्ता	last week
गज्	yard
गड्बड्	confusion, confused, upset
गणतन्त्र	republic
गत	last
गत वर्ष	last year
गते	date (of Vikram era only)
चार् गते	the fourth (of the month)
गन्नु	to count
गम्नु	to ponder, reflect
गरम्	see गर्म
गरीब्	poor, indigent
गरीबी	poverty
-ले गर्दा	because of
गर्नु	to do
गर्म	hot
गर्मी	heat, hot season
गलैंचा	carpet
गहिरो	deep
गहुँ	wheat
गह्रुँगो	heavy
गाई	cow
गाईको मासु	beef
गाउँ	village
गाउँले	villager
गाउनु	to sing
गाड़ी	cart, car, train
गान्	song
गार्ड्	guard
गाली	oath, abuse
गाली गर्नु	to swear, abuse
गाह्रो	difficult
गिरि	mountain
गीत्	song
गुच्छ	bunch (of flowers)
गुप्त	hidden

गुफा	cave
गुरु	guru, teacher
गुलियो	sweet, sugary
गुह्य	dark, obscure
गृहकृत्य	housework
गोचर्	cow-pasture, air-field
गोप्य	obscure, hidden
गोरु	bull
ग्रामीण्	rustic, vulgar

घ

घट्ना	event, accident
घट्नु	to become less, decrease
घटाउनु	to make less, bring down (a price)
घटीमा	at least
घण्टा	hour, bell
घण्टा-घर्	clock tower
घर्	house, home, building
घर्-बार्	family, household
घर्-बार् बसाल्नु	to start a family, set up house
घरै	at home
घाँस्	grass
घाँसी	grass-cutter
घाम्	sunshine
घाम् लाग्नु	to be sunny
घस्नु	to drag, push
घुइँचो	crowd
घुम्-फिर्	travelling, strolling
घुमाउनु	to take for a walk
घुम्नु	to travel, stroll
घेरिनु	to be surrounded
घेर्नु	to surround
घोड़ा	horse
घोड़ा चढ्नु	to ride/mount a horse
घोषणा	announcement

च

चकित्	surprised
चढ्नु	to mount, go up, ride (a horse)
चढ़ाउनु	to offer up
चमेना	cold meal, snack
चम्चा	spoon, spoonful
चरो	bird

चर्को	harsh, severe
चर्नु	to graze
चलन्	use, custom
चलाउनु	to make move, drive, operate
चल्नु	to move, run (of machinery)
चश्मा	spectacles
चाँड़ो	quick, fast
चाँड़ै	quickly, soon
चाँद्	moon
चाख्लाग्दो	interesting, tasty
चाख्नु	to taste
चामल्	rice (in grain)
चालाक्	clever, cunning
चालु	operating, running
चाहनु	to want, wish
चाहिनु	to be wanted, required
-चाहिं	(particle) -one, as for,
मचाहिं	as for me
राम्रोचाहिं	the good one
चिठी	letter
चित्त	heart, mind, feelings
चित्त दुखाउनु	to hurt the feelings
चित्त बुझाउनु	to console, satisfy
चित्र	picture
चिनी	sugar
चिन्ता	anxiety, worry, care
चिन्नु	to know, be acquainted with
चिप्लनु	to slip
चिप्लो	slippery
चिर्नु	to tear, split
चिया	tea
चियापसल्	teashop
चिसो	cold, damp
चीज्	thing, object
चीन्	China
चीनिया	Chinese
चुचुरो	peak (of mountain)
चुप्प लाग्नु	to be silent, shut up
चुरोट्	cigarette
चुरोट् खानु	to smoke
चोक्	square (in a city)
चोटी	time, occasion
चोर्	thief

छ

छ,छैन	is, is not (see हुनु)
छहारी	shade
छाड्नु	to abandon, leave
छाता	umbrella
छाती	breast, chest
छाना	roof
छापा	newspaper
छाप्नु	to print
छिटो	quick, quickly
छिन्	moment
एक् छिन्	just a moment, in a moment
छिमेकी	neighbour
छुट्टयाउनु	to separate
छुट्टी	holiday, leave
छेउ	side, vicinity
छेत्री	Chetri
छोटो	short
छोड्नु	to give up, leave
छोरा	boy
छोराछोरी	children, sons and daughters
छोरी	girl
छोपिनु	to be covered

ज

जंगी	military
जँचाउनु	to examine
जग्गा	land, landed property
जङ्गल्	jungle
जतन्	care, carefulness
जतन् गरेर	carefully
जता	wherever
जता ततै	here and there, everywhere
जति	however much, approximately
जत्रो	however big
जनता	people, populace
-जना	numeral classifier denoting human beings
जन्म	birth
जन्म हुनु	to be born
जन्मस्थल्	birth-place
जन्मनु, जन्मिनु	to be born
जब	whenever

जबसम्म	until the time that, as long as
जमीन्	land (for agriculture)
जमुना	Jamuna (river)
जम्मा	in all, altogether
जय्	long live
जरूरै	certainly
जरो (ज्वर्)	fever
जल्	water
जल्पान्	snack, breakfast
जल्-वायु	climate
जवान्	young, young man, private soldier
जवाफ्	answer
जस्तो	as, in the way which, like
जहाँ	where, wherever
जहान्	wife, family
जहिले	whenever
जहिले पनि	at any time
जाँच्	examination
जागीर्	official employment
जागीर् खानु	to be employed
जाड़ो	the cold, cold season
जाड़ो लाग्नु	to feel cold
जात्, जाति	caste
जात्रा (यात्रा)	procession
जान्कारी	information
जानु	to go
जान्नु	to know (a fact)
जापान्	Japan
जिउँदो	alive
जिउनु	to be alive
जिन्दगी	life
जिभ्रो	tongue
जिल्ला	district
-जी	see ज्यू
जिउ	body
जीवन्	life, way of life
जीविका	livelihood
जीविका चलाउनु	to exist, lead one's life
जुत्ता	shoe
जुन्	that which, whichever
जुनाफ्	presence
जूवा खेल्नु	to gamble
जे	whatever

जेठो eldest (of the family)
-जेल् as long as, until
जेल jail
जो who, whoever
जोई wife
जोगी jogi, religious ascetic
जोड्नु to join, link
जोर् pair
एक् जोर् जुत्ता a pair of shoes
जौ barley
ज्ञान् knowledge
ज्ञानी wise, good
ज्यादा more, much, very
ज्यापू peasant
ज्यू suffix added to a name denoting respect. Mr., sir
ज्योति light, gleam
ज्योतिषी astrologer
ज्वर् fever

झ

झगड़ा fight, battle
झण्डा flag
झण्डै almost
झरी shower
झर्नु to come down, descend
झाँट्नु to scold
झार्नु to shed (tears)
झिक्नु to pull out, take out
झीङ्गो a fly
झैं like, as
झ्याल् window

ट

टक्र्याउनु bestow, offer up, sound (a reveille)
टाउको head
टाकुरो top (of a hill)
टाढ़ा far
टिकट् ticket
टुक्रा piece, bit
टुप्पा summit
टेबुल् table
टोक्नु to bite (of an animal)

टोपी	hat
ट्याक्सी	taxi
ट्वालट्वाल्ती हेर्नु	to stare at

ठ

ठट्टा	joke
ठम्याउनु	to decide, ascertain
ठण्डा	cold
ठाउँ	place
ठाउँठाउँमा	in places
ठान्नु	to decide, imagine
ठीक्	all right, well, exactly
ठीक् चार् बजे	at four o'clock precisely
ठूलो	big, elder
ठेगाना	address, place of residence
ठेल्नु	to drag

ड

डर्	fear
डराउनु	to fear, be afraid
डाँक्	post, mail
डाँड़ो	ridge
डाक्टर्	doctor
डाक्नु	to summon, send for
डाम्	mark, stain, insect bite
डुब्नु	to sink
डुल्नु	to walk, stroll
डेढ़	one and a half
डोको	basket
ड्राइभर्	driver

ढ

ढाँकिनु	to be covered
ढाँट्नु	to tell lies
ढाइ	two and a half
ढाका	Dacca
ढीलो	late
ढीलो आउनु	to arrive late
ढुँगा	stone, pebble
ढोका	door
ढोग्नु	to greet, reverence

त

त	however, but, even
तँ	2 sing. pron. 'you'
तट्	bank (of river), level (of sea)
तथा	and
तपस्वी	religious ascetic
तपाईं	HGH 2 pers. pron. 'you'
तब	then, from then on
तबसम्म	up to that time
तयार्	ready
तर	but
तरकारी	vegetables
तराई	Terai
तरीका	way, method
तर्नु	to cross (a river)
तल	below, under
तलब्	wages
तला	storey, floor
तल्लो	lower
तस्वीर्	picture, photograph
तहिले	then, at that time
ताका	time, occasion
ताजा	fresh
तातो	warm, hot
तान्नु	to pull, tighten
तापनि	although, even so
तापक्रम्	temperature
ताप्नु	to warm oneself
तारा	star
तारीख्	date (of Christian calendar)
तारीफ्	praise
तालीम्	education
ताश्	cards (game)
तिनी	MGH 3 sing. pron. 'he', 'she'
तिब्बत्	Tibet
तिमी	MGH 2 pers. pron. 'you'
-तिर	towards, approximately
तिर्खा	thirst
तिर्खा लाग्नु	to feel thirsty
तिर्नु	to pay, hand over (money)
ती	pl. of त्यो
तीर्थ	pilgrimage

तुल्याउनु	to cause to be, make into
तेर्सिनु	to be scattered
तेल्	oil
तोप्	cannon
त्यता	in that direction
त्यति	so much, so
त्यतिको	so much, that much
त्यत्रो	that big
त्यसरी	in that manner
त्यसैले	therefore
त्यसो	thus
त्यसो भए	in that case
त्यस्तो	in that manner
त्यहाँ	there
त्यो	that, he, she, it
त्रिशूल्	trident

थ

थकाई	tiredness
थकाई लाग्नु	to feel tired
थरी	sect
थामिनु	to be stopped, to cease
थाम्नु	to stop
थाल्नु	to begin
थाहा पाउनु	to find out
थाहा हुनु	to know
मलाई थाहा छैन	I don't know
थुन्नु	to shut
थुप्रो	heap, quantity
थुप्रै	loads of, many
थोक्	thing, matter
थोरै	a few, a little

द

दक्षिण्	south
दगुराउनु	to make run
दगुर्नु	to run
दण्डवत्	respectful salutation
एक् दम्	absolutely
दया	pity, compassion
दर्बार्	court, palace
दर्शन्	seeing, meeting, visiting (a shrine, etc.)

दशा	plight
दह	pit, hole
दही	curd
दाँजो	comparison
दाँज्नु	to compare
दाँत्	tooth
दाइ	elder brother
दाउरा	firewood
दाज्यू	elder brother
दाम्	money, price
दाल्	lentils
दावी गर्नु	to claim
दिउँसो	afternoon
दिक्क	worry, trouble
दिक्क मान्नु	to be worried
दिदी	elder sister
दिन्	day
दिन्‌दिनै	every day
दिनहुँ	daily
दिनु	to give, allow
दिल्ली	Delhi
दिवस्	day, a special day
दिशा	direction
दिसा	dysentery
दीर्घायु	long life
दुःख	pain, grief
दुःखद्	painful
दुःखी	pained, grief-stricken
दुखाउनु	to hurt, give pain to
दुख्नु	to ache, pain
दुनियाँ	world
दुर्दशा	accident
दुलहा	bridegroom
दुलही	bride
दुवै	both
दुष्ट	wicked
दुहुनु	to milk
दूध्	milk
दृष्टि	sight, view
दृष्टिकोण्	point of view
देखाइनु	to be shown
देखाउनु	to show
-देखि	from, since

देखिनु	to be seen, appear
देख्नु	to see
देवता (देउता)	a god
देवल्	temple
देवस्थल्	temple
देवी	goddess
देश्	country
दैनिक्	daily
दोष्	blame
दोस्रो	second
दोहोत्याउनु	to repeat
द्वारा	by means of
द्वीप्	island

ध

धन्	riches
धनी	rich
धन्यवाद्	thank you
धर्म	duty, religion
धर्मबीरु	religious devotee
धाउनु	to run to and fro
धागो	thread
धातु	metal
धान्	paddy
धारा	stream, fountain, washing place
धार्मिक्	religious, pertaining to religion
धावा	battle, war
धुनु	to wash (things)
धूलो	dust
धूर्मपान्	smoking
धूर्त	cunning
धेरै	much, many
धेरैजसो	often, usually
धोका	deception
धोका दिनु	to deceive
धोबी	washerman
ध्यान्	attention, concentration
ध्वनित् गर्नु	to sound, make sound

न

न -	negative particle
न...न	neither . . . nor

नक्शा map
नगर् city
नजीक् near, nearby
नत्र otherwise
नदी river
नमस्कार् a greeting: 'hello', 'goodbye'
नमस्ते see (नमस्कार्)
नम्र polite, coaxing
नयाँ new
नर-नारी men and women
नराम्रो bad
नराम्रोसित badly
नवरात्रि Navaratri (Hindu festival)
नाउँ name
नाउँ गरेको by name, called
नाक् nose
नाग् cobra, a Naga
नागरिक् citizen, pertaining to a city
नाच् dance
नाच्-गान् dancing and singing
नाच्नु to dance
नानी baby, child
नाटक् play, drama
नाथ् Lord, God, the saint, Gorakhnath
नाम् name (see नाउँ)
नामक् by name, called
नायक् leader
नाश् हुनु to be destroyed
नि particle: 'you know', 'what about'
निकाल्नु to take out, let out
निको good, healthy
निक्कै emph. of निको, well, very good, very
निगम् corporation, company
निजामती civil
निदाउनु to fall asleep
निद्रा sleep
निद्रा लाग्नु to feel sleepy
निधो गर्नु to decide
निपुण् clever, expert
-को निमित्त for the sake of
को निम्ति for the sake of
निम्तो, निम्ता invitation
-निर see -नेर

निराश्	disappointed
निराशा	disappointment
निवेदन्	request
निश्चय	certainty
मलाई निश्चय छैन	I am not certain
निश्चय नै	certainly
निश्चिन्त	carefree, untroubled
निस्कनु	to come out
नीलो	blue
नुहाउनु	to bathe, have a bath
नून्	salt
नेपाल्	Nepal
नेपाली	Nepali
-नेर	near, nearby, next to
नेवारी	Newari
नै	only, just, indeed
नोकर्	servant
नोकर्नी	female servant
नोक्सान्	loss, damage
नौनी	butter
न्यानो	comfortable, warm
न्याय	justice
न्यायाधीश्	judge, a justice

प

पँखा	fan
पकाउनु	to cook
पक्का	certain, decided
पक्का गर्नु	to decide
पक्कै पनि	certainly
पक्षी	bird
पग्लनु	to melt
पच्छिम्	west, see पश्चिम्
पछि	behind, after
पछाड़ी	after, behind
पछिल्तिर	at the back of, behind
पछिल्लो	last, hindmost
पञ्चायत्	Panchayat
पटक्	time, turn
एक् पटक्	once
पहिलो पटक्	for the first time
-पट्टि	in the direction of

पढ़ाउनु	to cause to read, teach
पढ़नु	to read, study
पढ़े-लेखेको	literate
पण्डित्	pandit, scholar
पति	husband, master
पत्नी	wife, mistress
पत्र	letter
पत्रिका	magazine
पनि	also, even
परन्तु	but
परिर्वतन्	change, alteration
परिवार्	family
परिवार्-नियोजन्	family-planning
परिश्रम्	effort
परिश्रमी	hard working
परीक्षा	examination
परेवा	dove, pigeon
पर्खनु	to wait for
पर्नु	to fall, come about, be necessary, to have to, to cost
कति पर्छ?	how much does it cost?
पानी पर्छ	it is raining
पर्यटक्	tourist
पर्व	festival
पर्सी	the day after tomorrow
पल्टन्	army
पल्लो	the next, the farther
पशु	cattle, animal
पशुपतिनाथ्	Shiva, a temple in Kathmandu
पश्चिम्	west
पसल्	shop
पसले	shopkeeper
पस्नु	to enter
पहाड़्	hill, mountain, foothill
पहिरो	landslide
पहिला	first of all
पहिलो	first
पहिले	first of all, firstly
पहेंलो	yellow
पाइनु	to be found, be acquired
पाउनु	receive, get, find
पाउन्ड्	pound
पाकिस्तान्	Pakistan
पाक्नु	to be cooked

पागल्	mad
पाटन्	Patan
पाठ्	lesson
पानी	water, rain
पाप्	sin
पार्	across
पार् गर्नु	to cross
पार्नु	to cause to come about, to lay (eggs)
पाली	turn, time
पाल्नु	to look after, to enter, to come (hon.)
पाल्पा	Palpa
पाहुना	guest
पिउनु	to drink
पिट्नु	to beat, hit
पिठो	kind of rice cake
पिता	father
पितृ	ancestor
पिरो	hot (of food), spicy
पीठ्	the back
पुग् नपुग्	about, approximately
पुग्नु	to arrive, to suffice
पुजारी	worshipper
पुच्छर्	tail
पुणीत्	holy, auspicious
पुरानो	old, ancient
पुरिया	packet
पुर्‍याउनु	to cause to arrive, to fulfil
पुष्प-गुच्छा	bunch of flowers
पुस्तक्	book
पुस्तकालय	library
पूजा	worship
पूजा-आजा	worship
पूजा गर्नु	to worship
पूरा	full, entire
पूर्ण	full, entire
पूर्ण गर्नु	to fulfil
पूर्व, पूर्ब	east
पृथ्वी	earth
पृथ्वीनारायण् शाह्	Prithvinarayan Shah
पेट्	stomach
पैदल्	on foot
पैसा	money, pice
पैरो, पैले	see पहिरो, पहिले

पो	on the contrary, indeed
पोइ	husband
पोको	parcel, bundle
पोखरा	Pokhara
पोखरी	lake, pond
पोखिन्	to be spilt
पोल्नु	to burn, scald
पोहोर् (साल्)	last year
पौड़ी खेल्नु	to swim
पौने	minus a quarter
पौने चार्	three and three quarters
प्यारो	darling, dear
प्रकार्	kind, sort
यस् प्रकार्ले	in this fashion, of this sort
प्रख्यात्	famed
प्रगति	advance, progress
प्रणाम्	respect
प्रति	towards, for
प्रतिदिन्	every day
प्रतिनिधि	representative
प्रतिस्थापन् गर्नु	to set up, establish
प्रतीक्षा	waiting
-को प्रतीक्षा गर्नु	to wait for
प्रथम्	first
प्रधान्	chief
प्रधान्मन्त्री	Prime Minister
प्रभाव्	effect
प्रमुख्	most important, chief
प्रयत्न	effort, trial
प्रयोग् गर्नु	to use
प्रवेश्	entry
प्रवेश् गर्नु	to enter
प्रशस्त	much, many
प्रश्न	question
प्रसन्न	happy, delighted
प्रसिद्ध	famous
प्राचीन्	ancient
प्राप्त हुनु	to be acquired
प्रायः	usually
प्रिय	dear (in letters)
प्रेम्	love

फ

फरक्	difference
फर्फराउनु	to flutter, wave
फर्कनु	to return, come back
फर्काउनु	to give back
फल्	fruit, result
फल्फुल्	fruit
फाइदा	advantage
फिक्री	worry, care
फिक्री गर्नु	to worry
फिर्ता	back
फिर्ता दिनु	to give back, give change
फुट्	foot (measure)
फुर्ती	elegance
फुर्तीसाथ्	elegantly
फुर्सत्, फुर्सद्	leisure, time
मलाई फुर्सत् छैन	I do not have the time
फुल्	egg
फूल्	flower
फेरा	time, occasion
फेरि	again, once more
फेल् हुनु	to fail
फेला पर्नु	to be found, acquired
फैस्ला	decision
फोन् गर्नु	to telephone
फोहर्	dirty
फौज्	army
फ्याँक्नु	to throw
फ्रान्स्	France
फ्रान्सीसी	French (language)

ब

(See also under व)

बंग्लादेश्	Bangladesh
बक्सनु	to bestow, auxiliary used in forming the 'royal honorific'
बखत्	time
बगैंचा, बघैंचा	garden
बग्नु	to flow
बङ्गाल्	Bengal
बचन् (वचन्)	word, speech
बजाउनु	to play (an instrument)

बजार्	market
...बजे	at . . . o'clock
बज्नु	to strike, to sound (of a bell, etc.)
बज्यै	grandmother
...बज्यो	it is . . . o'clock
बड़ो	great, big, very
बढ़ाउनु	to increase
बढ़ी, बढ़्ता	more, greater
बताउनु	to tell, relate
बत्ती	lamp, light
बन् (वन्)	forest, jungle
बनाउनु	to make, construct
बन्द	closed
बन्दूक्	gun
बन्दोबस्त	arrangements
बन्नु	to be made, become
बरु	moreover, otherwise
बर्खा	rain, rainy season
बर्ष (वर्ष)	year
बर्सात्	rainy season
बर्सादी	raincoat
बलवान्	strong
बलि	sacrifice
बल्ल-बल्ल	with difficulty, finally
बस्	bus
बस्-बसौनी	bus-stop
बसाल्नु	to set up, establish
बस्तु (वस्तु)	cattle, household effects
बस्नु	to sit, stay, reside
बहाल्	rent
बहाल्मा	rented
बहिनी	younger sister
बहुत्	much, very
बहुतै	emph. of बहुत्
बाँकी	left over, remaining
बाँड़नु	to distribute
बाँध्नु	to bind, tie up
बा	father
बा	ugh, particle expressing disgust
बाक्लो	thick, sturdy
बाजे	grandfather
-बाट	from, by
-को बाद्	after

बादल्	cloud
बानी	habit
बाबु	father, boy, child
-बारे	about, concerning
-को बारेमा	about, concerning
बालक्	boy, son
बालिका	girl
बाली-नाली	crops
बाल्नु	to burn, to switch on
बास्	lodging
बासी	stale, bad (of food)
बाहिर्	outside
बाहुन	Brahmin
बाहेक्	except
बिगार्नु	to spoil, break
बिग्रनु	to be spoilt, broken
बिचरा	poor, unfortunate
बिचार्	see विचार्
बिजुली	electricity, lightning
बिताउनु	to spend (time)
बित्तिकै	as soon as
बिदा	holiday, leave
बिदा दिन्	to give leave
बिना	without
बिन्ती	request
बिराट्नगर्, विराट्नगर्	Biratnagar
बिरामी	ill
बिरामी पर्नु	to fall ill
बिरालो	cat
बिर्सनु	to forget
बिस्कुट्	biscuit
बिस्तारै	slowly, quietly
बिहा (बिहे)	marriage
बिहान	morning
बिहार्	Bihar, see विहार्
बिहिबार्	Thursday
बीच्	middle, in the middle, among, between
-को बीच्मा	in the middle of
बीरगंज्	Birganj
बुझाउनु	to explain, to hand back, return
बुझ्नु	to understand
बुद्ध	Buddha
बुद्ध-धर्म	Buddhism

बुद्धिमान्	intelligent
बुधबार्	Wednesday
बुवा	father
बूढ़ी	old woman
बूढ़ो	old man
बेच्नु	to sell
बेला	time, period
बेलायत्	England
बेलुका	evening
बेर्	delay, lateness, time
अलि बेर्	for some time
बेरा	waiter
बेस्	good, fine
बोको	he-goat
बोक्नु	to carry
बोल्-चित्र	film, talky
बोलाई	dialect, spoken language
बोलाउनु	to call
बोल्नु	to speak, talk
ब्याँकक्	Bangkok
ब्रम्हपुत्र	Bramhaputra
ब्राह्मण्	Brahmin

भ

भइगयो (भैगो)	very well, let it pass
भइहाल्यो (भैहाल्यो)	very well, that's that
भक्त	devotee (of God)
भक्तजन्हरू	devotees
भक्तपूर्	Bhaktapur
भक्ति	devotion, worship
भग्वान्	God
भत्कनु	to be broken, demolished
भत्के-बिग्रेको	smashed, demolished
भनिठान्नु	to imagine, suppose
भने	if, saying that
-भन्दा	than, in comparison with
भन्नु	to say, to think
भन्ने	by name, however
भयो	see हुनु
-भर्	all through, all over
भर्सक्	as much as possible, probably
-भरि	all through, all over
भरिभराउ	full, crowded

भरिया	porter, carrier
भरे	this evening
भर्खर्	recently
भर्नु	to fill, draw (water)
भविष्य	future
भाँच्नु	to break
भाइ	younger brother
भाउ	(see भाव्)
भाग्	section, part
भाग्नु	to run away
भाग्यले	fortunately
भात्	boiled rice, dinner
भानुभक्त	Bhanubhakta (Nepali poet)
भारत्	India
भारतीय	Indian
भाव्	state, quality, price, rate
भाषण्	speech
भाषा	language
भासिनु	to sink down
भिक्षु	beggar, Buddhist monk
भिज्नु	to get wet
भित्र	inside, in
भिन्न	separate, various
भिरालो	steep
भीड्	crowd
भूईं भैं	ground, floor
भेग् र विश्व	near and far
भेट्	meeting
भेट्नु	to meet
भेला	crowd
भेला हुनु	to crowd around
भैंसी	female buffalo
भैरव	Bhairava, Shiva
भो	see हुनु
भोक्	hunger
भोक् लाग्नु	to feel hungry
भोज्, भोजन्	dinner, feast
भोट्	Tibet
भोटिया	Tibetan
भोलि	tomorrow
भोलिपल्ट	the next day
भ्याउनु	to reach, to manage to do, to fit
भ्रमण्	tour

म

म	I
मंच्	stage, platform
मङ्गल्वार्	Tuesday
मजदूर्	labourer
मजा	fun, pleasure
मञ्जुश्री	Manjushrī
मण्डप्	canopy, pavilion
मत्लब्	meaning
मदेस् (मदेश)	plains, the Terai
मद्दत् गर्नु	to help
मध्ये	in the middle of, among
मन्	heart, mind, feelings
मन् पर्नु	to like (something)
मन् लाग्नु	to like (to)
मन् गर्नु	to feel like
मनाई (मनाही)	forbidden
मनाउनु	to celebrate, to spend (holidays)
मनि	under, underneath (see मुनि)
मनोहर्	enchanting
मन्त्री	minister
मन्दिर्	temple
मर्नु	to die
मल्ल	Malla
मसिनो	soft, good quality
महँगो	expensive
महत्त्व	importance
महत्त्वपूर्ण	important
महन्त	high priest
महान्	great, huge
महाराजा	king, emperor
महाराजाधिराज्	His Majesty (title of King of Nepal)
महारानी	queen
महाविद्यालय	college
महीना	month
महेन्द्र	Mahendra
-मा	in, on, at
माइत,माइती	the home of the wife
माग्नु	to ask for, to beg
माग्ने	beggar
माछा	fish
माता	mother
मात्र	only

मात्रै	only (emph. of मात्र)
माथि	above, upon, over
माथिल्लो	upper
मान् गर्नु	to honour
मान्मनितो गर्नु	to honour, to treat well
मानिनु	to be admitted, to be celebrated
मानिस्	person, man
माने	meaning
मान्छे	man, person
मान्नु	to admit, agree
माफ् गर्नु	to forgive
माफ गर्नुहोला	excuse me, forgive me
माया	love, enchantment
मार्नु	to kill, murder
माल्	property, goods
माल्-ताल्	goods, things
माल-सामान्	luggage
माला	garland
माल्यार्पन्	garlanding
मासु	meat
माहिलो	second eldest child in the family
मिजासी	polite
मिठाई	a sweet
मित्र	friend
मिनेट्	minute
मीठो	good tasting
मील्	mile
मुख्	face, mouth
मुख्य	chief, important
मुटु	heart
-मुनि	under, underneath
मुलुक्	country, state
मुश्किल्	difficult
मुश्किल्ले	with difficulty
मुसुक्क हाँस्नु	to smile
मूर्ती	statue
मूल्-सड़क्	main road
मृत्यू	death
मेच्	chair
मेला	fair, spectacle
मेहनत्	effort, hard work
मेहनती	hard-working
मैदान्	(unploughed) field, ground, plain

मैलो — soiled, dirty
मोज् — enjoyment
मोटर् — motor-car
मोटो — fat
मोल् — price
मोहर् — a coin of 50 *paisa*
मौका — occasion, opportunity
मौसम् — weather, climate, season
मौसूफ् — honorific title applied to a member of the Nepalese Royal Family
म्वाई — kiss

य

यता — hither, in this direction
यता-उता — here and there
यति — so, so much
यतिको — so much, such
यत्रो — so big
यदि — if
यस् — oblique of यो
यसरी — in this manner
यसो, यसै — thus, in this manner
यस्तो — of this kind, like this
यहाँ — here, hon. 3rd pers. pron.
यहीं — in this very place
यही — this very one
यात्रा — journey
यात्रु — traveller
यिनी — MGH 3rd pers. pron.
यिनीहरू — they (LGH, MGH)
यी — these (pl. of यो)
युरोप — Europe
युवक् — young man
येती — Yeti
यो — this, LGH 3rd pers. pron.
योगी — yogī, Hindu ascetic
योग्य — worthy of
योजना — plan
यौटा — see एउटा

र

र — and, exclamation of surprise

रँग् (रङ्ग)	colour
रक्षक्	keeper, defender
रक्षा गर्नु	to keep
रक्सी	**raksī**, Nepalese spirit
रगत् (रक्त)	blood
रमाइलो	enjoyable, interesting
रमाइलो गर्नु	to have a good time, enjoy oneself
रहनु	to remain
रहर्	desire, great interest
रहेछ	it seems to be, it is
राँगो	male buffalo
राइफल्	rifle
राख्नु	to put, to place, to keep
राज्कुमार्	prince
राज्कुमारी	princess
राज्दूत्	ambassador
राज्दूतावास्	embassy
राजा	king
राज्धानी	capital
राज्य	kingdom, rule
राज्य गर्नु	to rule
राणा	Rana
रात्	night
राति	at night
रातो	red
रानी	queen
राम्ररी	nicely
राम्रो	good, beautiful, handsome
राष्ट्र	state, nation
राष्ट्र-नायक	'leader of the nation', King of Nepal
राष्ट्रपति	president
राहदानी	passport, permit (to travel)
रिक्शा	rickshaw
रिक्शावाला	rickshaw driver
रिस्	anger
रिसाउनु	to become angry
रुघा	a cold
रुघा लाग्नु	to have a cold
रुचि	appetite
रुनु	to cry, weep
रुपियाँ (रूपैयाँ)	rupee
रूख्	tree
रूप्	form, face, manner

रूस्	Russia
रूसी	Russian
रे	particle used to report speech
रेडियो	radio
रेल्	rail, train
रोकिनु	to be stopped
रोक्नु	to stop
रोटी	bread
रोप्नु	to plant (rice, etc.)

ल

ल	there, look
लगाउनु	to join, fix, connect
लग्नु	to take away
लड़ाईं	war, battle
लड्नु	to slip, to fight
लम्किनु	to hurry, stride out
लय्	tune, air
लाइहेर्नु	to try on (clothes)
-लाई	to, for
लाउनु	to attach, put on (clothes), to oblige to, to close (a door)
लाख्	one hundred thousand
-को लागि	to, for, for the sake of
लाग्नु	to be attached, to seem, to happen, to begin to
लाज्	shame
लाज् लाग्नु	to feel ashamed
लानु	to take away, to lead to
लामो	long
लाम्खुट्टे	mosquito
लिनु	to take, to buy
लिएर आउनु	to bring
लुगा	clothes
लुट्नु	to plunder, rob, loot
लेख्	article, essay
लेखक्	author
लेख्नु	to write
लेराउनु	see लिएर आउनु
लैजानु	to take away, to lead
लोक्-गीत्	folk-song
लोग्ने	man, husband
लोग्नेमान्छे	man, male

लोभ्	greed
लौ	there, there you are
ल्याउनु	to bring
ल्हासा	Lhasa

व

(See also under ब)

वंश	race, lineage
वंशावली	chronicle
वचन् (बचन्)	word, saying
-वटा	numerical classifier for things
वन्	forest
वर्पर्	around
वरिपरि	around, all around
वर्ग	class
वर्गीय	class (adj.)
वर्ष (बर्ष)	year
वर्षा	rain, rainy season
वस्तु	thing, property, cattle
वहाँ (उहाँ)	HGH 3rd pers. pron., there
वहीं (उहीं)	in that very place
वा	or
वायुयान्	aeroplane
वास्ता गर्नु	to care for
वाहन्	carriage, conveyance, motor car
विकास्	progress
विक्रम	Vikram
विक्रम-संवत्	Vikram Samvat era
विक्रमाब्द	the Vikram era
विचार् (बिचार्)	opinion
मेरो विचारले	in my opinion
विचार् गर्नु	to think about, to intend
विज्ञान्	science
विदेशी	foreigner
विद्यार्थी	student
विद्वान	scholar
विना (बिना)	without
विपत्ति	trouble
विभाग्	department
विभिन्न	different, various
विमान्	aeroplane
विमान्सेवा	air service

विमान्स्थल्	airport
विरक्त	detached, indifferent
विवरण्	account, description
विवाह	marriage
विशाल्	spacious
विशेष्	special
विशेष गरी	especially
विशेषता	speciality
विश्व	universe
विश्वविद्यालय	university
विश्वास्	trust, belief
विश्वास् लाग्नु	to believe in
विषय्	subject
-को विषयमा	on the subject of
विस्तार्	expansion, detail
विहार् (बिहार्)	a Buddhist monastery, Bihar
वीर् (बीर्)	hero, warrior
व्यक्ति	individual, a person
व्यर्थ	useless, vain
व्यर्थै	in vain
व्यवस्था	arrangements
व्यवहार्	transactions, behaviour
व्यापार् (बेपार्)	trade, business

श

शंका	doubt
मलाई शंका छ	I doubt
शताब्दी	century
शनिवार्	Saturday
शब्द	word
शब्दकोश्	dictionary
शरीर्	body
शहर्	town, city
शाखा	branch
शान्ति	peace
शामिल्	included, joining in
शायद्	perhaps
शाह	Shah (name of ruling dynasty of Nepal)
शाही	royal
शिकार्	hunting
शिकार् खेल्नु	to hunt
शिखर्	peak (of a mountain)
शिव	Shiva

शीतल्	cold, cool
शुक्रबार्	Friday
शुभ	auspicious
शुभजन्मोत्सव	birthday (hon.)
शुभनाम्	name (hon.)
शुरू	beginning
शुरू गर्नु	to begin
शुरूमा	in the beginning
शेर्पा	Sherpa
श्री	honorific title used before the names of Gods, Lord, Mr.
श्री पाँच्	title of the King of Nepal
श्रीमती	wife, Mrs.
श्लोक्	verse of a poem

स

संख्या	number
-सँग	with
सँगसँगै	all together
संगठन्	association, organisation
संपन्न	completed, performed
संबन्ध	connection
संभव्	possible
संभावना	possibility
संयुक्त	joined, conjunct
संयुक्त अक्षर्	conjunct character
संसार	world
संस्कृत्	Sanskrit
सकेकम्म...	as . . . as possible
सकेसम्म छिटो	as quickly as possible
सकिनु	to be possible, to be finished
सक्नु	to be able
सगर्माथा	Mount Everest
सङ्ख्या	see संख्या
सङ्ग	see सँग
सङ्गसङ्गै	see सँगसँगै
सङ्गठन्	see संगठन्
सजिनु	to be decorated
सजिलो	easy
सजिलोसित	easily
सञ्चर्बार्	Saturday
-को सट्टा	instead of

सड़क्	street, road
सताउनु	to vex, tease
सदस्य	member
सधैं (सँधै)	always
सन्चो	in good health
सन्चै	emph. of सन्चो
सन्तान	issue, offspring, children
सफर्	journey
सफल्	successful
सफल्ता	success
सफा	clean
सब्	all, whole
सबै (सप्पै)	emph. of सब्
सभा	council
समय्	time
समस्त	entire, all
समस्य	problem
समाउनु	to catch
समाचार्	news
समाचारपत्र	newspaper
समात्नु	to catch (hold of)
समाप्त हुनु	to be finished
समारोह्	celebrations
समिति	committee
समीप्	presence, nearness
समुद्र	sea
सम्झनु	to remember
सम्झाउनु	to remind
सम्बन्ध	see संबन्ध
-सम्म	up to, until, as far as
सम्मान् गर्नु	to honour
सय्	hundred
सर्कार्	government, title of King of Nepal
सर्कारी्	official
सर्नु	to move, shift (intr.)
सलाई	match
सलामी	greeting, salute
सल्लाह्	advice
सवा	plus a quarter
सवा तीन्	three and a quarter
सवारी	conveyance
सवारी होइबक्सनु	to go (royal hon.)
सवाल्	question
सवेरै	early

सस्तो	cheap
सस्तोमा	cheaply
सहर्	see शहर्
सहायता	aid
साँचो	true
साँचो	key
साँचै	really, truly
साँझ्	evening
साँझ सवेरै	evening and morning
साइकल्	cycle
सागर्	sea
साट्नु	to exchange
साढ़े	plus a half
साढ़े तीन्	three and a half
साथ्	with, along with, as soon as
साथ्साथै	all together
-को साथ्मा	in the company of
साथी	friend
साधारण्	usual, ordinary
साधारण्तय	usually
सान्	see सानो
सानो	small, young
सानोमा	in one's childhood
सापट् दिनुँ	to lend
साफ्	clean, clear
साबुन्	soap
सामान्	luggage
सारा	whole, all
साल्	year
पोहोर् साल्	last year
साहस्	courage, inclination
साहित्य	literature
साहूजी	shopkeeper, money-lender
साहेब्	Mr., sir
साह्रै	very, quite
सिंगार्	make-up, decoration
सिंगार् पार्नु	to make oneself up
सिंगरिनु	to be made up
सिंधु	Indus
सिंह	lion
सिंह दर्बार्	Singha Darbar (Nepalese Secretariat)
सिउनु	to sew
सिकिस्त बिरामी	gravely (ill)

सिक्नु	to learn
सिङ्गार	see सिंगार
-सित	with
सिद्धिनु	to be finished
सिदध्याउनु	to finish
सिनेमा	cinema, film
सिपाही	soldier
सिफारिश्	recommendation
सीधा	straight
सीमा	border, boundary
सीमाना	border, frontier
सुका	coin of 25 *paisa*
सुकै	suffix added to relative pronouns and adverbs: जोसुकै 'whoever', etc.
सुक्खा	dry
सुक्नु (सुख्नु)	to dry up
सुख्	pleasure, peace of mind
सुटुक्क जानु	to go quietly
सुत्नु	to sleep
सुन्	gold
सुनाउनु	to cause to hear, relate
सुनिनु	to be heard
सुन्तला	orange
सुन्दर्	beautiful
सुन्नु	to hear
सुबेदार्	Subedar (military rank)
सुरिलो	sweet, pleasant
सुरु	see शुरू
सूझ्	perception, understanding
सूर्य	sun
सेतो	white
सेना	army
सैकड़ा	service
सेवा	per hundred
सैनिक्	military, soldier
सो	that, thus, so
सोझो	straight
सोझै	directly
सोच्नु	to think
सोध्नु	to ask
सोम्वार्	Monday
सोर्	see स्वर्
सोल्लास्	great pleasure

स्कूल्	school
स्तम्भ	pillar, column
स्थान्	place
स्थायी	local, fixed, standing
स्थानीय	local
स्थित्	situated
स्याउ	apple
स्याल्	jackal
स्याहार गर्नु	to look after
स्रोत्	stream, downpour
स्वर्	voice, noise
ठूलो स्वर्ले	in a loud voice, aloud
स्वरूप्	aspect, guise, in the guise of
स्वागत्	welcome
स्वागत् गर्नु	to welcome
स्वाद्	taste
स्वास्थ्य	health
स्वास्नी	woman, wife
स्वास्नीमान्छे	woman, female
स्वीकार् गर्नु	to accept

ह

हँसिलो	laughing
हजार्	thousand
हजारौं	thousands of
हजूर्	sir, Your Majesty, respectful pronoun
हड्ताल्	strike
हड्ताल् गर्नु	to be on strike
हत्पत्	hurry, fuss
हत्पताउनु	to hurry
हतियार्	weapon
हनुमान्	Hanumān
हप्ता	week
आउने हप्ता	next week
गएको हप्ता	last week
हम्ला गर्नु	attack
हर्एक्	see हरेक्
हराउनु	to lose, be lost
हरियो	green
हरेक्	every, each
हल्ला	noise, fuss
हवस्	so be it, very well

हवाई-घाट्	airport
हवाई-जहाज्	aeroplane
हाँक्नु	to drive
हाँगो	branch (of tree)
हाँस्नु	to laugh
हाड्	bone
हात्	hand, forearm
हात्ती	elephant
हामी (-हरू)	we
हाम्रो	our
हार्दिक्	heartfelt
हाल्	the present, now, recently
हालत्	state, condition
हाल्नु	to put (into), pour, tell (a story)
हावा	wind, air
हावापानी	climate
हिंड्-डुल्	strolling
हिंड्नु	to walk, go on foot
हिउँ	snow
हिउँ पर्नु	to snow
हिउँद्	winter
हिजो	yesterday
हिजो राति	last night
हिजोआज	nowadays
हिन्दी	Hindi
हिन्दुस्तान्	India
हिन्दू	Hindu
हिमाल्	mountain, range of mountains
हिमालय	Himalayas
हिलो	mud
हिसाब्	accounts, reckoning
हुकुम्	order
हुनु (हो,छ,हुन्छ भयो)	to be
हुलाक्	post, mail, postal system (of Nepal)
हुलाक्-घर्	post office
हृदय	heart
हेर्नु	to look at, see
हेर्-विचार् गर्नु	to look after
है	interrogative particle
हैजा	cholera
हो	see हुनु
होटेल्	hotel
होला	see हुनु , maybe, perhaps

होश्	sense(s)
होश् गर्नु	to be careful
होश्यार्	clever, careful

Made in the USA
Lexington, KY
24 December 2009